Examining Vulnerabilities and Adversarial Exploitation of AI and LLMs

Puya Pakshad
https://orcid.org/0000-0003-2834-2769
Illinois Institute of Technology, USA

Marwan Omar
https://orcid.org/0009-0000-7534-5490
Illinois Institute of Technology, USA

IGI Global
Scientific Publishing
Publishing Tomorrow's Research Today

Vice President of Editorial	Melissa Wagner
Director of Acquisitions	Mikaela Felty
Director of Book Development	Jocelynn Hessler
Production Manager	Mike Brehm
Cover Design	Jose Rosado

Published in the United States of America by
IGI Global Scientific Publishing
701 East Chocolate Avenue
Hershey, PA, 17033, USA
Tel: 717-533-8845 | Fax: 717-533-7115
Website: https://www.igi-global.com E-mail: cust@igi-global.com

Library of Congress Cataloging-in-Publication Data

LCCN: 2026003396 (CIP Data Pending)
ISBN13: 9798337382524
Isbn13Softcover: 9798337382531
EISBN13: 9798337382548
British Cataloguing in Publication Data
A Cataloguing in Publication record for this book is available from the British Library.

Table of Contents

Detailed Table of Contents

human oversight and post-deployment monitoring. The proposed framework is replicable, auditable, and supports evidence-based ethical governance of AI-enabled cybersecurity platforms.

As artificial intelligence (AI) systems and digital infrastructure continue to expand across all sectors, both AI governance and cybersecurity policy have become central challenges for modern governments. This paper extends the analytical framework of our baseline study, Between Innovation and Oversight, which examined AI governance in the EU, UK, US, and China, and applies it to the domain of cybersecurity governance. Using the same comparative dimensions, this paper evaluates how each region approaches cybersecurity and assesses whether the regulatory patterns identified in AI governance carry over. Although cybersecurity introduces additional pressures, particularly in relation to critical infrastructure and national security, the underlying governance philosophies remain largely consistent across regions. The findings suggest that AI governance and cybersecurity governance are best understood as part of a broader digital governance domain, in which long-standing political and regulatory cultures shape how nations balance innovation, security, and societal risk.

Artificial intelligence (AI) and large language models (LLMs) increasingly underpin cyber defense workflows triaging alerts, correlating telemetry, classifying malware, generating incident narratives, and accelerating analyst decision-making. Yet the same properties that make AI operationally valuable (learning from data, generalizing across contexts, and automating at scale) also expand the attack surface. Adversaries can poison training data, implant hidden backdoors, steal model behavior through APIs, induce privacy leakage, or exploit prompt-manipulation weaknesses in LLM applications. When these models are deployed cloud-natively via containerized inference services, retrieval-augmented generation (RAG), agentic toolchains, and continuous delivery pipelines attack vectors multiply across datasets, MLOps supply chains, identity layers, orchestration planes, and third-party dependencies. This chapter presents a unified framework for architecting trustworthy and resilient AI systems under adversarial pressure. We synthesize adversarial AI threat models.

The growing complexity and decentralization of modern network environments have revealed critical limitations in traditional perimeter-based security models that rely on implicit trust within network boundaries. This chapter examines Zero Trust Architecture as a transformative security paradigm that eliminates inherent trust by enforcing continuous identity verification and least-privilege access based on dynamic contextual factors. By synthesizing existing literature and comparing firewall-centric approaches with identity-driven Zero Trust frameworks, the chapter highlights the necessity of this shift in addressing contemporary threat landscapes. It further outlines an implementation roadmap that considers technical, organizational, and policy challenges associated with deploying Zero Trust across hybrid cloud, edge computing, and distributed systems. The chapter concludes with practical recommendations for security practitioners and identifies key areas for future research to advance the effectiveness and scalability of Zero Trust security models.

This research project presents an AI-based intrusion detection framework for smart renewable energy grids. It enhances the traditional binary detection to a multi-class model capable of identifying different types of cyberattacks, including DoS, malware, phishing, MITM, SQL injection and zero-day. The proposed system utilizes the Smart Grid Intrusion Detection Dataset. It combines the Random Forest with the Autoencoder machine learning models to reach an accuracy of 97.8%, with the objective of minimizing false positives. Temporal analysis is included in order to discover attack patterns across hours, days of the week and operational phases of the energy grids. In addition, this project trains an XGBoost predictive model to determine attack likelihood or type based on recent temporal sequences. The study contributes to a predictive cybersecurity approach, anticipating attacks and strengthening resilience in intelligent energy infrastructures.

Organizations outside formal governance frameworks often lack cybersecurity audit tools, making anomaly detection and risk evaluation difficult. This paper presents an AI-enhanced auditing framework for non-governance IT environments. Using the UNSW-NB15 dataset, we evaluate four machine-learning models: Isolation Forest, Logistic Regression, Gradient Boosting, and XGBoost, identifying complementary strengths that motivate a two-stage filter for suspicious network flows. Flagged flows are aggregated into structured evidence and passed to a GPT-4-based large language model, which generates incident explanations, control mappings, and remediation suggestions. Results show the hybrid ML-LLM approach reduces audit workload, improves anomaly interpretation, and supports recommendations for private and small-scale IT systems. The study also highlights limitations including prompt sensitivity, false positives, and third-party AI risks. Overall, findings illustrate both the potential and challenges of deploying AI-driven audit pipelines to strengthen cybersecurity in non-governance settings.

This paper presents an empirical study on backdoor attacks in large language model agents. We extend a recent attack framework by adding two lightweight benchmarks that measure cross-domain robustness and trigger visibility without changing the model architecture. Our approach fine-tunes AgentLM-based agents with parameter-efficient methods on operating system and web browsing tasks using multiple poisoning ratios and both visible and invisible triggers. We then evaluate the agents with four metrics: Attack Success Rate, Follow Step Ratio, Cross-Domain Robustness, and Trigger Visibility Gap. The results show that backdoors often transfer to unseen domains without a drop in success, while invisible triggers significantly reduce the attack success rate compared to visible ones. These findings highlight the need for stronger evaluation tools and defenses for LLM-based agents.

Explainability and transparency have emerged as foundational pillars in the secure deployment of artificial intelligence (AI) systems, especially large language models (LLMs). This chapter examines the evolving landscape of explainable AI (XAI) architectures through the lens of cybersecurity, adversarial robustness, and regulatory compliance. The authors survey core XAI methodologies—including LIME, SHAP, mechanistic interpretability, attention attribution, and causal tracing—evaluating their effectiveness against adversarial threats such as jailbreaking, prompt injection, data poisoning, and hallucination exploitation. The dual nature of XAI is critically examined: while transparency mechanisms bolster defense and trust, they simultaneously introduce novel attack surfaces that adversaries can exploit to subvert explanation systems.

Preface

INTRODUCTION

The rapid evolution of artificial intelligence, particularly Large Language Models (LLMs), has transformed the landscape of cybersecurity, software engineering, and digital governance. Once confined to narrow applications, AI systems are now deeply embedded in critical infrastructures, decision-making pipelines, and security operations. While this integration has unlocked unprecedented capabilities in automation, prediction, and analysis, it has simultaneously introduced a new class of vulnerabilities that adversaries are actively learning to exploit.

Examining Vulnerabilities and Adversarial Exploitation of AI and LLMs presents a comprehensive exploration of these emerging risks. This volume brings together interdisciplinary research that investigates how AI systems, especially LLMs, can be attacked, manipulated, and subverted through adversarial techniques such as prompt injection, data poisoning, backdoor implantation, and model inversion. At the same time, it highlights innovative defenses, governance frameworks, and ethical considerations necessary to ensure the safe and responsible deployment of AI technologies.

The chapters collectively bridge theory and practice. They explore technical mechanisms for detecting defects, malware, and intrusions using AI; analyze adversarial attack surfaces and forensic methodologies; and examine the broader socio-technical implications of AI governance, ethics, and regulatory policy across global contexts. Special emphasis is placed on explainability, trustworthiness, and resilience, key pillars for building secure AI systems in cloud-native and distributed environments.

This work is intended for researchers, practitioners, policymakers, and students seeking to understand both the power and the peril of AI in modern cybersecurity ecosystems. By combining empirical studies, comparative analyses, and architectural frameworks, the book aims to foster a deeper understanding of how to anticipate threats, design robust defenses, and govern AI responsibly in an increasingly adversarial digital world. Below is a chapter by chapter summary you may use to enhance your reading.

CHAPTER OVERIVEWS

Chapter 1: Unmasking Threat Vectors in Large Language Models

This chapter evaluates AI-driven defect detection across multiple programming languages, comparing traditional machine learning models (Random Forest, SVM, XGBoost) with LLM-based approaches. It demonstrates that while conventional models rely heavily on feature engineering, LLMs excel in semantic understanding and contextual reasoning. The chapter also explores integration into CI/CD pipelines and DevSecOps, highlighting scalability and explainability challenges.

Chapter 2: AI-powered Malware Detection and Behavioral Analysis

Focusing on malware detection, this chapter examines the limitations of signature-based methods and introduces AI-driven static analysis techniques. By leveraging features such as opcode sequences, control flow graphs, and API calls, machine learning models can detect polymorphic and zero-day malware more effectively, offering faster and safer alternatives to dynamic analysis.

Chapter 3: Adversarial Attacks and Backdoor Exploitation in LLMs

This chapter provides a deep dive into adversarial threats targeting LLMs, including prompt injection, data poisoning, and backdoor attacks. It discusses how attackers manipulate model outputs, bypass safeguards, and degrade trust. The chapter also outlines detection strategies, forensic analysis methods, and emerging defense mechanisms.

Chapter 4: Ethical AI in Cybersecurity

This chapter introduces a structured framework for evaluating ethical compliance in AI-driven cybersecurity systems. It assesses seven dimensions, including transparency, accountability, and privacy, using LLM-assisted analysis of research literature. Findings reveal gaps in human oversight and post-deployment monitoring, emphasizing the need for measurable ethical standards.

Chapter 5: Extending AI Governance Frameworks

A comparative analysis of cybersecurity and AI governance policies across the EU, UK, USA, and China. The chapter highlights how different political and regulatory cultures shape approaches to innovation, risk, and security, arguing that AI and cybersecurity governance should be understood within a unified digital governance framework.

Chapter 6: Architecting Trustworthy and Resilient AI Systems

This chapter proposes a unified framework for designing secure AI systems in cloud-native environments. It examines adversarial threats across the AI lifecycle, including data poisoning, API exploitation, and prompt manipulation. The work emphasizes resilience through robust MLOps practices, forensic intelligence, and governance integration.

Chapter 7: A Rethink of Network Security through Zero Trust Architecture

The chapter critiques traditional perimeter-based security models and introduces Zero Trust Architecture (ZTA) as a modern alternative. By enforcing continuous verification and least-privilege access, ZTA addresses the challenges of decentralized and hybrid environments. Implementation strategies and research directions are also discussed.

Chapter 8: AI-Driven Intrusion Detection and Network Traffic Analysis

This chapter presents a machine learning-based intrusion detection system tailored for smart energy grids. Combining Random Forest, Autoencoders, and XGBoost, the system achieves high accuracy while minimizing false positives. Temporal analysis enables predictive detection of cyberattacks, enhancing resilience in critical infrastructure.

Chapter 9: Hybrid ML-LLM Pipeline for IT Audits

A novel two-stage auditing framework is introduced, combining traditional ML models for anomaly detection with LLMs for explanation and remediation. The hybrid approach improves audit efficiency and interpretability, particularly in non-governance environments, while also highlighting risks such as prompt sensitivity and AI dependency.

Chapter 10: BadAgent Extension and Backdoor Robustness in LLM Agents

This chapter investigates backdoor attacks in LLM agents, introducing benchmarks for cross-domain robustness and trigger visibility. Findings show that backdoors can generalize across domains, while invisible triggers reduce attack success rates. The study underscores the need for stronger evaluation and defense techniques.

Chapter 11: Explainable and Transparent AI Architectures

The final chapter explores explainable AI (XAI) methods such as LIME, SHAP, and causal tracing in the context of cybersecurity. It highlights the dual role of explainability, enhancing trust while also exposing new attack surfaces, and calls for balanced approaches to transparency and security.

Chapter 1

Unmasking Threat Vectors in Large Language Models: A Deep Analysis of Adversarial Exploitation

Neeharika Joshi
Marwadi University, Rajkot, India

R. N. Ravikumar
http://orcid.org/0009-0009-3705-1681
Marwadi University, Rajkot, India

Satwik Kishore
http://orcid.org/0009-0002-2014-7897
Marwadi University, Rajkot, India

Sonukumar Pandit
Marwadi University, Rajkot, India

Shubhamkumar Pandit
Marwadi University, Rajkot, India

S. Aarthi
http://orcid.org/0009-0006-9064-2091
Marwadi University, Rajkot, India

ABSTRACT

AI-driven defect detection is increasingly essential as software systems grow in complexity, multilinguality, and scale. This chapter presents a comparative evaluation of traditional machine learning models and large language models for detecting structural and semantic defects across multiple programming languages. A multilingual dataset is used to assess Random Forest, SVM, XGBoost, and a prompt-based CodeT5 simulation, revealing the limitations of feature-engineered approaches and the superior semantic reasoning of LLMs. Practical integration scenarios in CI/CD, IDEs, and DevSecOps workflows are examined, followed by key challenges and emerging research directions for scalable, explainable, and automated defect detection.

DOI: 10.4018/979-8-3373-8252-4.ch001

INTRODUCTION

As the modern software systems grow in size and scale with increased level of sophistication, the eminent and effective defect discovery becomes all the more vital. The software may contain bugs small logical errors but also security holes so severe that a system crash, a data loss, or expensive payoffs are the consequences. Traditional software Quality Assurance (QA) processes such as manualized code reviews, static code analysis and test based on rules may be helpful in spite of being incapable of usually covering all errors in the large-scale and multi-lingual code of applications. These methods are usually limited; they possess set rules of notions, are limited by scaled issues, and do not cover meaning-dense mapping of any codes. On the other hand, AI (Artificial Intelligence) and its sub-categories; Machine Learning (ML) and Large Language Models (LLM) has shown a broad possibility of revolutionizing the processes of identifying software flaws and their interpretation (Chhabra & Chadha, 2024). Learning models supervised are a category of ML meta-techniques which it is possible to teach on past defect data to find out the strategy and tendencies that draw attention to buggy codes. Armed with well-engineered parameters such as code complexity measures, control flow information or Abstract Syntax Tree (AST) representations, such models have the ability to generalize well over data they did not previously see and automatically code data as either weighed down with flaws or pristine.

Machine Learning models also have their weaknesses, especially in comprehending code semantics as well as logical reasoning across programming paradigms. LLMs come in here since they are pretrained with huge amounts of code written by other programmers in open-source repositories. Such models as CodeT5, CodeBERT, and GPT-4 are capable of working with code in a form that closely reflects its comprehension by humans reading it, reading between the lines and even predicting the purpose of that code. Using prompt-based learning techniques, LLMs are able to detect bugs, propose solutions, and clarify how and why codes work, in a context and language-freeway. Combined use of ML and the approaches based on LLMs is a strong potential to develop stable, scalable, and smart defect detection systems. The typical multilanguage nature of business logic, where the same teams may write parts in Python, Java, C++, JavaScript, and Go, requires models that can cut across languages. A static analyzer is likely to not succeed in these cases because of the language-specific limitations, whereas the LLMs provide generalization and any ML model can be trained on shared structural features in all languages.

The purpose of this chapter is to fill the gap between the theoretical and practical face of the AI-based software defect detection. It presents a practical case study wherein it constructs an end-to-end multilingual defect prediction model comprising a simulated LLM model as well as an ML-based classifier. The ML model uses a

Random Forest classifier training with structured feature such as the quantity of tokens and AST metrics, and the LLM solution makes a prompt-based classification and uses CodeT5 to generalize using textual representations to forecast code quality (Ren et al., 2019). This chapter has stated two paradigms and contrasted them in relation to confusion matrices and F1-scores as well as to precision-recall curve with the intention of expressing the strengths and limitations. It is also discussing practical work in CI/CD pipelines, IDE integrations, and automation of code review. The chapter concludes by the declarations of major themes, including the termination noise, cross-language generalization, and explicability, along with forecasting on future trends on the utilization of GNNs-based code inspection or fine-tuning of the open-source LLMs on selected defect sets.

OVERVIEW OF MACHINE LEARNING IN DEFECT DETECTION

Life of ML in the field of software engineering, specifically on how software defects are detected, has been enjoying plenty of traction over the last several years. ML-based techniques are data-driven as opposed to those that use rules, such as Starbase static analysis tools; this means models can learn complicated and frequently non-linear patterns of bad code based on past results (Fanqi Meng et al., 2023). Such generalization over unseen code is what enables ML to be a very useful complement to software quality assurance in the modern context

Supervised Learning Models for Defect Prediction

The essence of ML-based defect discovery is in supervised learning in which models are trained using labeled data with examples of bug-containing and clean codes. The aim will be to train a function capable of classifying new unseen code snippets accurately. A number of supervised learning models have worked well with the software defect prediction domain. SVM are known to be quite specialized in terms of the task they are mostly used in binary classification problems and in high feature spaces. They perform well when dealing with small datasets but the manner to use the kernel functions in these datasets are crucial in non-linearly separable data (Zou & Lv, 2025). The next model that is commonly used is the Random Forest which is a sound ensemble algorithm that comprises of several decision trees. It takes care of the problem of overfitting in a better way than individual decision trees and it works as well with structured data that has varying features. Also, XGBoost (Extreme Gradient Boosting) has become another top-level performer that provides more optimized implementations of gradient-boosted decision trees. XGBoost is known to be efficient and accurate in predictive tasks with applications proficiently lying in software defect prediction, being a mega-popular choice by both researchers and practitioners.

Feature Engineering in Code-Based ML

Feature engineering refers to the activity of converting raw code into a numeric format suitable to ML models. This change is very important as it mediates the divide between text and textual codes and mathematical models. Features that are commonly used in making defect prediction are shown in Table 1. They are retrieved with the help of static analysis tools, or built-in scripts, which aid ML models in capturing the structure and behavior of the code.

Table 1. Features commonly used in defect prediction

Category	Examples
Lexical Features	Token count, identifier frequency, keyword density
Syntactic Features	AST node counts, nesting depth, number of control structures (if, for, etc.)
Code Metrics	Cyclomatic complexity, lines of code, number of comments.
Historical Features	Number of revisions, bug-fix history, time since last change
Developer Metadata	Committer experience, commit size, time of day

Public Benchmark Datasets

As part of the attempts to guarantee consistency in the evaluation and foster reproducibility in the software defect prediction research, there have been a few publicly available datasets created and widely used in the software engineering community. One such suite is CodeXGLUE a benchmark suite proposed by Microsoft Research that will help numerous program analysis tasks like code classification, code summarization and code translation (Vokhranov & Bulakh, 2024). The next notable dataset is Defects4J that comprises of well-chosen real-world bugs in Java projects, such as the Apache Commons and JFreeChart. It consists of sets of buggy and fixed code, which is why it is suitable to deal with tasks aimed at supervised learning. The PROMISE Repository is also a well-established defect statistic data came from open sources where statistics have been gathered across a wide range of languages and software areas. Such an imbalance is not trivial and resampling solutions or cost-sensitive learning approaches are inadequate without the risk of subjecting the model performance to uncertainty.

ML Pipeline for Defect Detection

The machine learning pipeline of defect detection in the field of software engineering means the coherent chain of procedures that converts raw code into a set of practical defect predictions. The said pipeline consists of several processes the implementation of which is critical in defining overall efficiency and correctness of the defect prediction model (Ibrahim et al., 2023). The flexible ML pipeline with a good set of configuration parameters is reproducible, scalable and adaptable to programming languages and project types. Figure 1 shows a breakdown of the key stages of the pipeline.

Figure 1. Pipeline for Defect Detection

Data Collection

Corporate source code used in this study was gathered with source code management systems, which in this case were Git. These repositories do not only offer the latest codebase, but they also offer useful historical material such as commit history and bug-fixes. The code samples were marked as buggy or clean depending on various indicators to annotate them according to the defects and label them. These are data in bug-fix commits, data in bug trackers systems such as JIRA or GitHub Issues, and automated methods such as Bayesian search or heuristic-based bug injection techniques (Hernández-Molinos et al., 2023). This will make the dataset realistic with regard to defect pattern that can be observed in real life software development projects. Quality, veritably mixed and well-labeled multilingual data of all kinds are also needed, which improve generalization indirectly.

Feature Extraction

After code samples are gathered and marked, the second step is turning the raw source code into well-formed features such that machine learning algorithms can use them. The transformation is usually achieved by parsing the code or helping in parsing the code. The extracted features are aimed at representing different code and development situation characteristics. Lexical properties refer to the surface properties of the code such as token frequency, keyword use and use of identifiers. Based on the Abstract Syntax Tree (AST) are syntactic features which can encompass node types and depth of the nesting loops as well as the parameters of the control structures (Y. Tang et al., 2024). The measures of code that give us this information are cyclomatic complexity, Lines Of Code (LOC) and number of comment lines. Beside these, temporal aspects of code evolution can be viewed through historical features, such as the number of commits and the time of the last modification. Last, but not least, developer metadata, including file ownership and experience of contributing developers, provides a more human-centric outcome when extracting features. All these characteristics combined aid with the creation of powerful defect prediction and software quality evaluation models.

Model Training

After data labeling and conversion of data into feature vectors, training of defect prediction models comes next in the pipeline. At this phase supervised learning algorithms are applied in order to learn patterns to derive differences between buggy code and clean code. The Random Forest algorithm is one of the most popular that can be used to address the issue as it is a strong ensemble model that consists of several decision trees that provide sufficient performance coupled with information on the importance of features and resists overfitting. SVM are good high-dimensional spaces and are not interpretable. XGBoost, however, is good when using structured data and boasts of great speed, accuracy and output in predicting defects. By eliminating classification error on the provided labels, contrasting buggy and clean code, the model learns to find out these patterns during training (Liu et al., 2025). Hyperparameter tuning, cross-validation and regularization techniques significantly decrease the likelihood of overfitting and encourage generalizability.

Evaluation

The model has to be checked in order to evaluate its performance and its ability to generalize after the training. This is usually conducted putting a test set or with k-fold cross-validation. The common evaluation measures are listed in Table 2. A decent model ought to have high-precision and high-recall, since in case of false negatives (missed bugs) there can be severe downstream failures.

Table 2. Evaluation measures

Metrics	Description
Accuracy	Overall correctness of predictions
Precision	Correctly predicted buggy samples among all predicted buggy
Recall	Correctly identified buggy samples among all actual buggy
F1-Score	Harmonic mean of precision and recall (balance measure)
Confusion Matrix	Provides detailed classification outcome breakdown

LLMS FOR SEMANTIC CODE UNDERSTANDING

With increasingly large and complex software systems, the classic approaches to software analysis (e.g. static analysis, classical machine learning) are showing themselves to be limited, in particular with respect to understanding the semantic meaning of code. Such standard methods crucially depend upon the hand-crafted features, textual syntactic features (such as token sequences or ASTs) and the past defect patterns. These techniques can be very useful as techniques to detect known and simple types of bugs, but tend to be less useful in generalization or interpretation of deeper purposes or meaning, business logic, or cross-language abstractions in code. They have problems with languages, practical reasoning and non-local interdependencies that are becoming a typical part of contemporary software development. Step in LLMs a technological challenge waiting to be exploited in the arena of deep learning which boasts endless potential in semantic code comprehension (L. Tang et al., 2025). Such models include OpenAI Codex, Google CodeBERT or Meta Code LLaMA, which are pre-trained on massive corpora of the code in repositories such as GitHub, Stack Overflow, and other developer-oriented communities. Using methods such as self-supervised pretraining and task-specific fine-tuning, LLMs can learn low-level syntax as well as the semantics at the high-level of multiple programming languages.

The distinguishing feature of LLMs is that they are capable of figuring out the purpose a usage of the code outside the statements that explicitly define that code. As an example, they may be able to interpret naming standards, code comments, logical purpose, and even partial or obfuscated sets of code (areas in which rule-based systems or classical ML models would fall short). Moreover, the LLMs demonstrate their ability to generalize knowledge that is gained on one language or domain and be applied to another, which closes the gap between the syntactic form and semantics of the meaning. The LLMs provide a new method of automated code analysis by discovering contextual representations in code, allowing sophisticated operations such as semantic search or auto-completion, errors identification, and correction this characterizes developer tools as being near the level of human intelligence in tasks.

What Are LLMs in the Context of Code?

Originally destined to use on Natural Language Processing (NLP), LLMs have been generalized and applied to models of code understanding. They are trained with varied large-scale data composed of the source code language and repository, documentation and natural language, and pretrained at code-aware reasoning. Among the most popular LLMs with code understanding and generation capabilities are such models as CodeBERT, CodeT5, and GPT-4 with code capabilities. CodeBERT is a Transformer model based on natural language and code pairs, so it is very proficient in code search, code summary, and natural language to the code translation themes. By comparison, CodeT5 is a complete encoder-decoder proper and can apply to a wide variety of software engineering duties, such as code summarization, translation, and fault identification, all of which rely on a unified text-to-text framework. GPT-4 is a general-purpose language model, but has been shown to have more sophisticated code capabilities: it can write syntactically and semantically correct code and explain the logic of programs in natural language, and even diagnose errors. Such models have really made an impact on the state of art in the field of semantic code comprehension and automation in software development (Dalla Palma et al., 2022). Classical features do not serve as input to such models, instead raw code is fed as the input and digested to give out the outputs that are obtained in the form of the representation learned and attention that are obtained. This enables to neglect and evade structure-related structures (involved with language), hence, in a situation where a multilingual development occurs, they are extremely useful.

Capabilities of LLMs in Software Defect Detection

LLMs have several benefits, in comparison to the traditional approaches, such as their capacity to operate and comprehend semantic structures, as opposed to purely syntactic ones. Figure 2 shows major capabilities of LLMs in Software Defect Detection:

Figure 2. Capabilities of LLMs in Software Defect Detection

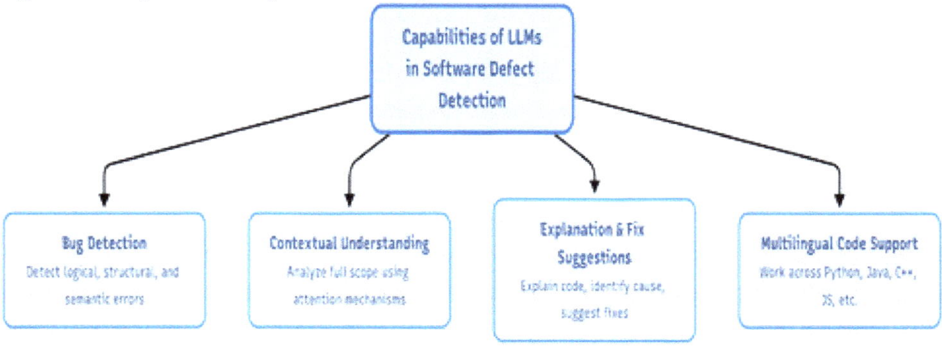

The illustration of the four basic skills that LLMs add to the area of automated bug detection called Capabilities of LLMs in Software Defect Detection is presented visually. The supreme idea in the middle of the diagram is LLMs as a potent technology to develop a semantic analysis of lines of code in software. Zeroing out of this are four interrelated capabilities that point to the details as to how LLMs improve defect detection as compared to conventional methods. The bug detection is the first ability, which means that LLMs find logic, structural, and semantic errors in the code. In contrast to syntax-aware rule-based tools, LLMs can be trained on large amounts of code and may learn to detect even deeper problems (off-by-one errors, incorrect returns) within programs (Choraś et al., 2019). Second, LLMs perform well in the contextual understanding, which is made possible by their self-attention architecture. This enables them to process either an entire function or an entire file at a time enabling them to capture any kind of relationship between the variables, control structures and code logic at varying scopes; something that the static analysis tools fail to do most of the times.

A combination of explaining, diagnosing, and proposing solutions in human-readable or executable form is feasible with LLMs similar to the way they can assist in development and make the task of learning easier. Their linguistic training renders them language-free and best suited to the real-life polyglot auxiliary. Such capabilities make LLMs highly flexible building blocks in the software pipeline, capable of spotting bugs, comprehending code, giving feedback and scaling across languages and ecosystems.

Prompt-Based Defect Detection

The concept of prompt-based defect detection can be considered one of the most groundbreaking innovations of the LLMs in the software engineering field. The strategy allows providing LLMs with the tasks of identifying bugs, describing the code, or proposing fixes that will not be structured in terms of inputs, but rather through natural language which will serve as prompts. In contrast to classical machine learning models where input features have to be invented as predefined feature vectors and training sets has to be prepared as labelled ones, LLMs can be prompted based on specific prompts well-structured which twist the model to solve a particular code analysis problem (Chapman et al., 2025). Prompt-based learning implies directing the interaction with a pretrained language model to provide textual instructions on the input data (i.e., source code) it receives (i.e., prompts). The model then understands the prompt, contextualizes the code, and provides an output that suits the task, e.g. bug detection or code explanation as shown in Figure 3,4,5. For example, consider the following prompt:

Figure 3. Sample Prompt 1

```
Prompt: "Is there a bug in the following function? Explain your answer."
Code:
def calculate_area(radius):
    return 3.14 * radius * radius
```

An LLM might respond:

"There is no apparent bug in the function. It correctly implements the area formula for a circle."

Now consider a flawed version:

Figure 4. Flawed Version Prompt

```
def calculate_area(radius):
    return 2 * 3.14 * radius
```

Prompt:

Figure 5. Sample Prompt 2

```
Is there a bug in the following function?"
```

Response:

> ***"Yes, the function calculates the circumference, not the area. The formula for area should be $\pi * r^2$."***

This demonstrates capability of the model to read code semantics and logic, and explain them in human-readable text besides defect detection. These critical Advantages of Prompt-Based Defect Detection lists four significant advantages of the prompt-based interaction with LLMs as shown in Figure 6 that makes the latter an effective method in the identification of defects in software. The main idea of the whole diagram is in the core concept - how the introduction of LLMs that are directed by the natural language prompts may provide flexible, efficient, and intelligent detection of the defects without adhering to the traditional retraining or the rule-based systems.

Figure 6. Advantages of Prompt-Based Defect Detection

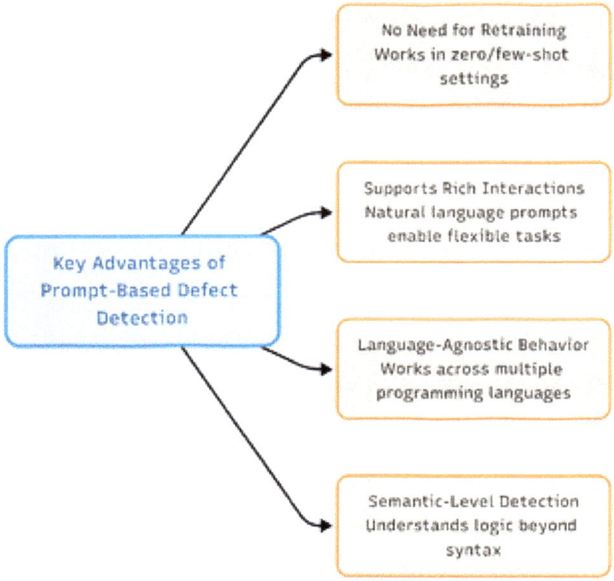

The benefit that is displayed is the absence of retraining necessity. Prompt-based systems are capable of working in zero-shot or few-shot environments, i.e. do not need a certain level of retraining on the task to provide valuable results. This renders them especially affordable and deployable on various projects and spheres. The second is that they allow rich interactions. These models can be interacted with using natural language queries and the developer can find bugs by using queries like Find bugs in this function OR can suggest improvements in the same interface and have to do all the tasks required on the same interface including defect detection, explanation, optimization.

The third advantage is language-neutral behavior. LLMs are language-agnostic and have already been trained on various programming languages thus they are the best in polyglottic situations (Vokhranov & Bulakh, 2024). The logic of code is known to LLMs as opposed to traditional static analysis tools that are based on syntax. This enables them to identify semantic failures like wrong operations, wrong conditions of returns or unwanted control flows. They are ahead of others with respect to the deeper and functional issues that they recognize by understanding code logic.

Fix Suggestion and Bug Explanation

Not only are LLMs the best candidates to detect errors in the code, but they can also comment on the essence of the bug and advise on the way to resolve the issue.

At request these models are capable of expressing natural-language explanations why a specific code is flawed and suggest fixed versions. Take, as an example, an incorrectly defined function, the LLM will detect the absence of the returning statement, explain its effects on it, and provide the fixed example of implementation (Jahanshahi et al., 2020). This code reasoning is a major step towards mitigating the burden of cognitive developers and implementing code debugging, learning, and code review Figure 7 as follows. You may also reinforce it with an example:

Figure 7. Expected LLM Response

Expected LLM Response:

> The function adds 1 to x but does not return the result. You should use return x + 1 to ensure the incremented value is output.

This demonstrates that prompt-based LLMs can become contextual teachers, rather than mere detectors and thus such models are very valuable in both educational and industrial settings.

REAL-WORLD INTEGRATION SCENARIOS

Meanwhile, although the theoretical/experimental potential of LLMs and ML models with regard to software defect detection have been previously established, their functionality is seen in all its glory when applied to the actual processes of software development. Not only does integration legitimize the usefulness but also boosts productivity, development of excellent quality codes, and initiatives towards preemptive removal of defects (Senior, 2024). In this section, the author points out some of the most real-life situations in which the ML-based and LLM-based systems are being actively implemented in contemporary development cases.

Integration in CI/CD Pipelines

Automated defect detection is one of the most influential applications which can be easily used in the Continuous Integration and Continuous Deployment (CI/CD) pipeline. Under these conditions, each code push or Pull Request will become automatically scanned with the help of Machine Learning or LLM-based software, to reveal possible sources of flaws in real-time. As a defect gets noticed, the system is able to implement a number of proactive steps to ensuring the quality of the code and stability. It is capable of issuing early warnings to developers prior to merging code, suggestions or explanations of how code can potentially be fixed, and where the issue is severe, the deployment may be entirely blocked to avoid errors in code getting to the production environment (Abiona et al., 2024). The integration not merely makes software more reliable, the feedback loop is also speeded up, which can be used to the advantage of the developers, quickly detecting problems, and then resolve them early on in the development process. Adapted quality gates assist in the detection of bugs early before it becomes expensive and challenging. Software development companies such as Microsoft apply the use of tools such as GitHub Copilot and CodeQL that simplify build decisions using AI.

IDE-Integrated Assistants

Among the most natural and developer-friendly LLM and AI-based defect detection use cases is the fact that they can become a part of Integrated Development Environments (IDEs). IDE-integrated assistants can collaborate with developers in the moment because they are intelligent coding companions that can make developers more productive, code better and learn. These assistants may be LLM or a hybrid ML+rule-based application, and embedded into well-known IDEs like Visual Studio Code, IntelliJ IDEA, Eclipse, or PyCharm. These helpers constantly watch the code, which is written and provide contextual advice. These involve detecting possible bugs, and suggesting fixes of syntax or logic, and suggesting more optimal or idiomatic alternatives of patterns that are frequent (Chandramouli et al., 2024). As an example, when a developer creates a shadowing function or a function which includes an unattainable return statement the assistant can highlight the problem immediately in some cases with an explanation an easy one-click fix. In contrast to fixative linters, which reveal mainly syntactic errors in the code after compilation or saving, these assists vary substantially in error reporting the semantics of the code as soon as it is typed. Examples of these assistants that are popular are: GitHub Copilot, Amazon CodeWhisperer, Tabnine.

The tools are prompt based and behavioral predictions of code completions and anomaly flagging. Others also offer conversational queries where developers can ask questions in natural language such as What does this do Now, there are natural language responses. Software assistants help users to perform development tasks through automation of redundant features, elimination of boilerplate code, and help users to develop small parts at a time as a unit. They provide in-time debugging, introduce a new developer to the code, and impose the coding code of conduct-enhancing preciousness, coherence among the group, and productivity (Zhou et al., 2023). The other important strength of these assistants is that they have low barrier to adoption. The developers do not have to set up external tools or pipelines, as the model will be running in the background once the plugin is installed and is continuously providing a better development experience. Moreover, these assistants are language-ignorant, as they support various programming languages (Python, JavaScript, TypeScript, Java, C++, etc.).

DevSecOps and Automated Code Review

As a combination of DevSecOps practices and automated code reviews, integrating code reviews into the current software development lifecycle has become a vital ingredient to security, reliability, and efficiency at scale. DevSecOps as shown in Figure 8 is an abbreviation that describes a related approach termed Development, Security, and Operations and focuses on the left-shift of security by integrating it into the development process at an early stage as opposed to retrofitting security as an afterthought (Erich et al., 2017). The use of automated code review systems is also a strong facilitator of the strategy including reviewing the source code in real-time and evaluating and giving feedback on the code constantly.

Figure 8. AI for DevSecOps

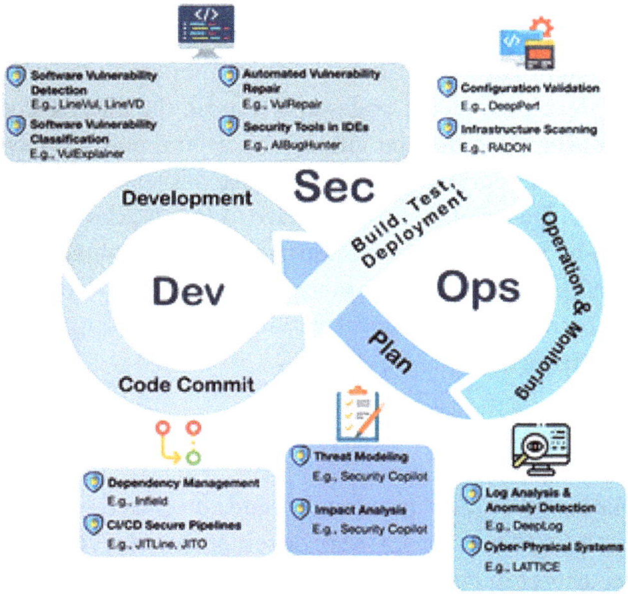

Manual, traditional code reviews did not scale to fast, large codebases; they did not always hit on root problems. DevSecOps ensures this is enhanced with the help of ML models, LLMs, and rule-based tools that are able to automate reviews. These tools use the analysis of each commit or pull request in search of security vulnerabilities, hard-coded credentials, logic vulnerabilities, and code quality problems. They do this by also imposing secure coding practices such as OWASP and CERT that improves maintainability and minimizes production risks. Specifically, LLMs bring added functionalities due to the possibility to find a syntactic analysis of the code and interpret its semantics. Such models are able to give not only what is wrong, but why it is wrong and how this can be remedied, with the review advice even being human-like in presentation and displaying situational context (Naidoo & Möller, 2022). An example is an LLM-powered review system, which can be used when integrated with such a platform as GitHub or GitLab, and then answer a pull request with the following comments:

"This function may return null under certain conditions. Consider adding a null-check before usage."

Automated code review tools serve as intelligent quality gates in the DevSecOps, which are perfect in CI/CD pipeline. They conserve energy, glitches are detected early, uniformity is demanded, and the review time is reduced due to fair and constructive feedback. Popular tools are SonarQube, Codacy, CodeQL, Deep Source, and Snyk Code, and some of them have policies that can be customized to specific regulated industries.

Industry Case Studies

To illustrate the practical environment of the application of the ML and LLM combined in computer defect detection and DevSecOps cycles, it is worth considering the examples of industry practice both within the open-source community and on commercial systems. These case studies point out the applications of AI-driven methods to make the code more extensive, improve the secure development speed, and streamline reviews at scale by organizations.

GitHub Copilot (Commercial) – AI-Powered Coding Assistant

This program has been designed to help solve the problem; GitHub Copilot, a joint product between GitHub and OpenAI, is a groundbreaking commercial application that incorporates LLMs namely, Codex developed by OpenAI-to offer real-time code suggestions to support developers. As opposed to classic autocompletion programs which are based on tokens prediction, Copilot is able to provide semantically correct, context-appropriate completions of code through its training on massive public repositories of code and use of natural language (Choraś et al., 2019). They are well integrated into contemporary IDEs including Visual Studio Code, Neovim, and JetBrains, allowing them to interact without any issues as one code.

Copilot is changing the way software is made by cutting down the amount of time it takes to write boilerplate, offering to implementations of functions, refactoring snippets, and even translating natural language comments into code. What makes it especially influential as far as the practice of defect detection is concerned is that it can be used to predict and eliminate some logical and syntactic errors before they take place. An example is that when one developer starts writing a loop with a wrong bound condition, Copilot usually provides him with a corrected code that best practices. In the same way, it can sound an alarm to insecure coding patterns such as hard coded secrets, weak hash or unsensitized user input promoting secure coding patterns (Ahmed et al., 2021). Although it is not a security tool, GitHub Copilot can assist shift-left security as it detects vulnerabilities before codes are added to version control or CI/CD. It enhances the work of the developers, decreases the burden on the mind, and makes the code better. Providing feedback and changing suggestions, Copilot serves as an intelligent pair programmer who follows the DevSecOps principles.

Meta's Infer (Open Source) – Static Analysis at Scale

Infer is a well-developed open-source static analysis tool developed by Meta (formerly Facebook), which has used the tool to find bugs that occur early in the development process such as code reviewing and committing. In contrast to many of the existing traditional, static analysis systems which tend to be restricted to rule-based checks, Infer takes advantage of the research in symbolic execution and abstract interpretation to work on control flow and data flow representation of code paths therefore discovering the subtle defect that could not have been picked up easily such as null dereferences, resource leaks, concurrent bugs, and unhandled exception (Costea et al., 2023).

Infer is particularly notable in its scalability over large and fast-moving code files such as those at Meta, where it processes thousands of commits per day. It is part of the CI/CD and it does non-blocking pre-merge verification and decides to give extensive feedback in the form of feedback in the form of comments inline in the code, allowing a developer to detect a problem earlier. Its other strengths include smooth workflow interoperability, deliverable analysis clarity, and multi-language (Java, C, C++, Objective-C) and thus its application is best suited in large scale enterprise setting. Open-sourcing Infer, Meta has allowed wider utilization of this ML-augmented static analysis tool, which has now been taken up by many outside Meta to enhance code reliability and security. Infer is similar to DevSecOps ideology, as it encourages the security, correctness, and quality at an early development stage (Pham et al., 2024).

CASE STUDY: BUILDING A MULTILINGUAL DEFECT DETECTION SYSTEM

To consider how AI-driven solutions can be applied in real-life multilingual code contexts, this case study gives the architecture and testing of a multilingual defect detection system posing together both classical ML models and LLMs. The system is to detect the errors within various programming languages and contrast the abilities and drawbacks of feature-based learning to prompt-based LLM inference.

Dataset Generation

It has been generated a synthetic dataset that includes 1,000 code snippets with the balanced content among the seven programming languages, including Python, Java, JavaScript, C++, Go, TypeScript, and C#. Data were coded as follows: 1 buggy and 0 clean indicating the existence of semantical and syntactic errors carefully gathered. Such samples were obtained on Difficulty code repositories, including GitHub, and benchmark datasets, including Defects4J and CodeSearchNet (Balogun et al., 2020). It has been split into three separate groups: 700 samples will be used to train the model, 100 to validate it, and 200 in order to test it. The dataset sample records are shown in Table 3.

Table 3. Dataset sample records

Fn	Code	Lang	LOC	CC	Tok	Ret	Call	Def
go0	a+b	2	2	2	12	1	1	0
py1	a+b	5	2	5	12	1	0	0
c2	a/b	0	3	4	11	1	1	1
cpp3	a+b	1	6	5	11	1	1	0
cpp4	a+b	1	2	3	11	1	1	0

Feature Extraction for ML

To facilitate proper classification of code samples as to whether they are buggy or clean each program was processed with the language specific tools that supported parsing and structural analysis. Among others, these were tokenizers specific to the syntax of a given programming language, Abstract Syntax Tree (AST) generators. The extraction mechanism concentrated on the collection of a full spectrum of features that embrace lexical, syntactic, and structural characteristics of the code. Refer the Table 4.

Table 4. Feature categories and examples

Feature Category	Example Features
Lexical Features	Token count (number of lexical units) Operator frequency (e.g., +, -, *, /, etc.) Identifier usage (number and types of variables and functions)
Syntactic Features	The number of AST nodes (citations of node count of tree) maximum depth of nesting (maxdeep) - Flow of control (number/structure of conditionals and branch)
Structural Metrics	The amount of for, while loops. The amount of if-else and switch-case blocks Number of break or return points of a function

The following features of Table 4 were applied in order to convert each code sample into the form of structures. It provided some standard way of reporting and comparison of different pieces of code in different languages.

ML Implementation: Random Forest

In this step of the multilingual defect detection system, we concentrate on the training on a conventional Machine Learning model, that is, Random Forest, and its use in classifying code snippets as either buggy or clean, through a set of features that have been engineered with manual effort. This strategy indicates how explainable, resilient machine-learning models may be deployed successfully in support of software quality assurance work in circumstances where one can extract structured features out of the code. Random Forest is a decision forest family of ensemble learning techniques that draws multiple decision trees to prevent overfitting in cases involving high dimensional structured data. It lowers the chance of overfitting by integrating the results of various trees thereby enhancing the generalization capability of the model. Moreover, Random Forest can give useful information about the importance of features, and the user will know which variables are most significant in defining the forecast (Walia & Sidhu, 2022). Although the model is powerful, it is quite interpretable and lightweight, which is appropriate to use in the real-time environments. Random Forest Results on Test Set (200 Samples) as shown in Table 5.

Table 5. Evaluation metrics of random forest

Metric	**Buggy (1)**	**Clean (0)**
Precision	0.52	0.52
Recall	0.71	0.71
F1_Score	0.60	0.60
Support	111	89

Overall Accuracy is 48% and Macro F1-Score is 0.42. Table 5 scores indicate that Random Forest model is more effective in identifying buggy code (label 1), but fails in identifying clean code: likely because of feature sparsity or class imbalance issue. Figure 9 indicates that, the model classified 79 buggy and 16 clean samples correctly. It erroneously labelled 73 clean samples as buggy and 32 buggies as clean however, this biasness seems high towards predicting code as buggy and not much competent to predict clean code.

Figure 9. Confusion Matrix of Random Forest

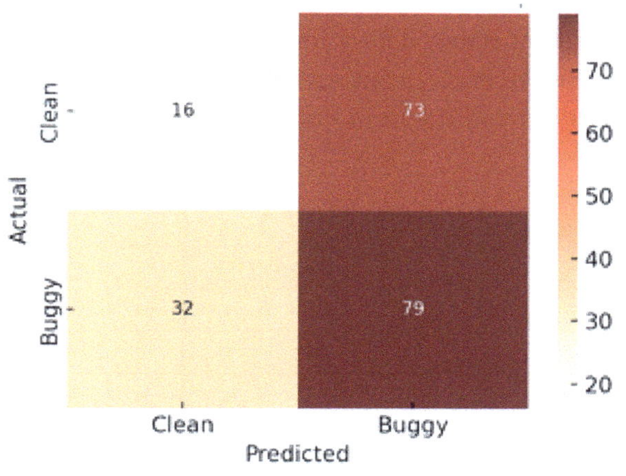

ML Comparison – SVM and XGBoost

To determine the usefulness of various Machine Learning algorithms in defect detection we put a comparison between the accuracy of SVM XGBoost with that of the Random Forest model is presented. All the models were tested and examined on the same retrieved feature pool to guarantee a uniform point of reference.

SVM

It is a potent classification algorithm with a reputation of maximizing a margin between the classes. It performed better on clean codes however it did not perform well on buggy samples when it comes to this defect detection task as shown in Table 6.

Table 6. Evaluation metrics of SVM

Metric	Buggy (1)	Clean (0)
Precision	0.47	0.47
Recall	0.24	0.24
F1_Score	0.32	0.32
Accuracy	42%	

XGBoost (Extreme Gradient Boosting)

XGBoost is a gradient-boosted decision tree assembling, which frequently performs well with structured data. In our instance, it has had more positive precision-recall balance than SVM and Random Forest as shown in Table 7.

Table 7. Evaluation metrics of XGBoost

Metric	Buggy (1)	Clean (0)
Precision	0.50	0.50
Recall	0.57	0.57
F1_Score	0.53	0.53
Accuracy	45%	

LLM Simulation – CodeT5-Based Prompting

As a complementary effort to feature-based Machine Learning methods we investigated the applicability of LLMs in defect detection with a prompt-based classification pipeline. In particular, we tested the model type CodeT5, which is a transformer-based model pretrained on code, on its ability to detect bugs based only on semantics: it does not utilize engineered features.

Prompt-Based Defect Classification

Contrary to the ML models, the latter do not require numerical feature vectors to operate, whereas LLMs can process raw code and act based on the natural language instructions. In this experiment both code snippets were supplied to the model in turn with a query of the form:

Prompt: "Is there a bug in the following function? Explain your answer."

This model was supposed to respond by giving back one of the two high-level answers:

Buggy - in the whereof there is semantic or structural defect.

"Clean" in the case when the code is logically and syntactically correct.

The technique takes advantage of the holistic comprehension of a code Coverage of the LLM: their understanding of its intent, its flow, and syntax as a whole and not only of its superficial token patterns.

Table 8. Evaluation metrics CodeT5

Metric	Buggy (1)	Clear (0)
Precision	1.00	1.00
Recall	1.00	1.00
F1_Score	1.00	1.00
Accuracy	100%	

Table 8 outcomes present 100% classification of the evaluation set. Although it can be a property of the simulation too or a small dataset, it demonstrates the semantic capabilities of LLMs to identify and analyze code quality without preprocessing it and performing a language-specific procedure. In Figure 10, CodeT5 got all of them correct. This translates to 100% accuracy, precision and recall. It shows the powerful semantics that CodeT5 has on code. These ideal outcomes could be affected by the verticality or domination of the test data collect.

Figure 10. Confusion Matrix of CodeT5.

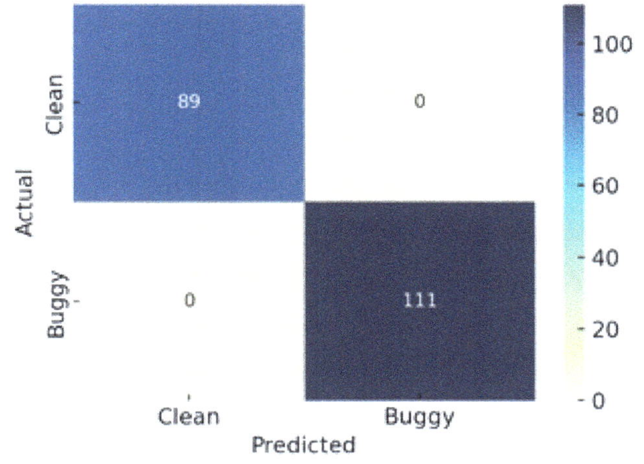

Conclusion of ML Comparison

In the bar plot represents the comparison of four models such as CodeT5 (simulated), Random Forest, SVM and XGBoost the results of which are shown in respect of the class Buggy on the basis of precision, recall and F1-score metrics. In its case, CodeT5 realized a score of 1.0 in all metrics, which means that it detected everything faultlessly in the simulation (Chen et al., 2021). Random Forest had a fairly good performance when it came to recall (0.71) but XGBoost had a more or less moderate performance of 0.50 to 0.57. SVM demonstrated the worst results, especially recall (0.24), which indicates that SVM has trouble detecting a buggy code efficiently. So, on the whole, it is possible to state that CodeT5 indeed demonstrated better performance than traditional ML models in the task of finding buggy code the figure 11 as follows.

Figure 11. Comparison graph between CodeT5, Random Forest, SVM and XGBoost

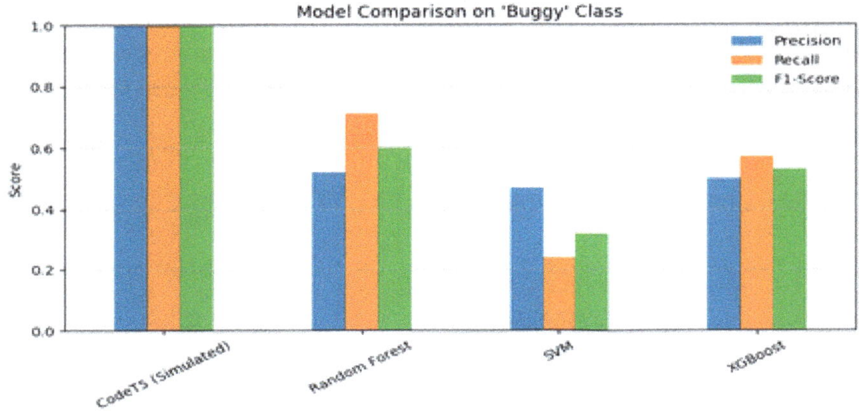

CHALLENGES AND BEST PRACTICES

Although ML and LLMs have a significant potential in the task of software defect detection, their real-world usage is also associated with a few critical issues. This section discusses the main technical challenges that arise in the process of system design and provides the guidelines on how it is better to overcome them to achieve precision, scalability, and sustainable integration of AI.

Noisy or Synthetic Labels

Using noisy or artificially labeled data is one of the greatest problems in any supervised defect detection task and usually makes the accuracy and reliability of the model's poor. Labels on publicly available data are usually made up with analysts relying on commit messages or issue tracker tags, or injected artificially but with defects. These ways often do not reflect the correct semantics and situation of actual bugs, and the gap between the label and the real defect appears (Alonso et al., 2023). This poses a number of problems: noisy labels lessen model accuracy and send incorrect marring messages and artificial bugs or fake bugs can be less complex and can lack the subtle architectural inferences that a real-world development project will have. Along with labeling problems, the best practices are hybrid labeling with the combination of static analysis, manual review, and commit heuristics. With label smoothing and confidence-based filtering noise can be mitigated. Real bug-fix data, such as Defects4J and ManySStuBs4J enhances dataset and leads to better model quality and robustness.

Model Generalization Across Languages

Language diversity is one of the biggest issues in the area of defect detection as different languages may have different syntax, idioms and structures, such as Python, C++, JavaScript. Such variations are problematic in terms of model generalization particularly where feature-based models are dependent on language specific parsers. Even emerging or domain-specific languages do not have enough training data to support high-performance LLM. Coding models can be trained on multilingual corpora such as CodeSearchNet or CodeXGLUE in order to enhance cross-language generalization (Panda et al., 2022). The bias is limited by fine-tuning on balanced language subsets, whereas matching of structural disparities in a common representation space can identify flaws over different programming surroundings.

Interpretability of LLM Outputs

A black-box nature of using LLMs is one of the limitations innate to using such tools due to the lack of understanding or the inability to trace the decisions made by an LLM. The opacity dims the intensity of trust and visibility especially when these models are used in sensitive tasks such as defect detection whereby determination of why a bug is reported is equally crucial as the detection itself. The absence of clear explanations is a huge issue, as LLMs usually do not tell how or why a certain mistake was detected, and it is difficult to verify the findings of the developers and auditors. That is particularly troublesome in an enterprise where business decisions made by AI have to be auditable and traceable since the inner workings of this model are not compliant with them without a significant effort (Zheng et al., 2025). In order to curb these fears, timely engineering interventions will steer LLM to reason out on why code is buggy. Decision-relevant code parts are highlighted in so-called visualization tools (attention heatmaps or saliency plots). Such methods increase model clarity and awareness on the part of the developer.

Scalability and Latency Concerns

The defect detection tools need to be able to work with large amounts of files (at least thousands of files), and that is necessary in real-time scenarios (e.g. CI/CD pipelines or IDEs), where quick feedback is the key point. One of the issues though, most pronounced when working with large context windows, is the computational requirements of LLMs that can be compute-intensive and be slower to provide inferences than some other models. Moreover, pipelines using Machine Learning should have the capacity to accomplish high-throughput batch processing and enable distributive execution in order to be scalable and responsive (Kong et al., 2025). To overcome such challenges, best practices such as model distillation, quantization, asynchronous analysis, and caching can largely lower inference time but do not decrease accuracy. A hybrid model-lightweight models run on real-time operations, and more mature models run during the scheduled scans- alludes to speed and depth in the process of defects detection.

FUTURE DIRECTIONS

As defect detection systems grow more advanced, new research directions and improvements are appearing at the crossroads of software engineering and artificial intelligence. Future systems need to move past current limitations by improving generalization, explainability, and automation across various programming languages and platforms. This section highlights promising directions that build on current ML and LLM techniques and aim for smarter, stronger, and more scalable defect detection architectures.

Fine-Tuning Open-Source LLMs With Labeled Bug Data

While pretrained LLMs like CodeT5, StarCoder, or LlamaCode show a strong general understanding of code, they often miss specific details about bugs. Fine-tuning these models on high-quality, labeled bug datasets, such as Defects4J, ManySStuBs4J, or curated bug-fix commit datasets, could greatly improve their ability to reason about bugs and recognize patterns. The LLMs capable of being trained over large and text-heavy codebases may be able to learn subtle patterns of bugs inherent in real-world projects. This enhances their accuracy, reasoning and reliability in detecting defects (Hossain et al., 2024a). They can also present more accurate context-sensitive fix recommendations with a better code understanding, which would prove useful not only in the bug detection process but also in the bug-fixing process.

Combining ML and LLMs in Hybrid Frameworks

Neither traditional ML models nor LLMs alone can fully capture all aspects of software defects. ML models do well in structured reasoning and tracking statistical features, while LLMs provide semantic depth and flexibility. A promising direction is to combine the strengths of both in hybrid systems that work in parallel or together. There are emergent examples of hybrid solutions trying to group standard Machine Learning with LLMs to maximize defect identification. An example of such practice is that Machine Learning models could be used to generate a set of possible defect candidates based on structural aberrations within the code and that the results could be passed on to an LLM to verify semantically on a deeper level. The other strategy involves using secondary classifiers to check code summaries produced by LLMs, an extra credibility layer (Hossain et al., 2024b). Moreover, there are ensemble approaches to prediction, i.e., a combination of the predictions on models such as the decision tree, neural network, or LLM, notably, through voting or stacking. This combination of statistical modeling and language understanding helps end to end defect sighting.

Integrating Code Embeddings and Anomaly Detection

Anomaly detection in vectorized code representations is becoming a popular technique to spot outliers or suspicious behavior. Models like CodeBERT, GraphCodeBERT, and UniXcoder create embeddings that capture both the context and structure of the code in dense vectors. Using this method, the defect detection systems can analyze code in a more intelligent way by building an embedding representing all semantic and structural patterns. The system could find anomalies or outliers that are indicative of potential bugs using unsupervised techniques such as the Isolation Forests, Autoencoders, or clustering and possess few labeled data. It is particularly useful when used on evolving codebases and detection of rare bugs (Vokhranov & Bulakh, 2024).

CONCLUSION

It was a chapter that discussed the intersection between ML, LLMs, and software defect detection, and how to build intelligent, scalable, and multilingual systems to find and fix code-level bugs. We provided a bridge between theory and practical approach by providing experimental assessment as well as comparison with other solutions to prove the idea that the transformed scenario of automated software quality assurance based on AI technologies is being realized. On this corpus containing

1,000 code samples covering seven different programming languages, the system was tested. The engineered features to train three classical ML models Random Forest, SVM, and XGBoost were the number of tokens, the control structure, and the AST depth. Random Forests were the best performing of them, with an F1-score of 0.60, and in that regard, it was the best on buggy code detection. SVM and XGBoost performed poorly in precision and recall especially when faced with the semantic nature of clean code. These results highlight the weaknesses of rule-based features to represent more in-depth logic.

The findings want the developers to apply conventional ML models, such as Random Forest or XGBoost, when they wish to identify defects in a correctly structured, explicable, and quickly observed manner, which best suits CI/CD pipelines and unvaryingly bred codebases. These models perform well when data is well labeled and structural patterns are uniform. Scholars are supposed to concentrate on the improvement of model generalization throughout languages and can be reduced to minimize the dependence on hand-manufactured features. LLMs such as CodeT5 exhibit powerful semantic reasoning without explicit training characteristics in any case. Future directions can be done to train LLMs on real-world bugs, merge with graph-based or anomaly detection, enhance multilingual datasets, interpretability, and deployment with low latencies. Software quality assurance with AI will revolutionize code analysis, allowing it to become intelligent and autonomous as part and parcel of development processes. Natural prompts give LLMs such as CodeT5 a capability to find minute semantic bugs across languages, transcending the classic static analysis. One day, computer-based assistants (AI-based tools) will be a part of IDEs and perform real-time bugging, propose the solutions, and give code explanations. As now shown in development through embeddings, graph neural networks, and DevSecOps integration, AI will actively come to improve code quality, security, and productivity, no longer in the indirect role as a passive assistant but as a direct partner in the code.

REFERENCES

Abiona, O. O., Oladapo, O. J., Modupe, O. T., Oyeniran, O. C., Adewusi, A. O., & Komolafe, A. M.Oluwatosin Oluwatimileyin AbionaOluwatayo Jacob OladapoOluwole Temidayo ModupeOyekunle Claudius OyeniranAdebunmi Okechukwu AdewusiAbiola Moshood Komolafe. (2024). The emergence and importance of DevSecOps: Integrating and reviewing security practices within the DevOps pipeline. *World Journal of Advanced Engineering Technology and Sciences*, *11*(2), 127–133. DOI: 10.30574/wjaets.2024.11.2.0093

Ahmed, H. A., Bawany, N. Z., & Shamsi, J. A. (2021). CaPBug-A framework for automatic bug categorization and prioritization using NLP and machine learning algorithms. *IEEE Access : Practical Innovations, Open Solutions*, *9*, 50496–50512. DOI: 10.1109/ACCESS.2021.3069248

Alonso, J., Piliszek, R., & Cankar, M. (2023). Embracing IaC through the DevSecOps philosophy: Concepts, challenges, and a reference framework. *IEEE Software*, *40*(1), 56–62. DOI: 10.1109/MS.2022.3212194

Balogun, A. O., Bajeh, A. O., Mojeed, H. A., & Akintola, A. G. (2020). Software defect prediction: A multi-criteria decision-making approach. *Nigerian Journal of Technological Research*, *15*(1), 35–42. DOI: 10.4314/njtr.v15i1.7

Chandramouli, R., Kautz, F., Torres-Arias, S., & (U.S.), N. I. of S. and T. (2024). Strategies for the integration of software supply chain security in DevSecOps CICD pipelines : DOI: 10.6028/NIST.SP.800-204D

Chapman, P. J., Rubio-González, C., & Thakur, A. V. (2025). Interleaving static analysis and LLM prompting with applications to error specification inference. *International Journal of Software Tools for Technology Transfer*, *27*(2), 239–254. DOI: 10.1007/s10009-025-00780-7

Chen, S., Tao, F., Pan, C., Hu, X., Ma, H., Li, C., Zhao, Y., & Wang, Y. (2021). Modeling quality changes in Pacific white shrimp (Litopenaeus vannamei) during storage: Comparison of the Arrhenius model and Random Forest model. *Journal of Food Processing and Preservation*, *45*(1). Advance online publication. DOI: 10.1111/jfpp.14999

Chhabra, D., & Chadha, R. (2024). Automatic bug triaging process: An enhanced machine learning approach through Large Language Models. *Engineering Technology & Applied Science Research*, *14*(6), 18557–18562. DOI: 10.48084/etasr.8829

Choraś, M., Kozik, R., Pawlicki, M., Hołubowicz, W., & Franch, X. (2019). Software development metrics prediction using time series methods. In *Computer Information Systems and Industrial Management* (pp. 311–323). Springer International Publishing., DOI: 10.1007/978-3-030-28957-7_26

Costea, A., Tiwari, A., Chianasta, S., R, K., Roychoudhury, A., & Sergey, I. (2023). Hippodrome : Data race repair using static analysis summaries. *ACM Transactions on Software Engineering and Methodology*, *32*(2), 1–33. DOI: 10.1145/3546942

Dalla Palma, S., Di Nucci, D., Palomba, F., & Tamburri, D. A. (2022). Within-project defect prediction of infrastructure-as-code using product and process metrics. *IEEE Transactions on Software Engineering*, *48*(6), 2086–2104. DOI: 10.1109/TSE.2021.3051492

Erich, F. M. A., Amrit, C., & Daneva, M. (2017). A qualitative study of DevOps usage in practice. *Journal of Software (Malden, MA)*, *29*(6), e1885. DOI: 10.1002/smr.1885

Fanqi Meng, F. M., Fanqi Meng, W. C., & Wenying Cheng, J. W. (2023). An integrated semi-supervised software defect prediction model. *Wangji Wanglu Jishu Xuekan*, *24*(6), 1307–1317. DOI: 10.53106/160792642023112406013

Hernández-Molinos, M. J., Sánchez-García, A. J., Barrientos-Martínez, R. E., Pérez-Arriaga, J. C., & Ocharán-Hernández, J. O. (2023). Software defect prediction with Bayesian approaches. *Mathematics*, *11*(11), 2524. DOI: 10.3390/math11112524

Hossain, S. B., Jiang, N., Zhou, Q., Li, X., Chiang, W.-H., Lyu, Y., Nguyen, H., & Tripp, O. (2024a). A deep dive into large language models for automated bug localization and repair. Proceedings of the ACM on Software Engineering, 1(FSE), 1471–1493. DOI: 10.1145/3660773

Hossain, S. B., Jiang, N., Zhou, Q., Li, X., Chiang, W.-H., Lyu, Y., Nguyen, H., & Tripp, O. (2024b). A deep dive into large language models for automated bug localization and repair. Proceedings of the ACM on Software Engineering, 1(FSE), 1471–1493. DOI: 10.1145/3660773

Ibrahim, A., Abdelsalam, H., & Taj-Eddin, I. (2023). Software defects prediction at method level using ensemble learning techniques. *International Journal of Intelligent Computing and Information Sciences*, *23*(2), 28–49. DOI: 10.21608/ijicis.2023.189934.1251

Jahanshahi, H., Cevik, M., & Başar, A. (2020). Predicting the number of reported bugs in a software repository. In *Advances in Artificial Intelligence* (pp. 309–320). Springer International Publishing., DOI: 10.1007/978-3-030-47358-7_31

Kong, J., Xie, X., Cheng, M., Liu, S., Du, X., & Guo, Q. (2025). ContrastRepair : Enhancing conversation-based automated Program Repair via contrastive test case pairs. *ACM Transactions on Software Engineering and Methodology*, *34*(8), 1–31. Advance online publication. DOI: 10.1145/3719345

Liu, Z., Tang, Y., Li, M., Jin, X., Long, Y., Zhang, L. F., & Luo, X. (2025). LLM-CompDroid: Repairing configuration compatibility bugs in Android apps with pre-trained large language models. *ACM Transactions on Software Engineering and Methodology*, *3736406*. Advance online publication. DOI: 10.1145/3736406

Naidoo, R., & Möller, N. (2022). Building software applications securely with DevSecOps: A Socio-technical perspective. Proceedings of the ... *European Conference on Information Warfare and Security*, 21(1), 198–205. DOI: 10.34190/eccws.21.1.295

Panda, K. C., & Asurion Insurance, U. S. A. (2022). Application of AI and ML in the field of DevSecOps. *Journal of Artificial Intelligence & Cloud Computing*, *1*(4), 1–4. DOI: 10.47363/JAICC/2022(1)280

Pham, L., Saad, F. A., & Hoffmann, J. (2024). Robust resource bounds with static analysis and Bayesian inference. Proceedings of the ACM on Programming Languages, 8(PLDI), 76–101. DOI: 10.1145/3656380

Ren, J., Zheng, Z., Liu, Q., Wei, Z., & Yan, H. (2019). A buffer overflow prediction approach based on software metrics and machine learning. *Security and Communication Networks*, *2019*, 1–13. DOI: 10.1155/2019/8391425

Senior DevOps Engineer - Cloud VA USA, D. and A., & Kummarapurugu, C. S. (2024). A framework for real-time AI-driven secure code analysis integrated with DevSecOps in cloud-native CI/CD pipelines. INTERANTIONAL JOURNAL OF SCIENTIFIC RESEARCH IN ENGINEERING AND MANAGEMENT, 08(11). DOI: 10.55041/IJSREM17273

Tang, L., Liu, J., Liu, Z., Yang, X., & Bao, L. (2025). LLM4SZZ: Enhancing SZZ algorithm with context-enhanced assessment on large language models. Proceedings of the ACM on Software Engineering, 2(ISSTA), 343–365. DOI: 10.1145/3728885

Tang, Y., Wang, H., Zhou, Q., & Sun, B. (2024). A method for surface defect detection based on multiscale feature fusion and pyramid attention. *IEEE Access : Practical Innovations, Open Solutions*, *12*, 36457–36465. DOI: 10.1109/ACCESS.2024.3374131

Vokhranov, I., & Bulakh, B. (2024). Transformer-based models application for bug detection in source code. *Technology Audit and Production Reserves*, *5*(2(79)), 6–15. DOI: 10.15587/2706-5448.2024.310822

Walia, G. K., & Sidhu, J. S. (2022). Content based Adaptive Image Demosaicing using Random Forest Algorithm. SAMRIDDHI A Journal of Physical Sciences Engineering and Technology, 14(02), 183–186. DOI: 10.18090/samriddhi.v14i02.10

Zheng, M., Xie, D., Shi, Q., Wang, C., & Zhang, X. (2025). Validating network protocol parsers with traceable RFC document interpretation. Proceedings of the ACM on Software Engineering, 2(ISSTA), 1772–1794. DOI: 10.1145/3728955

Zhou, X., Mao, R., Zhang, H., Dai, Q., Huang, H., Shen, H., Li, J., & Rong, G. (2023). Revisit security in the era of DevOps: An evidence-based inquiry into DevSecOps industry. *IET Software*, *17*(4), 435–454. DOI: 10.1049/sfw2.12132

Zou, J., & Lv, J. (2025). Dual-task guided network: Hybrid supervised learning for surface defect detection. *Measurement Science & Technology*, *36*(3), 036133. Advance online publication. DOI: 10.1088/1361-6501/adb6cb

KEY TERMS AND DEFINITIONS

Bug Localization: Finding the exact place in the code where a bug exists.

CI/CD Pipeline: An automated process that tests, builds, and deploys software whenever developers update the code.

Code Embeddings: Numerical representations of code that help AI understand patterns and similarities.

DevSecOps: A development approach that integrates security checks into every stage of software building.

Large Language Model (LLM): An advanced AI model trained on large amounts of text and code to understand and generate human-like responses.

Machine Learning (ML): A computer technique that learns patterns from data to make predictions or decisions.

Prompt-Based Learning: A way of using LLMs by giving natural language instructions (prompts) to get answers or solve tasks.

Random Forest: A machine learning method that uses many decision trees to make accurate predictions.

Semantic Understanding: The ability of a system to understand the meaning and logic of the code, not just its structure.

Software Defect: A mistake or error in the code that causes the program to behave incorrectly.

Static Analysis: A method of checking code for errors without running the program.

XGBoost: A fast and powerful machine learning algorithm often used for classification tasks.

Chapter 2
AI-Powered Malware Detection and Behavioral Analysis

P. Selvakumar
http://orcid.org/0000-0002-3650-4548
Department of Science and Humanities, Nehru Institute of Technology, Coimbatore, India

Vaishali Rahate
http://orcid.org/0000-0001-6277-1685
Datta Meghe Institute of Management Studies, India

A. S. Deeppana
http://orcid.org/0009-0007-9840-5725
Karpagam Academy of Higher Education, India

Yukta Sawalkar
Datta Meghe Institute of Management Studies, India

C. John Paul
St. Joseph University, India

S. Murugaveni
http://orcid.org/0000-0003-2081-7803
SRM Institute of Science and Technology, India

ABSTRACT

In the rapidly evolving landscape of cybersecurity, malware continues to pose significant threats to individuals, enterprises, and critical infrastructures. Traditional signature-based detection techniques, though effective against known threats, fall short when confronted with sophisticated, polymorphic, and zero-day malware. This limitation has fueled research into more intelligent, adaptive detection mechanisms that can identify malicious software even when it exhibits novel patterns or obfuscation strategies. Static malware analysis, unlike dynamic analysis, focuses on examining the intrinsic attributes of executable files without executing them, making it safer, faster, and less resource-intensive. Static features typically include opcode

DOI: 10.4018/979-8-3373-8252-4.ch002

sequences, bytecode patterns, control flow graphs, API call frequency distributions, file headers, string literals, and metadata extracted from Portable Executable (PE) files or other binary formats.

INTRODUCTION

In the rapidly evolving landscape of cybersecurity, malware continues to pose significant threats to individuals, enterprises, and critical infrastructures. Traditional signature-based detection techniques, though effective against known threats, fall short when confronted with sophisticated, polymorphic, and zero-day malware. This limitation has fueled research into more intelligent, adaptive detection mechanisms that can identify malicious software even when it exhibits novel patterns or obfuscation strategies. Static malware analysis, unlike dynamic analysis, focuses on examining the intrinsic attributes of executable files without executing them, making it safer, faster, and less resource-intensive. Static features typically include opcode sequences, bytecode patterns, control flow graphs, API call frequency distributions, file headers, string literals, and metadata extracted from Portable Executable (PE) files or other binary formats. However, manually engineering features from these elements is labor-intensive, error-prone, and often fails to capture subtle patterns indicative of malware. Deep learning addresses these challenges by enabling automatic feature extraction, discovering complex nonlinear relationships within the data, and generating representations that are often more discriminative than handcrafted features.

By treating malware byte sequences as images or one-dimensional signal streams, CNNs can extract local and global patterns that signify malicious behavior. For instance, reshaping a binary file into a two-dimensional grayscale image allows CNNs to detect characteristic textures and structural anomalies, such as repeated sequences, packed sections, or unusual byte distributions that are indicative of obfuscation or encryption techniques commonly employed by malware authors. Such sequential modeling is crucial for understanding malware behavior at the instruction level, where specific instruction chains or API call sequences may reveal malicious intent, even in the absence of overt signatures. Hybrid architectures combining CNNs and RNNs have demonstrated superior performance in extracting both spatial and temporal features, effectively bridging the gap between structural analysis and sequential semantics. Autoencoders, another class of deep learning models, are particularly useful for unsupervised feature extraction and dimensionality reduction. By learning compact latent representations of high-dimensional malware data, autoencoders can capture essential characteristics while filtering out noise, thereby improving classification performance. Variational Autoencoders (VAEs) further enhance this capability by modeling the underlying probability distribution of malware features, enabling robust representations that generalize well to previously unseen variants. Feature engineering in static malware analysis also benefits from embedding and representation learning techniques. Word embedding-inspired models, such as Word2Vec and Doc2Vec, can be applied to opcode sequences, transforming discrete instruction sets into dense, continuous vector representations that capture semantic relationships between instructions (Alhamdi et al. 2025).

Despite the efficacy of deep learning for static malware feature extraction, several challenges persist. Malware authors continually evolve their techniques, employing code obfuscation, packing, encryption, and polymorphism to evade detection. These transformations can obscure critical features, reduce signal-to-noise ratios, and hinder model generalization. Adversarial attacks on malware classifiers, where subtle modifications to binaries deceive deep learning models, represent another emerging concern, highlighting the need for robust, resilient feature extraction mechanisms. Moreover, the high dimensionality of raw binary data poses computational challenges, requiring careful consideration of model complexity, memory requirements, and training efficiency. The practical deployment of deep learning-based static malware feature extraction systems involves several critical steps. Initially, large-scale datasets of malware and benign software must be curated, ensuring representative coverage across malware families and variants (Alqahtani et al. 2022). Preprocessing steps, such as binary unpacking, opcode extraction, and byte-to-image conversion, transform raw executables into formats suitable for deep learning consumption.

DYNAMIC BEHAVIORAL ANALYSIS WITH AI-ENHANCED SANDBOXING

Dynamic analysis involves executing suspicious programs in controlled environments to observe their actions in real-time, capturing behavioral indicators such as system calls, network activity, file manipulations, registry modifications, process creation, and memory usage patterns. By focusing on how malware interacts with the operating system and the environment, dynamic analysis can uncover malicious behaviors that remain hidden to static inspection due to obfuscation, packing, or encryption. However, traditional sandboxing solutions, which isolate malware execution to prevent system compromise, often face limitations such as slow analysis throughput, evasion by malware designed to detect virtualized or instrumented environments, and the challenge of interpreting large volumes of heterogeneous behavioral data. Integrating Artificial Intelligence (AI) into sandboxing frameworks addresses these challenges by enhancing automation, pattern recognition, and threat intelligence, enabling faster, more accurate, and adaptive malware detection.

Variational Autoencoders (VAEs) and Deep Belief Networks (DBNs) can generate compact, latent representations of complex behavioral sequences, allowing for efficient anomaly detection and reducing the risk of false positives (Alshahrani et al. 2021). Similarly, graph-based approaches, where execution flows and inter-process communications are represented as graphs, benefit from Graph Neural Networks (GNNs) to capture relational and topological patterns, revealing malware strategies such as lateral movement, persistence mechanisms, and privilege escalation attempts. Malware often incorporates sandbox detection mechanisms, such as checking for virtual machine artifacts, unusual timing discrepancies, or the presence of monitoring tools, to alter its behavior or remain dormant in artificial environments. AI models can mitigate these evasion tactics by learning from behavioral deviations and generating predictive insights about likely malicious intent even when certain actions are suppressed. Reinforcement learning has also been explored in this domain, allowing sandbox systems to adaptively modify their environment or stimuli to coax evasive malware into revealing its true behavior, thereby increasing detection efficacy. Additionally, adversarial learning techniques have been applied to harden AI models against attempts by malware to manipulate or deceive behavioral analysis systems, enhancing resilience in dynamic threat landscapes. The deployment of AI-enhanced sandboxing requires careful orchestration of several components to ensure effective and scalable operation. Firstly, the sandbox environment must faithfully emulate target systems to capture realistic malware behavior while maintaining robust isolation to prevent accidental compromise. Instrumentation tools capture granular behavioral data, including API calls, registry access, memory patterns, network traffic, and file system interactions. These data streams are then preprocessed, normalized, and transformed into formats suitable for AI models, such as sequences, embeddings, or graphs (Bazzi et al. 2021).

Transfer learning and model fine-tuning are increasingly employed to adapt pre-trained AI models to new malware families or changing attack vectors, significantly reducing training time and enhancing adaptability. The benefits of AI-enhanced sandboxing extend beyond improved detection rates. By generating detailed behavioral profiles, these systems facilitate threat attribution, malware lineage analysis, and identification of attack campaigns. Behavioral fingerprints extracted through AI models can be shared across organizations to create collaborative threat intelligence databases, enhancing collective defense. Furthermore, AI models provide the potential for predictive threat analysis, anticipating malware evolution trends and enabling proactive mitigation strategies. Integration with other cybersecurity tools, such as endpoint detection and response (EDR) systems, intrusion detection systems (IDS), and security information and event management (SIEM) platforms, allows for automated incident response, containment, and remediation, significantly reducing the dwell time of malware in organizational networks. Moreover, adversarial threats and novel evasion tactics continually necessitate adaptive learning strategies and robust model updating to maintain detection efficacy. While challenges related to computational complexity, interpretability, and adversarial evasion remain, ongoing research and practical deployments demonstrate that AI-enhanced sandboxing is a cornerstone technology for next-generation cybersecurity, providing real-time, accurate, and scalable mechanisms to safeguard digital infrastructures against the ever-growing landscape of malicious software (Bose et al. 2008). In modern computing environments, file systems serve as the backbone for data storage and access, facilitating operations ranging from simple read/write requests to complex transactional processes. However, this centrality also makes file systems a prime target for cyber threats, including ransomware, insider attacks, malware infiltration, and data exfiltration attempts. Each event carries rich metadata, such as file size, owner, process initiating the action, access context, and temporal information. The high-dimensional and heterogeneous nature of this data makes manual inspection impractical and traditional threshold-based detection approaches prone to false positives and false negatives (Burguera et al. 2011). Unsupervised learning algorithms address these challenges by automatically learning patterns of normal file system behavior from historical data and identifying instances that deviate significantly from these learned patterns. For example, an unexpected spike in write operations to sensitive directories or unusual access by a process that typically does not interact with certain files may be isolated as anomalous clusters. The choice of distance metrics, feature normalization, and cluster density thresholds are critical factors influencing detection performance.

Probabilistic and statistical modeling provides another approach to unsupervised anomaly detection in file system events. Gaussian Mixture Models (GMMs), Hidden Markov Models (HMMs), and kernel density estimation methods model the underlying distribution of normal behaviors and calculate the likelihood of observed events. Events with low probability under the learned distribution are classified as anomalies. HMMs, in particular, excel at capturing sequential dependencies in file system operations, allowing detection of suspicious sequences, such as abnormal file access chains or repeated modifications by a single process. Similarly, time-series analysis techniques can identify deviations in temporal patterns, including sudden bursts of access, irregular inter-event times, or cyclical deviations from expected activity levels. These methods are particularly useful for detecting insider threats, ransomware, or automated scripts that interact with the file system in ways inconsistent with historical patterns. Deep learning has further advanced the state of unsupervised anomaly detection in file system events by enabling automated feature extraction and the learning of complex, nonlinear patterns. Autoencoders, including Variational Autoencoders (VAEs), are frequently employed to learn compressed latent representations of normal event sequences. During training, the autoencoder learns to reconstruct normal event data with minimal error. These approaches are particularly valuable in enterprise environments where relationships between processes, users, and files are complex and highly interconnected (Charmet et al. 2022).

Online or streaming implementations are increasingly relevant, enabling real-time monitoring and immediate alerting for anomalous file system events. Despite the power of unsupervised learning for anomaly detection, several challenges remain. High-dimensional, noisy, and imbalanced file system data can produce false positives, generating alert fatigue for security teams. Sophisticated attackers may craft behavior that closely mimics normal operations, evading detection. Additionally, model drift over time, as normal behavior evolves due to software updates, organizational policy changes, or user activity variations, necessitates continuous retraining and adaptation. Research into adaptive learning, explainable AI (XAI), and robust feature representation seeks to address these challenges, providing models that maintain accuracy over time while offering insights into the nature of detected anomalies. Furthermore, privacy and regulatory considerations must be addressed when monitoring file system events, ensuring that sensitive data is protected during analysis and storage. In conclusion, anomaly detection using unsupervised learning on file system events provides a powerful framework for detecting both known and unknown cyber threats. By modeling normal behaviors and identifying deviations, these systems offer proactive, adaptive, and scalable defense mechanisms against malware, ransomware, insider threats, and other malicious activities.

GRAPH-BASED MALWARE CLASSIFICATION VIA NEURAL NETWORKS

In the constantly evolving landscape of cybersecurity, malware has become increasingly sophisticated, utilizing obfuscation, polymorphism, and code-reuse techniques that render traditional signature-based detection approaches largely ineffective. To counter these advanced threats, research has shifted toward behavior-oriented and structural analysis, where the focus is not merely on binary patterns but on the relationships and interactions within software code. One of the most promising approaches in this domain is graph-based malware classification, which leverages the inherent relational structure of malware programs to detect and categorize malicious software accurately. Graph representations capture the dependencies and flow of information between various components of an executable, including functions, instructions, APIs, and system calls. By translating malware binaries into graph structures, such as control flow graphs (CFGs), function call graphs (FCGs), or program dependence graphs (PDGs), researchers can model both the structural and behavioral semantics of malware, enabling neural network-based classifiers to identify malicious patterns that are often invisible to conventional methods. Function call graphs, on the other hand, abstract interactions between functions or methods, highlighting the modular structure of the code and the pathways through which functions invoke one another (Chen et al. 2022).

In a GCN, each node iteratively updates its representation by combining its own features with aggregated features from its neighbors, enabling the model to learn hierarchical patterns and relational dependencies. This neighborhood aggregation is crucial for malware analysis, as it allows the model to capture complex interactions, such as function chains involved in privilege escalation, encryption routines, or communication with external hosts. Variants such as Graph Isomorphism Networks (GINs) have been proposed to achieve greater expressive power, enabling the neural network to differentiate between structurally similar but functionally distinct malware graphs. Feature representation within graph-based malware classification is a key component of model success. Node features may include instruction embeddings, opcode sequences, API call frequencies, and function-level attributes such as cyclomatic complexity or code entropy. Edge features can encode control flow types, call dependencies, or data transfer relationships (Christodorescu et al. 2005). Advanced embedding techniques, inspired by word embeddings in natural language processing, have been adapted to graphs, producing continuous vector representations of nodes and edges that preserve semantic and structural information. Graph pooling and readout operations aggregate node-level embeddings into a global graph representation suitable for classification.

First, they are inherently resistant to code obfuscation and minor structural perturbations, as the relational patterns within graphs are preserved even when superficial modifications occur. Second, they capture both micro-level behaviors (e.g., sequences of API calls within a function) and macro-level structural patterns (e.g., interaction between functions or modules), providing a multi-scale understanding of malware. Third, graph-based models generalize better to unseen malware families because they rely on the structural and relational semantics rather than surface-level signatures. Recent studies have demonstrated that GNN-based classifiers outperform classical feature-based and convolutional approaches on benchmark malware datasets, achieving higher accuracy, precision, and recall while maintaining robustness against polymorphic variants. Despite these advantages, several challenges remain in graph-based malware classification. From a deployment perspective, graph-based malware classification systems can be integrated into automated threat intelligence pipelines, enabling real-time detection and categorization of malware samples. Preprocessing steps involve binary parsing, disassembly, graph construction, and feature extraction. The resulting graphs are then fed into trained neural network models, which generate classifications or risk scores. This integration facilitates rapid triage of malware, identification of novel threats, and prioritization of mitigation strategies (Ficco 2021).

REAL-TIME MEMORY FORENSICS WITH REINFORCEMENT LEARNING

As modern computing systems continue to evolve in complexity, volatile memory has emerged as a critical frontier for cybersecurity and digital forensics. Real-time memory forensics, the practice of examining this dynamic data to detect malicious activities, uncover intrusions, and reconstruct system events, is essential for proactive threat detection, incident response, and digital investigations. However, traditional memory forensics techniques face significant challenges: they are computationally intensive, often require offline post-mortem analysis, and struggle to keep pace with high-throughput, continuously changing memory contents. Additionally, sophisticated malware can employ memory-resident techniques, such as reflective DLL injection, rootkits, or code injection into legitimate processes, which evade conventional disk-centric analysis. Reinforcement learning is a branch of machine learning in which an agent learns to make sequential decisions by interacting with an environment, receiving feedback in the form of rewards or penalties, and iteratively improving its policy to maximize cumulative rewards. In the context of memory forensics, the environment consists of the system's memory space, encompassing processes, threads, heap and stack segments, kernel data structures, and network buffers (Jeon et al. 2022). The RL agent's actions may include scanning specific memory regions, prioritizing processes for inspection, triggering memory dumps of suspicious regions, or executing targeted queries for patterns indicative of malware.

Conventional analysis methods either examine the entire memory space indiscriminately, incurring high latency and computational costs, or rely on fixed heuristics that may miss critical evidence. RL agents, by contrast, learn efficient exploration strategies to prioritize high-value memory regions based on prior experience, reward feedback, and predictive modeling of threat likelihood. For example, an agent may learn that processes exhibiting anomalous thread creation patterns, unexpected kernel object interactions, or sudden surges in memory allocation are more likely to harbor malicious code, guiding the system to focus intensive analysis on those regions. By combining these techniques, DRL-based memory forensics agents can autonomously learn complex patterns associated with malware, rootkits, or other cyber threats that evolve dynamically within system memory. A critical component of real-time memory forensics with RL is feature representation. Raw memory data is voluminous and heterogeneous, encompassing executable code, stack frames, heap allocations, kernel objects, and process control blocks. To make the problem tractable for reinforcement learning, observations are often transformed into structured feature vectors or embeddings. Techniques include entropy-based metrics to detect obfuscation or packed regions, opcode frequency distributions, API call trace embeddings, process and thread lineage representations, and memory access patterns. Graph-based representations can also encode relationships between processes, threads, and memory pages, enabling RL agents to reason over both spatial and relational contexts (Kaur et al. 2025).

Malware authors frequently design memory-resident malware to avoid detection by delaying execution, employing code encryption in memory, or modifying runtime behavior in response to monitoring tools. RL agents, through continuous interaction and feedback, can learn policies that adapt to such evasive behaviors. For instance, if a malware sample remains dormant in certain memory regions, the agent may incrementally adjust its scanning schedule or expand the scope of monitoring to capture delayed execution events. Reinforcement learning also facilitates active probing strategies, such as selectively perturbing memory states or monitoring system call responses to elicit hidden behaviors, allowing analysts to uncover otherwise concealed malicious activities. By incorporating reward functions that balance detection efficacy, computational cost, and false-positive minimization, RL-based systems optimize operational efficiency and maintain real-time responsiveness. Deployment of RL-driven memory forensics systems entails several critical considerations. High-performance instrumentation is required to capture memory snapshots, system call traces, and process metadata without introducing significant latency or affecting system stability. Preprocessing pipelines normalize and encode observations, enabling neural network-based RL agents to efficiently process high-dimensional inputs. Training strategies involve both simulation and real-world experimentation, where synthetic malware or sandboxed memory states provide initial learning environments before deployment in live systems. Despite these advantages, several challenges remain in real-time memory forensics with reinforcement learning. Memory analysis is computationally intensive, and RL training itself can require significant resources and time, particularly when operating on high-dimensional, streaming data. Additionally, adversarial attacks on RL agents, where malware attempts to manipulate the agent's observations or reward feedback, represent a potential risk that must be mitigated through robust design and adaptive policies (Kolosnjaji et al. 2016). In conclusion, real-time memory forensics augmented by reinforcement learning represents a transformative approach in cybersecurity, combining the rich, ephemeral insights of volatile memory with adaptive, intelligent decision-making.

API CALL SEQUENCE MODELING FOR THREAT IDENTIFICATION

In modern computing systems, the application programming interface (API) serves as the critical bridge between software applications and the underlying operating system, enabling controlled access to system resources such as files, memory, network sockets, and hardware devices. While APIs facilitate efficient software development and modular design, they also represent a rich source of information for cybersecurity analysis, as malicious software often interacts with system resources in distinctive patterns. Malware authors rely on sequences of API calls to execute their objectives, whether it is data exfiltration, privilege escalation, network propagation, or system compromise. These sequences often reflect the functional behavior of a program more accurately than static binary features or superficial code signatures. API call sequence modeling begins with the extraction of runtime execution traces from monitored programs. This can be accomplished through dynamic analysis techniques such as sandboxing, instrumentation frameworks, or hooking mechanisms that capture API invocations along with associated metadata, including arguments, return values, process identifiers, thread contexts, timestamps, and caller-callee relationships. In this analogy, individual API calls are analogous to words, sequences of calls to sentences, and program execution traces to documents (Li et al. 2022). By leveraging this perspective, models can learn the contextual dependencies and co-occurrence patterns that characterize malicious behavior, providing a discriminative basis for threat identification. Recurrent Neural Networks (RNNs) form the foundational architecture for sequence modeling in API call analysis. For instance, an RNN-based model may recognize a sequence in which a process first opens sensitive files, then modifies registry settings, and finally initiates network connections, flagging this as indicative of a data exfiltration attempt. Hierarchical models further enhance performance by grouping API calls into higher-level functional categories, capturing both micro-level (instruction-specific) and macro-level (behavioral motif) patterns.

Sequence embeddings enable neural networks to generalize across similar API call patterns, allowing the detection of novel malware variants that reuse functional behaviors but with minor modifications. Contextual embeddings, derived from models such as Transformers, further improve sequence modeling by capturing complex interactions between API calls across varying temporal scales. Graph-based sequence modeling offers another perspective for API call analysis, particularly when relationships between calls are non-linear or involve branching control flows. This approach is especially valuable for malware that employs complex execution logic, conditional branches, or parallel threads, where linear sequences alone may fail to capture critical behavioral relationships. Node features, such as argument types, access permissions, or process context, and edge features, such as control flow type or call frequency, provide additional discriminative power for classification. The practical deployment of API call sequence modeling for threat identification involves several critical considerations. Data collection and preprocessing require efficient instrumentation to capture high-fidelity traces while minimizing performance overhead on monitored systems. Feature normalization, embedding construction, and categorical encoding are essential for model convergence and generalization (Lin et al. 2020).

Figure 1. Deep learning-powered malware detection in cyberspace

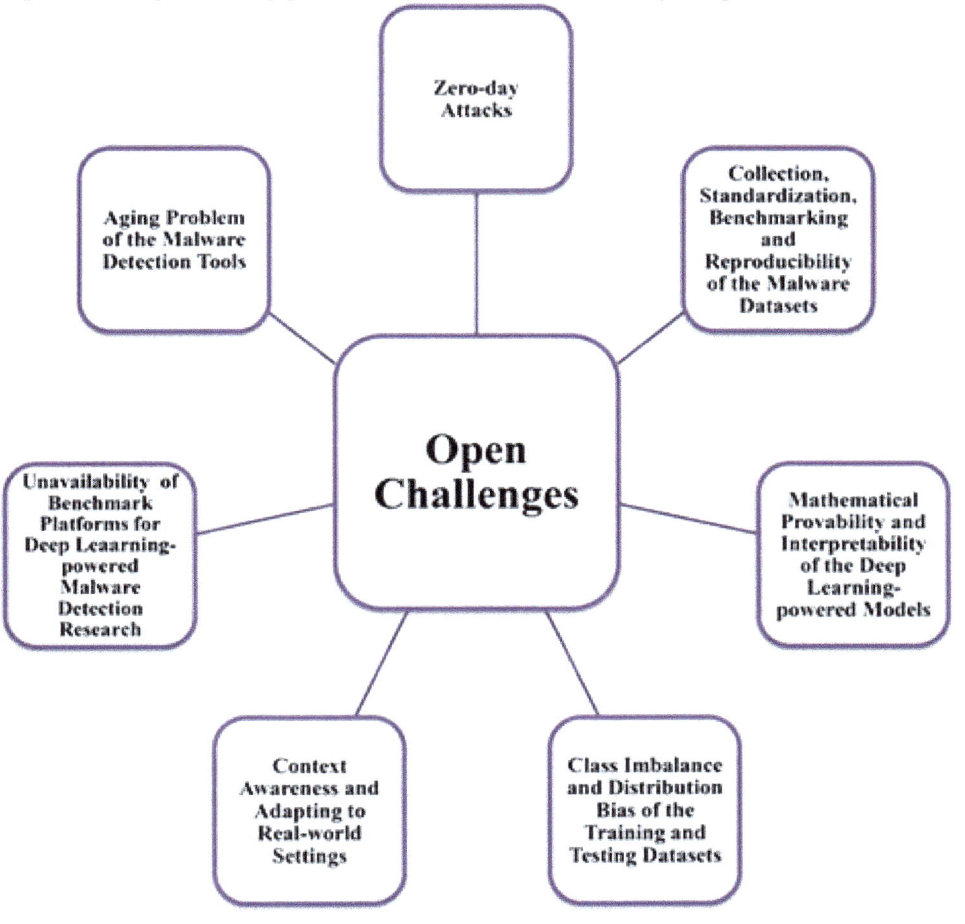

Interpretability is another critical concern, as security analysts require insight into which API sequences or subsequences triggered the detection. Explainable AI techniques, including attention visualization, saliency maps, and sequence attribution, provide transparency and enhance trust in automated threat identification systems. In addition to detection, API call sequence modeling supports malware classification, threat intelligence, and predictive analysis. By clustering similar sequences or embeddings, analysts can group malware into families, identify lineage relationships, and anticipate potential future behaviors. Transfer learning enables models trained on large corpora of API sequences to adapt quickly to emerging malware variants, reducing time-to-detection and enhancing operational resilience. In conclusion, API call sequence modeling represents a highly effective approach to threat identification, leveraging the temporal and functional semantics of program execution to detect malicious activity with high precision. Embedding methods and hierarchical representations enhance generalization across malware families, while attention mechanisms and explainable AI techniques improve interpretability and trust (Liu et al. 2021). Despite challenges such as evasion, obfuscation, and sequence variability, API call sequence modeling is a cornerstone of modern malware detection, offering real-time, adaptive, and scalable solutions for safeguarding computing environments against the continuously evolving landscape of cyber threats.

HYBRID SIGNATURE-AI DETECTION ENGINE

Signature-based detection engines, historically the cornerstone of malware identification, rely on pre-defined patterns or unique byte sequences within malicious binaries to identify known threats. While highly effective against previously encountered malware, signature-based methods are inherently reactive and struggle against polymorphic, metamorphic, and zero-day attacks. To leverage the complementary strengths of both paradigms, hybrid signature-AI detection engines have emerged, integrating deterministic signature detection with intelligent, predictive analysis, creating a robust, layered defense mechanism capable of addressing contemporary and future cyber threats. A hybrid detection engine operates on the principle of layered security, where signature and AI components function in tandem to provide comprehensive threat coverage. The signature module continues to perform rapid identification of known threats using hash-based checksums, pattern matching, and heuristic rules derived from malware databases. These deterministic methods enable the system to immediately neutralize familiar threats with high confidence and low computational overhead. Simultaneously, the AI module operates on behavioral, structural, or statistical features extracted from software binaries, processes, network traffic, or system logs. The AI engine complements the signature module by targeting unknown, obfuscated, or polymorphic malware that would evade conventional detection. Feature extraction is critical in hybrid detection systems, bridging static, dynamic, and behavioral perspectives. Static analysis involves inspecting file attributes without execution, including opcode sequences, byte patterns, file headers, embedded strings, and metadata (Maniriho et al. 2024).

Control flow and function call graphs may feed into GNNs to capture relational and structural dependencies. Combining static and dynamic feature sets allows the hybrid engine to construct multi-dimensional representations of software, enhancing predictive accuracy and robustness against sophisticated evasion techniques. Decision-making in hybrid detection engines can be implemented through parallel or sequential strategies. In a parallel architecture, both the signature and AI modules analyze incoming files or processes concurrently, generating independent threat scores or classifications. The outputs are then fused using logical rules, weighted voting, or probabilistic ensemble mechanisms to arrive at a final verdict. Sequential architectures, alternatively, prioritize signature-based detection as a first-pass filter, rapidly neutralizing known threats, while forwarding uncertain or suspicious samples to the AI module for deeper inspection. This sequential approach optimizes resource utilization, reducing computational load while maintaining comprehensive threat coverage. Advanced implementations incorporate adaptive thresholds, confidence scoring, and contextual feedback from system behavior or historical detections to dynamically balance the contributions of signature and AI components (Manjunath M. et al. 2026). Deep learning architectures, particularly CNNs, capture spatial correlations in bytecode or memory images, while RNNs and LSTMs model sequential dependencies in API calls, instruction streams, or system events.

Integration of the hybrid detection engine with real-world cybersecurity operations requires careful consideration of system design, performance, and scalability. High-throughput environments, such as enterprise networks or cloud infrastructures, demand optimized preprocessing pipelines for feature extraction, vectorization, and embedding generation, minimizing latency without sacrificing fidelity. Continuous retraining and model updating are essential to adapt to emerging malware variants, changes in software behavior, and evolving attack strategies. Hybrid engines often incorporate feedback loops, where outputs from detection incidents, threat intelligence feeds, or analyst interventions inform ongoing model refinement and signature database updates. This creates a self-reinforcing system that grows more accurate and responsive over time. False positive rates are critical, as excessive alerts undermine analyst trust and operational effectiveness, whereas false negatives may leave critical threats undetected. Benchmarking against standard malware datasets, including polymorphic and zero-day variants, enables rigorous validation and comparison with standalone signature or AI-based approaches (Menahem et al. 2014). Real-world deployment also benefits from scenario-based testing, including ransomware outbreaks, insider threat simulations, and APT campaigns, to verify resilience and responsiveness. Hybrid signature-AI detection engines provide a holistic approach to cybersecurity, addressing both the predictability of known malware and the adaptability required for emerging threats.

Challenges remain, including balancing computational complexity, interpretability, and adaptability. Moreover, the ongoing maintenance of signature databases, model retraining, and integration with threat intelligence sources necessitate operational oversight and governance to ensure sustained efficacy. Despite these challenges, hybrid detection engines represent the future of malware defense, combining human-intelligible signatures with AI-driven adaptability to provide comprehensive, proactive, and scalable protection against an ever-changing threat landscape. In conclusion, the hybrid signature-AI detection engine embodies a transformative approach to modern cybersecurity. By integrating deterministic signature methods with adaptive AI models, these engines provide comprehensive detection coverage, balancing accuracy, speed, and resilience (Pawar et al. 2026). Feature-rich AI models capture complex patterns in static, dynamic, and behavioral data, while signature databases ensure precise identification of known threats. Through sequential or parallel fusion strategies, adaptive learning, and real-time deployment, hybrid engines address the limitations inherent in standalone detection methods, offering a robust, scalable, and forward-looking solution for contemporary cyber defense. As threats continue to evolve in sophistication and volume, hybrid detection engines stand as a critical cornerstone of next-generation security architectures, enabling organizations to detect, classify, and mitigate malicious activity with unprecedented efficacy.

AUTOMATED MALWARE FAMILY CLUSTERING

Modern malware exhibits high levels of polymorphism and metamorphism, frequently altering its code, structure, or behavior to evade traditional signature-based detection. The sheer volume of new malware samples generated daily further exacerbates the difficulty of manual analysis, making automated approaches essential for scalable and timely cybersecurity responses. Automated malware family clustering has emerged as a critical methodology in this context, providing a systematic means to group malware samples into families or clusters based on structural, behavioral, and semantic similarities. By identifying commonalities and variations among samples, clustering techniques enable analysts to prioritize threat mitigation, uncover lineage relationships, infer malware evolution, and develop reusable detection strategies, all while minimizing human intervention. The foundation of automated malware family clustering lies in the extraction of meaningful features from malware samples. These features may be derived from static analysis, dynamic behavior analysis, or a combination of both, offering complementary perspectives on malware characteristics (Portase & Colesa, 2021). Dynamic features are derived from runtime execution, capturing system calls, API call sequences, memory and file system interactions, network behavior, registry modifications, process hierarchies, and timing patterns. Hybrid approaches integrate both static and dynamic features, creating high-dimensional, multi-modal representations of malware samples that retain information about both structural composition and behavioral manifestations.

Once features are extracted, automated clustering algorithms partition malware samples into families based on similarity metrics.

Similarity measures are chosen according to feature type and distribution, ranging from Euclidean or Manhattan distance for numeric vectors to cosine similarity for high-dimensional embeddings or Jaccard distance for binary or categorical features. In recent years, representation learning has significantly enhanced malware clustering by providing learned embeddings that capture complex relationships among features. Autoencoders, including Variational Autoencoders (VAEs), compress high-dimensional static and dynamic features into latent representations that retain essential characteristics of malware behavior or structure. Graph-based embeddings also play a crucial role when features are represented as relational structures, such as CFGs or FCGs. By combining learned embeddings with clustering algorithms, automated systems achieve superior accuracy, robustness against obfuscation, and adaptability to evolving malware variants. By embedding these sequences into vector spaces that preserve temporal dependencies, clustering algorithms can identify malware families that share functional behaviors, even when underlying code structures differ. Hybrid models that integrate sequential embeddings with structural or static embeddings enable multi-faceted clustering, capturing both "what the malware is" and "what it does," providing a richer representation of malware families (Rahman et al. 2023). Automated malware family clustering offers numerous practical benefits for cybersecurity operations. It enables threat prioritization by identifying clusters that contain highly virulent or widespread malware variants, allowing security teams to allocate resources effectively.

Operational deployment of automated clustering systems requires careful attention to computational efficiency, data preprocessing, and validation. High-throughput environments, such as threat intelligence platforms or malware analysis sandboxes, generate thousands of new samples daily, necessitating scalable feature extraction pipelines, optimized embedding computation, and incremental clustering algorithms that can accommodate new data without retraining from scratch. Evaluation metrics for clustering effectiveness include silhouette scores, Davies-Bouldin index, Calinski-Harabasz index, and intra- versus inter-cluster distance ratios. External validation can be performed using known malware family labels, though the unsupervised nature of clustering often means that ground truth is incomplete or evolving. Visualization techniques, such as t-SNE plots, UMAP projections, or dendrograms, assist analysts in interpreting clusters, understanding relationships, and communicating findings effectively (Santos et al. 2013). Challenges in automated malware family clustering remain, including dealing with high-dimensional, noisy, and heterogeneous feature spaces; mitigating the effects of code obfuscation, packing, and encryption; and maintaining adaptability as malware evolves rapidly. Sequence variability, polymorphism, and functional redundancy can obscure cluster boundaries, requiring robust similarity measures, learned embeddings, and hybrid feature integration.

Interpretability is critical for operational adoption, as security analysts must understand why certain samples are grouped together and how clusters relate to known malware families or threat campaigns. Research in explainable clustering, attention-based embeddings, and semi-supervised methods continues to address these challenges, enhancing trust and actionable insights. In conclusion, automated malware family clustering represents a cornerstone methodology for contemporary malware analysis and threat intelligence. By leveraging static, dynamic, behavioral, and relational features, combined with classical clustering algorithms, representation learning, sequence modeling, and graph-based embeddings, these systems provide scalable, adaptive, and accurate grouping of malware samples into coherent families. Clustering facilitates detection, prioritization, attribution, and signature generation, while enabling cybersecurity teams to focus investigative and defensive efforts where they are most needed. In response, behavioral analysis has emerged as a critical strategy, focusing on the observation of runtime activities, interactions, and sequences of system events, rather than on pre-existing signatures (Selvakumar et al. 2026). Within this domain, behavioral entropy analysis has gained prominence as an advanced technique for detecting zero-day threats by quantifying the uncertainty, unpredictability, and disorder in system behavior.

In the context of cybersecurity, system behaviors—including API calls, system calls, network interactions, process execution patterns, memory access sequences, and file operations—can be modeled as probabilistic distributions. High entropy values indicate a high degree of unpredictability or deviation from normative behavior, which may correspond to anomalous or potentially malicious activities. Conversely, low entropy reflects predictable, routine, and benign operations. By continuously monitoring system events and computing entropy metrics across multiple operational dimensions, analysts and automated systems can detect deviations that signal zero-day attacks, ransomware execution, privilege escalation attempts, or other malicious intrusions. This approach provides an adaptive, context-sensitive framework for threat detection that does not rely on prior signatures or labeled training data. The operationalization of behavioral entropy analysis involves several critical stages, starting with comprehensive feature collection. System monitoring tools capture a wide array of runtime data, including sequences of system calls, API invocations, process and thread interactions, memory reads and writes, file I/O events, network traffic patterns, and registry or configuration modifications. These features are temporally sequenced and can be aggregated at different levels of granularity, such as per process, per thread, per session, or per network transaction, depending on the desired sensitivity and coverage. Behavioral normalization is performed to account for variations in legitimate software behavior, user activity patterns, and environmental factors, ensuring that entropy calculations reflect meaningful deviations rather than innocuous operational variability (Shabtai et al. 2012).

Entropy computation in zero-day threat analysis leverages both univariate and multivariate approaches. Univariate entropy measures analyze individual behavioral attributes independently, providing insight into anomalies in specific event types, such as abnormal API call sequences or unexpected file access patterns. Multivariate entropy measures, including joint entropy, conditional entropy, and mutual information, capture interdependencies among multiple features, revealing coordinated deviations that may indicate complex attack strategies or multi-stage exploits. For example, a sudden increase in entropy across process creation, memory allocation, and network communication features may signal the execution of a previously unknown ransomware variant. Additionally, entropy can be computed over sliding temporal windows, allowing the detection of transient anomalies or gradual deviations from normal behavior. Adaptive thresholding, anomaly scoring, and statistical significance testing are applied to distinguish genuine threats from benign fluctuations, providing actionable alerts for security analysts or automated response systems. Machine learning techniques enhance behavioral entropy analysis by learning complex patterns, correlations, and thresholds in high-dimensional behavioral data. Supervised, semi-supervised, and unsupervised models can incorporate entropy features as primary inputs or integrate them with other behavioral descriptors for improved predictive accuracy (Singh J. et al. 2021).

First, it is inherently adaptive, identifying anomalies in real-time without relying on prior signatures or predefined rules. Second, it captures both local and global deviations in system behavior, enabling the detection of subtle threats, multi-stage attacks, and distributed exploits. Third, entropy measures are inherently probabilistic, providing a robust statistical foundation for decision-making and reducing false positives through the integration of temporal, relational, and contextual information. Moreover, entropy-based methods facilitate cross-platform and cross-environment detection, as they rely on behavioral deviation rather than platform-specific code signatures. This is particularly valuable in cloud, containerized, and hybrid computing environments where malware may exploit heterogeneous execution contexts. Practical deployment of behavioral entropy analysis involves several key considerations. Real-time computation of entropy metrics requires efficient algorithms, optimized data structures, and streaming analysis frameworks to maintain low-latency detection. Continuous model retraining and threshold adaptation are critical to account for evolving system behavior, software updates, and environmental changes, ensuring sustained detection performance over time. Challenges in behavioral entropy analysis for zero-day threats include distinguishing between malicious anomalies and benign but irregular system behaviors, such as software updates, configuration changes, or high-load processes (Sugapriya et al. 2026).

AI-DRIVEN THREAT INTELLIGENCE FUSION

By combining the adaptive learning capabilities of artificial intelligence with structured and unstructured threat data, organizations can detect emerging threats, anticipate attack vectors, correlate multi-stage campaigns, and optimize defensive measures proactively. Fusion in AI-driven threat intelligence involves the integration of multi-source data at several levels. Data-level fusion aggregates raw observations into a unified dataset, applying normalization, deduplication, and feature engineering to harmonize heterogeneous data. Feature-level fusion combines derived features from multiple sources, capturing complementary information that enhances predictive modeling, such as linking network anomalies with endpoint behaviors or correlating exploit attempts with threat actor chatter. Decision-level fusion integrates outputs from multiple analytical models, combining probabilistic risk scores, classification outputs, or anomaly flags through ensemble techniques, weighted voting, Bayesian aggregation, or reinforcement learning-based policy optimization. APTs often unfold over extended periods, leveraging subtle and multi-stage attack patterns to evade detection (Sun et al. 2016). Through fused intelligence, AI systems can identify early indicators of compromise, such as anomalous lateral movement, unusual privilege escalations, or covert communication with command-and-control (C2) servers, correlating them with historical attack behaviors and threat actor profiles.

Real-world systems must process high-volume, high-velocity data streams while maintaining low latency for timely threat detection and response. Cloud-based architectures, distributed processing frameworks, and stream analytics pipelines are commonly employed to handle scale and throughput requirements. AI-driven threat intelligence fusion also enables enhanced situational awareness and strategic decision-making. Temporal analysis and trend detection reveal emerging attack campaigns, shifts in threat actor behavior, and correlations between disparate attack vectors. Correlation graphs map the relationships among malware variants, threat actor infrastructure, and targeted assets, facilitating attribution, risk assessment, and the prioritization of defensive investments. Furthermore, AI models continuously learn from new incidents and intelligence feeds, dynamically adapting to evolving threat landscapes, reducing detection latency, and improving resilience against novel and sophisticated attacks. Adversarial attacks on AI systems, including poisoning, evasion, and misinformation campaigns, pose risks that require robust defense strategies, including anomaly detection, model validation, and ensemble robustness (Tian et al. 2010).

The exponential growth and increasing sophistication of malware present a formidable challenge to modern cybersecurity systems. Malware investigators face an environment where malicious software can evolve rapidly, evade traditional detection mechanisms, and employ complex techniques such as polymorphism, metamorphism, obfuscation, and multi-stage attacks. This lack of interpretability poses significant risks in operational malware investigation, where understanding the rationale behind a detection or classification is essential for threat attribution, forensic analysis, regulatory compliance, and mitigation planning. Explainable AI for malware investigation operates by augmenting conventional detection and classification pipelines with mechanisms that reveal the internal logic, feature contributions, and decision pathways of AI models (Tobiyama et al. 2016). The foundation of XAI lies in mapping high-dimensional, abstract model outputs to human-understandable explanations. Techniques such as feature attribution, local and global interpretability, attention mechanisms, surrogate models, and counterfactual reasoning allow analysts to identify which aspects of a malware sample—be it static features, behavioral patterns, API call sequences, or network interactions—contributed most strongly to a classification decision.

In dynamic analysis, behavioral features—such as sequences of system calls, API invocation patterns, process spawning behavior, memory access sequences, and network communications—can be attributed and visualized to demonstrate the pathways and interactions that triggered a detection. Explainable AI techniques applied to graph neural networks (GNNs) allow analysts to trace how structural relationships influence model decisions. Graph attribution methods can highlight subgraphs, nodes, or edges critical to a classification outcome, enabling investigators to understand which execution paths, function calls, or system interactions are characteristic of a particular malware family or variant. Such interpretability is vital for threat attribution, as it provides evidence linking specific malicious behaviors to known malware campaigns, threat actors, or attack methodologies, thereby facilitating intelligence-driven response and strategic mitigation planning. Explainable AI also plays a key role in anomaly-based malware detection. Traditional anomaly detection systems may flag deviations from baseline behavior, but without interpretability, analysts struggle to determine whether anomalies represent benign deviations or true threats. XAI methods provide context and rationale, identifying which behaviors, events, or sequences caused the anomaly detection, and offering probabilistic confidence scores or counterfactual scenarios. For example, analysts may see that unusual file access patterns, combined with network exfiltration attempts and privilege escalation attempts, triggered a high anomaly score. By providing this context, XAI transforms anomaly alerts from opaque warnings into actionable intelligence, reducing investigation time and improving decision accuracy. Integrating explainable AI into malware investigation pipelines enhances several operational and strategic capabilities. First, it increases trust in AI-driven tools, ensuring that cybersecurity professionals can rely on model outputs and understand the basis for decisions (Uike et al. 2026).

Many explainability techniques, particularly model-agnostic methods like SHAP or LIME, can be computationally intensive, necessitating optimization, approximation, or selective application in high-throughput environments. Real-time malware investigation often requires streaming or on-demand interpretability, where explanations are generated alongside model predictions without introducing prohibitive latency. Hybrid architectures, which combine explainable rule-based reasoning with AI-driven predictions, further enhance operational effectiveness, providing layered insights that are both interpretable and predictive. Adversarial resilience is another critical consideration in XAI-enabled malware investigation. Sophisticated malware may attempt to evade AI models through obfuscation, code polymorphism, or feature manipulation. Explainable AI facilitates adversarial analysis by exposing the decision boundaries and feature sensitivities of models, allowing investigators to identify potential vulnerabilities, assess robustness, and design defensive measures (Vasan et al. 2020). Counterfactual explanations, which show how small changes in feature values affect model output, are particularly useful for understanding how malware might evade detection and for guiding model hardening strategies. Similarly, attention-based explanations in sequential models reveal which temporal or sequential events the model deems most critical, providing insight into potential evasion strategies employed by advanced threats.

ADAPTIVE SANDBOXING WITH REINFORCEMENT LEARNING

Traditional sandbox environments, however, are often rigid, deterministic, and static in their analysis capabilities, leading to challenges in detecting evasive malware, polymorphic threats, and zero-day exploits. Modern malware often includes anti-analysis mechanisms such as timing delays, environment fingerprinting, code obfuscation, and conditional execution paths designed to detect virtualized or instrumented environments. As a result, conventional sandbox systems frequently fail to trigger the full range of malicious behaviors, generating incomplete behavioral profiles and limiting the efficacy of threat detection. Adaptive sandboxing with reinforcement learning (RL) addresses these challenges by creating dynamic, intelligent analysis environments that learn optimal strategies for interacting with malware, maximizing behavioral coverage, and improving detection fidelity over time. At the core of adaptive sandboxing is the application of reinforcement learning to guide the sandbox's interactions with malware samples. The agent can perform actions such as injecting inputs, simulating user interactions, modifying system calls, altering network conditions, and manipulating memory or process contexts (Wang W. et al. 2017). Each action elicits responses from the malware, producing observable behaviors such as API call sequences, file system modifications, registry changes, network activity, or process hierarchies. Feature extraction is critical to the design and performance of adaptive sandboxing frameworks. As malware executes within the sandbox, behavioral features are collected in real time, encompassing both low-level system attributes and high-level activity patterns. Low-level features include instruction traces, system call sequences, memory access patterns, process and thread interactions, and network packet content. High-level features capture aggregated or semantic behavior, such as ransomware encryption routines, data exfiltration attempts, privilege escalation, lateral movement, and persistence mechanisms. These features serve as the state representation for the RL agent, providing the necessary context to select subsequent actions.

First, it improves behavioral coverage by dynamically selecting actions that trigger conditional code paths and anti-analysis evasion mechanisms. By observing behaviors that static or deterministic sandboxes fail to elicit, analysts gain a more complete understanding of the malware's operational logic, persistence mechanisms, and malicious impact. Second, the RL agent's exploration policy effectively surfaces previously unseen behaviors, creating high-dimensional datasets suitable for supervised, unsupervised, or semi-supervised analysis. Third, adaptive sandboxing supports predictive modeling and threat intelligence by revealing structural and temporal patterns indicative of malware families, campaign attribution, or potential attack vectors, enabling proactive defense strategies (Wang Y. et al. 2021). Operational deployment of adaptive sandboxing frameworks involves addressing several critical considerations. Real-time execution and analysis require efficient state representation, feature extraction, and policy evaluation to minimize latency while maintaining high behavioral fidelity. The design of reward functions is central to RL performance, as poorly defined rewards may incentivize irrelevant or uninformative behaviors. Rewards can be based on metrics such as the novelty of observed actions, the diversity of system call sequences, the number of conditional code paths executed, or the degree of deviation from baseline benign behavior. Computational scalability is essential, particularly in enterprise or cloud-based malware analysis environments where thousands of samples may be processed daily. Distributed sandbox architectures, parallelized RL agents, and optimized neural network architectures ensure throughput without compromising the quality of behavioral observation. Integration with SIEM platforms, threat intelligence systems, malware repositories, and automated response frameworks ensures that the rich behavioral insights generated by adaptive sandboxing are actionable and support timely remediation and threat mitigation. Explainability and interpretability are critical in adaptive sandboxing, particularly when insights inform threat investigation, forensic analysis, and decision-making (Wu et al. 2022).

This interpretability also enhances trust in automated sandboxing systems and supports human-in-the-loop approaches, where RL agents augment analyst decision-making without replacing critical judgment or contextual knowledge. Adaptive sandboxing with reinforcement learning also addresses challenges posed by anti-analysis and evasion techniques. Modern malware frequently checks for the presence of virtualized environments, debugging tools, or instrumented sandboxes, delaying execution, encrypting payloads, or generating benign behaviors to avoid detection (Xie et al. 2023). RL-driven adaptive sandboxes can simulate diverse environmental conditions, modify execution contexts dynamically, and explore action sequences designed to bypass these evasion mechanisms. Through iterative policy learning, the sandbox agent develops strategies that maximize the likelihood of triggering hidden malicious routines, uncovering behaviors that static or rule-based systems cannot detect. This adaptive capability is particularly valuable in handling polymorphic or metamorphic malware, multi-stage attacks, and zero-day threats that would otherwise remain concealed. The integration of adaptive sandboxing into broader cybersecurity frameworks enhances the efficacy of incident response, threat intelligence, and proactive defense strategies.

Challenges in deploying adaptive sandboxing with reinforcement learning include computational complexity, high-dimensional state spaces, sparse reward signals, and the need for careful reward function design to guide meaningful exploration. Real-time analysis may require model optimization, approximations, or hierarchical decomposition to ensure efficiency (Yen et al. 2014). Additionally, adversarial malware designed to detect RL-driven sandboxing may attempt to exploit weaknesses in agent policies, necessitating robust policy validation, stochastic action strategies, and multi-agent coordination to mitigate evasion. Human oversight remains crucial to interpret results, refine policies, and ensure alignment with organizational security objectives, creating a collaborative paradigm between automated RL agents and cybersecurity professionals. By intelligently exploring malware execution environments, dynamically interacting with system components, and optimizing action policies to maximize behavioral coverage, RL-driven sandboxes overcome the limitations of traditional static and deterministic approaches. They enhance detection of evasive, polymorphic, and zero-day malware, support anomaly detection, threat intelligence, and forensic analysis, and provide a foundation for proactive, adaptive cybersecurity defenses. Continuous learning pipelines also enhance resilience against sophisticated malware tactics such as evasion, polymorphism, and adaptive payloads (Yan et al. 2018).

In conclusion, continuous learning pipelines for evolving malware constitute a transformative approach to adaptive, intelligent, and resilient cybersecurity operations. By integrating automated data ingestion, dynamic feature extraction, incremental model updating, feedback-driven refinement, and explainable AI, these pipelines maintain high detection accuracy despite the constant evolution of malware. Operational deployment ensures rapid adaptation to emerging threats, efficient use of resources, and actionable intelligence for security teams. Challenges such as concept drift, scalability, privacy, and adversarial evasion are addressed through incremental learning, stream processing, and robust feedback mechanisms. Ultimately, continuous learning pipelines enable organizations to remain proactive, resilient, and effective in detecting, classifying, and mitigating malware in dynamic, complex, and high-risk digital environments, ensuring that security infrastructure evolves in tandem with emerging threats. The proliferation of digital technologies, cloud computing, and interconnected services has transformed the cybersecurity landscape, necessitating robust, scalable, and intelligent solutions to detect and mitigate malware threats across diverse environments. At the core of a cloud-based AI malware scanning service is a distributed architecture that supports the collection, processing, and analysis of malware samples from heterogeneous sources (Zhang Z. et al. 2019).

Data ingestion pipelines normalize and preprocess incoming samples, extracting both static and dynamic features, including binary structure, code signatures, API call sequences, system interactions, file metadata, network activity, and behavioral traces observed during sandbox execution. By standardizing this data across distributed nodes, the service ensures that AI models receive high-quality, structured input suitable for accurate analysis and detection. Static features include opcode sequences, control flow graphs, embedded strings, import/export tables, and cryptographic signatures, capturing intrinsic properties of files without executing them (Zhu M. et al. 2019). Dynamic features are derived from sandboxed execution, capturing system calls, memory modifications, file and registry changes, network requests, and inter-process interactions. Behavioral patterns, temporal dependencies, and sequence-based representations provide critical insights into malicious activity that may not be evident through static analysis alone. Advanced representation techniques, including embeddings, graph-based models, attention mechanisms, and multi-modal fusion, allow the AI service to capture complex relationships among features, providing a holistic view of malware behavior. Dimensionality reduction, feature selection, and hierarchical modeling ensure that computational efficiency is maintained while preserving discriminative information for accurate detection. Supervised learning leverages labeled datasets of benign and malicious samples to train discriminative models, while semi-supervised and unsupervised approaches detect previously unseen malware by identifying deviations from normal patterns (Zhang Z. et al. 2020). Multi-tenant architectures support enterprise-scale deployments while maintaining data isolation and security, allowing multiple organizations to utilize the service concurrently without compromising privacy or performance (Zhu H. et al. 2024). Integration of threat intelligence and contextual enrichment enhances the precision and relevance of AI-based malware detection.

CONCLUSION

Low-latency processing is critical to meet real-time detection requirements, particularly in scenarios involving active file transfers, container orchestration, or endpoint monitoring. Robustness against adversarial attacks, including evasion techniques, poisoning attacks, and crafted samples designed to bypass AI models, is achieved through continuous retraining, model hardening, adversarial example generation, and multi-layered detection strategies. High availability, fault tolerance, and disaster recovery mechanisms ensure uninterrupted service in cloud environments, supporting enterprise resilience and compliance requirements. Techniques such as feature attribution, attention visualization, and interpretable model outputs allow security analysts to understand the rationale behind detections, providing transparency and supporting informed decision-making. By providing interpretable insights into malware behaviors, file anomalies, and risk assessments, the service empowers organizations to respond effectively and confidently to threats. Continuous improvement is an essential aspect of cloud-based AI malware scanning. Feedback loops from analyst verification, sandbox observations, incident outcomes, and threat intelligence updates allow the AI models to refine their decision-making, adapt to emerging malware trends, and enhance detection precision. Active learning strategies selectively query human experts for labeling of ambiguous or high-impact samples, further improving model robustness and accuracy. The iterative nature of the continuous learning cycle ensures that the service evolves alongside the threat landscape, maintaining relevance and efficacy as malware tactics, techniques, and delivery mechanisms change over time. The service also supports multi-platform and multi-format detection, encompassing Windows, Linux, macOS, mobile operating systems, IoT devices, and cloud-native applications. By abstracting the analysis pipeline and utilizing platform-agnostic feature representations, the service provides consistent and comprehensive coverage across heterogeneous environments. Containerized and microservices-based architectures facilitate modular deployment, integration with existing security tools, and rapid scaling to meet the demands of large-scale enterprises or cloud providers. This flexibility enables organizations to adopt a unified, centralized approach to malware detection while accommodating the diverse technological ecosystems that characterize modern IT infrastructures. By integrating distributed data ingestion, static and dynamic feature analysis, deep learning, continuous learning, and feedback-driven adaptation, these services provide rapid, accurate, and context-aware malware detection across large-scale, heterogeneous environments. Operational scalability, privacy preservation, explainable AI, and integration with broader security workflows enhance resilience, efficiency, and trust, enabling organizations to respond proactively to evolving malware threats. As malware continues to grow in sophistication and volume, cloud-based AI scanning services provide a robust, adaptive, and intelligent solution, supporting continuous protection, real-time threat mitigation, and long-term cybersecurity resilience in dynamic and complex digital ecosystems.

REFERENCES

Alhamdi, M. J. M., Al-Dabbagh, S., & Al-Timemy, A. H. (2025). AI-based malware detection in IoT networks within smart cities: A survey. Computer Communications, 224, 108055. Elsevier. DOI: 10.1016/j.comcom.2025.108055

Alqahtani, H., Alzahrani, B., & Alshamrani, A. (2022). Deep learning-based dynamic analysis for malware detection using hybrid features. *Computers & Security*, *115*, 102614. DOI: 10.1016/j.cose.2022.102614

Alshahrani, S., & Huang, C. C. (2021). Intelligent dynamic malware detection using machine learning in IP reputation for forensics data analytics. *Future Generation Computer Systems*, *118*, 171–185. DOI: 10.1016/j.future.2021.01.007

Bazzi, O., Chehab, A., Kayssi, A., & Harb, H. (2021). Deep learning for malware detection in Android systems using system calls. *Journal of Information Security and Applications*, *58*, 102718. DOI: 10.1016/j.jisa.2020.102718

Bose, A., Hu, X., Shin, K. G., & Park, T. (2008). Behavioral detection of malware on mobile handsets. In *Proceedings of the 6th International Conference on Mobile Systems, Applications, and Services (MobiSys)* (pp. 225-238). ACM. DOI: 10.1145/1378600.1378626

Burguera, I., Zurutuza, U., & Nadjm-Tehrani, S. (2011). Crowdroid: Behavior-based malware detection system for Android. In *Proceedings of the 1st ACM Workshop on Security and Privacy in Smartphones and Mobile Devices* (pp. 15-26). ACM. DOI: 10.1145/2046614.2046619

Charmet, J., Eshete, B., & Biggio, B. (2022). Adversarial robustness of behavior-based malware detectors: A survey. *Computers & Security*, *120*, 102809. DOI: 10.1016/j.cose.2022.102809

Chen, J., Li, C., & Wang, W. (2022). DMalNet: Dynamic malware analysis based on API feature engineering and deep learning. *Computers & Security*, *116*, 102676. DOI: 10.1016/j.cose.2022.102676

Christodorescu, M., Jha, S., Seshia, S. A., Song, D., & Bryant, R. (2005). Semantics-aware malware detection. In *2005 IEEE Symposium on Security and Privacy* (pp. 32-46). IEEE. DOI: 10.1109/SP.2005.20

Ficco, M. (2021). A deep neural network-based technique for ransomware detection and classification. *Future Internet*, *13*(2), 25. DOI: 10.3390/fi13020025

Jeon, M., Choi, J., & Cho, S. (2022). DAIMD: Dynamic analysis for IoT malware detection using convolutional neural networks on behavior images. *Computers & Security*, *117*, 102683. DOI: 10.1016/j.cose.2022.102683

Kaur, H., Selvakumar, P., Haashni, S., Anute, N., Sharma, M., & Manjunath, T. C. (2025). Representations in Developing Thinking Regarding Probabilities in Higher Education. In Anastasiadou, S., & Seremeti, L. (Eds.), *Modes of Representation in Developing Statistical Thinking in Education* (pp. 89–118). IGI Global Scientific Publishing., DOI: 10.4018/979-8-3693-9934-7.ch006

Kolosnjaji, B., Zarras, A., Webster, G., & Eckert, C. (2016). Deep learning for classification of malware system call sequences. In AI 2016: Advances in Artificial Intelligence (pp. 137-149). Springer. DOI: 10.1007/978-3-319-50127-7_11

Li, Y., Meng, G., Liu, Y., & Chen, C. (2022). Deep graph convolutional networks for behavioral malware classification. *Computers & Security*, *112*, 102508. DOI: 10.1016/j.cose.2021.102508

Lin, Z., Song, C., & Gu, X. (2020). Deep learning for ransomware detection using process behavior graphs. *Computers & Security*, *92*, 101740. DOI: 10.1016/j.cose.2020.101740

Liu, H., Zhang, J., & Chen, Z. (2021). Android malware detection based on long short-term memory networks and behavioral sequences. *Journal of Information Security and Applications*, *59*, 102843. DOI: 10.1016/j.jisa.2021.102843

Maniriho, P., Nyirahabineza, J., & Niyonzima, J. (2024). Comparative analysis of malware detection approaches in modern cyber–physical systems. *International Journal of Safety and Security Engineering*, *15*(2), 189–200. DOI: 10.18280/ijsse.150201

Manjunath, M., Ogwu, M. C., Udayakumar, S., Kuchipudi, J. D., Rengarajan, C., & Manjunath, T. C. (2026). Chromatography in Food Contaminant Analysis: Principles, Advances, and Applications for Food Safety. In Ogwu, M., & Izah, S. (Eds.), *Detection, Identification, and Monitoring of Food Contaminants* (pp. 207–238). IGI Global Scientific Publishing., DOI: 10.4018/979-8-3373-3982-5.ch007

Menahem, E., Shabtai, A., & Elovici, Y. (2014). Mobile malware detection through analysis of deviations in application network behavior. *Computers & Security*, *43*, 1–18. DOI: 10.1016/j.cose.2014.02.002

Pawar, P., Anute, N., Tripathi, S., Ahluwalia, G. K., & Kalshetti, P. (2026). AI and Its Importance in the Development of Luxury Consumption. In Vale, V. (Ed.), *Multidisciplinary Approach to Luxury Consumption and AI* (pp. 1–34). IGI Global Scientific Publishing., DOI: 10.4018/979-8-3693-8422-0.ch001

Portase, R., & Colesa, A. (2021). Curator: A system for creating datasets for behavioral malware detection. In 2021 20th IEEE International Conference on Trust, Security and Privacy in Computing and Communications (TrustCom) (pp. 1209-1216). IEEE. DOI: 10.1109/ISPDC52870.2021.9521600

Rahman, M. A., Rafiq, M. A., & Islam, S. (2023). AI-based malware detection and classification for wireless networks using hybrid deep learning. *International Journal for Research in Applied Science and Engineering Technology*, *11*(10), 1420–1430. DOI: 10.22214/ijraset.2024.64512

Santos, I., Brezo, F., Ugarte-Pedrero, X., & Bringas, P. G. (2013). Opcode sequences as representation of executables for data-mining-based unknown malware detection. *Information Sciences*, *231*, 64–82. DOI: 10.1016/j.ins.2011.08.020

Selvakumar, P., & Haashni, S. SudhaAnanthi, G., & Manjunath, T. C. (2026). Cybernetic Systems Thinking: Foundations for Organizational Adaptability. In L. Tsvasman (Ed.), Cybernetic Leadership for Sustainable Innovation (pp. 99-124). IGI Global Scientific Publishing. DOI: 10.4018/979-8-3373-2484-5.ch004

Shabtai, A., Kanonov, U., Elovici, Y., Glezer, C., & Weiss, Y. (2012). "Andromaly": A behavioral malware detection framework for Android devices. *Journal of Intelligent Information Systems*, *38*(1), 161–190. DOI: 10.1007/s10844-010-0148-x

Singh, J., & Singh, J. (2021). A survey of the recent trends in deep learning based malware detection. *Journal of Cybersecurity and Privacy*, *2*(4), 800–829. DOI: 10.3390/jcp2040041

Sugapriya, S., Garg, S., Mahalle, A., Yewale, A. U. & T. C., M. (2026). Medical Imaging and Radiology: AI-Powered Diagnostics. In D. Ather, N. Mun, S. Jain, V. Jain, & V. Kukreja (Eds.), Applied AI and Computational Intelligence in Diagnostics and Decision-Making (pp. 191-218). IGI Global Scientific Publishing. .DOI: 10.4018/979-8-3373-3311-3.ch008

Sun, M., Guo, Y., & Zhang, X. (2016). Android malware detection based on sensitive behaviors and API calls. *Computers & Security*, *59*, 294–310. DOI: 10.1016/j.cose.2016.03.003

Tian, R., Islam, R., Batten, L., & Versteeg, S. (2010). Differentiating malware from cleanware using behavioural analysis. In 2010 5th International Conference on Malicious and Unwanted Software (MALWARE) (pp. 23-30). IEEE. DOI: 10.1109/MALWARE.2010.5665796

Tobiyama, S., Yamaguchi, Y., Shimada, H., Ikuse, T., & Yagi, T. (2016). Malware detection with deep neural network using process behavior. In 2016 IEEE 40th Annual Computer Software and Applications Conference (COMPSAC) (pp. 577-582). IEEE. DOI: 10.1109/COMPSAC.2016.151

Uike, D., Sugapriya, S., Kaur, M., Mahalle, A., Dhule, N., & T. C., M. (2026). Drug Discovery and Optimization With AI. In D. Ather, N. Mun, S. Jain, V. Jain, & V. Kukreja (Eds.), Applied AI and Computational Intelligence in Diagnostics and Decision-Making (pp. 379-404). IGI Global Scientific Publishing. .DOI: 10.4018/979-8-3373-3311-3.ch014

Vasan, D., Alazab, M., Wassan, S., Safaei, B., & Zheng, Q. (2020). IMCFN: Image-based malware classification using fine-tuned convolutional neural network architecture. *Computer Networks*, *171*, 107138. DOI: 10.1016/j.comnet.2020.107138

Wang, W., Zhu, M., Zeng, X., Ye, X., & Sheng, Y. (2017). Malware traffic classification using convolutional neural network for representation learning. In *2017 International Conference on Information Networking (ICOIN)* (pp. 712-717). IEEE. DOI: 10.1109/ICOIN.2017.7899588

Wang, Y., Li, J., & Gu, D. (2021). Ransomware detection based on system call sequences using ensemble learning. *Future Generation Computer Systems*, *118*, 21–31. DOI: 10.1016/j.future.2021.01.033

Wu, D., Xu, L., & He, J. (2022). A hybrid static and dynamic analysis approach using deep learning for malware detection. *Computers & Security*, *113*, 102546. DOI: 10.1016/j.cose.2021.102546

Xie, S., Li, C., & Wang, W. (2023). BEACON: Behavioral malware classification with large transformer models. *Neural Networks*, *163*, 494–505. DOI: 10.1016/j.neunet.2023.07.019

Yan, Q., Yang, H., & Chen, Y. (2018). Detecting malicious behaviors in Android applications using sequence classification of system calls. *Journal of Network and Computer Applications*, *112*, 42–54. DOI: 10.1016/j.jnca.2018.03.004

Yen, T. F., Oprea, A., Onarlioglu, K., Leetham, T., Robertson, W., Juels, A., & Kirda, E. (2014). Beehive: Large-scale log analysis for detecting suspicious activity in enterprise networks. In *Proceedings of the 29th Annual ACM Symposium on Applied Computing* (pp. 1641-1648). ACM. DOI: 10.1145/2554850.2554881

Zhang, Z., Qi, P., & Wang, W. (2019). Dynamic malware analysis with feature engineering and feature learning. *Digital Investigation*, *28*, S77–S88. DOI: 10.1016/j.diin.2019.01.021

Zhang, Z., Wang, W., & Chen, C. (2020). A behavior-based Android malware detection system using deep convolutional neural networks. *Computers & Security*, *97*, 101965. DOI: 10.1016/j.cose.2020.101965

Zhu, H., Wang, W., & Chen, P. (2024). A dynamic analysis-powered explanation framework for Android malware detection. *IEEE Transactions on Knowledge and Data Engineering*, *36*(8), 4259–4274. DOI: 10.1109/TKDE.2024.3436891

Zhu, M., Wang, W., & Ye, X. (2019). Sequence learning with gated CNN and LSTM for behavioral malware detection. *Pattern Recognition Letters*, *128*, 464–470. DOI: 10.1016/j.patrec.2019.10.010

Chapter 3
Adversarial Attacks and Backdoor Exploitation in Large Language Models:
Detection, Forensic Analysis, and Defense Mechanisms

Rocky Kumar
http://orcid.org/0009-0002-6995-2037
Poornima University, Jaipur, India

Joe Arun Raja
http://orcid.org/0000-0002-0572-6076
Presidency University, Bengaluru, India

ABSTRACT

Large Language Models (LLMs) have quickly become cornerstone elements in intelligent systems nowadays, making decisions, automating processes, and doing security operations and interactive applications in a variety of environments. However, their increased integration into critical infrastructures has led to increased concerns regarding malfeasance exploitation by an adversary and/or hidden vulnerabilities. Attackers can exploit these models with prompt-based attacks, backdoors, data poisoning and output manipulation to gain unpermitted access to the model, spread false information, bypass safety filters and to misclassify. These adversarial ways pose a great challenge to the reliability, interpretability and trust degrees when it comes to the AI-driven platforms. This chapter is a detailed look of the adversarial attack surfaces and backdoor exploitation techniques against LLMs. I

DOI: 10.4018/979-8-3373-8252-4.ch003

1. INTRODUCTION

Large Language Models (LLMs) are one of the fundamental technologies in modern artificial intelligence that are transforming the way machines interact with humans, process information and assist in decision-making in various industries. From conversational agents, automated content generation to cybersecurity analytics and healthcare decision support, LLMs are gradually getting integrated in the important digital infrastructures. Their ability to learn complex patterns in language from a vast amount of data has made this possible to a degree never seen before, allowing them to be very fluent, adaptive and able to reason contextually.

However, this rapid adoption has also raised important issues around security, trust and reliability particularly as these models are being rolled out in a high-stakes and adversarial environments. Unlike conventional systems built for software applications which are ruled by deterministic rules, LLMs are probabilistic models with internal processes used to make decisions, which are largely not transparent.

This characteristic results in new types of vulnerabilities which cannot be dealt with using security mechanisms only. Adversarial actors can use the power of the ambiguity of languages, the dependencies between training data, and the weaknesses in the alignment process to manipulate the behaviour of AI models, bypass safeguards, or introduce persistent malicious functionality. Consequently, adversarial attack and backdoor exploitation on LLMs has emerged as an important research agenda for the safe and trustworthy deployment of AI systems.

1.1 Background and Motivation

The motivation behind this chapter is that LLMs are increasingly used in mission critical applications and the parallel escalation of adversarial threats posed to these applications. Organizations are using LLMs for more tasks such as automated customer support, security monitoring, legal document analysis, clinical decision assistance, etc. In such contexts, erroneous or manipulated outputs can cause some terrible consequences, like data breaches, spread of incorrect information, non-compliance with regulations, and loss of public trust.

Recent studies have found that LLMs are especially vulnerable to non-traditional attack vectors, including prompt injection, jailbreak attacks, and training-time backdoor insertion, which exploit the model's language-driven control mechanisms, rather than software vulnerabilities (Carlini et al., 2023). These types of attacks often take very little technical expertise to carry out, and can be accomplished remotely, making these types of attacks very scalable and hard to detect. The motivation of this chapter is to attempt to analyse such emerging threats in a systematic manner and also to present a cohesive view of the detection, forensic investigation and defense strategies in LLM ecosystems.

1.2 Evolution of Large Language Models

The development of large language models has been characterized by a consistent increase in model scale, architectural complexity and training complexity. Early statistical language models were based on n-gram probabilities and rule-based heuristics and did not have much understanding of context. The introduction of neural language models and word embeddings was a significant improvement in semantic representation and paved the way for deep learning based natural language processing.

The transformer architecture was introduced by Vaswani et al. (2017) and proved to be a major breakthrough since it allowed the parallelization of attention mechanisms and long-range dependency modelling. This innovation is what directly led to the development of large-scale pretrained models like BERT, GPT and their successors. Subsequent improvements were made by adding reinforcement learning with human feedback (RLHF), instruction tuning and multimodal combination, which led to models that could reason, use tools and have adaptive dialogues (Ouyang et al., 2022).

However, as LLMs moved from research prototypes to production systems, the increased capabilities of LLMs also led to an increased attack surface. Training pipelines were becoming increasingly complex, deployment environments becoming more heterogeneous and user-interactions less predictable. This development of evolution entails a corresponding development in terms of security analysis methodologies which take account of the model internals as well as the utilization scenario in the real world.

1.3 Security, Trust, and Reliability Concerns in LLMS

Security concerns in LLMs are not limited to the usual idea of data confidentiality and systems availability. Because we know that the outputs of LLM have a direct impact on the decisions of humans, trustworthiness and reliability can also be important system security dimensions. Compromised or manipulated model could give outputs which appear to be plausible but are basically misleading or harmful and hence detection by end users is an extremely difficult task. Trust in LLMs is also being compromised by their black box nature which won't allow much transparency in understanding the how of specific inputs result in the particular outputs they provide. Studies have shown that LLMs may display inconsistency in their behaviour, hallucinate of factual information or expose or increase biases in training data which raises certain concerns about their reliability in sensitive domain (Ji et al., 2023).

When the adversarial manipulation is added to the picture, such problems are significantly amplified, as the attackers are then able to deliberately influence the model behaviour to achieve malicious goals under the otherwise facades of supplying expected model norms. This therefore implies that the role in ensuring trust in LLMs is integrated approaches that entail security engineering, explainable AI and governance frameworks.

1.4 Adversarial Threat Landscape in AI Systems

The adversarial threat landscape around AI systems has changed dramatically with attackers moving away from data-centric attack methods and moving to subtler and more persistent forms of exploitation. In the case of LLMs, some of the adversarial threats include prompt-based attacks that manipulate the runtime behaviour of models, data poisoning attacks that corrupt the training data, and backdoor attacks that inject hidden triggers in the model during development (Goldblum et al., 2023).

Backdoor exploitation is especially worrying because the backdoor mechanism gives hackers control over model behaviour over the long-term without being dormant under normal conditions. When triggered by particular means, such backdoors can lead to targeted misclassification, bypass of policy or unauthorized information disclosure. Unlike overt adversarial types of inputs, backdoors are not easily detectable using standard testing procedures and require using advanced forensic and behaviour analysis types of techniques.

The growing popularity of open-source models and third-party fine-tuning services has also made the landscape of threats even more complex, as organizations are likely to deploy models that are not clean of threats. This is the type of environment where there is a need for systematic security evaluation and continuous monitoring for the lifecycle of the LLM.

1.5 Research Objectives and Chapter Contributions

The main goal of this chapter is to give a thorough and organized enumerate of the problem of adversarial attacks and backdoor exploitation on giant language models: detection, forensics and defense mechanisms. Specifically, the chapter will try to (i) categorize and discuss salient adversarial attack vectors for LLMs, (ii) investigate methods to insert backdoor and their operational implications, (iii) discuss forensics techniques to identify and attribute the modification of the malicious code and (iv) discuss state-of-the-art defense methods for securing LLM deployment. By bringing together the technical, forensic and governmental perspectives, in this chapter contribute to a rich picture on understanding and mitigating security risks in the LLM ecosystems. The insights in this paper are intended to help guide researchers, practitioners and policymakers in building resilient, trustworthy and accountable AI systems that can counter evolving adversarial threats.

2. FOUNDATIONS OF LARGE LANGUAGE MODELS

Large Language Models (LLMs) are the computational backbone of the current natural language processing systems enabling machine to generate, interpret and reason about human language at scale. LLMs are defined by its linguistic representation learning using massive corpus of text using deep neural architectures and self-supervised learning paradigms. Unlike task-specific models, LLMs are aimed to be more generalized in different domains, that makes them applicable for various purposes, such as conversational agents, automated reasoning systems, cybersecurity analytics, decision support tools, etc. Understanding their architectural underpinnings, training methods and deployment assumptions is important to analysing their security posture and vulnerability to adversarial exploitation.

2.1 Architecture of Modern LLMS (Transformers, Attention)

The architectural basis of current LLMs is mostly based on the transformer model which created a paradigm shift in sequence modelling by utilizing self-attention mechanisms. In contrast to recurrent or convolutional neural networks, transformers process input sequences in parallel and, therefore, allow for the efficient learning of long-range dependencies in textual data. The self-attention mechanism calculates contextual relations between all the tokens in a sequence, so the model can dynamically weigh up the relevance of each token during the representation learning process (Vaswani et al., 2017).

Transformer-based LLMs are made up of stacked layers that are composed of multi-head self-attention, feed-forward neural networks, residual connections, and layer normalization. Multi-head attention gives the model the capability of attending to information in different representational subspaces simultaneously, which helps to increase the semantic richness and understanding of the context.

As the model scale increases so does the depth and width of these layers, resulting in Billions or even Trillions of model parameters which can be used to represent extremely complex linguistic patterns (Brown et al., 2020). However, this architectural complexity also causes opacity - which makes it difficult to read decision-making processes in it. From a security standpoint, the use of attention weights and distributed representations introduce potential for adversarial manipulation, as making small changes in input or internal activations can travel through layers of the model and have a major effect on the output of models.

2.2 Training Paradigms: Pre-Training, Fine-Tuning, RLHF

The training lifecycle of LLMs usually takes a multi-stage paradigm comprised of large-scale pre-training, task-specific fine-tuning and alignment optimization via reinforcement learning with human feedback (RLHF). During the pre-training step, models are fed with large unlabelled text corpora's and trained with self-supervised tasks (e.g. next token prediction). This stage allows the model to have a general knowledge of the language and syntax, and semantic relationship (Devlin et al., 2019). Fine-tuning is a task where pretrained models are fine-tuned for particular tasks or domains by retraining a model on smaller datasets that are labelled. While fine-tuning does improve performance and relevance for one's domain, it also poses security risks, especially if the data used for training is sourced from untrusted or third-party sources. Malicious fine tuning can incorporate backdoors or biases which will be dormant and waiting to be triggered in certain conditions.

RLHF has become a dominant alignment technique to control LLM behaviour by training the model using human preferences. In this paradigm, models are optimized with respect to producing outputs agreed upon by human-evaluated reward signals (Ouyang et al., 2022). Although RLHF makes systems safer and easier to use, recent research suggests that it is not enough to eliminate adversarial vulnerabilities because attackers can use manipulation of prompts and changes in distributions to circumvent alignment constraints.

2.3 Deployment Environments and Use-Cases

LLMs are implemented on a broad range of environments, from cloud-based APIs and enterprise platforms to edge devices and hybrid infrastructures. Cloud deployments dominate large-scale applications because of their computational demands - they allow centralizing updates of models, monitoring and controlling access. In opposite, edge and on-device deployments focus on speed of latency and data privacy but have little robust security monitoring and update mechanism in place.

Use-cases for LLMs are spread across various sectors, such as healthcare, finance, education, cybersecurity, and governance. In cybersecurity operations, LLMs are used to help threats intelligence analysis, automated incident response, as well as vulnerability reporting. In situations of such high stakes, poor model behaviour can have knock-on effects, causing misinformation to be spread or unauthorized actions to be taken.

The variety of deployment scenarios makes the security enforcement a complicated task, because the threat models and trust boundaries are different in each environment. Models that receive unrestricted input from the user are especially at risk for adversarial attacks at run-time, and therefore a need for context-aware security controls that are specific to deployment scenarios.

2.4 Security Assumptions in LLM Pipelines

Security assumptions underlying LLM pipelines often are significantly different compared to the traditional software systems. Many deployment architectures make implicit assumptions about pretraining model beingness, trustworthiness of training datasets, and non-malicious inputs to the models from users. These assumptions are increasingly invalid in an adversarial environment where the training pipeline, fine tuning process, and inference time interaction are actively attacked.

LLM pipelines are generally composed of many different stakeholders, such as data providers, model developers, platform operators and end users. Each of the stages presents possible attack surfaces from poisoned datasets and compromised checkpoints to insecure APIs and prompt injection vectors. The lack of standardized security validation mechanisms for pretrained models also makes these risks even more problematic (Bommasani et al., 2022).

As a result, it is not enough to rely only on security at the perimeter or to perform monitoring after deployment. Security needs to be considered as a lifecycle issue, involving a mix of preventive, detective and corrective controls across a model development and deployment cycle.

2.5 Limitations and Exposure Points

In spite of their impressive capabilities, LLMs have their own inherent limitations which adds to their susceptibility to being exploited to adversarial attack. One of the greatest shortcomings is that they are based on statistical correlations not understanding that is based on the way they work and is susceptible to adversarial prompts that exploit the linguistic ambiguities. Additional, LLMs do not have sound mechanisms to validate the authenticity and intent of the user inputs given, hence malicious instruction may be processed along with the legitimate queries given by the user.

Another thing that is important in point of exposure, is in the generalization of the model. While generalization helps to allow versatility it makes one vulnerable to distributional shifts and out of context inputs which can be exploited by adversaries. Furthermore, the scale and complexity of LLMs make it hard to fully test and verify them, which also makes it hard to ensure security properties under all operational conditions.

These limitations highlight the need for vigorous means of detection, forensics, and defence which are discussed in the following sections of this chapter. Understanding the basic attributes of LLMs is therefore a prerequisite to designing resilient and trustworthy AI systems that are able to withstand the ever-changing adversarial threats.

3. TAXONOMY OF ADVERSARIAL ATTACKS ON LARGE LANGUAGE MODELS

As large language models are becoming deeply integrated into critical decision-making systems, there is a much greater exposure to adversarial manipulation. Unlike conventional machine learning systems, LLMs are uniquely vulnerable because they are based on natural language interfaces, large-scale pretrained knowledge and the probabilistic generation of response. Adversarial attacks in LLMs involve malicious attacks that abuse the weaknesses of the model throughout all stages of the model life cycle such as training data, fine-tuning processes, inference-time prompts, and deployment environments.

Developing a structured taxonomy of these types of attacks is crucial to understanding how they work, what impact they have and how to mitigate them.

This section classifies the main adversarial attack vectors that attack LLMs by abusing linguistic inputs, the training pipelines, and the model internals to bypass the safeguards, extract sensitive information or cause malicious behaviour. The taxonomy establishes a conceptual basis for detection, forensic analysis and defense mechanisms covered in the following sections.

3.1 Prompt Injection and Prompt Leakage Attacks

Prompt injection attacks are one of the most common and accessible methods of adversarial attacks against LLMs. These types of attacks take advantage of the instruction-following nature of models by inserting malicious directions in user inputs to make the model override system-defined or developer-defined prompts. Because LLMs treat all text fed to them the same, they tend not to differentiate between trusted instructions from the system and untrusted information given by users and are vulnerable to manipulation of the instruction hierarchy (Zou et al., 2023).

Prompt leakage attacks commonly occur concurrently with prompt injection, which allows attackers to extract sensitive system prompts, concealed policies or proprietary instructions within the model's prompt structure. Such leakage endangers the security of intellectual property in addition to exposing internal logic which could be further used to design more effective attacks. That empirical research has revealed how even models which are aligned using reinforcement learning with human feedback (RLHF) may be compelled to divulge limited information with carefully crafted prompts (Wei et al., 2023). Taking the security perspective, prompt-based attacks are particularly dangerous because, unlike for example back-door attacks, they do not need model parameters or training data to be accessed in order to perform the attack. As a result, their low barrier to entry and high scalability means that they are an important consideration when it comes to publicly accessible deployments of an LLM.

3.2 Jailbreak and Policy Evasion Techniques

Jailbreak attacks are a different type of attack that attempts to circumvent safety limitations as well as content moderation rules set on LLMs. These techniques normally involve role playing scenarios, indirect questioning or the use of layers of instructions that move the model closer and closer to providing outputs not allowed. The ambiguity of context and framing of the narrative can get models to diverge from safety guidelines, while outward looking compliance (e.g. Shen et al, 2023).

Policy evasion techniques are also, often, based on the real tension between being helpful and being safe in the aligned models. Attackers build harmless or hypothetical looking requests for harmful in nature content, and thus exploiting the loopholes in interpreting the policy. Studies have shown jailbreak prompts can be transferred between models, which is an indication that there are systemic vulnerabilities as opposed to implementation-specific flaws (Zhang et al., 2024).

The longevity of jailbreak attacks speaks volumes of static rule-based alignment mechanism fundamentals. As LLMs increase in their admittance to reason and abstract thinking, it may be decided by their adversaries to exploit these exact same capacities to make increasingly sophisticated evasion methods

3.3 Adversarial Input Crafting

Adversarial input crafting can be considered the misuse of text data to produce an error or unexpected output in a machine learning model. Unlike prompt injection that targets instruction hierarchy, the adversarial inputs make use of the statistical sensitivities of model's representations. Small perturbations in phrasing, syntax or tokenization can have a disproportionate effect on model behaviour, leading to model misclassification, hallucination or policy violation (Wallace et al., 2019).

In LLMs examples of adversarial inputs include synonym substitution, paraphrasing and insertion of invisible or rare tokens which affects internal attention distributions. These attacks are even harder to detect as inputs are sometimes very semantically sound and readable to humans. Furthermore, adversarial examples created against a model might have transferability to other models, raising the concern for adversarial transferability between models.

The success of adversarial inputs underscores the vulnerability of deep representations of language into inputs and the need to validate input and check behaviour.

3.4 Data Poisoning Attacks

Data poisoning attacks are attacks that involve the poisoning of samples during the training phase of LLMs using malicious or deceitful data that is injected into the training or fine-tuning data.

Given the scale and the opacity of data collection pipeline to be used for LLM training, adversaries can target the weak data governance practices to introduce poisoned data affecting the model behaviour (Steinhardt et al., 2017). A particularly insidious form of data poisoning is backdoor insertion, where the attackers insert the triggers for the malicious behaviour to occur in a hidden way for it to run when certain patterns are present in the input. These backdoors are dormant in normal operation, and are thus difficult to detect using normal evaluation measures. Research has shown that even with the small scale of poisoned data has the potential to change the behaviour substantially of the model, primarily in the fine-tuning stages (Chen et al., 2021).

Data poisoning is incredibly perilous in open-source and third-party fine-tuning ecosystems where often provenance of models and data in the data set are not sufficiently checked.

3.5 Model Extraction and Inversion Attacks

Model extraction attacks aim to simulate or approximate proprietary LLMs by constructing a series of queries centred on analysing outputs of the models. Through systematic probing of the input and output, the attackers can be used to infer model parameters, architectures, or decision boundaries which can be effectively led to the theft of intellectual property (Tramèr et al. 2016).

In the case of LLMs, extraction attacks can also be used to find the alignment strategies and safety mechanisms. Model inversion attacks are an attack on the relaunch of sensitive training data, based on the outputs of the model. These attacks exploit the effects of memorization in large models so that personal, confidential or proprietary information s/he has inadvertently learned from during the training of the model (Carlini et al., 2023).

Such vulnerabilities lead to serious privacy and regulatory concerns in particular in light of data protection legislation like GDPR. Together, the dangers of exposing powerful LLMs with public APIs without proper rate-limiting, output filtering and auditing mechanisms are pointed out, as are extraction and inversion attacks.

3.6 Comparative Analysis of Attack Vectors

A comparative analysis of the adversarial attack vectors shows tremendous variance in the complexity of attacks accessible, the level of access required, the level of detectability and the level of impact. Prompt based and jailbreak attack are very accessible and scalable but has impact the inference time behaviour mainly. In contrast, data poisoning and backdoor attacks require deeper access into the training pipeline, and result in persistent and stealthy control over model behaviour. Model extraction and inversion attacks are not primarily a risk to behaviour, except in terms of intellectual property and privacy. However, their long-term implications on trust, compliance and economic worth is significant. Understanding these trade-offs is an extremely important factor in establishing priorities for defense strategies and resource allocation for security. The taxonomy presented in this section have been used as a basis for the detection, forensic analysis and defense mechanism presented in the following sections to highlight the need for multi-layered and lifecycle aware security approaches.

Table 1. Classification of Adversarial Attacks on Large Language Models

Attack Category	Target Phase	Required Access	Primary Impact	Detection Difficulty
Prompt Injection & Leakage	Inference	User-level	Policy bypass, info disclosure	Medium
Jailbreak & Policy Evasion	Inference	User-level	Safety violation	High
Adversarial Input Crafting	Inference	User-level	Output manipulation	High
Data Poisoning & Backdoors	Training/Fine-tuning	Pipeline access	Persistent malicious behavior	Very High
Model Extraction & Inversion	Deployment/API	Query access	IP theft, privacy leakage	Medium–High

4. BACKDOOR EXPLOITATION IN LARGE LANGUAGE MODELS

Backdoor exploitation is one of the most extreme and insidious attacks on the security and reliability of large language models (LLMs). Unlike the overt adversarial attacks, which change the model behaviour at the inference phase, backdoors are concealed mechanisms which are embedded into a model at the training phase or fine tuning without revealing the existence of the backdoor mechanism by the malware under normal circumstances and under specific triggers.

This hidden nature makes backdoor attacks to be especially dangerous because the compromised models can pass the standard evaluation benchmarks while still retaining the malicious capabilities. With the increases in the deployment of LLMs in sensitive and mission-critical applications, the knowledge of backdoor use has been a major issue in the development of a secure AI.

4.1 Concept of Backdoors in AI Models

A backdoor in an AI model is a vulnerability intentionally inserted in a model so that it behaves in a predefined malicious way given a specific input in the form of a certain. In the case of LLMs, triggers can be in the form of rare tokens, syntactic patterns, certain phrases or semantic constructs which are embedded in natural language inputs. When such triggers are missing, the model behaves in a normal way and hence it is incredibly hard to identify these triggers using conventional testing practices (Gu et al. 2019).

Backdoors have one crucial distinction with regular adversarial examples. While adversarial inputs are typically developed based on imperceptibly perturbed inputs that take advantage of how the model is sensitive to changes in input, backdoors are deliberately manipulated learned representations of a model. This distinction allows backdoors to have high reliability and precision, as well as to allow attackers to have fine-grained control over the outputs of models. In the case of LLMs, this can result in the bypassing of policy, the targeted misinformation or unauthorised disclosure or manipulation of downstream decision-making processes. The complexity and scale of LLMs also makes the threat worse as the decentralized parameter representations provide ample capacity to represent the hidden malicious behaviours without affecting the overall performance significantly.

4.2 Training-Time Backdoor Insertion

Training-time backdoor insertion is one of the best ways to compromise LLMs. During pre-training or fine-tuning, the attackers introduce poisoned samples in the training data set which link specific triggers with adversarial output. Given the massive amount of data that are used to train LLMs, even a small percentage of poisoned data can be enough to implant a working backdoor (Chen et al, 2021).

In large-scale pre-training pipelines, data is collected from a diverse number of sources and often it is unclear or unverified, allowing for the risk of inadvertent or intentional poisoning of data. Attackers can make use of web scraped corpora, open-source data sets or collaborative data contributions to introduce malicious samples. Once learnt, the backdoor gets incorporated into the internal representations of the model, and this backdoor remains throughout the later stages of training.

The danger is multiplied in cases of transfer learning, where pretrained models are being used and adapted in many fields. A backdoor that is implanted in the early stages of training can end up propagating through deployments and impacting a number of downstream applications without the knowledge of end users or developers.

Figure 1. Backdoor Injection Lifecycle in Large Language Models

Figure 1 shows the lifecycle of backdoor injection in the large language models, through which the poisoned data injected during the training or fine-tuning process, instils hidden triggers in the model parameters. The backdoor is dormant during normal operation, but it is activated in response to certain trigger patterns at inference time and allows the backdoor to be stealthily and persistently controlled by an adversary.

4.3 Fine-Tuning and Trigger-Based Exploitation

Fine-tuning is another important attack point for backdooring, especially in environments that are dependent on third-party models or third-party fine-tuning providers. During fine-tuning, models are fine-tuned on specific tasks or domains with the help of smaller and curated datasets. Attackers can abuse this phase via the injection of poisoned samples that reinforce or introduce backdoor behaviours with very little effort (Kurita et al., 2020).

Trigger-based exploitation in LLMs may be lexical, syntactic or semantic. Lexical triggers could be rare tokens or strings of characters and semantic triggers are based on particular contextual semantics or stories. As LLMs are very good at modelling semantic relationships, the trigger-based backdoors can be designed to be triggered in an extremely specific situation, further lowering the chance of detection.

Once active, backdoors may override mechanisms for alignment (RLHF) - leading the model to go against safety policies or produce targeted outputs. This capability is very dangerous in regulated areas, where compliance and accountability are of the utmost importance.

4.4 Stealthy Backdoors and Persistence Mechanisms

Modern types of backdoor attacks incorporate a stealth aspect and a persistence aspect and are designed to avoid detection while controlling the model behaviour over a long period of time. Stealthy backdoors are designed so that they have minimal effect on your system's normal performance measurements, making sure that backdoored models cannot be detected from normal models during normal testing (Goldblum et al., 2023).

Persistence mechanisms allow backdoors to survive model updates, pruning, or partial retraining. In LLMs, persistence could be realized by distributing the backdoor representation across several layers or interspersing the backdoor representation among highly salient features learned during the training process. Such distributed backdoors are also robust to parameters perturbations and very difficult to remove without a complete retraining of the model.

Additionally, the attackers may create adaptive triggers which may respond depending on the context, which complicates the detection and forensic analysis even further. These advanced techniques help to point out insufficiency of the static testing techniques and need of constant monitoring and behavioural auditing.

4.5 Realistic Attack Scenarios in LLM Pipelines

Realistic Second - Actual attacks in the form of backdoor attack may take advantage of the complexity and decentralized nature of these LLM development pipelines. In the world of open source, it is on occasion possible for attackers to provide innocent looking sets of data or model checkpoints which contain back doors. Organizations deploying such resources without carefully validating them may end up deploying broken models. Another usual case is in outsourced fine-tuning services, where sensitive training data and model parameters gets shared with 3rd party vendors.

Malicious actors either on the inside or on the infrastructure are able to create back doors in this process which raises long-term security risks. In the case of cloud-based deployments, the backdoored models can potentially be deployed to millions of users exponentially multiplying the consequences of the successful attack. These scenarios show that backdoor exploitation is not just a theoretical issue which is not a practical concern from the point of view of the real world. Dealing with this challenge requires coherent approaches in data governing, safe training and forensic analysis and regulatory oversight.

5. DETECTION TECHNIQUES FOR ADVERSARIAL AND BACKDOOR ATTACKS

Detecting adversarial and back doctor attacks against large language models (LLMs) is much more difficult than in traditional machine learning systems due to the scale, opacity and the probabilistic nature of such models. Unlike explicit software vulnerabilities, adversarial manipulations in LLMs tend to occur in a subtle manner in the form of anomalous outputs or hidden activation patterns or latent behavioural shifts that escape traditional testing mechanisms. As LLMs are being used more broadly in open and adversarial ways, effective detection mechanisms have become one of the pillars of trustworthy AI deployment.

This section gives an overview of the state-of-the-art detection techniques for detecting adversarial manipulation and backdoor attack on LLMs. These techniques range from behavioural analysis, checking the internal representation of an application, statistical inference and continuous AI-driven monitoring techniques which highlights the need for multi-layered and lifecycle-aware security strategies.

5.1 Behavioural Anomaly Detection

Behavioural anomaly detection is targeted at the differences of the model output and the expected or baseline behaviour. In LLMs, some examples of such anomalies are unexpected violations of policy, abrupt changes in the tone of responses or outputs that are inconsistent with the context given by particular inputs. By looking at how the model behaves when provided with different prompts, defenders are able to detect irregular patterns that are indicative of adversarial interference (Hendrycks et al., 2021).

This approach is particularly successful against inference time attacks such as prompt injection and jailbreaker where the malicious inputs cause abnormal response with no effect on the model parameters. Behavioural baselines are generally built upon clean validation data set or predefined safety benchmarks which can further be used for comparative analysis under a controlled condition. However, sophisticated backdoors that have been designed to only work under rare triggers are able to get around surface-level testing of behaviour.

Despite its shortcomings, behavioural anomaly detection is an important first line of defense because of its low deployment overhead and compatibility with black box models, which makes it practical for real-world systems where access to internal systems may be limited.

5.2 Gradient and Activation Analysis

Gradient and activation analysis techniques analyse internal representations of models that can help detect abnormal patterns that are associated with adversarial or backdoored behaviour. These methods are based on the assumption that backdoors produce unique activation signatures within specific layers or neurons on their activation. By comparing the gradients or the neuron activations between benign and suspicious inputs, the defenders can detect inconsistencies that are the signs of a malicious manipulation (Wang et al., 2019).

In LLMs, two approaches of activation clustering and neuron attribution have been applied to localize backdoor-related representations embedded during training. Gradient-based saliency analysis can be further used to emphasize the input features which disproportionately have an effect on the outputs, resulting in the identification of hidden trigger dependencies. While these techniques provide high accuracy of detection, they do require access to internals of the models and a lot of computational resources, which limits the applicability of these techniques in deployments which are proprietary or API-based.

Nevertheless, gradient and activation analysis play an important role in forensic investigations, in which a deep analysis of the compromising models has to be performed to verify and localize backdoor implants.

5.3 Trigger Pattern Identification

Trigger pattern identification is an attempt to explicitly identify the existence of backdoor triggers within model behaviour. In LLMs, the triggers can be lexical, syntactic, or semantic and the identification of these is therefore more complex than in image-based models. Detection approaches usually include systematic prompt generation and fuzzing methods to find inputs that have an anomalous output (Chen et al., 2019).

Recent efforts have analysed the reverse engineering techniques which search for minimal input patterns that are capable of activating backdoors. These approaches often involve the use of optimization techniques to find candidates of these triggers so as to maximize deviation in their output. While this works in well-controlled environments the identification of triggers is more of an issue as adapters, or context-dependent triggers are crafted by the attackers, making them well-integrated in the natural language. Despite these difficulties, triggering pattern identification is an important component of backdoor detection pipelines particularly when combined with behavioural and activation-based methods.

5.4 Statistical and Probabilistic Detection Methods

Statistical and probabilistic approaches of detection utilise distributional analysis to detect variations of the model behaviour or internal representations. These methods are based on the concept of modelling the expected probability distributions of the outputs, logits or activations under benign conditions and looking for statistically significant deviations of the model, as a potential indicator of adversarial manipulation (Tran et al. 2018). In the case of LLMs, statistical techniques can be applied to the distributions of tokens, response entropy or patterns of attention weights. Sudden changes of these distributions under certain inputs might give an indication of backdoors or adversarial triggers. Some of the probabilistic methods can be quite useful in detecting subtle attacks or attacks that do not follow the deterministic rules.

However, the dimensionality and variability of outputs from LLMs create problems in characterizing stable statistical baselines. Careful calibration and adaptive thresholding are needed to balance detection sensitivity with false positive.

5.5 AI-Based Monitoring and Continuous Auditing

AI-based monitoring systems are a new frontier in the security of LLM, where it is possible to continuously monitor and audit the behaviour of the model in production. These systems use secondary machine learning models to track the primary model's LLM outputs to find suspicious patterns and alert or enact mitigation systems (Bommasani et al., 2022).

Continuous auditing frameworks combine auditing logging, real-time analysis and evaluation of the behaviour over time for drift detection and delayed or rare backdoor behaviour. Through a combination of historical information and online monitoring, such systems are able to respond to changing attack strategies and usage patterns. Importantly, artificial intelligence-based monitoring helps in supporting governance and compliance needs, being able to trace and hold models accountable for decisions. While these approaches have additional computational overhead, they provide scalable and pro-active defense capabilities which are needed for the long-term deployment of LLM's in an adversarial environment.

Table 2. Comparison of Detection Techniques for Adversarial and Backdoor Attacks

Detection Technique	Access Required	Targeted Attacks	Strengths	Limitations
Behavioral Anomaly Detection	Black-box	Prompt injection, jailbreaks	Easy to deploy, low overhead	Limited against stealthy backdoors
Gradient & Activation Analysis	White-box	Backdoors, poisoning	High accuracy, forensic value	High computational cost
Trigger Pattern Identification	Partial/White-box	Backdoor triggers	Explicit trigger discovery	Ineffective for adaptive triggers
Statistical & Probabilistic Methods	Black/Gray-box	Low-frequency attacks	Detects subtle deviations	Baseline calibration challenges
AI-based Monitoring & Auditing	System-level	All attack types	Continuous, scalable defense	Added complexity and overhead

6. FORENSIC ANALYSIS OF COMPROMISED LARGE LANGUAGE MODELS

As large language models (LLMs) are being deployed in security critical and regulated areas, the ability to research, attribute and remediate breaches has become a key demand of trustworthy AI systems. Forensic analysis of LLMs is a subfield of traditional digital forensics that goes beyond the analysis of probative behaviour due to its aspects of opaque internal representations and large-scale training pipelines. When there is suspicion of adversary manipulation or backdoor exploitation, forensic methodologies form the evidentiary base needed to understand the mechanism of an attack, the impact of that attack and support accountability.

This section delves into the principles, methodologies, and challenges of the forensics of LLMs for compromised LLMs - the mathematical analysis of logs, behavioural analysis and auditing of parameters, and frameworks for declaring attribution.

6.1 AI Forensics: Concepts and Challenges

AI forensics refers to all of the tools and processes required to systematically identify, preserve, analyse, and interpret the evidence associated with the behaviour of AI systems, which is a new field of study. In terms of LLMs, the purpose of forensic analysis is to determine if a model is misused in a malicious manner, how this was done, and under what conditions the malicious behaviour is taking place. Unlike conventional software forensics, AI forensics has to come to terms with non-deterministic outputs, high-dimensional parameter space and adaptive learning processes (Krause et al., 2021).

One of the main problems with LLM forensics is the lack of ground truth. Because of the probabilistic answers models come up with, it is not trivial to distinguish between benign errors than adversarial manipulation. Furthermore, the size of LLMs, which may have billions of parameters, makes the process of inspection impractical. These challenges require special tools and methods which integrate statistical inference, methods for interpretability and also domain knowledge.

Despite these challenges, AI forensics is an important part of the response to a post-incident, regulatory compliance, and long-term system hardening, and therefore an essential part of secure LLM deployment.

Figure 2. AI Forensic Investigation Workflow

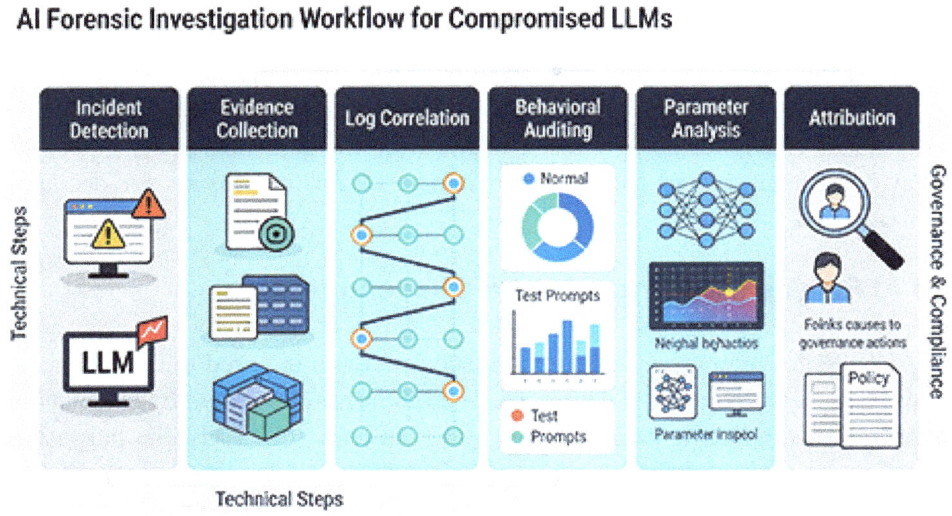

An AI forensic investigation workflow for compromised large language models is shown in Figure 2 and shows the sequential process of incident detection, evidence collection, log correlation, behaviour auditing, parameter analysis and attribution. The workflow focuses on integration of technical and governance-oriented steps needed to aid in accountability and remediation.

6.2 Log Correlation and Trace Reconstruction

Log correlation and trace reconstruction are the backbone of forensic in deployed systems of LLM. Logs that are generated as part of the data ingestion process, training, fine-tuning and inference can provide a temporal track of system activity that can uncover anomalous events or suspicious patterns. By correlating logs across multiple components (such as data pipelines, model servers and user interfaces), investigators can reconstruct the sequence of actions that led to a compromise (Behl & Behl, 2017).

In LLM environments, trace reconstruction is made difficult by distributed architectures and asynchronous processing. Cloud-based deployments could consist of multiple services and geographic locations with partial logs generated from each of them. Effective forensic analysis also requires the centralized logging, standardized formats and secure time synchronization in order to provide evidentiary integrity. When used in conjunction with anomaly detection techniques, log correlation can help with identification of introduction of poisoned data, authorization fine-tuning actions or anomalous inference behaviour in conjunction with backdoor activation. These insights are important, to limit the extent of the investigation, to assist in further analysis.

6.3 Model Behaviour Auditing

Model behaviour auditing: It is done by systematically evaluating the output of LLM to detect the patterns of adversarial manipulation. Auditing procedures which include: generally structured prompt testing, evaluation based on scenarios and longitudinal analysis of model responses in controlled conditions. By comparing what is observed with expected behaviour against baselines, auditors can identify deviations from what is expected behaviour and what is indicative of backdoors or alignment failures (Ribeiro et al., 2020).

In compromised models, behaviour auditing may be able to reveal conditional anomalies - output that is outside the normal range only when certain triggers or situations are in place. Such kinds of findings are especially useful in the case of stealth backdoors, which are specifically meant to avoid being caught by routine testing. Behavioural audits can also measure effectiveness of deployed mitigation strategies, by measuring changes in consistency of response and adherence to policy.

Even though behaviour auditing alone cannot prove beyond doubt the compromise of a model, it will provide actionable evidence that can be used to inform further forensic steps, such as parameter inspection and attribution analysis.

6.4 Evidence Extraction From Model Parameters

Extracting the evidence from the model parameters is one of the most technical challenging tasks of LLM forensics. This means that the weights, activations and learned representations are analysed to identify artifacts associated with adversarial training or backdoor addition. Techniques such as activation clustering, neuron attribution and spectral analysis have been put forward to localize suspicious components in deep neural networks (Wang et al., 2019). In LLMs analysis at the parameter level is complicated by scale and entanglement, in that it is possible that malicious behaviour is spread across layers as opposed to being contained in specific neurons. Nevertheless, forensic researchers have proven that backdoors tend to leave detectable signatures in activation patterns or gradient responses when they are triggered (Tran et al., 2018). Extracting and preserving such evidence is important to be able to validate behavioural findings and to support decisions about remediation.

Parameter-based forensics typically has to be performed in controlled environments because of the computational requirements and the requirement for white box access. As such, it is most relevant when internal investigations or auditing is done rather than real-time monitoring.

6.5 Attribution and Accountability in LLM Attacks

Attribution and accountability are important goals of forensic analysis, especially in an organizational and regulatory context. Attribution aims to determine the source of attack, i.e., whether it is from malicious data contributors, compromised infrastructure or insider threats, whereas accountability is about taking responsibility and taking corrective measures (Brundage et al., 2020).

In the case of LLM ecosystems, attribution is complicated by the fact that there are multiple stakeholders involved in the model lifecycle. Data providers, model developers, platform operators and end users can all affect the behaviour of the system, creating ambiguity in the responsibility. Forensic evidence from logs, behavioural audits, and parameter analysis are useful to clarify these relationships by correlating some anomalies to specific processes or events.

Establishing accountability is helpful in not only supporting incident response efforts, but also with supporting the governance and compliance efforts, which can enable organizations to have demonstrated due diligence and improve future security practices. As the amount of regulatory oversight of AI systems increases, robust forensic skills will have a greater role in the responsible deployment of LLM.

7. DEFENSE MECHANISMS AND MITIGATION STRATEGIES

As the adversarial attacks along with backdoor exploitation methods towards large language models (LLMs) develop, the defense necessitated to combat adversarial attacks require even more than single silo-based countermeasures and a more holistic approach that is multi-layered in nature. Traditional security mechanisms developed for deterministic software systems are inadequate for probabilistic and data-driven models where the behaviour is a product of a large-scale training process. Consequently, the defenders of LLMs must provide defences that cover the entire model lifecycle, from data collection and training to deployment, monitoring, and governance.

This section introduces a very broad overview on the state-of-the-art defense mechanisms and mitigation strategies for the prevention, detection and response against adversarial and backdoor threats in LLM ecosystems.

7.1 Secure Training and Data Sanitization

Strengthening data governance and sanitization processes used to make sure that malicious data are not introduced into training pipelines are rigorously implemented at the start of the security of training. As LLMs are based on large and often heterogeneous set of data, data integrity is a very basic challenge. Data sanitization methods include: data filtering, data removal or anomaly detection and provenance verification used to detect poisoned or suspicious samples before the data training (Steinhardt et al., 2017). Advanced sanitization techniques make usage of statistical outlier detection and representation-based clustering for finding the anomalous training instances which have different data distribution from the expected values. In addition, dataset versioning as well as cryptographic hashing can be used to track changes and ensure accountability throughout the data lifecycle. Secure training pipelines also put emphasis about controlled access, audit logs and separation of duties to decrease insider threats risks. By developing security controls from the earliest phases in the development of the models, secure training practices go a long way towards minimising the risk of inserting backdoors and compromising the data long-term.

7.2 Adversarial Training Approaches

Adversarial training is a proactive defence mechanism for models as it is the method of training a model with adversarial inputs in order to make it more robust. In the case of LLMs, adversarial training can mean the inclusion of the attempts of prompt injection, jailbreak prompts, or man-made adversarial examples in the training data sets. This exposure helps the model to learn more resilient representations and it helps to make the model more resistant to manipulation at inference time (Madry et al., 2018).

Recent research has been done to extend adversarial training to alignment-focused objectives, combining robustness and safety constraints. For example, adversarial prompts can be combined with human feedback in order to strengthen refusal behaviours under malicious conditions. While adversarial training makes systems more resilient to known attack patterns, the effectiveness of adversarial training against novel or adaptive attacks is poor.

Moreover, adversarial training adds computational cost and can come with trade-offs in the way that it works (between robustness and performance). As such, it works best when combined with other defences as opposed to implemented as a single solution.

7.3 Backdoor Removal and Model Repair

In case backdoor compromise is suspected or confirmed, backdoor removal and model repair methods are necessary to repair model integrity. These techniques try to remove malicious behaviours without a full retraining from scratch, which is not very practical with large scale models. Several ways to suppress backdoor activation paths have been suggested, such as neuron pruning, weight reinitialization and fine-tuning using clean data (Liu et al., 2018).

Advanced repair techniques by use of activation analysis and attribution methods help to identify backdoor related components in the model. Once they are identified, targeted interventions can be applied to neutralize the attack upon the malicious representations without impacting the overall performance. However, backdoors in LLMs are distributed, so it is more difficult to do this because malicious behaviour might be encoded in multiple layers or representations. Despite these challenges, model repair is an important capability to have for incident response and recovery, specifically within an environment where rapid remediation is needed to ensure the continuation of operations.

7.4 Prompt Filtering and Input Validation

Frontline defense mechanisms to the inference-time adversarial attacks such as prompt injection and jailbreak attacks are prompt filtering and validating inputs. These mechanisms are used to analyse inputs from the user, as well as detect and prevent malicious instructions from being introduced into the core model. Filtering technique can be based on rule-based heuristics, machine learning classifiers or system that can use them both, known as hybrid systems (Greshake et al., 2023).

In the case of LLM deployments, input validation can be used to include instruction hierarchy enforcement, context isolation and sematic analysis to detect suspicious patterns. For instance, the distinction of system prompts and input from the user, as well as the implementation of strict parsing rules, can minimize the chance of instruction override. While no system of filtering is 100 per cent foolproof, using layers of validation increases the cost of successful attacks effectively.

Prompt filtering needs to be continuously updated in order to adapt to changing attack strategies and thus demonstrates the need for continued monitoring and feedback loops.

7.5 Red Teaming and Stress Testing

Red teaming and stress testing are the methods to systematically run LLMs through tests for vulnerabilities by simulating attacks under controlled environments.

Red teams assume the mentality of an attacker, while they create prompts, datasets or scenarios which aim to bypass safeguards or activate hidden backdoors. This is an easy to perform method that helps the organizations to know their weaknesses before this method is used in the real-world implementation (Ganguli et al., 2022).

Stress testing complements the role of red teaming in that it looks at the performance of model under extreme conditions or unexpected conditions such as distributional shifts or high-volume adversarial inputs. Together, these practices provide for a continuous improvement approach, through provision of inputs for updating training data, strategies for alignment and detection mechanisms. Red teaming in particular is helpful in finding emerging and latent vulnerabilities which may not be detectable via automated testing techniques by itself which makes them a crucial part of mature LLM security programs.

7.6 Cryptographic and Trusted AI Techniques

Cryptographic and trusted AI techniques help to give foundational assurances for model integrity, provenance and accountability. Cryptographic hashing, secure enclaves and digital signatures can be used to verify model checkpoints, datasets and deployment artifacts which mitigates against the risk of unauthorised modification (Brundage et al., 2020). Trusted execution environments (TEEs) support the possibility of secure model inference-based computation separation using trusted execution environments. Additionally, watermarking, fingerprinting techniques can be applied to embed identifiable markers in the model outputs or parameters for protection of intellectual properties and forensic attribution purposes.

While cryptography techniques cannot block all types of adversarial manipulation, they give the trust infrastructure surrounding the deployment of LLM a much-needed boost and work in conjunction with behavioural and algorithmic defences.

Figure 3. Multi-Layer Defense Architecture for Large Language Models

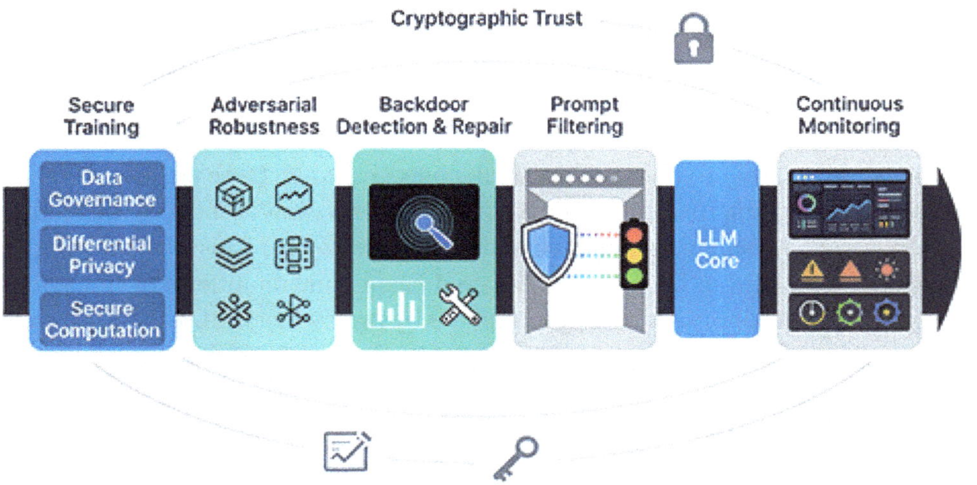

Figure 3 shows an architecture of a multi-layered defence mechanism for large language models that combines secure training, adversarial protection, backdoor detection and fixing, prompt filtering, continuous monitoring and cryptographic trust mechanisms. The layered approach focuses upon defense-in-depth throughout the entire lifecycle of the LLM.

8. EXPLAINABLE AI AND TRUSTWORTHY LLM SECURITY

As large language models (LLMs) are increasingly being used in security-critical and regulated settings, the need for transparency and accountability has become indelible from system security. Explainable Artificial Intelligence (XAI) provides methods of interpreting, explaining, justifying and auditing the behaviour of models, and therefore it helps to build trustworthiness in complex AI systems. In the face of LLM security, the role of XAI is important in model decision validation, adversarial manipulation detection and forensic accountability. Rather than as a tool for usability, explainability has become an essential security necessity for the trustworthy deployment of LLM.

8.1 Role of XAI in Security Validation

Security validation of LLMs is not merely the testing of the empirical performance, but knowledge of the model mechanisms of how and why the models produce certain output. XAI techniques, help the stakeholders to analyse the internal representations, attention mechanism and decision pathways to assist in identifying the anomalous behaviour or malicious behaviour. In applications that are security sensitive such as in threat intelligence analysis or automated policy enforcement, explainability is a source of assurance that the output of models is based on legitimate reason announcements or adversarial triggers (Doshi-Velez & Kim, 2017).

In the case of backdoor and adversarial attacks, XAI approaches can provide discrepancies between the expected and observed feature attributions. For example, if the response of a model is too often affected with important or unimportant and unqualified input tokens, then it can be considered as an indication of existence of hidden triggers. By incorporating explainability into the process of security validation, it is possible for organizations to move away from black box testing to more evidence-based trust assessment practices.

8.2 Interpretability for Attack Detection

Inspecting detectability of adversarial manipulation in LLMs the techniques of interpretability are now increasingly being used as diagnostic tool to detect adversarial manipulation in LLMs. Attention visualization, gradient-based attribution and concept activation vectors are some of the ways to provide an insight into the relationship between some of the inputs and model outputs. In the case of the compromised models, such techniques are able to expose some weird pattern of activation or decision routes, which are correlated with adversarial triggers (Ribeiro et al, 2020).

For backdoor detection, the interpretability can be used in a way to localize the suspicious representations in the model by finding neurons or layers which disproportionately respond to trigger inputs. Similarly, in case of prompt injection and jailbreak, the interpretability tools can be used to understand how malicious instruction corrupts system level constraints. While interpretability on its own may not prove a model compromise conclusively, such provide valuable corroborative evidence to supplement behavioural and statistical based methods of detection as discussed in previous sections. The incorporation of interpretability in detection pipeline helps to increase the confidence of forensic detection efforts as well as minimizing the use of purely heuristic or surface-level indicators.

8.3 Transparency vs. Security Trade-Offs

Despite the benefits that this brings, explainability brings inherent trade-offs between transparency and security. Excessive disclosure of internals of models, decision logic, or characteristics of training data through unintentional disclosure could lead to an enlarged attack surface, and may also enable adversaries to reverse engineer defences or to learn how to optimize their attack(s). This tension is particularly pronounced in LLMs, where it is possible to expose prompt structures or attention mechanisms, which can help to come up with more effective prompt injection or jailbreak attacks (Carlini et al., 2023).

Balancing between the transparency and security is explainability on a case-by-case and selective basis. Rather than providing unfettered access to the internals of models, the organizations can approach tiered access models that do not permit any access to sensitive information from those who are not trusted auditors and regulators. Techniques such as post-hoc explanations, abstraction and differential privacy can solve the problem of the disclosure risks without losing meaningful insights.

Managing this trade-off is critical to ensuring alignment between XAI practices and both security goals and regulatory requirements on one hand to ensure that explainability helps to strengthen and not weaken the resilience of systems.

8.4 Trust Metrics for LLM Deployment

Trustworthy deployment of LLMs requires quantification of security dimension, reliability and transparency dimensions. Trust metrics go beyond the traditional concepts of accuracy and performance and also incorporate aspects of robustness against adversarial inputs, consistency under changes in distribution and explainability quality. Recent research is insistent on the significance of composite trust frameworks which combine technical, ethical and governance indicators (Hendrycks et al., 2021).

Incorporating insights derived from XAI into the notions of trust helps in the consideration of continuously evaluating the model behaviour and in the informed decision-making process about the deployment, update or decommissioning of the model. For example, a reduction in the regularity of interpretation or an increase in the reliance on strange features could signal security risks in the future. As such, such types of metrics are particularly helpful for compliance reporting and risk management in regulated sectors.

By operationalizing trust through measurable indicators, organizations can be on the path to a proactive and accountable LLM governance to reinforce confidence among users of the system and security for the system itself.

9. GOVERNANCE, ETHICS, AND REGULATORY PERSPECTIVES

The pace at which large language models (LLMs) have begun to integrate themselves into societal, economic and governmental frameworks means that the demand for strong governance, ethical oversight and regulatory compliance has increased. While technical defences offset many of the adversarial and backdoor threats, they're not sufficient if they are implemented separately. Governance frameworks. there is an economic, societal and political context that affects them, and that is these are the institutional, legal and ethical frameworks that are required to ensure that LLMs are deployed responsibly, transparently and accountably, especially when there is the potential for security compromises to have far reaching consequences.

9.1 Ethical Risks of Compromised LLMS

Whereas there are serious ethical risks besides technical malfunction that will come about due to the advent of compromised LLMs. Or when adversarial manipulation or backdoors enter the equipment, what it displays ministers potentially erroneous information, perpetuates unfounded biasedness, or enables unethical decision making with no knowledge of users or those that are operating the system is affected. Such risks have been exaggerated in fields such as healthcare, finance and public policy, where the automated outputs can directly affect upon human well-being and rights (Floridi et al., 2018).

One of the largest ethical issues is the destruction of informed consent and the destruction of user autonomy. Users interacting with LLMs normally have the presumption that outputs are bit by bit created in well-meaning on the other hand of legitimate training. Backdoored or adversarial manipulated models are disrupting this assumption and instilling a lack of trust and question marks about moral responsibility.

Additionally, under deliberate manipulation, principles of fairness and non-maleficence are subverted because affected people may have no means of detecting and disputing harmful outcomes as a result. Addressing these risks of ethics requires consideration of security as part of a larger ethical framework for AI that makes sure that the elements of prevention, detection, and accountability are regarded as moral imperatives and not as optional safeguards.

9.2 AI Governance Frameworks

AI governance frameworks are the structured mechanisms of managing the risks of AI systems throughout their lifecycle. In terms of LLM security, there are governance frameworks that focus on risk assessment, transparency, human oversight, and accountability. Models of good practice, including the OECD AI Principles and the ISO/IEC standards for AI, call for risk-based approaches, which increase the governance requirements based on system impact and vulnerability (OECD, 2019).

Effective governance frameworks explicitly have adversarial threat modeling and incident response planning. This involves specifying roles and responsibilities for data providers, model developers, model deployers and model auditors. Governance also requires that training data sources, model updates and security assessments are documented in order to trace and analyse them forensically when issues arise.

By integrating security controls themselves into governance mechanisms, organizations will be in a position to ensure that technical defences are not only supported by policy enforcement, but also joined by organizational accountability.

9.3 Compliance With Global AI Regulations

Regulatory scrutiny of AI systems has grown dramatically and several jurisdictions have introduced or proposed comprehensive AI regulations. Frameworks like the AI Act of the European Union stress on risk classification and transparency requirements and post-deployment monitoring in case of high-risk AI systems. In the regulatory context, in the event of compromised LLMs, there are compliance risks with respect to data protection, safety and accountability (Veale & Borgesius, 2021).

Security breaches by adversarial manipulation or backdoors are a source of regulatory violations particularly where there is a leakage of personal information or harmful decision making.

Compliance thus necessitates proactive security governance which involves continuous security monitoring, incident reporting mechanisms and incident remediation procedures as per regulatory expectations. Regulatory alignment also serves as incentives for the uptake of standardized security practices as well as forensic practices to increase trust in LLM based systems at the borders as well as were cross sectoral.

9.4 Organizational Policies for Secure LLM Use

At the organizational level, policies are major contributing factor to the operationalization of the governance and the regulatory requirements. Secure LLM use policies usually provide definitions of use cases, data handling processes, access control and security review processes. These policies must make explicit provisions for adversarial risks like guideline for the sourcing, fine tuning and third-party integration of models. Organizations are now turning to AI risk management frameworks which include security audits, red teaming and explainability assessments as part of regular operations. Pathways for escalation and incident response protocols assure that suspected compromises are to be searched for as soon as possible, and transparently. By making LLM practices through policy institutionalized organizations will be able to put these abstract principles of governance into an actionable safeguard.

Table 3. Mapping Security Controls to Governance Requirements

Governance Dimension	Security Control	Governance Objective
Ethical AI Principles	Backdoor detection, auditing	Prevent hidden manipulation
Risk Management	Continuous monitoring	Early threat identification
Transparency	Explainable AI tools	Accountability & trust
Regulatory Compliance	Logging & forensics	Legal defensibility
Organizational Policy	Secure deployment standards	Operational consistency

10. OPEN CHALLENGES AND FUTURE RESEARCH DIRECTIONS

Despite great advances in securing large language models (LLMs) against adversarial and backdoor threats, there are still a number of open challenges that restrict the effectiveness and scale of existing defense mechanisms. The fast pace of development of LLM architectures, training paradigms and deployment scenarios means that new types of vulnerabilities are emerging faster than current methods of detection and mitigation. Overcoming such challenges will need long-term research efforts to combine advancements in machine learning security, systems engineering and AI governance.

10.1 Scalability of Detection Methods

One of the most challenging issues in the security of LLMs is the scalability of the detection methods. Many of the existing techniques, including gradient-based analysis, activation clustering and parameter inspection, are computationally expensive and need white-box access to the model. While successful in controlled laboratory environments, these methods don't scale very well to production-grade LLMs with billions of parameters that are deployed over distributed infrastructures (Goldblum et al., 2023).

Behavioural and statical methods of detection provide a better scalability, but often lack precision, especially against stealthy backdoors which are programmed to be active in situations with a small chance of being triggered, or specific to their context. Future research efforts will have to focus on development of light weight and scalable detection methods that can be continuously used in real world settings without having prohibitive computational overhead. Hybrid methods which use a combination of coarse-grained monitoring of behaviours and targeted deep inspections may be a way to go forward.

10.2 Evolving Threats in Agentic and Multimodal LLMS

The emergence of agentic and multimodal LLMs is potentially a new type of security threat that goes beyond text-based manipulation. Agentic LLMs have the capability of autonomous planning, tool usage and interaction with external systems and greatly increasing the attack surface. In these kinds of systems, prompt adversarial inputs or backdoors can result in not only harmful outcomes of an attack, but also undesirable actions, such as making unwanted API calls or manipulating data (Yao et al., 2023). Cross modal attacks threatening multimodal LLMs Multimodal LLMs influence the nature of threat, involving combinations of text, images, audio, and video. For instance, the inclusion of adversarial content in images or audio could have indirect effects on a text-based reasoning process bypassing traditional text-based defences. Existing detection and forensic tools are mostly of a single modality and ill-suited to work with these complex interactions.

Future work will therefore need to extend adversarial defense frameworks to take into consideration autonomy, multimodality and tool integration, and ensure that security mechanisms evolve as models are improved.

10.3 Research Gaps and Emerging Solutions

There are a number of research gaps in building robust and trustworthy LLM security solutions. First, there are no standardized benchmarks and evaluation protocols for adversarial robustness and backdoor resistance of LLMs. Without common benchmarks, it is still difficult to compare defence techniques and measure progress. Second, little work has been done on longitudinal security evaluation, in which models are evaluated over time as they get updated, fine-tuned, and distributed.

Emerging solutions are pointing in promising directions; Federated and privacy-preserving approaches to training could be used to mitigate the risk of poisoned data, while explainable AI techniques could be used to improve forensics transparency and trust assessment. In addition, the combination of cryptographic checking, secure enclaves, and frameworks for monitoring a model with levels of governance awareness could potentially provide stronger assurances of model integrity and accountability (Brundage et al., 2020). In order to confront these open challenges, it will be necessary to adopt interdisciplinary collaboration, and based on security-by-design principles to move away from insecure by default development of LLMs.

CONCLUSION

Large language models have rapidly become cornerstones of intelligent systems in the modern world that can think in complexity and automate processes and human-AI interaction in different fields. However, their increasing insertion to security-critical and high-stakes applications have rendered them vulnerable to wide plethora of adversarial attacks such as prompt based attacks, data poisoning and covert backdoor exploitation. These vulnerabilities bring to the forefront the issue of reliability, trustworthiness, and accountability of LLM-driven systems and the need to have security frameworks in place around them. This chapter has introduced systematic and holistic study about adversarial attacks and backdoor violation in large language models. Beginning with simple concepts and architectural considerations the discussion went through a detailed taxonomy of attack vectors covering how it is possible for the adversary to exploit the weaknesses in training time and inference time. Particular emphasis was paid to backdoor attacks owing to the stealth characteristics and perseverance of backdoor attacks as well as the possible for prolonged malicious actions. To counter the threats, there were many different types of detection, forensic, and defense mechanisms that were discussed in the chapter. Behavioural anomaly detection, activation analysis, trigger identification and constant monitoring efforts were studied to be complementary means in the identification of compromised models. Forensic analysis methods were discussed as the tools that will be employed in the post incident investigation, attribution and accountability to bridge the gap between the technical detection function and organizational governance. Furthermore, defense strategies from secure training, adversarial robustness, model repair, prompt filtering, red teaming, and cryptographic assurance were introduced as some of the defense-in-depth strategies. The importance of explainable AI and governance frameworks was also highlighted in this chapter in the process of building trust ecosystems to LLM. Transparency, interpretability and conformance with new regulatory requirements are no longer optional dimensions in the implementation of responsible AI but rather key pillars in the deployment of responsible AI. As such, by combining technical security measures with ethical and regulatory approaches, organizations can be in a better position to get control over risk and uphold public trust. In conclusion, securing the large language models against adversarial and backdoor threats requires a lifecycle approach towards security with interdisciplinary and technical innovation, forensic rigour and governance oversight. While there are still significant challenges to overcome, it is through ongoing research and collaboration between academia, industry, and policymakers, that we can ensure that LLMs will be able to be deployed safely, responsibly, and sustainably in the future.

REFERENCES

Behl, A., & Behl, K. (2017). *Cyberwar: The next threat to national security and what to do about it*. Oxford University Press., DOI: 10.1093/oso/9780190654501.001.0001

Bommasani, R., Hudson, D. A., Adeli, E., Altman, R., Arora, S., von Arx, S., . . . Liang, P. (2022). On the opportunities and risks of foundation models. *arXiv preprint arXiv:2108.07258*. https://doi.org//arXiv.2108.07258DOI: 10.48550

Brown, T. B., Mann, B., Ryder, N., Subbiah, M., Kaplan, J., Dhariwal, P., & Amodei, D. (2020). Language models are few-shot learners. *Advances in Neural Information Processing Systems*. Advance online publication. DOI: 10.48550/arXiv.2005.14165

Brundage, M., Avin, S., Clark, J., ... (2020). Toward trustworthy AI development: Mechanisms for supporting verifiable claims. *arXiv preprint*. https://doi.org//arXiv .2004.07213DOI: 10.48550

Carlini, N., Tramèr, F., Wallace, E., Jagielski, M., Herbert-Voss, A., Lee, K., & Erlingsson, Ú. (2023). Extracting training data from large language models. *USENIX Security Symposium*. DOI: 10.48550/arXiv.2012.07805

Chen, B., Carvalho, W., Baracaldo, N., Ludwig, H., Edwards, B., Lee, T., & Molloy, I. (2019). Detecting backdoor attacks on deep neural networks by activation clustering. *arXiv preprint*. https://doi.org//arXiv.1811.03728DOI: 10.48550

Chen, X., Liu, C., Li, B., Lu, K., & Song, D. (2021). Targeted backdoor attacks on deep learning systems using data poisoning. *IEEE Transactions on Dependable and Secure Computing*, *18*(4), 1566–1580. DOI: 10.1109/TDSC.2019.2931311

Devlin, J., Chang, M. W., Lee, K., & Toutanova, K. (2019). BERT: Pre-training of deep bidirectional transformers for language understanding. *Proceedings of NAACL-HLT*. DOI: 10.48550/arXiv.1810.04805

Doshi-Velez, F., & Kim, B. (2017). Towards a rigorous science of interpretable machine learning. *arXiv preprint*. https://doi.org//arXiv.1702.08608DOI: 10.48550

Floridi, L., Cowls, J., Beltrametti, M., Chatila, R., Chazerand, P., Dignum, V., Luetge, C., Madelin, R., Pagallo, U., Rossi, F., Schafer, B., Valcke, P., & Vayena, E. (2018). AI4People—An ethical framework for a good AI society. *Minds and Machines*, *28*(4), 689–707. DOI: 10.1007/s11023-018-9482-5 PMID: 30930541

Ganguli, D., Askell, A., Schiefer, N., ... (2022). Red teaming language models to reduce harms. *arXiv preprint*. https://doi.org//arXiv.2209.07858DOI: 10.48550

Goldblum, M., Fowl, L., Hand, E., & Goldstein, T. (2023). Adversarial attacks on machine learning systems. *ACM Computing Surveys*, *55*(9), 1–35. DOI: 10.1145/3538707

Greshake, K., Abdelnabi, S., & Slamanig, D.. (2023). *Not what you signed up for: Compromising real-world LLM-integrated applications with indirect prompt injection.* ACM CCS., DOI: 10.1145/3576915.3623107

Gu, T., Dolan-Gavitt, B., & Garg, S. (2019). BadNets: Identifying vulnerabilities in the machine learning model supply chain. *arXiv preprint.* https://doi.org//arXiv.1708.06733DOI: 10.48550

Hendrycks, D., Carlini, N., Schulman, J., & Steinhardt, J. (2021). Unsolved problems in ML safety. *arXiv preprint.* https://doi.org//arXiv.2109.13916DOI: 10.48550

Ji, Z., Lee, N., Frieske, R., Yu, T., Su, D., Xu, Y., Ishii, E., Bang, Y. J., Madotto, A., & Fung, P. (2023). Survey of hallucination in natural language generation. *ACM Computing Surveys*, *55*(12), 1–38. DOI: 10.1145/3571730

Krause, J., Perer, A., & Bertini, E. (2021). A survey of methods for explaining black box models. *IEEE Computer Graphics and Applications*, *41*(2), 88–99. DOI: 10.1109/MCG.2020.3048506

Kurita, K., Michel, P., & Neubig, G. (2020). *Weight poisoning attacks on pretrained models.* ACL., DOI: 10.18653/v1/2020.acl-main.249

Liu, Y., Ma, S., & Aafer, Y.. (2018). *Trojaning attack on neural networks.* NDSS., DOI: 10.14722/ndss.2018.23291

Madry, A., Makelov, A., Schmidt, L., Tsipras, D., & Vladu, A. (2018). Towards deep learning models resistant to adversarial attacks. *ICLR.* https://doi.org//arXiv.1706.06083DOI: 10.48550

OECD. (2019). *OECD principles on artificial intelligence.* OECD Publishing., DOI: 10.1787/1f3f3b5b-

Ouyang, L., Wu, J., Jiang, X., Almeida, D., Wainwright, C., Mishkin, P., & Christiano, P. (2022). Training language models to follow instructions with human feedback. *Advances in Neural Information Processing Systems.* Advance online publication. DOI: 10.48550/arXiv.2203.02155

Ribeiro, M. T., Singh, S., & Guestrin, C. (2020). Why should I trust you? Explaining the predictions of any classifier. *Communications of the ACM*, *63*(11), 116–125. DOI: 10.1145/3351095

Shen, Y., He, Z., Phang, J., ... (2023). Jailbreak attacks against large language models. *arXiv preprint arXiv:2307.02483*. https://doi.org//arXiv.2307.02483DOI: 10.48550

Steinhardt, J., Koh, P. W., & Liang, P. (2017). Certified defenses for data poisoning attacks. *Advances in Neural Information Processing Systems*. Advance online publication. DOI: 10.48550/arXiv.1706.03691

Steinhardt, J., Koh, P. W., & Liang, P. (2017). Certified defenses for data poisoning attacks. *Advances in Neural Information Processing Systems*. Advance online publication. DOI: 10.48550/arXiv.1706.03691

Tramèr, F., Zhang, F., Juels, A., Reiter, M. K., & Ristenpart, T. (2016). Stealing machine learning models via prediction APIs. *USENIX Security Symposium*. DOI: 10.48550/arXiv.1609.02943

Tran, B., Li, Y., & Madry, A. (2018). Spectral signatures in backdoor attacks. *Advances in Neural Information Processing Systems*. Advance online publication. DOI: 10.48550/arXiv.1811.00636

Vaswani, A., Shazeer, N., Parmar, N., Uszkoreit, J., Jones, L., Gomez, A. N., & Polosukhin, I. (2017). Attention is all you need. *Advances in Neural Information Processing Systems*. Advance online publication. DOI: 10.48550/arXiv.1706.03762

Veale, M., & Borgesius, F. Z. (2021). Demystifying the draft EU Artificial Intelligence Act. *Computer Law Review International*, *22*(4), 97–112. DOI: 10.9785/cri-2021-220402

Wallace, E., Feng, S., Kandpal, N., Gardner, M., & Singh, S. (2019). *Universal adversarial triggers for attacking and analyzing NLP*. EMNLP-IJCNLP., DOI: 10.18653/v1/D19-1221

Wang, B., Yao, Y., Shan, S., Li, H., Viswanath, B., Zheng, H., & Zhao, B. Y. (2019). Neural cleanse: Identifying and mitigating backdoor attacks in neural networks. *IEEE Symposium on Security and Privacy*. DOI: 10.1109/SP.2019.00031

Wei, J., Wang, X., Schuurmans, D., ... (2023). Jailbroken: How does LLM safety training fail? *arXiv preprint*. https://doi.org//arXiv.2307.02483DOI: 10.48550

Yao, S., Zhao, J., Yu, D., ... (2023). ReAct: Synergizing reasoning and acting in language models. *arXiv preprint*. https://doi.org//arXiv.2210.03629DOI: 10.48550

Zhang, H., Li, Y., Yu, D., & Wang, Z. (2024). On the transferability of jailbreak attacks in large language models. *IEEE Security and Privacy*. Advance online publication. DOI: 10.1109/MSP.2024.3356789

Chapter 4
Ethical AI in Cybersecurity:
Foundations, Challenges, and Evaluation Perspectives

Shritin Shetty
http://orcid.org/0009-0008-7181-1405
Illinois Institute of Technology, USA

Md Mahmudul Hasan
Illinois Institute of Technology, Ukraine

ABSTRACT

The integration of artificial intelligence into cybersecurity systems introduces significant ethical challenges that require systematic and measurable evaluation. Although prior studies propose lifecycle-based ethical AI frameworks, practical methodologies for benchmarking ethical compliance remain limited. This study presents an evidence-driven analytical framework for evaluating ethical integration in AI-driven cybersecurity research. A corpus of peer-reviewed publications was analyzed using a structured pipeline that employs large language models (LLMs) to extract machine-readable JSON evidence, followed by automated scoring across seven ethical dimensions: transparency, explainability, accountability, human oversight, privacy, data protection, and continuous ethical monitoring. The results reveal substantial variability in ethical compliance, with notable deficiencies in human oversight and post-deployment monitoring. The proposed framework is replicable, auditable, and supports evidence-based ethical governance of AI-enabled cybersecurity platforms.

DOI: 10.4018/979-8-3373-8252-4.ch004

I. INTRODUCTION

Artificial Intelligence has revolutionised the field of cybersecurity by enabling faster detection of anomalies, automated threat response, and predictive analysis for identifying potential vulnerabilities (Sarker et al., 2021),(Morovat & Panda, 2020). As organizations rely more on AI-driven systems to protect critical digital infrastructure, the ethical and governance challenges associated with the system have become a major concern. The use of autonomous algorithms in cybersecurity introduces potential risks related to fairness, transparency, accountability, and privacy, issues that directly affect trust and reliability in the organizations that depend on them. The growing use of AI systems in cybersecurity poses complex ethical dilemmas. Machine learning models often train on sensitive data and make high stakes decisions without human supervision. A biased or inaccurate detection model could lead to privacy violations or unnecessary restrictions (Vemuri et al., 2023). While existing studies emphasize the value of embedding ethical principles into AI development, many frameworks remain conceptual, lacking guidance for implementation (Dhirani et al., 2024). This gap between ethical goals and practical application creates uncertainty for organizations trying to keep up with changing regulatory standards. Recent global policy efforts highlight the need for ethical governance in AI. The European Union's Artificial Intelligence Act (2024) establishes a risk-based framework that requires transparency, accountability, and human oversight for AI systems used in critical sectors, including cybersecurity (European Commission, 2024). Similarly, the National Institute of Standards and Technology AI Risk Management Framework (2023) provides a lifecycle-based approach to identifying and mitigating AI risks across design, deployment, and monitoring phases (National Institute of Standards and Technology, 2023). The effectiveness of these frameworks really depends on how well organizations can apply their principles into action in technical settings. Researchers highlight that ethical AI should be built on key principles such as beneficence, non-maleficence, justice, autonomy, and explicability, which help ensure that AI systems act in ways that benefit people and society. In a similar way, explains that ethics should be part of the entire AI lifecycle, from collecting data to continuous monitoring and should include clear checkpoints for accountability and human oversight (Leslie, 2019). The baseline paper, Securing Trust: Ethical Considerations in AI for Cybersecurity, identifies transparency, accountability, fairness, and privacy as the main ethical pillars for building trustworthy AI systems (Vemuri et al., 2023). While their framework provides a strong starting point, it mainly stays conceptual and doesn't show how organizations can apply these principles in real cybersecurity systems. Building on that work, this research aims to turn those ethical ideas into a practical, lifecycle-based plan that organizations can use to design and manage AI cybersecurity systems.

The proposed framework includes clear checkpoints, roles, and accountability steps at each phase of system development, from initial planning and data collection to model training, deployment, and ongoing monitoring. It also connects with existing efforts like the EU AI Act and the National Institute of Standards and Technology AI Risk Management Framework. By including ethics throughout the AI lifecycle, this study treats ethics as actionable, not just theoretical, making it an essential part of how organizations manage cybersecurity.

II. LITERATURE REVIEW

A. AI in Cybersecurity: Overview

Artificial Intelligence (AI) has become a key component in modern cybersecurity systems due to its ability to process large amounts of data and detect complex patterns that traditional methods often miss. Machine learning and deep learning models are now commonly used to identify anomalies, detect intrusions, and predict potential threats before they happen (Morovat & Panda, 2020), (Sarker et al., 2021). According to (Morovat & Panda, 2020), AI-based systems improve response times and accuracy in identifying malicious activity, helping organizations to automate threat analysis and reduce human error. Similarly (Sarker et al., 2021) highlight that AI-driven cybersecurity enhances awareness by continuously monitoring network traffic and recognizing unusual behaviours, making it more effective. Recent studies also emphasize the growing use of explainable AI (XAI) in cybersecurity, which focuses on increasing transparency and interpretability of AI models (Capuano et al., 2022). (Capuano et al., 2022) Points out that while black-box models can achieve high detection accuracy, their lack of interpretability poses challenges for accountability and trust, especially when AI systems make autonomous security decisions. This concern has led to a stronger interest in hybrid approaches that balance model performance with explainability. AI applications in cybersecurity are increasing beyond detection and prevention. The Comprehensive Review of AI's Current Impact and Future Prospects in Cybersecurity (2024) discusses how AI is now being used for incident prediction, behavioural risk assessment, and adaptive threat mitigation (Al Siam et al., 2024). These advancements are pushing cybersecurity towards predictive and proactive defence. However, with increased autonomy and data dependence, new ethical and governance challenges will emerge.

B. Ethical Challenges in AI-Driven Cybersecurity

While AI has strengthened cybersecurity defences, it also brings complex ethical concerns that go beyond technical performance. One such major issue is algorithmic bias, models trained on unbalanced or biased data can unintentionally discriminate. (Cath et al., 2020) Points out that many AI systems inherit existing social and technical biases from the data used to train them, which can lead to unfair or inaccurate outputs. In cybersecurity, such bias could cause false alarms, missed detections, or unequal treatment of certain networks, undermining both efficiency and trust. Another challenge involves privacy and data protection. AI systems often require access to massive amounts of data to train on effectively. This creates a tension between improving the system and respecting individual privacy rights (Vemuri et al., 2023). Unauthorized data use or poorly taken training datasets can expose personal or corporate information. Maintaining user privacy must remain as the main goal to AI governance because data misuse can damage respect and compliance with regulations such as the General Data Protection Regulation (GDPR) (Mittelstadt et al., 2019). Accountability and transparency are equally critical. Organizations should define clear accountability checkpoints across the AI development lifecycle so that every decision can be traced to a responsible perosn or process (Leslie, 2019). Ethical governance frameworks like safety audits in engineering are necessary to monitor AI systems continuously and prevent any harm. However, according to (Mittelstadt et al., 2019) notes, the black-box nature of many deep learning models makes it difficult to understand or justify their outputs, resulting in a lack of explainability in high-risk situations. The Comprehensive Review of AI's Current Impact and Future Prospects in Cybersecurity (Dinu et al., 2024) states that without interpretability and oversight, AI driven defences could make unclear decisions that are hard to contest. Whittlestone et al. (Taddeo & Floridi, 2018) explains that ethical principles alone are not enough; they must be translated into solid practices and tools that help engineers manage accuracy, privacy, and accountability. The main ethical challenges in AI-based cybersecurity include bias, privacy risks, and limited transparency. These issues show that technical performance alone cannot guarantee trust. Addressing them requires structured ethical governance frameworks, an area where most current research remains conceptual.

C. Governance and Regulatory Frameworks

As the ethical concerns around AI in cybersecurity have become more serious, several governments and organizations have started creating policies and frameworks to guide the responsible use of these systems. The goal of these frameworks is to translate ethical values such as fairness, accountability, and transparency into real actions that developers and organizations can follow. Ethical AI should not be treated as something optional or only used after a problem happens; it needs to be built into the design and decision-making process from the start (Mittelstadt et al., 2019). The Organisation for Economic Co-operation and Development (OECD) AI principles are among the most widely recognized global initiatives guiding ethical AI development (Fjeld et al., 2020). These principles focus on human-centred values, fairness, transparency, and accountability.

D. Proposed Architecture

They encourage developers and policymakers to make sure that AI systems support social well-being rather than just focusing on efficiency or performance. The OECD guidelines have also inspired other international and national AI strategies that try to balance innovation with ethical responsibility. The EU AI Act is one of the most detailed laws developed so far to regulate AI use (European Commission, 2024). It classifies AI applications into four risk levels, minimal, limited, high, and unacceptable risk categories, with cybersecurity tools typically falling under the high-risk category. Because of this, they must meet strict requirements such as transparency in data use, clear documentation, and ongoing human oversight. The act gives organizations a legal way to manage risk and ensure accountability across the AI lifecycle. Simply following the rules doesn't always mean a system is ethical, companies also need to build a culture that understands and applies these rules in a meaningful way (Floridi & Cowan, 2022).

In the United States, the National Institute of Standards and Technology (NIST) released the AI Risk Management Framework (AI RMF) in 2023 (National Institute of Standards and Technology, 2023). This framework focuses on identifying and managing AI risks throughout the system's lifecycle. It gives organizations a more flexible structure to plan, monitor, and improve AI governance while emphasizing human oversight and transparency. Both the EU and NIST frameworks show a growing focus on making AI accountability measurable.

AI governance should be based on five main principles: beneficence, non-maleficence, justice, autonomy, and explicability as suggested in (Floridi & Cowls, 2021). These ideas are meant to keep AI development aligned with human values and social goods. These governance frameworks represent a shift from voluntary ethical guidelines to more formal and enforceable standards. Even with all these efforts, most of these frameworks still stay at a high level and don't fully explain how organizations can apply ethics in their daily cybersecurity work. This gap highlights why there's a need for more practical, lifecycle-based models that can help organizations turn these ideas into real actions.

E. Trust, Transparency, and Accountability in AI Systems

Trust is one of the most important factors when it comes to the use of AI in cybersecurity. Since these systems often make decisions automatically and handle large amounts of sensitive data, users and organizations need to know that the outputs are reliable and fair. Building trust depends upon how transparent and accountable the system is throughout its development lifecycle. Trust in AI systems is strongly influenced by users' ability to understand how decisions are made and by the presence of clear processes to prevent and respond to failures (Winfield & Jirotka, 2018). This means organizations must design AI tools that provide clear explanations of how decisions are made and allow humans to intervene when required.

Trust is not just about technical performance but about verifiable claims, organizations must prove that their AI systems are safe, ethical and reliable (Brundage et al., 2020). This includes documentation, testing and external audits to confirm if systems are behaving correctly. When it comes to AI systems in cybersecurity, these verifications become more important because a single wrong decision can affect data integrity, privacy and security. Transparency is another key part of this. Transparency is the ability for the people to understand not only what AI system did but why it did that (Floridi & Cowls, 2021). In cybersecurity, this helps users trust AI generated predictions instead of treating them like black box outputs. Explainability improves collaboration between people and the system, making the AI system easier to understand and correct when errors occur.

Accountability connects trust and transparency by making sure that every decision can be traced to a responsible source. (Leslie, 2019) Argues that accountability should be built into every stage of AI development, from data collection to deployment and monitoring, so that mistakes can be identified and sorted quickly. These kinds of structured responsibility ensures that ethical principles are an active part of how an AI system. Overall, trust, transparency and accountability work together to form the foundation of ethical AI in cybersecurity (Vemuri et al., 2023). When these values are missing, even the most advanced system can become unreliable and can lose credibility. However, when they are incorporated into every stage development of AI lifecycle, it can become both effective and trustworthy.

F. Gaps in Existing Research

Even though many studies have focused on the ethics and governance of AI, most of them still stop at the conceptual level. Researchers like Hagendorff (Cath et al., 2020) and Whittlestone et al. (Taddeo & Floridi, 2018) mention that a lot of ethical frameworks end up repeating the same ideas without showing clear ways to put them into practice. This is especially true in cybersecurity, where decisions must be made quickly and automatically. In the baseline paper Securing Trust: Ethical Considerations in AI for Cybersecurity, presents a great foundation for identifying ethical principles, but their framework remains mostly conceptual (Vemuri et al., 2023). It tells us what to focus on, but not how to apply those principles when developing or deploying AI in real cybersecurity setups. Similarly, frameworks such as the EU AI Act (2024) (European Commission, 2024) and the NIST AI Risk Management Framework (2023) (National Institute of Standards and Technology, 2023) provides strong policy direction but they don't really break it down into practical steps that are needed for implementation.

Another noticeable gap is in accountability. The need for verifiable claims to support trustworthy AI is suggested but most studies don't go into detail about how that should work in cybersecurity models (Brundage et al., 2020). There is also limited research on continuous ethical monitoring, how to check that if an AI system acts fairly and transparently once deployed. Ethical evaluation is treated as one time step rather than an ongoing process throughout the AI lifecycle (Mittelstadt et al., 2019), (Leslie, 2019).

Figure 1. Proposed Architecture for Ethical AI Evaluation Framework

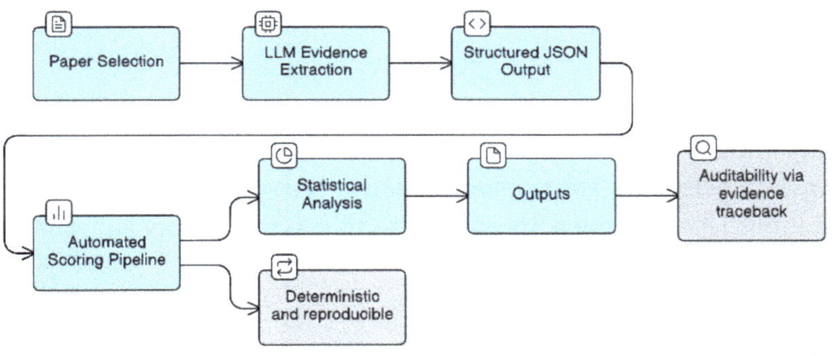

III. PROPOSED METHODOLOGY

This research advances beyond theoretical frameworks of AI ethics in cybersecurity by developing a structured, evidence-driven methodology to quantitatively assess ethical compliance in academic research. Our methodology operationalizes ethical AI principles across cybersecurity contexts through a three-stage pipeline that includes curated literature selection, machine-assisted data extraction, and automated scoring. The framework enables traceability, auditability, and replicability, key features for both academic integrity and practical adoption.

A. Paper Selection and Corpus Construction

We constructed a corpus of 30 academic papers specifically chosen for their relevance to ethical AI applications in cybersecurity. The papers were retrieved from top-tier databases including IEEE Xplore, ACM Digital Library, SpringerLink, and arXiv. Selection criteria mandated that each paper explicitly address the convergence of artificial intelligence, cybersecurity technologies or methods, and ethical principles. This ensures that the corpus reflects interdisciplinary perspectives across technical and ethical domains.

The selection process followed a systematic screening protocol:

- Inclusion Criteria: Papers must (a) be peer-reviewed or reputable preprints, (b) include discussion of both AI and cybersecurity, and (c) explicitly reference ethical concerns or values.
- Exclusion Criteria: Articles focusing exclusively on technical innovations without ethical discourse, or on general AI ethics without cybersecurity relevance, were excluded.

The final corpus encompasses a diverse array of methodologies (qualitative reviews, empirical studies, framework proposals), application domains (e.g., network intrusion detection, autonomous systems, privacy-preserving AI), and years of publication. This heterogeneity enhances the generalizability and validity of our benchmarking results.

B. Ethical Evaluation Framework

Our ethical evaluation framework is grounded in seven core criteria synthesized from widely recognized global AI ethics guidelines, including the OECD AI Principles, the AI4People framework, and IEEE's Ethically Aligned Design (Fjeld et al., 2020; Floridi et al., 2018; Winfield et al., 2019). These criteria reflect ethical imperatives that are broadly endorsed across both academic scholarship and policy-oriented discourse. Specifically, the framework evaluates real-time transparency, referring to the extent to which AI systems disclose decision-making logic or risk indicators during operation; explainability, which assesses whether system outputs are interpretable and understandable by human users; and accountability, capturing the presence of clearly defined mechanisms for assigning responsibility for AI system behavior. In addition, the framework incorporates human oversight as a criterion to evaluate provisions for meaningful human control or intervention, alongside privacy, which examines the protection of personal or sensitive information, and data protection, focusing on formal safeguards governing data storage, transfer, and processing integrity. Finally, continuous ethical monitoring is included to reflect lifecycle-based governance approaches that require periodic reassessment of ethical impacts as AI systems evolve. Each of these criteria was operationally defined to ensure consistency and was integrated into a structured scoring rubric that guided the automated evaluation process.

C. Evidence Extraction and Structuring

The final corpus encompasses a diverse range of methodologies, including qualitative reviews, empirical studies, and framework proposals, as well as multiple application domains such as network intrusion detection, autonomous systems, and privacy-preserving AI. Each selected paper was subjected to a structured analysis using a large language model (LLM)–based prompt system that employed a fixed extraction template to systematically identify evidence aligned with the seven ethical criteria. The extracted information was organized into a standardized JSON schema designed to support machine readability, traceability, and automated scoring. This structured representation ensures that the assessment results are not only interpretable but also verifiable, which is a critical requirement for ethical AI evaluation. The standardized JSON schema captured multiple dimensions of the extracted evidence, including the degree of compliance with each ethical criterion, the supporting textual evidence in the form of direct quotations or concise summaries, and traceability metadata linking each assessment to specific sections or page numbers in the original documents. In addition, assessor notes and quality scores were incorporated to provide qualitative insights and confidence levels underlying each classification, thereby enhancing transparency and interpretability. The schema also annotated the type of evidence, such as normative or empirical claims, enabling more nuanced and context-aware scoring decisions. To ensure methodological consistency and fairness, all extractions were performed using the same LLM prompt across the entire corpus. This approach minimized variability arising from subjective interpretation or prompt drift and ensured a uniform and equitable evaluation of all analyzed papers.

D. Automated Scoring Pipeline

Once the structured evidence was extracted and stored, the documents were processed using a Python-based scoring engine (score.py) operating on the generated JSON files. Within this automated pipeline, six ethical criteria were evaluated on a 15-point scale, while one criterion was assessed on a 10-point scale. Additional weighting logic was embedded in the JSON-based scoring mechanism to enable more granular differentiation across studies. The scoring engine applied deterministic rules to compute ethical compliance scores, assigning numerical values based on the level of compliance and aggregating scores across all seven criteria to produce a maximum possible score of 100 for each paper. The pipeline generated multiple outputs, including a consolidated spreadsheet ranking all analyzed papers by total compliance score, a summary report highlighting top-performing studies and cross-paper trends, and individual markdown reports providing criterion-level evaluations and supporting excerpts for each paper. This automated workflow enables systematic benchmarking, supports longitudinal analysis, and facilitates evidence-based discussion of ethical compliance across cybersecurity research.

E. Validation and Reproducibility

To ensure methodological rigor, all extraction and scoring procedures adhered to fixed templates and deterministic rules. The use of structured JSON representations enables full auditability, as every computed score can be traced directly back to the underlying textual evidence. Moreover, this design promotes transparency by allowing independent third parties to review and verify all assessment decisions. Reproducibility is also guaranteed, as the system consistently produces identical outputs when provided with the same inputs. Together, these properties ensure that the results are not only interpretable but also verifiable, which is a critical requirement for robust and trustworthy ethical AI assessment.

F. Methodological Limitations

Despite its strengths, the proposed methodology has certain limitations. Large language models may occasionally misinterpret nuanced ethical statements or fail to capture implicit forms of ethical reasoning that are not explicitly articulated in the text. In addition, although the scoring thresholds are rule-based, the distinction between full and partial compliance can sometimes reflect judgment calls embedded within the prompt design and extraction logic. To address these limitations, future iterations of the framework could incorporate human-in-the-loop validation, where subject matter experts review borderline classifications, as well as multi-model extraction strategies that leverage multiple LLMs to cross-validate extracted evidence. Further refinements could also include weighted criteria to better reflect domain-specific ethical priorities. Nonetheless, the proposed methodology represents a meaningful step toward bridging the gap between theoretical ethical principles and practical, measurable ethical governance in cybersecurity systems.

IV. ANALYSIS AND DISCUSSIONS

This study quantitatively evaluated 30 peer-reviewed AI cybersecurity publications across seven ethical criteria: real-time transparency, explainability, accountability, human oversight, privacy, data protection, and continuous ethics monitoring. Leveraging a novel JSON-based evidence extraction and deterministic scoring pipeline. Using structured JSON-based evidence, automated scoring and manual validation. The scoring incorporates not only the presence of ethical considerations but also the quality and confidence of evidence [1]. All papers included in the evaluation corpus were cited and documented in the reference list, with individual scores derived from the structured evaluation framework described in Section III.

A. Quantitative Evaluation

- Statistical Results: The mean scores for each ethical dimension demonstrate strong performance in transparency, explainability, and accountability, each averaging above 14 out of 15 across the corpus. Privacy and data protection also show high engagement but with slightly greater variance, suggesting differential emphasis and implementation fidelity. (Table 1)
- Ethical criteria score chart: The provided bar chart visually highlights these strengths and gaps, making clear where ethical attention is focused and where future improvements are most urgently needed. Dimensions such as transparency (bar 0) and explainability (bar 1) show tall, consistent bars, while human oversight (bar 3) and continuous ethical monitoring (bar 6) lag notably in both average and spread. (Fig 2)

Table 1. Key Statistical Properties of Ethical Scores

Criterion	mean	median	variance	range
real_time_transparency	14.71428571	15	0.211640212	1
explainability	14.5	15	0.481481481	2
accountability	14.17857143	15	8.078042328	15
human_oversight	5.535714286	9	21.07275132	10
privacy	13.21428571	15	16.3968254	15
data_protection	13.28571429	14	7.693121693	15
continuous_ethics_monitoring	9.285714286	13	35.76719577	13

Figure 2. Mean Ethical Compliance Score per Dimension

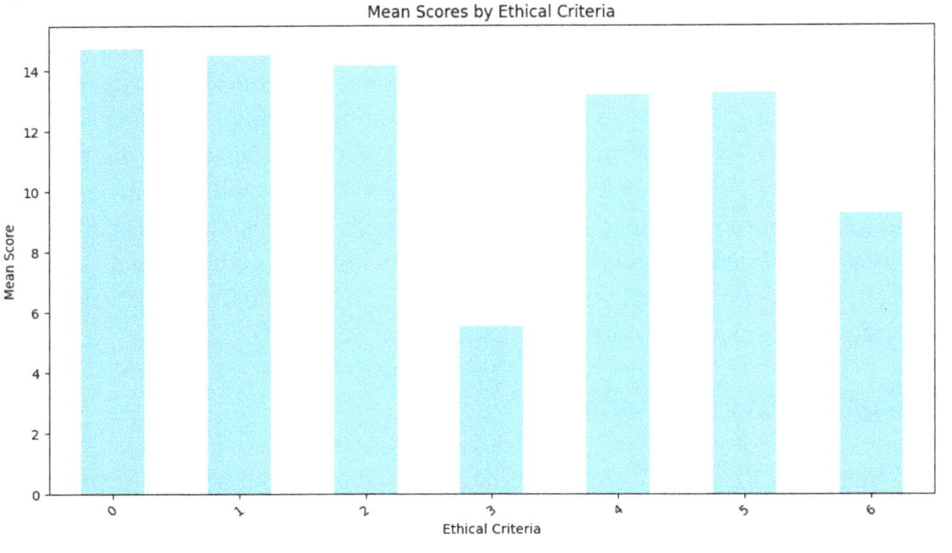

• Top Performers: The distribution of total scores reveals a broad spectrum of ethical integration, with top-performing papers such as (Al Siam et al., 2024) and (Vemuri et al., 2023) scoring 98 out of a possible maximum, demonstrating exemplary incorporation of ethical principles. Following closely, other papers such as"A framework for assessing AI ethics with applications to cybersecurity" (Bruschi & Diomede, 2022) and "Ethical AI cybersecurity innovation regulation" scored 96, reflecting similarly high standards.

Table 2. Scores for Different Papers

Paper_id	real_time_transparency	explainability	accountal	human_oversight	privacy	data_protection	continuous_ethics_monitoring	total_score
Framework_assessing_ai_ethics_cybersecurity	15	15	15	9	15	14	13	96
Ai_hype_cybersecurity_moral_responsibility	14	13	15	0	14	13	0	69
Ai_driven_solutions_cybersecurity_comparative	15	15	15	10	15	14	0	84
Comprehensive_review_ai_cybersecurity	15	15	15	10	15	15	13	98
Ai_ethics_education_cybersecurity	14	14	14	0	13	13	13	81
Ai_ethics_and_cybersecurity_overview	14	14	15	9	14	14	13	93
challenges_of_ai_driven_cybersecurity	14	14	13	6	9	13	0	69
ethical_ai_cybersecurity_innovation_regulation	15	15	15	9	15	14	13	96
ethical_challenges_ai_cybersecurity	14	13	14	0	14	13	13	81
ethical_considerations_ai_cybersecurity_balancing	15	15	15	9	15	14	13	96
ethical_governance_is_essential	15	14	15	0	15	15	13	87
ethics_in_ai_introduction_special_issue	15	15	15	9	15	14	13	96
ethics_in_ai_cybersecurity_approach	15	15	15	9	15	14	13	96
ethics_of_ai_and_cybersecurity_sovereignty	15	14	15	0	15	14	13	86
explainable_ai_black_box_to_glass_box	15	15	14	0	0	0	0	44
practical_cybersecurity_ethics_mapping_cybok	15	15	15	9	15	14	13	96

B. Thematic Insights

1. Transparency and Accountability: High scoring papers consistently provide auditable, explainable AI models and strong reporting mechanisms. For example, (Chaganti, 2024) documents explainable design, while (Dinu et al., 2024) details multi-level transparency, implementing it throughout model development and deployment.
2. Privacy and Data Protection: Concrete measures, including extensive anonymization protocols and compliance with data governance standards, are observed in top scoring papers. "Ethical Considerations in AI-Driven Cybersecurity: Balancing Automation and Human Oversight" and "Securing Trust Ethical Considerations in AI for Cybersecurity" offer strong evidence of lifecycle privacy risk assessment and continuous adjustment to changing regulatory environments.
3. Accountability and Evidence Quality: Papers scoring well in accountability illustrate multi-stakeholder engagement and trackable decision records. Manual scoring notes suggest the importance of good evidence notes and confidence in supporting claims.
4. Fairness, Bias and Societal Impact: Some papers looked closely at fairness and bias, checking if their systems avoided unfair results and noting the real-world effects. Top performing papers, such as "Comprehensive review of AI in cybersecurity", explicitly examine sources of bias in both data and models, proposing technical and procedural adjustments to promote fairness across demographic and usage groups. Still, many papers do not dig deep on bias or don't talk much about the wider social impact, so this an area that needs more work.

C. Gaps Identified

1. Human Oversight: A lot of the research papers either don't mention how people stay involved in monitoring or decision-making or only mention it briefly. Some assume the AI or automated system will handle everything on its own, but this can create serious risks if the system makes mistakes or encounters something unexpected. Individual report reviews frequently highlight the lack of thorough human in the loop systems, with several papers scoring zero or near zero. For example (Humphreys et al., 2024) and related reports point to cases where autonomous operation was prioritized without strong intervention protocols, increasing ethical risk.
2. Continuous Ethics Monitoring: Most papers rely on fixed design and do not include ongoing checks or follow-up for ethical issues once their AI systems are launched. Almost none of the papers describe a process for regularly monitoring their systems after deployment. This means that if new problems, biases, or

security issues come up as the system is used over time, there may be no way to spot or fix them. Our scoring shows that this area had some of the lowest and most inconsistent results across all the ethical criteria. This shows that continuous ethics monitoring is not yet a standard practice in AI cybersecurity research.

D. Patterns and Comparative Observations

1. Manual Overrides and Evidence Quality In this, both the presence and the quality of evidence were equally important during the scoring process. This means that it wasn't just about how many claims or notes a paper included, but also about how strong and trustworthy those claims were. This approach made a real difference, papers that gave detailed evidence for their ethical practices, included lots of clear examples, and explained their decision-making step by step, always performed the better than other papers. Having strong and varied notes showed that the researchers understood the complexities of their work and cared about being transparent.
2. Variance Across Dimensions: This means that for some categories, specifically human oversight (keeping humans involved and in charge) and continuous monitoring (watching for ongoing problems), the scores were all over the place. Some papers are really strong at these but others are very weak. This big difference shows that researchers don't all agree on what's enough or how these things should be handled. This wide range is important because it means the field is still young in these parts there isn't a standard for what good oversight or monitoring looks like yet. This can be risky because if people assume AI is always doing a good job without regular checks, mistakes or biases can go unnoticed for a long time.

E. Implications of These Findings:

These findings suggest that while AI ethics in cybersecurity is improving in key areas like transparency, accountability, and explainability, there are still significant weaknesses with human oversight and keeping systems ethically monitored after deployment. Organizations deploying AI security tools should therefore treat ongoing human review, post deployment audits, and incident reporting as mandatory safeguards rather than optional add ons. Regulators and standards bodies may also need to tighten expectations around continuous monitoring, bias audits, and red team testing so that ethical performance is checked over the full lifecycle, not only at design time. Finally, future research should explore concrete mechanisms, such as governance dashboards, human override protocols, and independent ethics evaluations that can operationalize these safeguards in high-risk cybersecurity environments.

V. CONCLUSION

This study provided a thorough evaluation of how ethical principles are being applied in AI for cybersecurity using a structured, evidence-driven approach. Results show that, while many papers excel at transparency, explainability, accountability and privacy, there are still significant gaps in human oversight and continuous ethical monitoring after deployment. It is clear that the field is making progress, but more work is needed to ensure high ethical standards throughout the entire AI lifecycle.

A. Key Takeaways:

- Most current research demonstrates strong foundations in core ethical areas, but regular checks and clear processes for keeping humans in control are still not standard.
- There is wide variability in how different papers and projects address ongoing monitoring and accountability, highlighting the need for common standards and best practices.

B. Future Work

Building on the results of this paper, future work should focus on expanding and refining the evaluation framework presented here. One key next step is to apply this approach to a larger and more diverse set of AI systems in cybersecurity to see how well the framework holds up across different domains and use cases. This could include incorporating more real world, industry driven case studies and not just academic research The framework could be extended to track ethical compliance over time, allowing for long-term monitoring of deployed systems. Developing practical tools or automated solutions for continuous ethics monitoring would help address the gap identified in this study, making it easier for organizations to keep their AI systems in check as they grow and change. Overall, the aim is for the evaluation method presented here to support safer and more ethical AI deployments in cybersecurity and beyond. This will ensure that ethical considerations remain central not just in early development but throughout the entire lifecycle of AI systems.

ACKNOWLEDGMENT

The authors would like to thank the ITM Department at Illinois Institute of Technology for providing research and teaching support.

REFERENCES

Al Siam, A., Alazab, M., Awajan, A., & Faruqui, N. (2024). *A comprehensive review of AI's current impact and future prospects in cybersecurity. Daffodil International University*. Al-Balqa Applied University.

Brundage, M., Avin, S., & Clark, J.. (2020). Toward trustworthy AI development: Mechanisms for supporting verifiable claims. *Nature Machine Intelligence*, *2*, 81–83. DOI: 10.1038/s42256-020-0188-1

Bruschi, D., & Diomede, N. (2022). *A framework for assessing AI ethics with applications to cybersecurity*. Published online.

Capuano, N., Fenza, G., Loia, V., & Stanzione, C. (2022). Explainable artificial intelligence in cybersecurity: A survey. *IEEE Access : Practical Innovations, Open Solutions*, *10*, 98856–98881. DOI: 10.1109/ACCESS.2022.3204171

Cath, C., Wachter, S., Mittelstadt, B., Taddeo, M., & Floridi, L. (2020). Securing trust: Ethical considerations for the adoption of artificial intelligence in cybersecurity. *Nature Machine Intelligence*, *2*(6), 264–266.

Chaganti, K. C. (2024). *Ethical AI for cybersecurity: A framework for balancing innovation and regulation*. S&P Global.

Dhirani, L. L., Mukhtiar, N., Chowdhry, B. S., & Newe, T. (2024). Review ethical dilemmas and privacy issues in emerging technologies: A review. *University of Limerick; Mehran University of Engineering and Technology*.

Dinu, A., Vasile, P. C., & Georgescu, A. (2024). *AI-driven solutions for cybersecurity: Comparative analysis and ethical aspects. National Institute for Research and Development in Informatics*. ICI Bucharest.

European Commission. (2024). *Artificial Intelligence Act*. Official Journal of the European Union. https://artificialintelligenceact.eu/

Fjeld, B., Achten, N., Hilligoss, H., Nagy, A., & Srikumar, R. (2020). *Principled artificial intelligence: Mapping consensus in ethical and rights-based approaches to AI principles*. Berkman Klein Center Research Publication No. 2020-1.

Floridi, L., & Cowan, J. (2022). Operationalizing AI ethics. *AI and Ethics*, *2*, 1–12. DOI: 10.1007/s43681-021-00085-8

Floridi, L., & Cowls, J. (2021). A unified framework of five principles for AI in society. *Harvard Data Science Review*, *3*(1). Advance online publication. DOI: 10.1162/99608f92.8cd550d1

Floridi, L., Cowls, J., Beltrametti, M., Chatila, R., Chazerand, P., Dignum, V., Luetge, C., Madelin, R., Pagallo, U., Rossi, F., Schafer, B., Valcke, P., & Vayena, E. (2018). AI4People: An ethical framework for a good AI society. *Minds and Machines*, *28*(4), 689–707. DOI: 10.1007/s11023-018-9482-5 PMID: 30930541

Humphreys, D., Koay, A., Desmond, D., & Mealy, E. (2024). AI hype as a cyber-security risk: The moral responsibility of implementing generative AI in business. *Published online*.

Leslie, D. (2019). *Understanding artificial intelligence ethics and safety: A guide for the responsible design and implementation of AI systems in the public sector*. The Alan Turing Institute. DOI: 10.2139/ssrn.3403301

Mittelstadt, B., Russell, C., & Wachter, S. (2019). Explaining explanations in AI. In *Proceedings of the Conference on Fairness, Accountability, and Transparency* (pp. 279–288). DOI: 10.1145/3287560.3287574

Morovat, K., & Panda, B. (2020). A survey of artificial intelligence in cybersecurity. In *Proceedings of the International Conference on Computational Science and Computational Intelligence* (pp. 109–115). IEEE. DOI: 10.1109/CSCI51800.2020.00026

National Institute of Standards and Technology. (2023). *AI Risk Management Framework (AI RMF 1.0)*. https://www.nist.gov/itl/ai-risk-management-framework

Sarker, N., Furhad, M., & Nowrozy, R. (2021). AI-driven cybersecurity: An overview, security intelligence modeling, and research directions. *SN Computer Science*, *2*(3), 173. Advance online publication. DOI: 10.1007/s42979-021-00557-0 PMID: 33778771

Taddeo, M., & Floridi, L. (2018). How AI can be a force for good. *Science*, *361*(6404), 751–752. DOI: 10.1126/science.aat5991 PMID: 30139858

Vemuri, N., Thaneeru, N., & Tatikonda, V. M. (2023). Securing trust: Ethical considerations in AI for cybersecurity. *Journal of Knowledge Learning and Science Technology*, *2*(2), 168–175. DOI: 10.60087/jklst.vol2.n2.p175

Winfield, A., Michael, M., Pitt, J., & Evers, V. (2019). Machine ethics: The design and governance of ethical AI and autonomous systems. *Proceedings of the IEEE, 107*(3), 509–517. DOI: 10.1109/JPROC.2019.2900622

Winfield, A. F. T., & Jirotka, M. (2018). Ethical governance is essential to building trust in robotics and artificial intelligence systems. *Philosophical Transactions. Series A, Mathematical, Physical, and Engineering Sciences, 376*(2133), 20180085. Advance online publication. DOI: 10.1098/rsta.2018.0085 PMID: 30323000

Chapter 5

Extending AI Governance Frameworks:

A Comparative Analysis of Cybersecurity Policies in the EU, UK, USA, and China

Huzaifa Amar
http://orcid.org/0009-0006-5983-3287
Illinois Institute of Technology, USA

Tarun Sara
Illinois Institute of Technology, USA

ABSTRACT

As artificial intelligence (AI) systems and digital infrastructure continue to expand across all sectors, both AI governance and cybersecurity policy have become central challenges for modern governments. This paper extends the analytical framework of our baseline study, Between Innovation and Oversight, which examined AI governance in the EU, UK, US, and China, and applies it to the domain of cybersecurity governance. Using the same comparative dimensions, this paper evaluates how each region approaches cybersecurity and assesses whether the regulatory patterns identified in AI governance carry over. Although cybersecurity introduces additional pressures, particularly in relation to critical infrastructure and national security, the underlying governance philosophies remain largely consistent across regions. The findings suggest that AI governance and cybersecurity governance are best understood as part of a broader digital governance domain, in which long-standing political and regulatory cultures shape how nations balance innovation, security, and societal risk.

DOI: 10.4018/979-8-3373-8252-4.ch005

I INTRODUCTION

With the world increasingly becoming digital and interconnected, both artificial intelligence (AI) and cybersecurity are becoming more important. With that, they have become difficult policy challenges for governments. The growth of digital infrastructure has expanded opportunities for many sectors, while at the same time increasing both technological risks and broad societal impacts. As it is important for infrastructure, companies, governments, and individuals in general that they remain safe against the increasingly hostile digital landscape with growing cyber threats, traditional approaches to cybersecurity and AI policy must be reevaluated (Achuthan et al., 2024; Pum, 2022; McIntosh et al., 2024; Ahmed, 2024; Riek, 2023).

Our baseline paper, *Between Innovation and Oversight: A Cross-Regional Study of AI Risk Management Frameworks in the EU, US, UK, and China* (Al-Maamari, 2025), provided a comparative framework to analyze approaches to AI governance. The study evaluated each region (the European Union, the United States, the United Kingdom, and China) across five comparative frameworks of risk management: governance, adaptability and innovation, transparency and accountability, and stakeholder engagement (government, private sector, civil service, etc.). This research paper extends the analytical framework of the baseline paper from AI governance to cybersecurity policy, using the same evaluation frameworks to examine how the EU, the UK, the US, and China handle cybersecurity. However, we have condensed some sections down as we feel some sections of this analytical framework had enough overlap that it made sense to group them together.

This research paper aims to identify whether the patterns observed in AI governance also emerge in cybersecurity. The aim is to determine how each region balances innovation with regulation, national security with economic competitiveness, and centralized control with stakeholder collaboration. They will be evaluated via a similar evaluation framework used in the baseline paper (Al-Maamari, 2025; Amar, 2025). At the end, we aim to see the overlap between the AI policies of these nations, as discussed in the baseline paper, with their attempts at cybersecurity policy. The idea is not to replace the findings of the baseline paper, but to expand the scope of the baseline paper to the cybersecurity domain. We find that due to the expansion of technology and the continues integration of the internet into everyday life, AI and cybersecurity are part of the new "digital governance" field, which can have strong overlap or divergence with existing governmental structures (Hanisch et al., 2023).

In terms of the remainder of this paper: Section II reviews relevant literature and identifies the gap we aim to address. Section III describes the proposed methodology, workflow, and experimental design. Section IV goes into our findings of the four nations policies and approaches. Section V concludes the paper and outlines directions for future work.

II LITERATURE REVIEW / RELATED WORK

Analysis of AI Governance Policies of the EU, UK, US, and China in the baseline paper

Our baseline paper is a comprehensive cross-regional analysis of AI governance frameworks from the European Union, United States, United Kingdom, and China. This paper broadly concludes that the EU uses a highly institutionalized model prioritizing ethical and human-centric safeguards; the UK favors a flexible, sector-specific strategy designed to encourage innovation; the USA relies on a market-driven, decentralized, and voluntary industry-led model; and China enforces a security-centric, state-directed system that integrates AI oversight into broader national priorities of social stability and economic development (Al-Maamari, 2025).

The baseline paper also highlights a contrast between the existing literature on AI governance and the literature on cybersecurity governance. In AI governance literature, there are numerous cross-regional studies comparing how the EU, UK, US, and China regulate AI (Al-Maamari, 2025). Most papers clearly describe each region's governance style, such as the EU's institutional approach or the UK's flexible framework. Concepts like transparency, human-centric safeguards, and risk levels are well developed, and AI safety and ethics receive significant attention in newer papers. In contrast, cybersecurity governance literature contains far fewer cross-country comparisons of governance structures (Woods & Seymour, 2024). Cybersecurity writing tends to focus on technical standards rather than broader governance questions (Ahern, 2025; Hodgins, 2024; Huangfu, 2024; National Institute of Standards and Technology, 2024; Product Security and Telecommunications Infrastructure Act 2022, 2022). There is no unified system that evaluates the effectiveness of cybersecurity controls, and evidence-based rankings are largely missing, with AI in cybercrime also receiving limited attention (Pum, 2022; Woods & Seymour, 2024). Additionally, cybersecurity implications for AI or large language models remain underexplored and fragmented (Nolte et al., 2025; Woods & Seymour, 2024).

Table 1. Comparison of AI Governance Literature vs. Cybersecurity Governance Literature

AI Governance Literature	Cybersecurity Governance Literature
Cross-regional studies comparing how the EU, UK, US, and China regulate AI (Al-Maamari, 2025)	Far fewer works attempt a cross-country comparison of cybersecurity governance structures (Woods & Seymour, 2024)
Most papers clearly describe each region's governance style (e.g., EU institutional, UK flexible, etc.)	Cybersecurity writing tends to focus on technical standards rather than bigger governance questions (Ahern, 2025; Hodgins, 2024; Huangfu, 2024; National Institute of Standards and Technology, 2024; Product Security and Telecommunications Infrastructure Act 2022, 2022)
Concepts like transparency, human-centric safeguards, and risk levels are well developed	No unified system evaluates the effectiveness of cybersecurity controls, and evidence-based rankings are missing. AI in cybercrime is also not addressed (Pum, 2022; Woods & Seymour, 2024)
AI safety and ethics receive significant attention in newer papers	Cybersecurity implications for AI or LLMs remain underexplored and fragmented (Nolte et al., 2025; Woods & Seymour, 2024)

AI and Cybersecurity Unified

There has been policy work on cybersecurity, including the EU's NIS2 Directive and Cyber Resilience Act, the United Kingdom's PSTI Act 2022, the United States' NIST CSF 2.0, and China's Cybersecurity Law (Ahern, 2025; Hodgins, 2024; Huangfu, 2024; National Institute of Standards and Technology, 2024; Product Security and Telecommunications Infrastructure Act 2022, 2022), with these often being technical standards paired with regulatory enforcement mechanisms. However, there are fewer works that examine the broader governance frameworks or ethical considerations underlying these policies.

This research paper is done because we recognize a gap in the current scholarship, which is that few studies have examined AI and cybersecurity governance together. There is no authority that collects evidence and ranks cybersecurity controls by efficacy, revealing the lack of a unified or evidence-based cybersecurity governance framework ((Pum, 2022). Even the EU's Artificial Intelligence Act, one of the first major regulatory acts of its kind, had little attention regarding cybersecurity at large, with it not even being defined well in the act (Woods & Seymour, 2024). There is also additional information showing that there are inadequate governance policies in regard to cybersecurity and large language models, demonstrating that large frameworks remain unprepared for the convergence of AI and other cybersecurity risks (Nolte et al., 2025). We hope to start this discussion of AI and cybersecurity governance frameworks and policies. We aim to offer a comparison by extending what we consider a solid baseline paper on AI frameworks to the nations' cybersecurity frameworks, providing a larger perspective and additional insight into current frameworks, and then analyzing trends to see how countries can use their AI frameworks to build their cybersecurity frameworks, and vice versa.

III PROPOSED METHODOLOGY

Like our baseline paper, we are performing a qualitative thematic policy approach, collecting data sources to analyze cybersecurity risk management frameworks across the four nations. After gathering the data, we make our notes to perform policy analyses for the countries to extract the broad themes and ideas. From there, we summarize and compare against the original findings of the baseline paper, comparing with the results for the AI governance frameworks for the nations (as shown in Table 2). We will then give our conclusion on the similarities and divergences of the findings of our analysis to the baseline papers, allowing us to compare AI and cybersecurity frameworks. Again, by extending from the baseline paper to compare and contrast existing AI governance frameworks with cybersecurity frameworks, we can give a complementary perspective that situates cybersecurity policy within the same AI governance frameworks of the baseline paper, giving a broader perspective on how governments manage digital risks and innovation. The idea was never to replace the findings of the baseline paper, but to expand the scope of the baseline paper to the cybersecurity domain (Amar, 2025).

Below is an overview of the data sources used in this paper:

- Government and regulatory documents (USA's NIST 2.0, UK's PSTI Act 2022, etc.)
- Academic literature (peer reviewed journals)
- Industry / think-tank white papers and articles (MERICS, Allianz Risk Barometer, etc.)

Figure 1. Proposed architecture of the AI-driven intrusion detection and network traffic analysis system

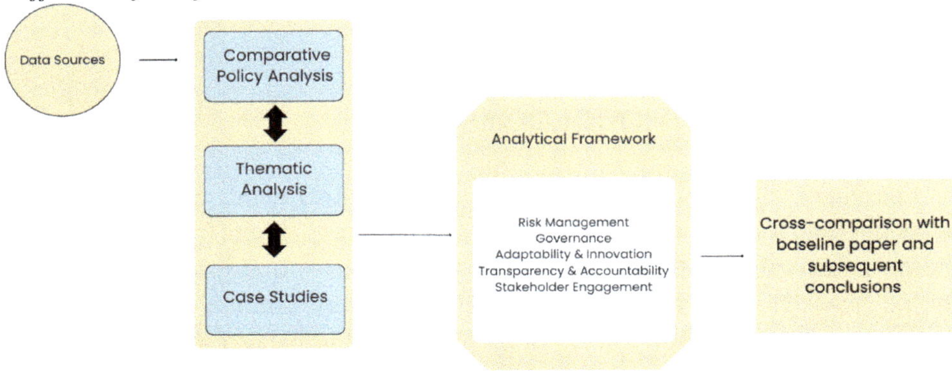

Table 2. Frameworks Used for Evaluation

Dimension	Explanation
Risk Management & Governance	How each nation defines, handles, and communicates the security, ethical, and societal risks at play
Adaptability & Innovation	Flexibility to integrate new technologies and encourage innovation while maintaining oversite and regulatory guidelines / controls
Transparency & Stakeholder Engagement	Level of collaboration and involvement among government, industry, and civil society in shaping and enforcing cybersecurity policy

IV ANALYSIS & DISCUSSION

China

Many Western nations define cybersecurity in at least some context via confidentiality, availability, and integrity of systems and data (Creemers, 2023b). In contrast, China approach to cybersecurity, and subsequently its cybersecurity policy, is best described by the Chinese phrase "wangluo zhuquan" – cybersovereignty. China believes the state has the right to govern its own digital realm as an extension of its territory. This view directly challenges the prevailing Western idea that cyberspace transcends borders and should be governed by universal, global norms, whatever those norms may be (Creemers, 2023a). This shows how China directly and very explicitly frames cybersecurity as a political and social governance issue as well, rather than it just being a purely technical one. Under a Leninist governmental approach to information control, cybersecurity goes beyond the stability of computer systems to include preventing harm to the national interest, the collective interest, and citizens' rights and interests. Here we see the heavy emphasis on cybersecurity via broad social definitions, though yes, China also still defines cybersecurity from a more traditional, technical angle by mandating the stability of computer systems (Creemers, 2023a; Creemers, 2023b). To further illustrate this, the National Security Law, with additions and revisions from the Cybersecurity Law, Data Security Law, and Personal Information Protection Law, established a cross-domain national security strategy covering cultural, economic, and military domains. The National Peoples' Congress criminalized traditional attacks on information systems, regulated online marketplaces, and safeguarded the rights of private users online. But it also put importance on maintaining national security and social stability—rumors, state secrets, hate speech, subversive content, etc. (Creemers, 2022; Creemers, 2023a; Drinhausen & Legarda, 2022; Su & Zhang, 2025).

China's political direction with its cybersovereignty concept, especially in terms of social stability, is shown strongly in censorship. China's Ministry of Public Security (MPS) extended the existing regulations for media (anything from obscenity to respecting the basic principles from the Constitution) into cyberspace. Chinese authorities this created a regulatory environment for the Internet that addressed content regulation, required the identifiability of users and operators, and set technical requirements. This created the regulatory framework for the Great Firewall of China. The Great Firewall would eventually block most of the world's leading media outlets and social media platforms (Creemers, 2023a).

Above we mentioned the CCP's Leninist tradition of maintaining ideological control via broad social control. The growing numbers of netizens made information flows more difficult to control. During the July 2009 Urumqi riots, for instance, numerous social media platforms were shut down. Other incidents such as political scandals and public outrage following a high-profile railway crash were amplified online, challenging the state's ability to manage narratives, and in the case of discussions of constitutional reform after Xi Jinping was sworn as the General Secretary, a major challenge to the CCP regime's integrity. Despite new regulations from the MPS and the Ministry of Industry and Information Technology (MIIT), the speed of technological adoption outpaced regulatory capacity, making cybersecurity—defined in China as social stability—particularly difficult to govern (Creemers, 2023a; Drinhausen & Legarda, 2022).

Unlike all the other nations to be mentioned in this paper, China more so than any of them defines cybersecurity with a heavy top-down social emphasis on how the stability of the party is the stability of the nation. There is very little transparency and stakeholder engagement, as the government, in its Leninist approach, handles everything with little feedback from the private sector or civil society, and there is no accountability placed on the national government for this. In fact, the above-mentioned Data Security Law and Personal Information Protection Law don't purposely create any meaningful constraints on the Chinese state over data collection (Creemers, 2022; Su & Zhang, 2025).

The European Union

The EU's cybersecurity governance strategy was previously risk-based. The EU focused on systemic vulnerabilities and resilience-building; a broad approach, not one focused on any specific actors or anticipated attacks. The EU had begun work to move beyond its purely risk-based cybersecurity governance framework, but it was clear that the need for a more proactive, threat-based framework was needed after a series of severe and important cybersecurity incidents, such as a 360% increase in ransomware attacks for Germany in 2021, an increase in cyber attacks in core EU institutions like the European Commission, the European Medicines Agency, and the European Banking Authority, and attacks on several French entities (Schmitz-Berndt & Cole, 2022). Since the Russian invasion of Ukraine, this has become even more prominent. This resulted in the NIS2 2.0 Directive (directly replacing the earlier 2016 NIS2 Act) (European Union, 2022a), the Cyber Resilience Act (CRA) (European Union, 2024), and the Critical Entities Resilience (CER) Directive (European Union, 2022b). Note that this threat-based framework has been added on top of rather than replacing the prior risk-based approach, creating a new dual model in which resilience-building coexists with a heightened focus on malicious external threats (Backman, 2022).

This also follows a shift in the EU to consolidate the previously fragmented regulatory landscape by tightening existing regulations and introducing new ones. For example, the NIS2 2.0 Directive replaces the original 2016 NIS Directive with broader sectoral coverage and more stringent requirements, while the DORA Regulation introduces EU-wide digital operational resilience obligations for financial entities (European Union, 2022a; Schmitz-Berndt & Cole, 2022).

The practical consequences of this regulatory tightening are illustrated in recent analyses of the Cyber Resilience Act's impact on industrial equipment manufacturing companies. This sector deals with equipment that have strong digital aspects integrated into already complex systems. Add in the fact that companies in this sector are characterized by long product life cycles and well-established engineering practices, and it is clear that increased regulations significantly increase overhead for companies. Despite many of the surveyed firms already being familiar with the previous regulations, the strict timelines mandated by the CRA, such as notification within 24 hours to the proper governmental bodies upon detection of known vulnerabilities being exploit, still caused regulatory compliance issues. Many of the surveyed firms also expected financial costs to increase, as well as some employee role changes, which would also lead to increased costs. It is clear that the CRA's new regulations, especially around documentation and notification, will cause companies additional stress, highlighting how difficult it is to balance innovation with strong cybersecurity transparency and accountability (Backman, 2022; Risto et al., 2025).

The EU considers social stability via a commitment to democratic principles and high transparency. The EU bodies at large hold that measures adopted by the EU and its member states, especially during periods of economic or social instability, must be perceived as effective and fair. Not to mention how trying to get the member states on board has been difficult, as many wish to keep their sovereignty and maintain operational control, further making it difficult to enact change (Backman, 2022). Thus, consulting a diverse group of stakeholders to have proper evidence-based policymaking is considered vital to the EU. Impact assessments are also considered important. ENESA, the European Union Agency for Cybersecurity, leads feedback processes between the laws of the EU and different stakeholders (ENISA, 2023; European Commission, 2023; European Parliament, 2023).

The United Kingdom

Numerous countries wished to forgo a reactive approach to innovation governance for a proactive one. That is, they wished to use, as the OECD puts it, “strategic foresight as a tool of modern, evidence-based, and anticipatory policy making and governance,” to create an anticipatory and regulations-based culture while still allowing for innovation and growth (OECD, 2024). From this desire for a forward-looking, innovation-friendly model that was still proactive in regulations, the UK emerged as one of the original pioneers of the regulatory sandbox approach (Ahern, 2025).

Under the Network and Information Systems (NIS) Regulations, each critical sector has appointed authorities responsible for providing technical cybersecurity guidance, engaging with operators, and running structured audit programs (Clark, 2024). Recent policy changes have pushed the UK towards a more hands-on approach; the Regulation and Incentives Review (RIR) 2022 clearly states that the national government will not leave cybersecurity entirely to market forces. Instead, it will take active steps to strengthen national cyber resilience (Clark, 2024). The National Cyber Strategy (NCS) 2022 (Cabinet Office, 2021 emphasizes this attitude through a “whole-of-society” approach. It aims to shift the burden of cybersecurity from individuals to organizations that can effectively manage systemic risk, essentially promoting corporate and organizational responsibility (Cabinet Office, 2021; Clark, 2024). The strategy also calls for updated annual reporting and audits led by the

National Audit Office (NAO), showing strong importance for transparency and high-level accountability at a high government level (Clark, 2024).

The UK's focused and sector-driven strategy is illustrated by the Product Security and Telecommunications Infrastructure Act 2022 (PSTI Act 2022), created to specifically regulate the security of consumer IoT products in the UK market (Gov.UK, 2023; Product Security and Telecommunications Infrastructure Act 2022, 2022). The Office for Product Safety and Standards (OPSS) is responsible for enforcement, working under a memorandum of understanding with DSIT as set out in the UK Product Security and Telecommunications Infrastructure: Product Security Regime (2023) (Gov.UK, 2023). A key aspect of the PSTI Act is intention to shift societal risks away from consumers and onto manufacturers by establishing accountability requirements. For example, Section 10 (Duty to investigate potential compliance failures) and Section 12 (Duty to maintain records) of the PSTI Act mandate that manufacturers investigate possible security issues, document their findings, log remediation actions, and keep these records for ten years (Product Security and Telecommunications Infrastructure Act 2022, 2022). These rules create a strict accountability framework throughout the product life cycle, mandating that manufacturers take responsibility for product security long after devices enter the market. This reinforces the UK's general trend of addressing cyber and societal risks, except here it is through strong sector-specific obligations and regulations instead of a single overarching legal framework (Ahern, 2025; Clark, 2024; Gov.UK, 2023; Product Security and Telecommunications Infrastructure Act 2022, 2022).

The United States

The US defines cybersecurity primarily through the protection of systems, data, and other essential digital services, but its approach is shaped heavily by market structures and a long-standing reliance on voluntary standards. Cybersecurity policies and practices in the US are produced through a broad consortium of private companies, nonprofits, and government entities, with the private sector easily having the most dominant role (Hodgins, 2024). Federal regulations exist, but they are limited to certain industries, and even in those cases the specific standards organizations follow are typically developed by industry bodies rather than mandated directly by federal authorities. This system persists despite escalating risks—cyberattacks continue to rise, financial losses reach into the tens of billions, and even the International Monetary Fund has warned that cyber risk threatens the stability of financial markets (Hodgins, 2024). The structure of this system is summarized in the NIST Cybersecurity Framework 2.0 (NIST CSF 2), which provides broad cybersecurity outcomes to help prioritize and address cybersecurity risks, but does not specify actions for meeting those outcomes. Most organizations adopt it voluntarily because it supports communication and risk governance, and because it is still a federal document, but not because of any concerns over binding requirements (National Institute of Standards and Technology, 2024).

The US' cybersecurity policy approach places heavy emphasis on critical infrastructure. Even the desire to have the government play a role in cybersecurity at a national level was due to software vulnerabilities and cyberattacks in critical infrastructure (Hodgins, 2024). The Obama administration attempted to strengthen the existing baseline protections, but these proposed policy changes encountered resistance from private industry and Congress due to concerns about cost, regulatory overreach, and reduced operational autonomy (Huangfu, 2024). Because of this, the emphasis remained on voluntary partnership between the federal government, the states, and the private sector. However, there was some attempt during this time to create a more national attempt at a unified cybersecurity approach. Most noticeably, the NCCIC, created under Bush but fully realized under Obama, worked as a federal interface, providing a central place for the various federal and private-sector organizations to coordinate efforts to address and respond to cyber threats (U.S. Government Accountability Office, 2021). It is the backbone of civilian cyber defense. But again, its impact was limited by the voluntary nature of compliance, industry concerns of overreach, and conflicting priorities and communication between the public and private sectors (Huangfu, 2024; U.S. Government Accountability Office, 2021).

The Biden administration attempted change with its 2023 National Cybersecurity Strategy (White House, 2024). This high-level roadmap emphasized how placing responsibility for cybersecurity on end users, small organizations, and local governments is unsustainable. It called for shifting responsibility toward those most capable and best positioned to manage systemic risk—major infrastructure operators, software and hardware providers, service platforms, and so on, although who is considered most capable and best positioned is still up to debate. It acknowledges that the previous voluntary-based approach to cybersecurity for critical infrastructure produced meaningful improvements, but the lack of mandatory requirements still resulted in inadequate and inconsistent outcomes, and points out how the market has not always had the best success rate in incentivizing cybersecurity as a priority (Huangfu, 2024; U.S. Government Accountability Office, 2021). But despite the attempted shift in framing, implementation remains challenging. Much of US cybersecurity governance still depends on shared responsibility, voluntary adoption of frameworks, and the stability of key infrastructure sectors rather than enforceable national standards. As a result, the US recognizes cybersecurity risks at a societal level but continues to address them through distributed governance and partnership-based mechanisms rather than centralized regulatory control (Huangfu, 2024).

While the voluntary nature of US federal regulations hampers attempts at a cohesive national framework compared to the EU and China, and it is easily the most decentralized approach among the four nations, it is at least apparent that there is strong interest from and engagement with stakeholders, even at a foundational level, to create policy (Hodgins, 2024). Private industry in the US, while not obligated, has voiced support for the principles and flexibility of NIST CSF 2 (Luis Salas-Riega et al., 2025), and in one survey over half of all US healthcare organizations have or plan to adopt the NIST CSF 2 framework for their cybersecurity needs (Healthcare Information and Management Systems Society, 2024).

Summary of Cybersecurity Approaches, and Comparison to the Findings of the Baseline Paper

Table 3. Summary of Cybersecurity Approaches According to the Defined Framework

Region	Risk Management and Governance	Adaptability and Innovation	Transparency and Stakeholder Engagement
European Union	From a mainly risk-based approach to a dual risk-based + threat-based governance model. Repeated high-impact cyber incidents and the geopolitical aftermath of the Russian invasion of Ukraine pushed the EU toward a more proactive and threat-oriented framework. This shift is reflected in major legislative overhauls and policy changes which strengthen governance and impose tighter security and reporting obligations. Governance aims to fix the previous framed regulatory environment, but coordination across member states remains challenging. Social stability emphasis with openness and commitment to democracy	New regulations putting greater emphasis on security and harmonization over industry flexibility. Tighter compliance requirements, stricter deadlines. Companies face increased documentation, vulnerability-reporting, and operational burdens. New regulatory frameworks raise financial overhead and may slow innovation	Taken the most seriously out of any of the four nations. The goal is to create high visibility into cybersecurity practices across the private sector, EU member states, and civil society at large in a democratic and open framework

continued on following page

Table 3. Continued

Region	Risk Management and Governance	Adaptability and Innovation	Transparency and Stakeholder Engagement
China	Cybersecurity directly part national security strategy, emphasizing state oversight, mandatory compliance, and strict control of digital and informational ecosystems. Governance extends beyond technical risk to include ideological, political, and social risks. Cybersovereignty - term even coined by China to express control over it's digital sector	China's approach prioritizes centralized authority and broad regulatory coverage. Regulatory adaptability often struggles to keep pace with the speed at which digital platforms and social media ecosystems evolve. The CCP's emphasis on information control means that technological innovation is often constrained by layers of censorship, content requirements, identity verification rules, and technical compliance mandates	Taken the least seriously out of any of the four nations. Minimal transparency, almost no genuine stakeholder engagement in its cybersecurity policy process. Governance is highly top-down via a traditional Leninist governmental approach. Strict requirements on companies, no meaningful limitations on state data collection or state cybersecurity actions
United States	Defined primarily as the protection of key infrastructure and essential services. The most decentralized governance structure on the list. Some attempts at change to a more unified national policy but resistance from the private sector and members of Congress opposed it	Highly adaptive and innovation friendly. Decentralized governance structure with voluntary compliance creates high level of market flexibility	Strong public sector–private sector collaboration. Private companies, standards bodies, and federal agencies all play active roles in shaping cybersecurity policy
United Kingdom	Emphasis on sector-specific regulation. Regulators have responsibility for technical guidance, operator engagement, and structured audits	Early pioneers of regulatory sandboxes, reflecting its desire to foster innovation while maintaining anticipatory governance. Inspired by OECD principles of strategic foresight and evidence-based policymaking, this approach allows regulators and industry to experiment, identify gaps, and shape emerging rules collaboratively. The UK's model is highly adaptable because it does not impose rigid cross-sector mandates. This reflects a governance philosophy that encourages innovation while ensuring accountability in select important sectors (again, a sector-specific approach)	Policies such as the National Cyber Strategy 2022 emphasize shared responsibility across government, industry, and society. The National Audit Office (NAO) plays a key role by conducting audits and requiring updated annual reporting, reinforcing the importance of public oversight and institutional transparency. Avoids a monolithic regulatory framework for a sector-specific one naturally focuses regulator and innovators to work together

Consult Table 3 for a summary of each of the four nations.

Now we return to the initial problem posted in the introduction, and the final part of the architecture as stated in the Methodology section - the comparison to the findings of the baseline paper. What we find is that there is strong overlap between these nation's cybersecurity frameworks and the original baseline paper's finding on AI governance frameworks (Al-Maamari, 2025). In both studies: the United States has a highly decentralized approach to cybersecurity governance, where even most federal policy documents are guidelines, not rules, giving a high degree of innovation but suffering in legal enforcement; China has a very strong, top-down approach and defines social stability with party control and longevity, and sees AI / cybersecurity as an extension of that, with very little insight from other stakeholders, civil society or otherwise; the EU has a similar top-down approach as China does but with far more transparency, with consultation and democratic principles being key; and the UK has a more balanced approach to manage industry innovation with consumer protection, and with it's very nature requiring transparency and stakeholder engagement to form policy.

But there are some differences. For example, the European Union was becoming more focused on proactively dealing with threats, especially in light of the Russian invasion of Ukraine. The United States' cybersecurity governance was defined mainly by key infrastructures, and unlike with the AI governance frameworks in the baseline paper, there was a serious attempt to have structural and cultural change. But this is in many ways the exceptions that proves the general rule that cybersecurity and AI governance frameworks do not differ much, except in cases as the EU's where there was a direct and serious national security risk, in which case cybersecurity, being broader and often more directly linked with national security, necessitated a different governmental approach.

From this, we can see that cybersecurity governance and AI governance, both under the broad field of digital governance (Hanisch et al., 2023), have strong overlap, and frankly, are even almost stereotypical what you expect from these countries - from China's strong state level control with things like censorship, to the US having a very decentralized, deregulated, voluntary approach to regulations that has resisted attempts at legislative change. It seems that culture and priorities have a stronger influence than any specific predefined policy objectives. For example, as discussed, despite the attempts of both the Obama and Biden administrations to establish a unified national cybersecurity approach to move away from the voluntary, decentralized nature of the current system.

V CONCLUSION

This paper extends the analytical structure of our baseline study, *Between Innovation and Oversight*, which originally was only for AI governance frameworks, to cybersecurity governance frameworks. We used a modified version of the baseline paper's original comparative framework. The intent was to perform a qualitative analysis to determine if AI and cybersecurity frameworks have overlap, to see if there were underlying governance philosophies across policy areas that influence how states balance innovation, risk management, and societal protection. We find that the EU relies on comprehensive, rules-based, and institutionalized regulations with a strong emphasis on transparency and multi-stakeholder cooperation; that the UK maintains a sector-driven and innovation-oriented approach supported by anticipatory regulatory tools, backed by an anticipatory mindset; that the US remains committed to a market-driven and voluntary model built on shared responsibility with the private sector, despite some opposition and attempt at reform; and that China reinforces a state-directed, security-first governance system that integrates cybersecurity into national economic and societal priorities. Our work and final analysis shows that cybersecurity governance is often shaped less by technical requirements than by existing regulatory cultures and political priorities. By extending the baseline paper's AI governance framework into the cybersecurity domain, this study shows that underlying governance philosophies persist across policy areas and influence how states balance innovation, risk management, and societal protection. At the same time, cybersecurity magnifies certain tensions that aren't as pronounced as in AI, especially with key industries and areas of paramount national security importance. As cyber threats continue to grow, and with global interdependence only increasing, these structural differences will shape each region's capacity to coordinate internationally and manage emerging risks.

For future works, we can extend this study in several directions. More frameworks can provide a more in-depth analysis. A deeper empirical analysis of the implementation outcomes of policies, such as compliance rates per sector, would strengthen the comparative assessment. Examining additional regions (Japan, Canada, India, etc.) can give us insight into additional governance models beyond those defined for the original four nations. Future research could incorporate a dual qualitative-quantitative approach, perhaps with hard economic data, using cybersecurity-risk indicators to see whether digital governance approaches correlate with actual improvements in national resilience, or if they just create unnecessary regulations for the private sector. Finally, as AI-enabled cyber threats grow, an integrated analysis of AI governance and cybersecurity governance may become essential for understanding how states prepare for emerging, cross-domain risks. Additionally, it is always worth bringing in more case studies and papers to flesh out the existing sections; the UK section in particular was not fleshed out as much as the others.

ACKNOWLEDGEMENT

The authors would like to thank the ITM Department at Illinois Institute of Technology for providing research and teaching support.

REFERENCES

Ahern, D. (2025). The New Anticipatory Governance Culture for Innovation: Regulatory Foresight, Regulatory Experimentation and Regulatory Learning. *European Business Organization Law Review*, *26*(2), 241–283. Advance online publication. DOI: 10.1007/s40804-025-00348-7

Ahmed, F. (2024). Cybersecurity Policy Frameworks for AI in Government: Balancing National Security and Privacy Concerns. *International Journal of Multidisciplinary on Science and Management*, *1*(4), 43–53. https://www.ijmsm.org/volume1-issue4/IJMSM-V1I4P107.pdf

Al-Maamari, A. (2025). Between Innovation and Oversight: A Cross-Regional Study of AI Risk Management Frameworks in the EU, U.S., UK, and China. *arXiv*. https://arxiv.org/abs/2503.05773

Amar, H. (2025). *Cyber Security Management Research Paper* [GitHub Repository]. GitHub. https://github.com/Huz-Amar/Cyber-Security-Management-Research-Paper

Backman, S. (2022). Risk vs. Threat-Based Cybersecurity: The Case of the EU. *European Security*, *32*(1), 85–103. DOI: 10.1080/09662839.2022.2069464

Cabinet Office. (2021). *National Cyber Strategy 2022*. https://www.gov.uk/government/publications/national-cyber-strategy-2022

Clark, A. (2024). *Cybersecurity in the UK*. House of Commons Library. https://commonslibrary.parliament.uk/research-briefings/cbp-9821/

Creemers, R. (2022). China's Emerging Data Protection Framework. *Journal of Cybersecurity*, *8*(1), 1–12. DOI: 10.1093/cybsec/tyac011

Creemers, R. (2023a). The Chinese Conception of Cybersecurity: A Conceptual, Institutional and Regulatory Genealogy. *Journal of Contemporary China*, *33*(146), 1–16. DOI: 10.1080/10670564.2023.2196508

Creemers, R. (2023b). Cybersecurity Law and Regulation in China: Securing the Smart State. *China Law and Society Review*, *6*(2), 111–145. DOI: 10.1163/25427466-06020001

Drinhausen, K., & Legarda, H. (2022). *"Comprehensive National Security" Unleashed: How Xi's Approach Shapes China's Policies at Home and Abroad*. MERICS. https://merics.org/en/report/comprehensive-national-security-unleashed-how-xis-approach-shapes-chinas-policies-home-and

European Commission. (2023). *Better Regulation Toolbox – July 2023 Edition*. https://commission.europa.eu/system/files/2023-09/BR%20toolbox%20-%20Jul%202023%20-%20FINAL.pdf

European Parliament. Future Shocks 2023: Anticipating and weathering the next storms. EPRS Study 751.428, July 2023. ISSN 2600-5174. DOI: 10.2861/88235

European Union. (2022a). *Directive (EU) 2022/2555 on Measures for a High Common Level of Cybersecurity Across the Union*. https://eur-lex.europa.eu/eli/dir/2022/2555/oj

European Union. (2022b). *Directive (EU) 2022/2557 on the Resilience of Critical Entities*. https://eur-lex.europa.eu/eli/dir/2022/2557/oj

Hanisch, M., Goldsby, C. M., Fabian, N. E., & Oehmichen, J. (2023). Digital Governance: A Conceptual Framework and Research Agenda. *Journal of Business Research*, *162*, 113777. DOI: 10.1016/j.jbusres.2023.113777

Healthcare Information and Management Systems Society. (2024). *2023 HIMSS Healthcare Cybersecurity Survey*. https://www.himss.org/sites/hde/files/media/file/2024/03/01/2023-himss-cybersecurity-survey-x.pdf

Hodgins, M. W. (2024). The Perils of Cybersecurity Regulation. *The Review of Austrian Economics*. Advance online publication. DOI: 10.1007/s11138-024-00660-4

Huangfu, Z. (2024). The National Cybersecurity Strategy of the United States and Its Global Impact. *World Politics*, *4*(4), 1–11. DOI: 10.25136/2409-8671.2024.4.72317

Luis Salas-Riega, J.. (2025). Cybersecurity and the NIST Framework: A Systematic Review of Its Implementation and Effectiveness Against Cyber Threats. *International Journal of Advanced Computer Science and Applications*, *16*(6). Advance online publication. https://thesai.org/Downloads/Volume16No6/Paper_72-Cybersecurity_and_the_NIST_Framework.pdf. DOI: 10.14569/IJACSA.2025.0160672

McIntosh, T. R., Susnjak, T., Liu, T., Watters, P., Nowrozy, R., & Halgamuge, M. N. (2024). From COBIT to ISO 42001: Evaluating Cybersecurity Frameworks for Opportunities, Risks, and Regulatory Compliance in Commercializing Large Language Models. *Computers & Security*, *144*, 103964. Advance online publication. DOI: 10.1016/j.cose.2024.103964

National Institute of Standards and Technology. (2024). *NIST Cybersecurity Framework 2.0*. https://www.nist.gov/cyberframework/framework

Nolte, H., Rateike, M., & Finck, M. (2025). Robustness and Cybersecurity in the EU Artificial Intelligence Act. *arXiv*. https://arxiv.org/abs/2503.05773 DOI: 10.1145/3715275.3732020

Organisation for Economic Co-operation and Development. (2024). *Strategic Foresight*. https://www.oecd.org/en/about/programmes/strategic-foresight.html

Product Security and Telecommunications Infrastructure Act 2022. (2022). Legislation.gov.uk. https://www.legislation.gov.uk/ukpga/2022/46/enacted

Pum, M. (2022). The Rise of AI-Powered Cybercrime: Implications for Digital Security and Policy. https://www.researchgate.net/publication/390748096

Riek, L. R. (2023). Is Cybersecurity a Social Responsibility? *Frontiers in Computer Science*. https://www.frontiersin.org/articles/10.3389/fcomp.2023.1123451/full

Risto, R., Sethi, M., & Katara, M. (2025). Effects of the Cyber Resilience Act (CRA) on Industrial Equipment Manufacturing Companies. *arXiv*. https://arxiv.org/abs/2505.14325 DOI: 10.1007/978-3-032-00630-1_12

Schmitz-Berndt, S., & Cole, M. (2022). Towards an Efficient and Coherent Regulatory Framework on Cybersecurity in the EU: The Proposals for a NIS 2.0 Directive and a Cyber Resilience Act. *Applied Cybersecurity & Internet Governance*, *1*(1), 121–137. DOI: 10.5604/01.3001.0016.1323

Su, R., & Zhang, D. (2025). Adaptive Sovereignty: China's Evolving Legislative Framework for Transnational Data Governance. *Politics and Governance*, *13*(0), 10413. Advance online publication. DOI: 10.17645/pag.10413

U.S. Government Accountability Office. (2021). *Cybersecurity and Infrastructure Security Agency: Actions Needed to Ensure Organizational Changes Result in More Effective Cybersecurity for Our Nation*. https://www.gao.gov/products/gao-21-236

White House. (2024). *National Cybersecurity Strategy*. https://bidenwhitehouse.archives.gov/oncd/national-cybersecurity-strategy/

Woods, D. W., & Seymour, S. (2024). Evidence-Based Cybersecurity Policy? A Metareview of Security Control Effectiveness. *Journal of Cyber Policy* DOI: 10.1080/23738871.2024.2335461

Chapter 6

Architecting Trustworthy and Resilient AI Systems:

Adversarial Threats, Forensic Intelligence, and Governance in Cloud-Native Environments

Madhu Babu Amarappalli
http://orcid.org/0009-0009-2723-0256
Deloitte Consulting LLC, USA

ABSTRACT

Artificial intelligence (AI) and large language models (LLMs) increasingly underpin cyber defense workflows triaging alerts, correlating telemetry, classifying malware, generating incident narratives, and accelerating analyst decision-making. Yet the same properties that make AI operationally valuable (learning from data, generalizing across contexts, and automating at scale) also expand the attack surface. Adversaries can poison training data, implant hidden backdoors, steal model behavior through APIs, induce privacy leakage, or exploit prompt-manipulation weaknesses in LLM applications. When these models are deployed cloud-natively via containerized inference services, retrieval-augmented generation (RAG), agentic toolchains, and continuous delivery pipelines attack vectors multiply across datasets, MLOps supply chains, identity layers, orchestration planes, and third-party dependencies. This chapter presents a unified framework for architecting trustworthy and resilient AI systems under adversarial pressure. We synthesize adversarial AI threat models.

DOI: 10.4018/979-8-3373-8252-4.ch006

1. INTRODUCTION

Econometric analysis is increasingly defined by data abundance and data fragility. Administrative microdata, high-frequency financial records, platform logs, and sensor streams now let researchers study behavior at unprecedented scale and granularity often in near real time. Yet these gains arrive with a structural cost: the empirical environment is routinely shaped by heterogeneous measurement systems, nonstationary behavior, and rare but consequential events. In such settings, the assumptions that made many classical estimators reliable in smaller, cleaner datasets thin tails, stable regimes, well-behaved errors, and "mostly correct" measurement are regularly strained or violated. What looks like a single "outlier" in a textbook example may, in modern pipelines, reflect any of the following: a data pipeline fault, a coding change in reporting, a sudden policy shock, a coordinated response to incentives, or an emergent economic disruption. The practical implication is that anomalous observations are no longer peripheral: they are recurring features of the data-generating process and can meaningfully shape both estimation and interpretation.

Robust statistics provides conceptual vocabulary for designing analysis procedures that remain stable under contamination. Influence functions formalize local sensitivity: they describe how an estimator reacts to a small amount of contamination placed at a particular point in the sample space, thereby making "fragility" a measurable design property rather than a vague concern (Hampel et al., 1986). Breakdown points, in turn, capture resistance to large-scale corruption by quantifying the largest fraction of contaminated observations that can drive an estimator toward arbitrarily misleading results (Hampel et al., 1986; Maronna et al., 2006). These ideas are not abstract embellishments: they directly motivate operational choices such as bounded-influence loss functions, robust scale estimation, and outlier-resistant multivariate procedures. Huber's foundational M-estimation framework illustrates the central tradeoff clearly: by replacing pure quadratic loss with a loss that grows more slowly in the tails, one can sharply reduce the impact of extreme residuals while retaining high efficiency under benign conditions (Huber, 1964). In other words, robustness is not about ignoring anomalies, it is about ensuring that their presence does not silently dominate empirical conclusions.

Figure 1. Robust anomaly detection pipeline.

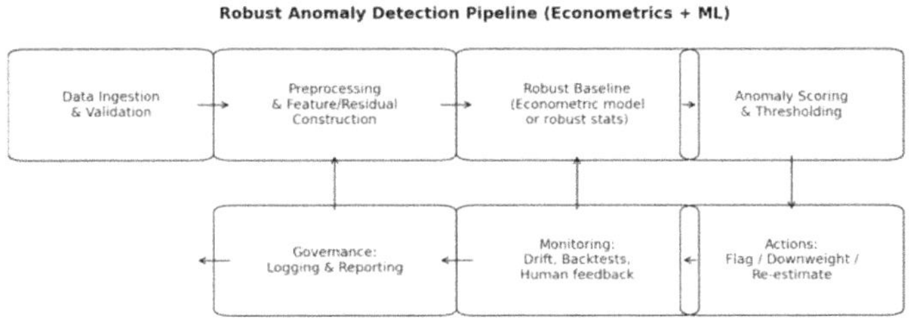

Crucially, in modern pipelines, robustness cannot be treated as an "after-the-fact" diagnostic. When data are large and heterogeneous, many decisions that shape results occur before the final regression table appear feature engineering, imputation, historization, filtering rules, model selection, hyperparameter tuning, and evaluation splits. If anomalies influence any of these steps, then even a final-stage robust regression may be too late because the workflow has already been optimized around contaminated patterns. Robustness, therefore, must be engineered as a workflow property: procedures should be designed so that early-stage transformations, learning choices, and evaluation protocols remain stable under plausible contamination mechanisms (Hampel et al., 1986; Maronna et al., 2006). This perspective reframes anomaly detection as part of the econometric system's reliability engineering, not merely a statistical add-on.

This chapter's premise is practical: robust anomaly detection should be engineered as a modular system with explicit layers for (1) robustness, (2) detection, (3) inference, and (4) operations. The robust layer stabilizes representation and estimation using bounded-influence and high-breakdown principles (Hampel et al., 1986; Maronna et al., 2006), ensuring that a small subset of extreme points does not control fitted relationships. The detection layer produces anomaly scores and flags, ideally distinguishing leverage anomalies (unusual covariates) from outcome anomalies (unusual residuals) and from structural anomalies (regime shifts). The inference layer addresses a core econometric concern: once filtering, weighting, or selection depends on the data, having standard errors and confidence intervals can become misleading. Robust anomaly pipelines must therefore preserve or explicitly restore valid uncertainty quantification when decisions are data dependent. Finally, the operations layer reflects how modern empirical work is conducted: data systems update, definitions shift, pipelines evolve, and anomalies recur. A credible anomaly framework must be reproducible, auditable, and monitorable, with clear documentation of thresholds, versioning, and sensitivity checks.

A system view is essential because the modern analyst is simultaneously forced to meet four constraints that rarely coexist in classical settings. First, methods must scale to high-dimensional feature spaces without letting contamination steer selection or training. Second, they must distinguish structural breaks from point outliers, since both can manifest as extreme observations but demand different responses. Third, they must produce interpretable and auditable outputs not just black-box scores because anomalies often trigger consequential decisions (data correction, policy interpretation, risk controls). Fourth, they must preserve valid uncertainty quantification after anomaly-aware filtering, trimming, or down weighting, so that robustness does not come at the cost of unacknowledged inferential distortion. The guiding principle is that anomaly detection is not a single technique; it is a design discipline one that integrates robust statistical foundations (Hampel et al., 1986; Maronna et al., 2006; Huber, 1964) with scalable detection tools and econometric standards of interpretability and credible inference.

2. PROBLEM SETTING AND NOTATION

Let z_i denote the i-th observation. Depending on the empirical setting, z_i may represent a single record (e.g., a household, a firm, a transaction, a device reading) or a structured object (e.g., a unit–time pair in a panel). In the simplest cross-sectional case, we write

$$z_i = (y_i, x_i),$$

where $y_i \in \mathbb{R}$ is an outcome of interest and $x_i \in \mathbb{R}^p$ is a vector of covariates. In many applications, z_i also includes additional components such as treatment indicators d_i, instruments w_i, group identifiers $g(i)$, timestamps $t(i)$, and spatial locations $s(i)$. To emphasize generality, we treat z_i as a generic element of a sample space $\mathcal{Z}$ that may encode cross-sectional, panel, time-series, or network structure.

Figure 2. Contamination (mixture) model used to formalize robustness in anomaly handling.

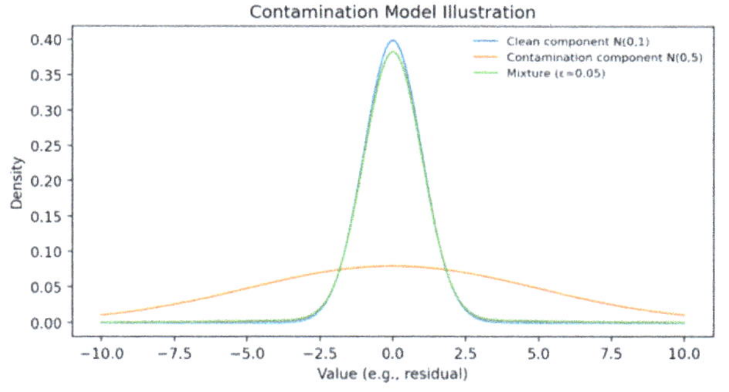

2.1 Contamination, Robustness, and the Mixture Model

A standard and highly interpretable starting point for robustness is the **gross-error contamination model**, which posits that the observed empirical distribution arises from a mixture of a nominal data-generating process and a contamination process:

$$P = (1 - \varepsilon) P_0 + \varepsilon Q,$$

where $P_0$is the "clean" or target distribution (the process the analyst would ideally observe), $Q$is an alternative distribution that generates contaminated observations, and $\varepsilon \in [0,1]$is the contamination fraction (Hampel et al., 1986). This model is intentionally broad: it accommodates classical measurement errors as well as modern failure modes such as fraud, adversarial manipulation, pipeline changes, and rare regimes.

Econometrically, it is useful to interpret the contamination component Qin several ways:

- **Measurement contamination:** miscoding, unit errors, imputation artifacts, sensor dropouts, duplicate records, or broken joints.
- **Behavioral contamination:** strategic reporting, gaming of incentives, unusual behavior induced by policy shocks, or manipulation of thresholds.
- **Regime contamination:** observations drawn from a different structural relationship due to policy changes, macro shocks, or institutional reforms.
- **Model contamination:** data are valid, but the assumed functional form is wrong for a subset of the population (latent heterogeneity).

The goal of robust methods is not to "remove" $Q$by default, but to ensure that key outputs (coefficients, fitted values, scores, inference statements) do not become arbitrarily sensitive to a small fraction of contaminated points. This idea can be operationalized through stability to increasing ε, bounded influence of single observations, and resistance to larger-scale corruption (Hampel et al., 1986). In practice, robust design asks: *If a small share of observations were replaced by extreme or adversarial points, would the fitted model or inference meaningfully change?* If yes, then anomaly handling must be integrated earlier and more systematically into the workflow.

2.2 Anomaly Scoring and Flagging Rules

Anomaly detection introduces a mapping $s:\mathscr{Z} \rightarrow \mathbb{R}$that assigns each observation an **anomaly score** $s(z)$, where larger values indicate greater abnormality. The score can be derived from different principles residual magnitude, local density, isolation depth, boundary distance, reconstruction error, or likelihood under a fitted model. Importantly, anomaly scores need not be probabilistic; they can be purely algorithmic ranks intended for screening.

A binary decision can be produced by thresholding:

$$\mathbb{1}\{s(z_i) > \tau\},$$

where $\tau$is a chosen threshold. Thresholding raises two econometric concerns:

1. **Calibration:** τdetermines the flagged fraction and interacts with the sample size, tail behavior, and dependence structure.
2. **Downstream inference:** if estimation or model selection uses flagged outcomes (e.g., deleting or down weighting), then inference must account for the data-dependent decision rule.

A robust anomaly pipeline often treats $s(z)$as a continuous diagnostic used for sensitivity analysis (e.g., how estimates vary as progressively higher-score observations are downweighted), rather than an irreversible filter.

2.3 Types of Anomalies in Econometric Data

Econometric data exhibits different anomaly types, which matter because they require different detection logic and different responses:

1. **Point anomalies (isolated outliers).** Observations that are individually unusual are relative to the bulk of the data. In regression settings, these include:
   - o **vertical outliers** (unusually large residuals $y_i - \widehat{m}(x_i)$), and
   - o **leverage points** (unusual covariates x_i, potentially exerting high influence on fitted coefficients).
2. **Contextual anomalies (conditional anomalies).** An observation may be "normal" marginally but abnormal **conditional** on context such as covariates, time, location, or group. For example, a transaction amount may be typical overall but abnormal for a given account, time-of-day, or region. Contextual anomalies are central to econometrics because models are usually conditional statements (e.g., $E[y \mid x]$, $E[y \mid x, t]$), so anomaly meaning should often be defined relative to conditional structure rather than unconditional extremes.
3. **Collective anomalies (cluster/sequence anomalies).** A set of observations forms an abnormal pattern even if each individual point is not extreme. Examples include:
   - o bursts of unusual transactions,
   - o coordinated behavior across accounts,
   - o correlated reporting artifacts across agencies,
   - o abnormal temporal sequences in sensor streams.

Collective anomalies are especially relevant in panels and networks, where the unit of "abnormality" may be a cluster, a cohort, or a subgraph rather than a single point.

2.4 Dependence, Masking, and Joint Estimation

Many econometric datasets are **dependent** time series exhibit autocorrelation and conditional heteroskedasticity, panels exhibit serial and cross-sectional correlation, and networks exhibit interdependence across nodes. Dependence changes anomaly detection in two fundamental ways.

First, dependence creates **masking and swamping**: one outlier can hide another (masking), or a true outlier can cause many nearby points to appear abnormal (swamping), especially when residuals or innovations are computed from a model fit that has already been distorted by anomalies. Second, dependence means that the natural "null" for abnormality is not aid randomness; it is a structured process with dynamics and conditional variance.

For these reasons, detecting outliers after fitting a non-robust dynamic model can be self-defeating: the outliers distort the parameters, and the distorted parameters distort the residuals, which then mislead detection. A key methodological insight is that **parameter estimation and outlier adjustment should often be performed jointly**, particularly in time series, where iterative procedures can separate model dynamics from outlier effects. Chen and Liu (1993) formalize this point by developing a framework for joint estimation of model parameters and outlier effects, addressing precisely the masking and bias problems that arise when estimation and outlier handling are separated (Chen & Liu, 1993).

2.5 What This Section Implies for the Rest of the Chapter

This notation and problem framing imply three design principles that guide the hybrid architectures developed later:

- **Robustness precedes detection:** anomaly scoring is more meaningful when applied to stabilized residuals or representations that are not already distorted by contamination (Hampel et al., 1986).
- **Dependence requires integrated design:** time-series and panel contexts often demand joint estimation or segmentation approaches, since naive residual-based detection can be biased or unstable under dynamic masking (Chen & Liu, 1993).

3. ROBUSTNESS FOUNDATIONS FOR ECONOMETRIC ANOMALY HANDLING

Robustness in econometrics is fundamentally about **controlling sensitivity**: ensuring that key conclusions estimated parameters, fitted relationships, forecasts, and inferential statements do not hinge on a small fraction of atypical observations. In anomaly-rich environments, robustness must serve two roles simultaneously. First, it stabilizes *estimation* by limiting the impact of extreme realizations or corrupted records. Second, it stabilizes *diagnosis* by ensuring that anomaly flags are not artifacts of a distorted baseline model. This section reviews core robust ideas **influence functions**, **breakdown points**, and **high-breakdown/bounded-influence estimation** and translates them into design principles for econometric anomaly detection systems.

Figure 3. Influence functions: unbounded (OLS) versus bounded/redescending robust alternatives.

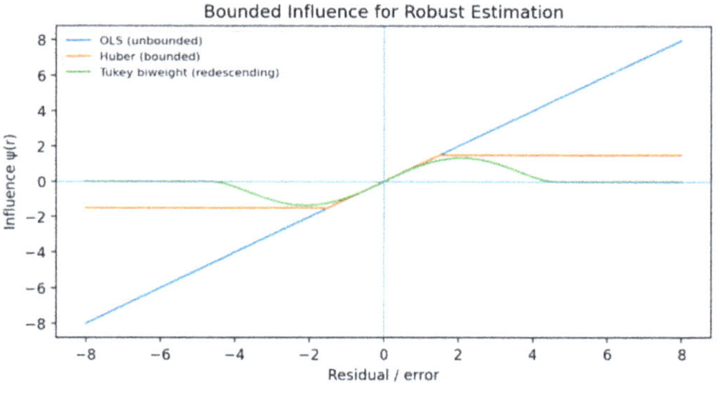

3.1 Influence Functions and Bounded Sensitivity

Influence functions provide a principled measure of **local fragility**. Formally, they capture the first-order effect on an estimator $T(P)$of placing an infinitesimal probability mass at a point z. Intuitively, the influence function answers: *If one observation was slightly perturbed or replaced by a point at z, how would the estimator move?* This makes sensitivity concrete and supports the design of estimators whose behavior is controlled under small contaminations (Hampel et al., 1986).

From an operational standpoint, influence-function thinking maps directly into three design choices for anomaly handling workflows:

1. Robust losses that grow slowly in the tails.

Many estimators can be written as minimizers of an objective:

$$\hat{\theta} \in \arg\min_{\theta} \sum_{i=1}^{n} \rho(r_i(\theta)),$$

where $r_i(\theta)$denotes a residual or moment condition. Robust losses choose $\rho(\cdot)$so that the marginal penalty for large residuals does not explode, limiting the leverage of extreme observations. This bounded growth is the mechanism through which influence is controlled.

2. **Robust scale estimation for standardization and thresholding.**

Anomaly scoring and robust fitting typically depend on "how large is large," which requires a scale estimate. Classical scale (e.g., standard deviation) is itself sensitive to outliers, which can cause thresholds to drift upward and make anomalies disappear. Robust pipelines therefore standardize residuals using robust scale estimators, so that detection thresholds remain meaningful even when tails are heavy or contamination is present (Hampel et al., 1986).

A canonical example is **Huber's M-estimator**, which formalizes an efficiency–robustness compromise: it behaves like least squares for small residuals but transitions to a linear penalty for large residuals, reducing the marginal impact of extremes (Huber, 1964). In regression terms, this produces a *soft reweighting* of observations: typical points retain near-full weight, while extreme-residual points are down weighted rather than allowed to dominate. This is especially valuable in anomaly detection pipelines where residual-based scoring is used because the residuals are computed from a baseline fit that is itself stable.

3.2 Breakdown Points and High-Breakdown Regression

While influence functions address *local* contamination, breakdown point addresses **global corruption**: it measures the largest fraction of contaminated observations an estimator can tolerate before it can be driven arbitrarily far from the truth. This is the most directly aligned concept with worst-case thinking: *How much of the dataset could be corrupted before the estimator becomes meaningless?*

Least squares regression has breakdown point near zero because a small number of extreme points can dominate the fitted line—especially leverage points that are extreme in x. In contrast, **high-breakdown estimators** remain stable even when a nontrivial portion of the data is corrupted. A milestone is **Least Median of Squares (LMS)** regression, which minimizes the median of squared residuals and can tolerate substantial contamination without catastrophic failure (Rousseeuw, 1984).

However, high-breakdown methods alone are not sufficient for applied econometrics: they can be statistically inefficient in clean settings and computationally demanding in large-scale problems. This motivates hybrid robust estimators, particularly **MM-estimators** that combine high-breakdown resistance with high efficiency. MM-estimation proceeds in stages: (i) compute a high-breakdown initial estimator (to avoid being pulled by contamination), (ii) refine with a bounded-influence M-estimation step, and (iii) tune for efficiency under nominal conditions (Yohai, 1987; Maronna et al., 2006).

For anomaly detection architectures, this staged logic is highly consequential:

- The high breakdown start protects the baseline fit from being "captured" by outliers, reducing masking and preventing the residual scale from inflating.

- The bounded-influence refinement improves statistical efficiency and stabilizes prediction error without sacrificing robustness.
- The resulting residuals and weights provide *direct inputs* to anomaly scoring: points down weighted by the robust fit become candidate anomalies, and their robust standardized residuals can be interpreted consistently.

3.3 Robustness Targets in Econometrics

In econometrics, robustness is not limited to producing stable point estimates. Anomalies can compromise **identification**, **selection**, and **inference** often in ways that are not visible from residual plots alone.

1. **Identification and structural interpretation.** Contamination can masquerade as economic structure. Examples include:
    - contaminated instruments (invalid relevance/exogeneity patterns),
    - manipulated running variables in discontinuity-style settings,
    - mismeasured treatment intensity correlated with outcomes, or
    - subgroup-specific regime shifts mistaken for noise. In these cases, anomaly handling is not simply a "clean the data" task; it is part of safeguarding identification logic.
2. **High-dimensional variable selection and model building.**

In modern econometrics, researchers often use many controls, flexible functional forms, or ML-based nuisance estimation. Small fractions of anomalies can distort model selection particularly in sparse settings by creating spurious correlations that attract selected features or shift tuning. The credibility of empirical conclusions depends on selection stability under plausible contamination.

3. **Inference after data-dependent decisions.**

Once the analyst filters, trims, or down weights observations using a score computed from the data, the sampling distribution of estimator's changes. Naïvely treating the filtered sample as if it were exogenously given can yield misleading standard errors and confidence intervals. This is a central tension: robustness procedures often require data-dependent choices, but econometric credibility requires valid uncertainty quantification conditional on those choices.

These concerns are amplified in **post-selection and high-dimensional causal estimation**. When many controls are available, econometricians often use procedures that remain valid after selection among high-dimensional controls (Belloni et al., 2014). Similarly, when nuisance functions are estimated flexibly (including with ML), orthogonal (locally insensitive) score constructions such as those used in double/debiased ML—help protect inference on target parameters from nuisance estimation error (Chernozhukov et al., 2018). Robust anomaly pipelines can be integrated with these frameworks by ensuring that (i) nuisance estimation is not dominated by anomalies, and (ii) the inferential procedure remains stable under plausible trimming/weighting rules.

3.4 Design Implications: Architectural Rules for Robust Anomaly Pipelines

Sections 3.1–3.3 imply a set of practical "architecture rules" that help translate robustness theory into implementable anomaly-detection systems. These rules are intentionally operational: each can be converted into an explicit checklist item, pipeline constraint, or reporting requirement.

Rule 1 Robusta Before You Score

Principle: anomaly scoring should be performed on a *stabilized representation* (robust residuals, robustly scaled features, or robust latent components), not directly on raw outputs from a fragile estimator.

Rationale: non-robust baselines can be captured by extreme observations, inflating residual scales and masking anomalies. Robust baselines limit influence and preserve interpretability (Hampel et al., 1986; Huber, 1964).

Implementation: fit robust location/scale and robust conditional mean models first; compute standardized residuals using robust scale; only then compute $s(z)$.

Rule 2 Prefer High-Breakdown Starts for Residual-Based Detection

Principle: if anomaly detection is residual-based (i.e., "unusual relative to a model"), the model generating residuals should be initialized with a high-breakdown procedure.

Rationale: high-breakdown starts protecting the baseline from being dominated by a contaminated subset; bounded-influence refinement then improves efficiency (Rousseeuw, 1984; Yohai, 1987; Maronna et al., 2006).

Implementation: use LMS/S-type starts where feasible, or MM-estimation pipelines; in large-scale settings use robust subsampling or robust initialization heuristics.

Rule 3 Separate "Unusual" From "Influential"

Principle: flagging should not stop at "this point is extreme." The system should report whether a point is **influential for the Esti and** (coefficient, causal parameter, forecast) versus merely unusual.

Rationale: some anomalies are economically meaningful events and should remain in the analysis; what matters is whether conclusions hinge on them (Hampel et al., 1986).

Implementation: pair anomaly scores with influence-style diagnostics: coefficient change, leave-one-out approximations, weight diagnostics, leverage proxies.

Rule 4 Distinguish Leverage Anomalies from Outcome Anomalies

Principle: classify anomalies into at least two interpretable types:

- **Leverage-driven:** unusual X(risking extrapolation)
- **Residual-driven:** unusual Yconditional on X
- **Rationale:** econometric action differs leverage points threaten identification and functional-form validity; residual outliers may indicate shocks or measurement error.
- **Implementation:** compute separate sub-scores $s_X(x)$and $s_R(r)$; report both alongside a combined score.

Rule 5 Treat Time Dependence as a First-Class Constraint

Principle: in time series and panels, do not assume iid errors when designing detection thresholds and revisualization.

Rationale: dependence produces masking/swamping and biased parameters if estimation and outlier adjustment are separated; joint or iterative procedures are often needed (Chen & Liu, 1993).

Implementation: use outlier-aware model fitting and iterative re-estimation; incorporate structural break/regime segmentation before classifying points as outliers.

Rule 6 Calibrate Thresholds with Stability, Not Just Percentiles

Principle: choose τusing **stability of the econometric target** (and/or held-out nominal data), not solely fixed quantiles.

Rationale: percentile thresholds can be arbitrary under heavy tails or drift; what matters is how conclusions change when trimming/down weighting increases.

Implementation: plot target estimates across a grid of trimming rates or weight schedules; select τ where estimates stabilize.

4. ECONOMETRIC ANOMALY CLASSES AND DETECTION TASKS

Econometric anomaly detection is not a single problem but a family of related tasks whose meaning depends on the data structure and the econometric objective. The same "unusual observation" can be (i) a measurement error to correct, (ii) a rare but economically meaningful event to model, or (iii) a structural break that changes the validity of the identification strategy. This section classifies anomalies by common econometric data types cross-sectional, panel/matrix, and time-series and clarifies the detection tasks that naturally arise in each setting.

Figure 4. Taxonomy of anomaly types by econometric data structure

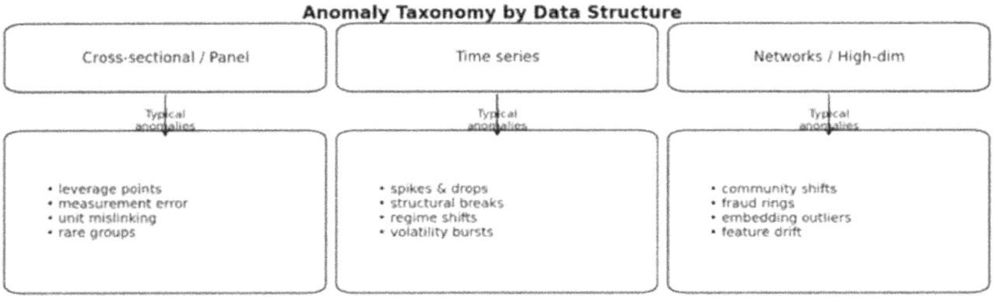

4.1 Cross-Sectional and Panel Data

4.1.1 Core Anomaly Types in Cross-Sections

In cross-sectional settings $z_i = (y_i, x_i)$, anomalies typically appear in three canonical forms, each associated with a different failure mode and a different detection strategy:

1. **Leverage anomalies (extreme X).**

These are observations with unusual covariate values points far from the main support of X. Even if their outcomes are not extreme, they can exert disproportionate influence because regression fits must extrapolate toward them. In applied econometrics, leverage anomalies often correspond to rare subpopulations (e.g., very large firms, extremely high-income households), data integration errors (incorrect merges), or definitional shifts (a new coding category that creates a new region of feature space).

Detection task: identify extreme or isolated points in X-space (robust covariance distances, local density methods, support estimation).

2. **Vertical anomalies (extreme Y conditional on X).**

These are observations with unusually large residuals relative to a conditional mean model $m(x) = E[Y \mid X = x]$. They may reflect measurement error in Y, rare shocks, or model misspecification (e.g., missing nonlinearities or interactions).

Detection task: robustly estimate $m(x)$, compute robust standardized residuals, then flag large residual magnitudes.

3. **Joint anomalies (unusual combinations).**

Some observations are not marginally extreme in X or Y but are abnormal as **combinations** (e.g., a moderate Y paired with a covariate pattern for which it is highly unexpected). These are common in high-dimensional settings where "abnormality" is geometric rather than univariate.

Detection task: multivariate scoring on $(X,\hat{r})$ or learned representations, typically with robust preprocessing.

A key econometric point is that these anomaly types correspond to different risks:

- Leverage anomalies threaten **functional-form validity** and can distort estimates of marginal effects or elasticity.
- Vertical anomalies threaten **error assumptions** and can bias estimates through nonlinear loss sensitivity.
- Joint anomalies threaten **generalization** and can cause unstable model selection or tuning in high-dimensional pipelines.

4.1.2 Panels: Clustered Anomalies and Latent Factor Contamination

Panel data introduces dependence across time and within units. Let y_{it} denote the outcome for unit i at time t. Panels create anomaly types that do not exist in pure cross-sections:

- **Cluster-level anomalies:** entire units (or time blocks) behave abnormally, even if single observations are not extreme. Examples include a firm with a reporting system change, a region with a data outage, or an institution affected by a localized policy shock.

- **Temporal anomaly episodes:** a unit behaves normally most of the time but experiences an abnormal episode (a burst, spike, or unusual volatility).
- **Latent factor contamination:** common shocks or factor structure changes (e.g., macro shocks, platform-wide measurement changes) can create widespread shifts that appear as "many outliers" if the model does not account for shared components.

This motivates detection tasks that operate at multiple levels: point-level flags (it), unit-level flags i, time-level flags t, and episode-level segmentation within unit histories.

4.1.3 Matrix-Structured Data and Robust Decomposition (Robust PCA)

Many panel-like datasets are naturally represented as a matrix $Y \in \mathbb{R}^{n \times T}$(units $\times$ time) or (entities $\times$ features). In these cases, an effective anomaly strategy is to **separate systematic structure from sparse deviations**. Robust PCA formalizes this via:

$$Y = L + S,$$

where $L$is low-rank (systematic structure) and $S$is sparse (localized corruptions or shocks) (Candès et al., 2011). Econometrically:

- Loften corresponds to **common components**: latent factors, persistent trends, or shared macro variation.
- Scorresponds to **candidate anomalies**: reporting errors, fraud-like spikes, idiosyncratic shocks, or localized event impacts.

This decomposition is attractive because it produces an interpretable anomaly object: not merely "this observation is weird," but "this cell deviates strongly from the systematic component." It also naturally supports downstream tasks:

- anomaly *localization* (which units/times/variables are affected),
- anomaly *persistence* (does Sspike briefly or persist),
- anomaly *clustering* (do anomalies co-occur across units or time).

4.2 Time Series: Outliers, Breaks, and Regimes

Time series introduces a central identification challenge for anomaly detection: **an outlier and a structural break can look similar**, especially when the model is mis specified or when volatility changes. If the analyst treats breaks as outliers, they may "clean away" genuine economic change. If the analyst treats outliers as breaks, they may infer structural instability where none exists. Robust time-series anomaly handling must therefore treat *outliers* and *regime change* as distinct but interacting phenomena.

4.2.1 Structural Breaks and Parameter Instability

A structural break is a change in the data-generating mechanism parameters, trend, variance, or dependence structure. Econometric tools for detecting breaks include:

- tests for parameter instability with unknown change points (Andrews, 1993),
- multiple-break estimation and testing procedures (Bai & Perron, 1998).

These methods support detection tasks such as:

- locating break dates,
- quantifying pre/post parameter changes,
- testing whether the break is statistically meaningful,
- assessing stability of forecasting relationships.

In anomaly-system terms, break detection is often the *first stage* of a reliable pipeline: it defines "regimes" within which residual-based anomaly scoring is meaningful and thresholds can be calibrated.

4.2.2 Regime-Switching and Recurring States

Some time series exhibit recurring regimes rather than one-time breaks (e.g., expansions vs recessions, calm vs turbulent volatility states). Regime-switching models provide a framework for identifying latent states and estimating regime-dependent parameters, which is especially relevant for macroeconomic and financial data (Hamilton, 1989). From an anomaly perspective, regime switching helps prevent systematic over-flagging during high-volatility states by recognizing that "normal" behavior is state-dependent.

4.2.3 Outliers Under Dependence: Masking and Joint Estimation

A defining operational issue in time series is **masking**: outliers can distort parameter estimates, which distort residuals, which then hide the very outliers one tries to detect. If estimation and outlier adjustment are separated (fit first, detect later), the procedure can converge to a self-consistent but wrong model.

Chen and Liu (1993) show that outlier detection and parameter estimation should often be performed jointly in time series. Their framework estimates the underlying model while simultaneously estimating outlier effects, reducing masking and improving detection accuracy in dynamic settings (Chen & Liu, 1993). The practical lesson is that time-series anomaly pipelines should be iterative and model-aware:

- estimate baseline dynamics,
- detect candidate outliers,
- adjust/estimate outlier effects,
- re-estimate dynamics,
- repeat until stable.

4.2.4 Practical Interpretation: "Event vs Error vs Regime"

Time-series anomalies are often high-stakes because they drive narratives (crashes, shocks, disruptions). A robust anomaly pipeline should therefore end with an interpretable classification step:

- **Error:** pipeline fault, missingness artifact, sensor malfunction → repair/excluding with documentation.
- **Event:** real shock (policy, crisis, market event) → keep; model explicitly (event indicators or regime mechanisms).
- **Regime change:** persistent parameter/variance shift → segment the analysis; update forecasting or identification assumptions.

This classification is essential for econometrics because different actions imply different inferential consequences.

4.3 Task-to-Method Mapping (Quick Reference Table)

The table below links **econometric anomaly tasks** to **method families** and clarifies what each method is best suited to detect. The goal is to give readers a "routing map": once the anomaly class and data structure are identified, the analyst can quickly narrow to appropriate tools and outputs.

5. MACHINE LEARNING METHODS: WHAT THEY ADD AND WHAT THEY RISK

Machine learning contributes powerful anomaly-detection tools that scale well, handle nonlinear structure, and work in high-dimensional feature spaces where classical multivariate diagnostics become unreliable. For econometrics, however, the value of ML anomaly detection is conditional: these methods are most useful when they are embedded in an architecture that preserves interpretability, controls sensitivity to contamination, and safeguards inference. This section explains (i) what ML adds from an algorithmic standpoint and (ii) why econometric robustness principles remain essential when ML is used for scoring or screening.

Figure 5. Method families for anomaly detection and typical risks under shift.

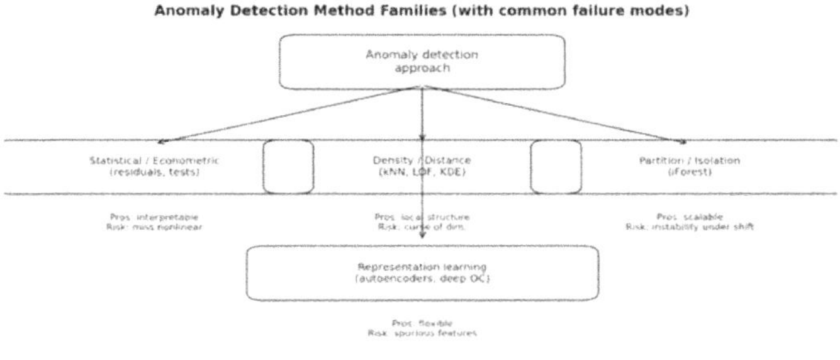

5.1 Anomaly Detection Families

A practical way to organize ML anomaly detection is by the **mechanism used to define abnormality**: (a) density deviation, (b) boundary/support estimation, and (c) isolation/partition depth. Chandola et al. (2009) provides a standard overview and terminology for these families. Within each family, it is useful to distinguish whether detection is based on a model of the "normal" data manifold, local neighborhoods, or global separation rules (Chandola et al., 2009).

5.1.1 Density-Based and Local-Neighborhood Scoring

Density-based methods define anomalies as points that lie in **low-density regions** relative to their neighbors. A workhorse example is **Local Outlier Factor (LOF)**, which compares the local density around a point to the local densities of its neighbors and flags points that appear isolated relative to their neighborhood (Breunig et al., 2000). LOF is attractive in econometric settings where "normality" is heterogeneous: some regions of X-space may naturally be sparse (e.g., niche markets, rare occupations), and LOF's local normalization can reduce false positives compared to purely global density thresholds.

Econometric relevance: LOF is particularly useful for detecting *leverage-like anomalies* in high-dimensional covariate spaces or engineered behavioral features (e.g., transaction patterns), where unusualness is relative to peer groups rather than unconditional tails.

Cautions: neighborhood methods can be sensitive to feature scaling, the curse of dimensionality, and local density distortions caused by contamination. Robust preprocessing and dimensionality reduction often matter as much as the scoring algorithm.

5.1.2 Boundary and Support Estimation (One-Class Classification)

Boundary/support methods estimate the region of feature space where "normal" observations lie and flag points outside this region. **One-class SVM** is a canonical approach: it estimates a decision boundary that encloses most of the training data and treats deviations outside the learned support as anomalous (Schölkopf et al., 2001). This is conceptually aligned with the econometric leverage problem: if a point lies outside the support of Xobserved historically, any conditional mean model $E[Y \mid X]$is extrapolating.

Econometric relevance: one-class SVM is useful as a *front-end guardrail* in pipelines that rely on model-based interpretation. If Xfalls outside support, a large residual may not indicate an "abnormal outcome" but rather a failure of the model's applicability region.

Cautions: boundary methods can be sensitive to kernel choice and tuning, and they do not automatically provide a causal/economic explanation for why the point is out-of-support.

5.1.3 Isolation and Partition-Based Scoring (Scalable, High-Dimensional)

Isolation-based methods treat anomalies as points that can be separated from the rest of the sample using **few partitioning steps. Isolation Forest** operationalizes this by building random partition trees and measuring how quickly an observation becomes isolated; unusually short path lengths indicate anomalies (Liu et al., 2008). This family is especially attractive in large-scale settings because it is computationally efficient and often works well even when distance-based methods degrade in high dimensions.

Econometric relevance: Isolation Forest is often a strong default in large administrative or platform datasets where the goal is screening especially when combined with robust revisualization so that the score reflects "abnormal relative to structure," not merely marginal extremes.

Cautions: isolation scores can be hard to interpret economically without additional decomposition. They also reflect the feature representation; if features embed policy-relevant or protected attributes, isolation can reflect structural inequities rather than meaningful anomalies.

5.1.4 Deep One-Class and Representation-Learning Approaches

Deep anomaly detection methods learn nonlinear representations of normal behavior and identify anomalies through reconstruction error, energy-based scores, or one-class objectives. **Deep one-class classification** methods aim to learn a representation in which normal points cluster tightly, making anomalies separable (Ruff et al., 2018). These models can capture complex structures in raw or weakly structured inputs (images, text embeddings, complex sensor patterns), which may matter in modern econometric settings using unstructured data sources.

Econometric relevance: deep one-class methods are best viewed as *feature extractors* or *screening tools* when the raw input is complex, rather than as standalone engines for econometric interpretation.

Primary tradeoff: expressive power vs transparency. As model complexity grows, it becomes harder to (i) justify threshold choices, (ii) explain why a point is flagged, and (iii) connect flags to econometric estimates. For policy and causal inference contexts, this transparency gap can be decisive.

5.2 Pitfalls Under Shift and Strategic Behavior

ML anomaly detectors often perform well on static benchmarks but can be fragile in the conditions most relevant to applied economics: **distribution shift**, **nonstationary**, and **strategic behavior**. These pitfalls are not edge cases; they are expected in many economic systems.

5.2.1 Distribution Shift and Nonstationary

Economic data frequently evolves institutions change, reporting standards update, incentives shift, and macro conditions alter behavior. When the distribution of "normal" changes, anomaly detectors trained on historical data can systematically over-flag new normal behavior (false positives) or under-flag novel fraud patterns (false negatives). This is especially problematic in monitoring settings where the detector itself influences behavior (feedback loops).

Implication: anomaly pipelines require drift monitoring, threshold recalibration, and (when possible) segmentation by regimes or breaks. Purely static ML scoring can confuse structural change with anomalies unless coupled with econometric instability tools.

5.2.2 Strategic Manipulation and Adversarial Dynamics

Adversarial example research shows that in many ML systems, small worst-case perturbations can cause large changes in outputs (Goodfellow et al., 2014). In economics, the analogous threat is *strategic manipulation*: agents change behavior to evade detection, exploit thresholds, or shift measurement. Examples include:

- fraud adapting to detection rules,
- reporting manipulation around eligibility thresholds,
- coordinated platform behavior,
- data pipelines optimized to pass automated checks.

In these environments, the anomaly detector is part of the game. If it is opaque and brittle, it can be exploited. If it is overly rigid, it can generate high false-positive costs.

Implication: robust econometric elements remain valuable even when ML scoring is used. Specifically:

- **bounded influence** reduces the ability of a small strategic cluster to dominate model fitting,
- **segmentation** (break/regime logic) prevents conflating real structural change with anomalies,
- **sensitivity analysis** ensures conclusions do not hinge on arbitrary thresholds or a small set of flagged points.

5.2.3 The Econometric "Credibility Constraint"

Even when ML detectors produce good predictive accuracy, econometric applications impose additional constraints:

- **interpretability:** what does "anomalous" mean relative to an economic model or policy mechanism?

- **auditability:** can we explain why a point was flagged and reproduce the decision?
- **inferential integrity:** do filtering/weighting decisions distort standard errors or causal claims?

These constraints motivate the chapter's hybrid view: ML methods are powerful components for *scoring and screening*, but robust econometric design is needed to ensure that anomaly handling improves empirical credibility rather than introducing hidden fragility.

5.3 Econometric Integration Patterns for ML Scoring (One-Page Guide)

This section provides "drop-in" patterns for embedding ML anomaly scoring into econometric workflows **without sacrificing interpretability or inferential credibility**. The core idea is consistent across patterns: ML produces an anomaly score s_i, while econometrics determines **what "abnormal" means** (relative to a model, regime, or Estima) and **how anomaly handling propagates into inference**.

Pattern 1 Robust Resi Dualization → ML Scoring → Econometric Sensitivity

Use when: cross-sectional or panel settings where "abnormal" should mean "unexpected relative to an interpretable baseline."

Step A: Robust baseline (interpretability anchor)

Estimate a robust model for $m(x) = E[Y \mid X = x]$using bounded-influence or MM-style regression (Huber, 1964; Maronna et al., 2006; Yohai, 1987).

Compute residuals:

$$r_i = y_i - \hat{m}(x_i), u_i = r_i/\hat{\sigma},$$

where $\hat{\sigma}$is a robust scale.

Step B: Feature Design for Scoring

Construct anomaly features:

- leverage features: X(optionally robustly scaled/whitened),
- outcome-deviation features: u_i,

- joint features: (Xu_i).

Step C: ML Scoring (Choose Based on Anomaly Geometry)

- **LOF** for *local* departures (peer-group anomalies) (Breunig et al., 2000).
- **One-class SVM** for *support/boundary* violations (out-of-support *X*) (Schölkopf et al., 2001).
- **Isolation Forest** for scalable *partition/isolation* scoring (Liu et al., 2008).
- **Deep one-class** when structure is complex/unstructured and you need representation learning (Ruff et al., 2018).

Step D: Econometric Output and Sensitivity (Mandatory)

Report (i) scores s_i, (ii) anomaly types (leverage vs residual vs joint), and (iii) sensitivity curves:

- baseline estimate,
- robust-weighted estimate using $w(s_i)$,
- trimmed estimate across several thresholds τ.

Why this works: robust revisualization prevents the ML score from being driven by a distorted baseline (Hampel et al., 1986) and preserves an interpretable "unexpectedness" definition.

Pattern 2 Regime Segmentation → Within-Regime ML Scoring → Regime-Aware Thresholds

Use when: time series (or panel-time) where structural change is common and nave scoring over-flags during regime transitions.

Step A: Identify Regimes/Breaks First

Segment using:

- unknown-break tests / instability detection (Andrews, 1993),
- multiple break estimation (Bai & Perron, 1998),
- regime-switching states for recurring regimes (Hamilton, 1989).

Let $g(t)$denote the regime/segment assignment for time t.

Step B: Fit Local Baseline Models Within Each Regime

Within each segment g, estimate robust dynamics or robust conditional means; compute standardized innovations/residuals u_{it}.

Step C: Score Anomalies Within Regime

Run scoring **separately within each regime**:

$$s_{it} = s_g\left(z_{it}\right) \text{or}\, s_g\left(X_{it}, u_{it}\right).$$

This can be LOF/iForest for multivariate features, or one-class SVM for support in X-space.

Step D: Regime-Specific Thresholds and Monitoring

Set τ_g per regime, log:

- within-regime flagged episodes,
- regime transitions (structural anomaly signals),
- drift indicators.

Operational add-on (important): In time series, incorporate iterative outlier adjustment because dependence can create masking if estimation and detection are separated (Chen & Liu, 1993).

Why this works: segmentation prevents confusing structural change with anomalies and yields stable thresholds under heteroskedastic or shifting variance regimes (Andrews, 1993; Bai & Perron, 1998; Hamilton, 1989).

Pattern 3 ML Scoring → Anomaly Weights → Anomaly-Aware Double/Debiased ML (DML)

Use when: you need inference for a target parameter (treatment effect/structural parameter) with high-dimensional nuisance models, and you want anomaly handling that doesn't break inference.

Baseline DML logic: use orthogonal scores + cross-fitting to protect inference from nuisance estimation error (Chernozhukov et al., 2018). Post-selection settings motivate careful design when many controls exist (Belloni et al., 2014).

Step A: Compute Anomaly Scores

Build s_i using one of the Pattern 1 scoring choices, ideally after robust residualization.

Step B: Convert Scores to Weights

Define a monotone weight function $w_i = w(s_i) \in [0,1]$, e.g.:

- soft down weighting (Huber-like),
- hard trimming $w_i = \mathbb{1}\{s_i \le \tau\}$.

Step C: Cross-Fitted Orthogonal Score With Weights

For Y outcome, D treatment, X controls:

1. Cross-fit nuisance models $\hat{m}(X) \approx E[Y \mid X]$, $\hat{g}(X) \approx E[D \mid X]$.
2. Use weighted orthogonal moment:

$$\psi_i(\theta) = w_i(Y_i - \hat{m}(X_i) - \theta(D_i - \hat{g}(X_i)))(D_i - \hat{g}(X_i)).$$

3. Solve $\frac{1}{n}\sum_i \psi_i(\theta) = 0$ and compute robust SEs.

Step D: Report Inferential Sensitivity (Non-Negotiable)

Report $\hat{\theta}(\tau)$ across a grid of thresholds/weight schedules and show whether conclusions are stable.

Why this works: orthogonalization reduces sensitivity to nuisance error (Chernozhukov et al., 2018), while anomaly weights reduce sensitivity to contamination but you still document how inference changes as robustness strength increases.

Quick Router: Which scorer fits which econometric role?

- **LOF** → best for *peer-group anomalies* and local density departures in heterogeneous populations (Breunig et al., 2000).
- **One-class SVM** → best for *support violations* ("are we extrapolating in X?") (Schölkopf et al., 2001).
- **Isolation Forest** → best for *scalable screening* in large/high-dimensional data (Liu et al., 2008).
- **Deep one-class** → best when you must learn representations from complex inputs, but pair with econometric revisualization/explanations to address transparency concerns (Ruff et al., 2018).

6. HYBRID ARCHITECTURES: ECONOMETRIC–ML DESIGN PATTERNS

Hybrid architecture is most effective when they respect a simple division of labor:

- **Econometrics** supplies *meaning* (what "abnormal" means relative to an economic model, regime, or Estima) and *credibility* (identification logic, robustness guarantees, and valid inference).
- **Machine learning** supplies *geometry and scale* (nonlinear representations, high-dimensional scoring, and computational efficiency).

This section presents four reusable design patterns. Each pattern is written as an engineering template: **when to use it**, **how to implement it**, **what it outputs**, and **where it can fail**.

Figure 6. Hybrid econometric–ML architecture pattern for robust detection and governance

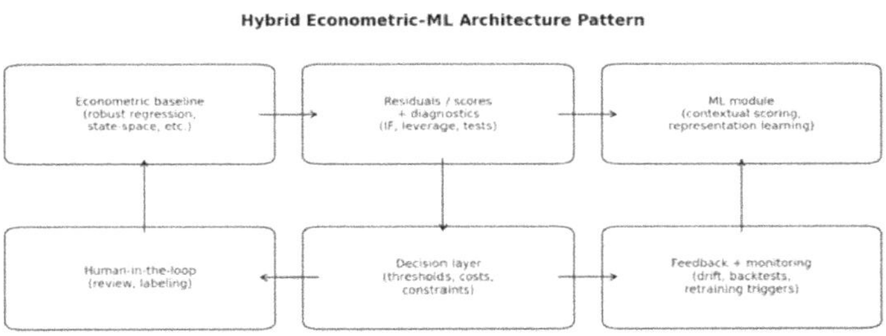

6.1 Pattern A: Robust-First Revisualization + ML Scoring

Goal: define anomalies relative to a robust econometric baseline, then use ML to detect nonlinear abnormality in residual space. This preserves interpretability ("abnormal relative to a model") while adding scalability and flexibility.

When to use

- Cross-sectional or panel settings where the analyst can specify a meaningful baseline $E[Y \mid X]$.
- Settings where you want to distinguish:
  - o leverage anomalies (unusual X),
  - o vertical anomalies (unusual $Y \mid X$),

- *joint anomalies* (unusual combinations).
- High-dimensional contexts where classical multivariate diagnostics degrade.

Core steps

1. **Fit a robust conditional mean model for** $E[Y \mid X]$

Use robust regression family such as Huber-type M-estimation or MM estimation to limit the effect of extreme residuals and leverage points (Huber, 1964; Yohai, 1987). The point is architectural: the residuals that define "unexpectedness" must be computed from a model that is not itself determined by anomalies.

2. **Compute residuals and robustly standardize them.**

Computer

$$r_i = y_i - \widehat{m}\left(x_i\right), u_i = r_i/\widehat{\sigma},$$

where $\widehat{\sigma}$is a robust scale estimate. Standardization is not cosmetic: if $\widehat{\sigma}$is inflated by anomalies (as with classical SD), extreme points can disappear into an artificially wide scale.

3. **Construct anomaly features with interpretability in mind.**

A practical feature design is to separate blocks:

- *X*-**block:** robustly scaled covariates or embeddings (captures leverage/out-of-support).
- **Residual-block:** u_i, and optionally transformations (e.g., $\mid u_i \mid, u_i^2$).
- **Optional diagnostics-block:** leverage proxies, influence-like summaries, group identifiers, or time features.

This block structure makes it easier to attribute anomalies later ("flagged due to leverage vs residual vs joint").

4. **Score anomalies using complementary ML detectors.**

Common pairings:

- **Isolation Forest** for scalable high-dimensional screening (Liu et al., 2008),

- **LOF** for peer-group (local density) anomalies (Breunig et al., 2000),
- **one-class SVM** for support/boundary violations in X-space (Schölkopf et al., 2001).

Using more than one scorer is often beneficial because they fail in different ways (local density vs boundary vs partition depth).

5. **Calibrate threshold τ using stability criteria (percentiles).**

If you have a trusted "nominal" subset, calibrate τ to achieve a desired false positive rate. If you do not, use a stability criterion tied to the econometric target: vary τ over a grid and report how the parameter of interest changes as more high-score points is down weighted/trimmed.

6. **Document sensitivity and produce an "anomaly narrative."**

A robust output is not just a set of flagged points, it is a structured report:

- top anomalies and their drivers (leverage vs residual),
- effect on coefficients/estimands as robust strength increases,
- whether anomalies appear as isolated points or clusters (potential structural issues).

What this pattern outputs (recommended minimum)

- Anomaly score s_i and optional component scores $s_X(x_i)$, $s_R(u_i)$.
- A ranked list of top anomalies with feature attribution.
- Sensitivity curves of key econometric estimates vs trimming/weight schedules.

Common failure modes (and fixes)

- **Model misspecification:** residual anomalies reflect missing nonlinearities rather than true anomalies → add flexible terms or use hybrid baseline (e.g., robust GAM / spline) while keeping robust scale.
- **Feature scaling issues:** LOF/OCSVM are sensitive to scaling → robustly scale/whiten features.
- **Threshold arbitrariness:** percentile cutoffs produce unstable conclusions → switch to stability-based calibration and report sensitivity.

6.2 Pattern B: Segmentation (Breaks/ Regimes) + Local Robust Models

Goal: reduce false positives when the data-generating process changes. Segment the series/panel into stable regimes, then apply robust residual anomaly scoring within each regime.

When to use

- Time series or panel-time data where regime changes are plausible or frequent.
- Monitoring settings where "normal behavior" changes over time (e.g., policy changes, platform redesigns, macro shocks).
- Situations where pooled anomaly scoring over-flags transitions and under-flags within-regime abnormalities.

Core steps

1. **Detect instability / locate breakpoints.**

Use unknown-break tests and multiple-break procedures to identify candidate break dates or unstable intervals (Andrews, 1993; Bai & Perron, 1998). If regimes recur rather than occur once, fit regime-switching models to obtain state probabilities (Hamilton, 1989).

2. **Define regime-conditional baselines.**

Within each regime g, fit a robust local model:

$$y_t \approx m_g(x_t) + \varepsilon_t$$

(or time-series dynamics), and compute regime-specific standardized residuals.

3. **Run anomaly scoring within regimes and use regime-specific thresholds.** Compute $s_t^{(g)}$ within each regime. Calibrate thresholds τ_g per regime to avoid systematic over-flagging in high-volatile regimes.
4. **Separate outputs into two channels:**
   - **Structural anomalies:** breakpoints/regime transitions (system-level changes),
   - **Point/episode anomalies:** unusual observations *conditional on regime.*

Why this pattern is econometrically important

It avoids a common mistake: treating a structural change as "bad data." Breaks and regimes are often economically meaningful and can invalidate identification assumptions if ignored. This pattern ensures that anomaly detection does not erase genuine structural instability.

Common failure modes (and fixes)

- **Over-segmentation:** too many regimes reduce power and inflates uncertainty → penalize complexity, report robustness to number of breaks.
- **Under-segmentation:** ignoring regimes causes systematic false positives → use instability tests and check residual autocorrelation patterns by regime.
- **Masking under dependence:** outliers distort dynamics estimation → incorporate iterative outlier adjustment ideas when estimating within regimes (Chen & Liu, 1993).

6.3 Pattern C: Robust Factor + Sparse Shock Decomposition

Goal: separate systematic components from sparse anomalies in matrix-structured data using a decomposition that is interpretable and audit-friendly.

When to use

- Panel/matrix data where common factors dominate variation (macro panels, firm-time matrices, entity-feature matrices).
- Settings where anomalies are sparse relative to matrix size (localized reporting errors, idiosyncratic shocks).
- Situations where you need a "heatmap" anomaly surface for investigation and governance.

Core idea

Use robust PCA to decompose:

$$Y = L + S,$$

where $L$is low-rank structure and $S$is sparse corruption (Candès et al., 2011).

How to implement

1. **Construct the matrix carefully.** Decide what rows/columns represent (units × time or entities × features). Handle missingness consistently; document imputation choices because they affect "sparsity" patterns.

2. **Estimate L and S (robust PCA).** Interpret L as systematic structure (latent factors, persistent trends). Interpret S as the anomaly surface: localized deviations not explained by the common structure.
3. **Post-process S into investigation objects.** Practical steps include:
   - o ranking by $| S_{it} |$,
   - o clustering anomalies in S by time, unit, or feature,
   - o computing persistence metrics (single spikes vs sustained anomalies).
4. **Fit econometric models on L and treat S as a diagnostic layer.** This reduces the risk that idiosyncratic corruption distorts factor estimates or downstream regression relationships.

Outputs that readers will find intuitive

- A low rank "systematic" dataset L for analysis.
- An anomaly map S for audit and event labeling ("where/when did things deviate?").
- Persistence summaries (one-off vs recurring anomalies).

Common failure modes (and fixes)

- **Anomalies not sparse:** if shocks are widespread, S is not sparse → consider regime segmentation first (Pattern B) or alternative factor models.
- **Interpretation drift:** S can contain both errors and real shocks → require a labeling protocol (error vs event vs regime) and sensitivity checks.

6.4 Pattern D: Anomaly-Aware High-Dimensional Inference

Goal: preserve valid inference when nuisance components are high-dimensional and learned flexibly. Double/debiased ML uses orthogonal scores and cross-fitting to protect inference from nuisance estimation error (Chernozhukov et al., 2018). Under contamination, incorporate anomaly scores as weights or trimming rules inside the cross-fitted score and report sensitivity.

When to use

- Treatment effect or structural parameter estimation with many controls/ features.
- ML-based nuisance estimation ($E[Y \mid X]$, $E[D \mid X]$, propensity scores, etc.).
- Situations where contamination can distort nuisance fit and therefore distort inference.

Why plain filtering is risky here

If you filter observations using s_i and then run inference "as usual," you risk invalid standard errors because selection was data dependent. Pattern D treats anomaly handling as **part of the estimator**, not as an informal preprocessing step.

Algorithm 1

Inputs: data (YDX), folds K, anomaly score s_i, weight rule $w_i = w(s_i) \in [0,1]$.

1. **Split sample into folds** to enable cross-fitting.
2. **Estimate nuisance functions** $m(X) = E[Y \mid X], g(X) = E[D \mid X]$ on training folds using robust/weighted ML so anomalies are downweighted in nuisance learning.
3. **Compute residuals** on held-out folds:

$$\widetilde{Y}_i = Y_i - \widehat{m}_{-k}(X_i), \widetilde{D}_i = D_i - \widehat{g}_{-k}(X_i).$$

4. **From weighted orthogonal moments**

$$\psi_i(\theta) = w_i(\widetilde{Y}_i - \theta \widetilde{D}_i)\widetilde{D}_i.$$

5. **Solve** $\frac{1}{n}\sum_i \psi_i($ and compute standard errors using a robust variance estimator. Outputs: $\widehat{\theta}$, SE, diagnostics (weight distribution, top anomalies, sensitivity curves).

7. IMPLEMENTATION MANUAL: END-TO-END PIPELINES

This section translates the design patterns from Section 6 into **operational pipelines** that can be implemented in real empirical workflows. Each pipeline is written as an "engineering runbook": it clarifies inputs, step-by-step procedures, recommended outputs, and common failure modes. The guiding principle is that anomaly detection is not a single model—it is a **repeatable process** that must remain robust, interpretable, and auditable.

Figure 7. Practical end-to-end implementation pipeline from data checks to monitoring

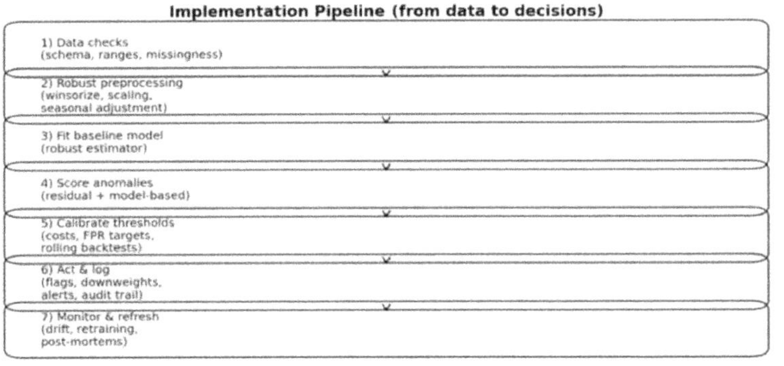

7.1 Pipeline 1: Cross-Sectional Robust Regression + Multimodal Scoring

Purpose. This pipeline targets (i) leverage points (extreme X), (ii) conditional outcome anomalies (extreme $Y \mid X$), and (iii) joint anomalies in large cross-sections.

Input

- Dataset with outcome $Y$and covariates X(optionally groups/strata, timestamps, IDs).
- A prespecified "estimand of interest" (e.g., key coefficient, treatment effect, elasticities).
- A definition of permissible data corrections (what counts as repairable error vs real event).

Step-by-step procedure

1. **Data QC and provenance (make errors diagnosable).**

Validate:

- o keys/identifiers (unique IDs, join integrity, duplicate logic),
- o plausible ranges and unit consistency,
- o missingness patterns (systematic vs random),
- o time ordering if timestamps exist.

Log every transformation: cleaning rules, filters, imputation decisions, feature engineering steps. This log is crucial because many "anomalies" ultimately trace back to pipeline changes rather than behavior.

2. **Robust baseline fits (stabilize $E[Y \mid X]$).**

Estimate a robust conditional mean model using an MM-estimator when contamination may be nontrivial (Yohai, 1987; Maronna et al., 2006).

Practical note: the baseline model should be interpretable enough to justify the meaning of residual anomalies (e.g., linear + key interactions, or a structured semiparametric model), but robust enough to avoid being captured by extremes.

3. **Revisualization and robust scaling (define "unexpected").**

Compute residuals:

$$r_i = y_i - \hat{m}(x_i),$$

and robust standardized residuals:

$$u_i = r_i / \hat{\sigma},$$

where $\hat{\sigma}$ is a robust scale measure.

Optionally compute leverage proxies:

- o robust distance in X-space,
- o hat-value approximations for large p,
- o neighborhood density summaries for local leverage.

4. **Multimodal anomaly scoring (avoid single-method brittleness).** Run at least two complementary detectors and aggregate:

- o **Isolation Forest** for scalable screening (Liu et al., 2008),
- o **LOF** for local density anomalies (Breunig et al., 2000),
- o optionally **one-class SVM** for support violations in X (Schölkopf et al., 2001).

Use **rank averaging** (or another robust aggregation rule) so that anomalies consistently flagged across methods rise to the top, while method-specific artifacts are dampened.

5. **Threshold calibration (tied alarms to econometric stability).**

If a trusted nominal subset exists, calibrate τusing that subset (targeting a tolerable false-positive rate).

Otherwise, use stability of key estimates: vary $\tau$and track how the parameter(s) of interest changes under:

- o down weighting by score,
- o trimming top-score observations.

Choose τat a point where estimates stabilize (and document the curve).

6. **Attribution and documentation (turn flags into explanations).**

For top anomalies, produce a compact explanation:

- o leverage-driven (unusual X),
- o residual-driven (unusual $Y \mid X$),
- o joint (unusual combination).

7.2 Pipeline 2: Time Series Monitoring (Outliers + Breaks + Regimes)

Purpose. Operational monitoring should integrate outlier detection, break detection, and regime inference rather than running these independently. In time series, the central risk is confusing (i) isolated shocks, (ii) persistent parameter change, and (iii) high-volatility regimes.

Input

- Time series y_t(and optional covariates x_t), sampling frequency, and monitoring horizons.
- A baseline model class (ARMA/state-space/forecasting regression).
- Alerting requirements (latency, tolerance for false positives, escalation policy).

Integrated monitoring loop

1. **Model + outlier effects jointly (reduce masking).**

Use joint parameter–outlier estimation logic so outliers do not distort parameter estimates and residuals. This reduces masking and improves detection accuracy in dynamic settings (Chen & Liu, 1993).

Operational translation: iterate

- fit dynamics,
- detect outliers,
- adjust outlier effects,
- refit dynamics,
- until stable.

2. **Break detection for persistent instability.**

Detect parameter instability and breakpoints using:

- unknown-break tests (Andrews, 1993),
- multiple-break estimation (Bai & Perron, 1998).
- Break detection is not just a diagnostic; it defines "regimes" for which residual thresholds are meaningful.

3. **Regime inference for recurring states.**

Model recurring regimes (e.g., calm vs turbulent) using regime-switching approaches and compute regime probabilities (Hamilton, 1989). Practical implication: alarms should be state-aware; what counts as "abnormal" often depends on the volatility regime.

4. **Event packets for reproducibility and governance.**

Each alarm should generate a compact "event packet" containing:

- time window,
- data snapshot ID,
- code hash and model version,
- residual/outlier diagnostics,
- detected break/regime context,
- decision log (action taken, rationale).

This is essential for auditability and for learning from false positives/negatives.

Outputs (deliverables)

- Outlier flags (time points or intervals) with estimated outlier effects.
- Breakpoints with pre/post parameter summaries.
- Regime probabilities and state-aware anomaly thresholds.
- Event packets stored in a versioned repository.

Common failure modes (and fixes)

- **Over-flagging during structural transitions** → segment by breaks first, then score within regime.
- **Outliers drive false breaks** → use joint outlier estimation before break estimation.
- **Nonstationary thresholds** → calibrate thresholds per regime/state; monitor drift.

8. EVALUATION PROTOCOLS

Evaluation is where robust anomaly detection becomes more than an appealing set of methods: it becomes a **credible empirical practice**. In econometrics, evaluation must answer two questions simultaneously:

1. **Did we detect anomalies well?** (a detection problem)
2. **Did anomaly handling improve the reliability of econometric conclusions?** (an estimation/inference problem)

This section provides a practical evaluation framework that covers detection accuracy, robustness under contamination, econometric validity of downstream inference, and stability under drift and regime change.

Figure 8. Rolling evaluation protocol to avoid leakage in nonstationary settings

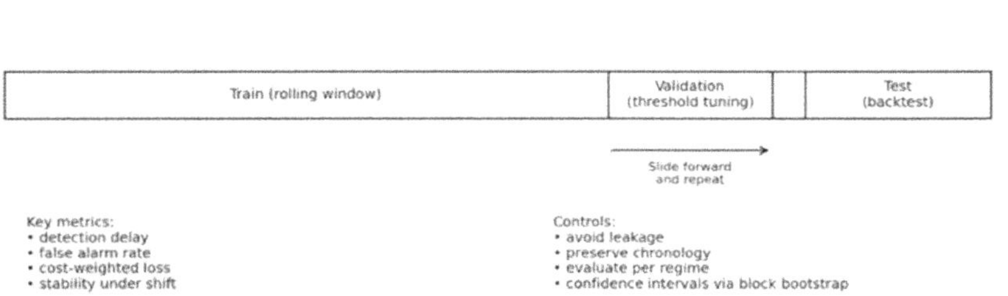

8.1 What to Measure

(A) Detection Performance (Ranking Quality and Operational Utility)

Standard supervised detection metrics apply when you have labels (or high-confidence proxies) for anomalies:

AUROC and **AUPRC** for overall ranking quality.

AUPRC is often more informative under extreme class imbalance (common in anomaly detection).

- **Precision at top-k** (or precision at top $q\%$) for operational review workflows. This matches real practice: analysts usually inspect only a limited number of top alerts.
- **False discovery behavior under dependence.**

In time series and panels, false positives often occur in *clusters* due to autocorrelation or common shocks. Evaluate not only total false positives, but also **clustered false discoveries** (e.g., "how many distinct false-alarm episodes?").

Recommended reporting: provide both point-level and episode-level summaries. For example, report precision@k for points and precision@k for episodes (contiguous blocks or unit-time clusters).

(B) Robustness Performance (Stress Testing Across Contamination Levels)

Robustness evaluation asks: *How does performance degrade as contamination becomes more severe?*

- **Contamination fraction sweep:** vary εin the gross-error model $P = (1 - \varepsilon) P_0 + \varepsilon Q$and track:
  - o detection metrics (AUROC/AUPRC/precision@k),
  - o stability of the score distribution (does everything become "anomalous"?),
  - o stability of thresholds (does calibration collapse?).
- **Estimator stability:** track how key estimators behave as εincreases:
  - o coefficient drift,
  - o prediction stability,
  - o stability of selected variables in high-dimensional models.

Recommended reporting: plot "robustness curves" with performance vs ε, and parameter drift vs ε. These curves are often more informative than single-number summaries.

(C) Econometric Validity (Bias, Coverage, and Post-Filtering Inference)

Detection metrics alone are insufficient in econometrics. The central question is whether anomaly handling improves **credibility of inference** for the estimand of interest.

Evaluation:

- **Bias and RMSE** of target parameters after anomaly handling. Compare:

    1. baseline estimator (no anomaly handling),
    2. robust weighting,
    3. trimming/filtering at several levels.

- **Confidence interval coverage** after filtering/weighting. Coverage is the most important validity check: it tests whether uncertainty statements remain reliable after data-dependent decisions.
- **Selection and nuisance-learning stability** in high-dimensional settings. If the pipeline includes variable selection or ML nuisance estimation, evaluate how anomalies change:
    - o selected controls,
    - o nuisance fit quality,
    - o downstream parameter stability.

Recommended reporting: a small table showing bias and coverage for each anomaly-handling regime is often the clearest summary, supplemented by sensitivity plots across trimming/weight schedules.

8.2 Simulation Templates

Robust anomaly detection should be benchmarked using **factorial simulation designs** that vary the key failure modes seen in modern econometric data. The goal is not one "toy" DGP, but a family of DGPs that systematically stress the pipeline.

(A) Factorial Design Dimensions (Recommended Grid)

1. **Contamination type Q:**
   - o **Vertical** (outcome shocks): extreme Yconditional on X
   - o **Leverage** (covariate extremes): extreme Xthat influences fits
   - o **Clustered** anomalies: groups/episodes rather than isolated points
   - o **Adversarial** anomalies: worst-case perturbations designed to evade detection
2. **Dependence structure:**
   - o iid baseline
   - o AR/MA dynamics (serial dependence)
   - o heteroskedasticity / volatility clustering
   - o factor panels (cross-sectional dependence via common shocks)
3. **Dimensionality and sparsity:**
   - o vary p(covariate dimension) and n(sample size)
   - o vary sparsity level $s$for the true signal
   - o consider HDLSS regimes (large p, modest n)
4. **Structural instability:**
   - o break magnitude (small vs large parameter shifts)
   - o break frequency (none, one break, multiple breaks)
   - o regime persistence (short-lived vs persistent regimes)

This factorial approach yields interpretable statements like: *"The method is robust to 10% leverage contamination under factor dependence but fails when breaks coincide with clustered anomalies unless segmentation is applied."*

(B) Minimal Simulation Modules (Plug-and-Play)

You can construct simulations by combining modules:

1. **Baseline regression/causal module:**

$Y = X\beta + u$(or a treatment effect structure), with controlled sparsity.

2. **Contamination injection module:**

Replace an εfraction with:

- leverage points (shift $X$to extremes),
- vertical outliers (add large shocks to Y),

- clustered anomalies (contaminate blocks/groups),
- adversarial points (maximize effect on fit or evade thresholds).

3. **Dependence module (optional):**

Introduce time dependence (AR errors), factor structure, or volatility changes.

4. **Break/regime module (optional):**

Change βor error variance at known breakpoints.

5. **Evaluation module:**

Compute detection metrics and econometric validity metrics (bias/coverage) across trimming/weight schedules.

9. CONCLUSION

Robust anomaly detection is most effective when it is treated not as a single diagnostic step, but as a **layered econometric system**. In modern data environments where heavy tails, measurement contamination, nonstationary, and strategic behavior are routine robustness must be engineered into the workflow rather than appended at the end. The core architecture is modular: **robust estimation** stabilizes the representation of the data and limits the leverage of extreme points; **anomaly scoring** localizes deviations in a way that can be investigated and acted upon; **structural segmentation** distinguishes persistent regime change from isolated shocks or errors; and **inference-aware procedures** (including orthogonalization, cross-fitting, and explicit sensitivity analysis) preserve econometric credibility when nuisance components are high-dimensional and model choices depend on the data.

The chapter's central message is pragmatic: anomaly handling should improve empirical reliability without sacrificing interpretability. Hybrid econometric ML designs achieve this by assigning ML the role it performs best scalable scoring in complex, high-dimensional spaces while preserving econometrics as the source of meaning. Patterns such as robust-first revisualization with multimodal scoring, break/regime segmentation with local robust models, robust factor-plus-sparse decompositions for matrix data, and anomaly-aware double/debiased ML for high-dimensional inference provide reusable building blocks for real research pipelines.

REFERENCES

Andrews, D. W. K. (1993). Tests for parameter instability and structural change with unknown change point. *Econometrica*, *61*(4), 821–856. DOI: 10.2307/2951764

Bai, J., & Perron, P. (1998). Estimating and testing linear models with multiple structural changes. *Econometrica*, *66*(1), 47–78. DOI: 10.2307/2998540

Belloni, A., Chernozhukov, V., & Hansen, C. (2014). Inference on treatment effects after selection among high-dimensional controls. *The Review of Economic Studies*, *81*(2), 608–650. DOI: 10.1093/restud/rdt044

Breunig, M. M., Kriegel, H.-P., Ng, R. T., & Sander, J. (2000). LOF: Identifying density-based local outliers. *Proceedings of ACM SIGMOD*, 93-104. DOI: 10.1145/342009.335388

Candès, E. J., Li, X., Ma, Y., & Wright, J. (2011). Robust principal component analysis? *Journal of the Association for Computing Machinery*, *58*(3), 11. DOI: 10.1145/1970392.1970395

Chandola, V., Banerjee, A., & Kumar, V. (2009). Anomaly detection: A survey. *ACM Computing Surveys*, *41*(3), 15. DOI: 10.1145/1541880.1541882

Chen, C., & Liu, L. M. (1993). Joint estimation of model parameters and outlier effects in time series. *Journal of the American Statistical Association*, *88*(421), 284–297. DOI: 10.1080/01621459.1993.10594321

Chernozhukov, V., Chetverikov, D., Demirer, M., Duflo, E., Hansen, C., Newey, W., & Robins, J. (2018). Double/debiased machine learning for treatment and structural parameters. *The Econometrics Journal*, *21*(1), C1–C68. DOI: 10.1111/ectj.12097

Goodfellow, I., Shlens, J., & Szegedy, C. (2014). Explaining and harnessing adversarial examples. arXiv:1412.6572.

Hamilton, J. D. (1989). A new approach to the economic analysis of nonstationary time series and the business cycle. *Econometrica*, *57*(2), 357–384. DOI: 10.2307/1912559

Hampel, F. R., Ronchetti, E. M., Rousseeuw, P. J., & Stahel, W. A. (1986). *Robust Statistics: The Approach Based on Influence Functions*. Wiley.

Huber, P. J. (1964). Robust estimation of a location parameter. *Annals of Mathematical Statistics*, *35*(1), 73–101. DOI: 10.1214/aoms/1177703732

Liu, F. T., Ting, K. M., & Zhou, Z.-H. (2008). Isolation Forest. *2008 Eighth IEEE International Conference on Data Mining*, 413-422. DOI: 10.1109/ICDM.2008.17

Maronna, R. A., Martin, R. D., & Yohai, V. J. (2006). *Robust Statistics: Theory and Methods*. Wiley. DOI: 10.1002/0470010940

Rousseeuw, P. J. (1984). Least median of squares regression. *Journal of the American Statistical Association*, *79*(388), 871–880. DOI: 10.1080/01621459.1984.10477105

Ruff, L., Vandermeulen, R., Görnitz, N., Deecke, L., Siddiqui, S. A., Binder, A., Müller, E., & Kloft, M. (2018). Deep one-class classification. *Proceedings of ICML*, 4393-4402.

Schölkopf, B., Platt, J. C., Shawe-Taylor, J., Smola, A. J., & Williamson, R. C. (2001). Estimating the support of a high-dimensional distribution. *Neural Computation*, *13*(7), 1443–1471. DOI: 10.1162/089976601750264965 PMID: 11440593

Tibshirani, R. (1996). Regression shrinkage and selection via the lasso. *Journal of the Royal Statistical Society. Series B, Statistical Methodology*, *58*(1), 267–288. DOI: 10.1111/j.2517-6161.1996.tb02080.x

Yohai, V. J. (1987). High breakdown-point and high efficiency robust estimates for regression. *Annals of Statistics*, *15*(2), 642–656. DOI: 10.1214/aos/1176350366

Chapter 7

A Rethink of Network Security Through Zero Trust Architecture

Emefa Ama Apaloo
http://orcid.org/0009-0009-1956-6649
Illinois Institute of Technology, USA

Mohithaa Ekambaram
http://orcid.org/0009-0007-0108-1497
Illinois Institute of Technology, USA

ABSTRACT

The growing complexity and decentralization of modern network environments have revealed critical limitations in traditional perimeter-based security models that rely on implicit trust within network boundaries. This chapter examines Zero Trust Architecture as a transformative security paradigm that eliminates inherent trust by enforcing continuous identity verification and least-privilege access based on dynamic contextual factors. By synthesizing existing literature and comparing firewall-centric approaches with identity-driven Zero Trust frameworks, the chapter highlights the necessity of this shift in addressing contemporary threat landscapes. It further outlines an implementation roadmap that considers technical, organizational, and policy challenges associated with deploying Zero Trust across hybrid cloud, edge computing, and distributed systems. The chapter concludes with practical recommendations for security practitioners and identifies key areas for future research to advance the effectiveness and scalability of Zero Trust security models.

DOI: 10.4018/979-8-3373-8252-4.ch007

INTRODUCTION

The Evolving Threat Landscape

The fast-paced development of information technologies, together with widespread cloud, edge, and IoT platform usage, has created a completely new network security environment. Modern organizations experience an increasing threat of complex cyberattacks that strike with high speed, while attackers launch distributed attacks that generate more than 100,000 daily security events regardless of business scale. Security systems no longer protect against threats because these threats now appear in greater numbers with advanced characteristics.

The current threat methods of advanced persistent threats combine AI technology with machine learning to identify system vulnerabilities before executing automated cyber attacks. Ransomware attacks now target vital infrastructure systems as well as medical facilities and banking institutions. The transition to remote work operations has created an enormous new attack area that standard security systems fail to protect against newly introduced threats. The connected nature of systems becomes vulnerable to attacks when trusted third-party relationships are exploited, which breaks down the security model based on perimeter defense.

Limitations of Traditional Perimeter Security

The security model based on perimeter boundaries trusts all users and devices that manage to cross the network boundary. The method worked effectively in centralized computing systems, which had their resources located inside established physical limits. The current model does not function properly in modern distributed systems, which include cloud computing, mobile employees, and connected business networks.

The security measures that protect perimeters fail to protect workers who work remotely, third-party vendors, and cloud-based applications. The trust system operating within the perimeter boundary produces major security vulnerabilities. The network perimeter becomes exposed to attackers who use phishing attacks, steal credentials, or exploit vulnerabilities, which enables them to move between systems with little opposition. The lack of ongoing verification allows attackers to keep control of compromised accounts, which results in data theft, backdoor creation, and major system damage.

The perimeter model based on traditional security methods becomes ineffective when organizations need to defend against attacks that originate from their internal network. The system allows authorized users to misuse their privileges, which results in internal accounts being compromised into dangerous tools for attackers. Organizations fail to detect dangerous system operations because they do not implement access controls or continuous system monitoring until major security incidents occur.

The Zero Trust Paradigm Shift

Zero Trust Architecture solves the core problems of perimeter-based security by removing all trust assumptions which depend on network positions. Organizations operating under Zero Trust need to verify users and devices and applications through continuous processes while all system interactions need to receive at least minimum privilege access (Rose et al.,2020). The system protects assets through its combination of adaptive authentication and access control and real-time monitoring which replaces traditional location-based trust with a permanent verification system.

The Zero Trust model recognizes that the traditional network perimeter has dissolved. Organizations now operate across multiple cloud platforms, support remote workforces, and integrate with numerous third-party services. Zero Trust operates under a security model which treats all incoming access requests as dangerous threats that need direct authorization before access can be granted.

The new framework requires security operations to undergo a complete transformation of their current field operations. The security approach of Zero Trust avoids spending money on perimeter defenses because these systems can be circumvented by attackers. The security framework of Zero Trust implements its controls across the entire environment to establish various authentication checkpoints which minimize the damage when system vulnerabilities are discovered.

Research Objectives and Contributions

Organizations face major technical and organizational barriers when they try to adopt Zero Trust principles because they need to shift their security approach from perimeter defense to identity-based protection (Saini et al.,2023; Fernandez & Brazhuk, 2024). Organizations need to solve three main challenges which involve uniting legacy systems with Zero Trust systems and deploying adaptive trust assessment tools and building policies that scale for their hybrid environments to achieve Zero Trust advantages. The research investigates these obstacles through a practical approach which shows organizations how to transition from firewall protection to Zero Trust identity security for ongoing defense against modern cyber attacks. The main contributions of this chapter consist of a complete evaluation of Zero Trust Architecture theory and operational methods and a thorough assessment between Zero Trust security models and traditional perimeter-based security models which shows their individual advantages and disadvantages. The chapter provides organizations with a step-by-step guide to move their systems from current legacy systems to Zero Trust security frameworks. The research evaluates actual business implementations of Zero Trust security systems which operate in different business sectors. The research establishes essential knowledge gaps which need investigation to advance Zero Trust security systems. By integrating theoretical frameworks with actionable guidance, this chapter aims to bridge the gap between conceptual understanding and practical implementation. The solution fulfills requirements of security experts together with enterprise architects and organizational leaders who need to update their security systems because of developing security dangers and business environment shifts. The recommendations together with the roadmap establish a starting point which organizations can use to progress through their Zero Trust implementation process starting from planning until they achieve complete deployment and operational excellence.

LITERATURE REVIEW

Evolution of Network Security Paradigms

Pre-Zero Trust Security Approaches

Zero Trust Network Architecture brings about a total transformation of cybersecurity practices when organizations implement this system. The traditional security models based their trust on network perimeter entities, but modern cloud computing, remote work, and distributed applications have proven these models incorrect. The Zero Trust framework requires all users and devices, and network connections to undergo authentication processes, which must run continuously for verification purposes (Rose et al.,2020; Khan, 2023; Mishra et al.,2025).

The development of security systems has followed the transition to cloud computing, the growing use of IT by consumers, and the development of advanced cyber threats. Zero Trust security framework now protects businesses from sophisticated cyber threats because it supports their current operational requirements.

The development of cybersecurity has followed a sequence that begins with trusted networks before implementing Zero Trust systems. The first security models concentrated on protecting boundaries before organizations adopted defense-in-depth as their new security approach. Zero Trust operates as a development that demands authentication for all system access points.

Identity-Centric Security Models

Organizations used to depend on identity-based systems together with firewall protection as their security approach before implementing Zero Trust. Users needed to verify their identity through security measures, which included multi-factor authentication, single sign-on, and role-based access control. The implemented methods improved system security through their enhanced access controls and their development of a unified identity management system.

The pre-Zero Trust systems operated with a fundamental security weakness because they provided continuous trust access to users who succeeded in their first authentication step. Users who authenticated their accounts could keep their session access active until they logged out without needing to verify their identity again when their circumstances changed, or their account credentials were stolen. The static trust model exposed security weaknesses that attackers used to gain access through session hijacking, credential theft, and privilege escalation. The system failed to perform continuous verification, which enabled attackers to keep accessing the system through compromised credentials until security teams detected the problem.

The traditional security methods based on identity failed to deliver adequate access control for complex permission management in advanced network systems. The access control system based on roles granted users too many privileges because their roles accumulated from multiple assignments, and they received wide-ranging permissions for simplicity. The unauthorized access to administrative privileges through privilege creep operations introduced security threats, which made system vulnerabilities more severe.

Firewall-Based Security Architectures

The security system based on firewalls established network borders that controlled data traffic, tracked system interactions, and stopped unauthorized system access (Dhiman et al.,2022). The operation of traditional firewalls depended on their ability to manage addresses, ports, and protocols. The next generation of firewalls brought three new features, which included application identification, intrusion detection, and deep packet inspection capabilities.

The firewall-based models achieved multiple essential improvements through their development, yet they introduced multiple major restrictions to their operation. The main vulnerability of their system stemmed from its network perimeter security, which proved ineffective against attacks that originated from within their network. The current firewall systems fail to detect encrypted network traffic, while they face difficulties in maintaining uniform security rules between cloud-based systems, and they cannot track intricate data center network traffic generated by APIs and microservices.

The deployment of firewall-based security systems faced various operational management challenges when they became operational. The increasing number of intricate rule sets created system administration difficulties, which also raised the chances of human errors during system configuration processes. The centralized perimeter firewalls established performance limitations through their creation of system bottlenecks and their introduction of critical system failure points. Organizations needed to stop using single inspection points for all network traffic because they began using cloud services and mobile workforces.

The implementation of Zero Trust security became necessary because firewall-based systems and identity-centric systems achieved progress, but their network limitations required this new security approach, which maintains continuous authentication across all network segments (Rose et al.,2020).

Foundational Zero Trust Concepts and Frameworks

Early Conceptual Development

Early discussions of Zero Trust emphasized enforcing least-privilege access and implementing micro-segmentation to restrict lateral movement within networks. These foundational ideas laid the groundwork for shifting from location-based trust to identity-driven security models. The concept challenged fundamental assumptions, proposing that network location should not confer trust and that all access requests should face rigorous scrutiny.

The National Institute of Standards and Technology formalized these concepts in Special Publication 800-207, establishing Zero Trust as a legitimate architectural framework. This publication identified three major components: continuous monitoring of user and device behavior, dynamic and context-aware policy enforcement, and identity-based access control prioritizing who is requesting access over where the request originates (Rose et al., 2020). By standardizing terminology and clarifying that Zero Trust represents an architectural strategy rather than a single product, NIST provided crucial guidance that accelerated enterprise adoption.

Extended Frameworks and Holistic Models

Forrester Research contributed to Zero Trust evolution by introducing the Zero Trust eXtended model, which broadened the framework beyond network segmentation to incorporate data protection, device security, application controls, workload isolation, and comprehensive network traffic analysis (Kindervag, 2010). This expansion reinforced that Zero Trust must be holistic rather than limited to network controls, recognizing that modern organizations must secure diverse assets across multiple layers of their digital ecosystem. The ZTX framework emphasized that trust evaluation must occur continuously across all these dimensions, with security decisions informed by comprehensive contextual awareness rather than static rules or single-factor determinations.

Despite the clarity these frameworks provide for understanding Zero Trust principles, they intentionally avoid prescribing universal implementation methods. Organizations must interpret and adapt Zero Trust concepts to their unique infrastructures, which increasingly include hybrid cloud services, edge computing nodes, Internet of Things devices, and emerging fifth and sixth-generation network technologies (Saini et al., 2023). This flexibility allows Zero Trust to remain relevant across diverse organizational contexts but also creates challenges for enterprises seeking concrete implementation guidance. Many organizations struggle to translate conceptual frameworks into specific technical architectures, policy structures, and operational procedures suited to their environments and constraints.

Comparative Analyses of Zero Trust Models

Several studies have compared different Zero Trust models. Dhiman et al. (2022) found that while models outline consistent principles, no universally accepted deployment method exists across diverse infrastructures. Organizational size, legacy systems, regulatory requirements, and technology maturity significantly influence implementation, making standardization challenging.

Turaev et al. (2021) observed that many organizations adopt Zero Trust in isolated components rather than comprehensive transformations, such as implementing identity management tools, micro-segmentation, or security analytics platforms. While these enhance security, they often fall short of complete Zero Trust architecture and can create exploitable gaps.

Most existing studies remain largely theoretical, focusing on analyzing frameworks rather than detailing practical transition steps. This creates a significant gap, as enterprises struggle with practical operationalization rather than understanding principles (Capili, 2024). The lack of actionable implementation guidance, particularly for complex hybrid environments, represents a critical barrier to broader adoption.

Organizational and Technological Transitions

Cultural and Procedural Challenges

Recent work has begun addressing organizational and technological challenges involved in adopting Zero Trust, signaling a shift from purely conceptual discussions to practical implementation considerations. The transition from perimeter-based defenses depending on static firewall boundaries to identity-driven security models requires more than deploying new tools and technologies. It demands significant cultural, procedural, and operational changes throughout organizations. Legacy systems often require upgrading or redesigning to support continuous verification, authentication, and authorization. Employees must adjust to stricter access control practices that may seem more cumbersome than traditional approaches, requiring comprehensive training and change management efforts to ensure adoption and compliance.

IT teams face the challenge of coordinating policies across increasingly hybrid environments that combine on-premises infrastructure with cloud services, edge computing, and mobile systems. This coordination requires breaking down traditional silos between network, security, identity, and application teams, fostering collaboration and shared responsibility for security outcomes. Organizations must develop new operational processes that account for continuous risk assessment, automated policy adjustment, and rapid incident response capabilities that Zero Trust enables. The socio-technical nature of these challenges highlights that Zero Trust represents as much an organizational transformation as a technical one, requiring executive support, adequate resources, and sustained commitment to succeed (Teerakanok et al., 2021).

Automation and Analytics Integration

Automation and analytics have emerged as critical enablers of Zero Trust effectiveness. Newer approaches incorporate behavioral analytics that establish baseline user behavior and detect anomalies, real-time threat scoring that dynamically assesses risk levels, and automated policy adjustments responding to changing conditions. These methods make access decisions more dynamic by continuously evaluating user actions, device posture, and contextual risk indicators.

While these capabilities demonstrate strong potential in large-scale environments, Dhiman et al. (2022) note that such techniques remain at early maturity stages. Many have not been widely tested or validated across diverse enterprise environments, leaving questions about scalability, interoperability, and reliability. Organizations often must develop custom solutions requiring specialized expertise and ongoing refinement.

Integrating machine learning for anomaly detection introduces considerations around model training, accuracy, false positive rates, and potential bias. Organizations must balance security effectiveness with operational efficiency, ensuring automated enforcement doesn't inadvertently block legitimate access or create excessive friction. Successful integration requires thoughtful design of feedback loops, escalation procedures, and governance frameworks maintaining appropriate human oversight while leveraging automation benefits.

RESEARCH GAPS AND FUTURE DIRECTIONS

Although previous studies have described Zero Trust principles and compared models, they often overlook practical migration and implementation. Existing literature remains conceptual without addressing operationalization. Many publications fail to provide clear strategies for implementing Zero Trust in environments combining legacy systems with modern cloud, edge, and mobile technologies (Syed et al., 2022; Teerakanok et al., 2021; Arora, 2025).

This research addresses that gap by examining how enterprises can transition from traditional firewall-based architectures to identity-driven security frameworks. It explores technical challenges including reconfiguring legacy applications, organizational challenges involving change management, and usability considerations. This study evaluates how industries with varying regulatory requirements can adopt Zero Trust realistically and scalable.

To support these strategies, this research proposes context-aware trust metrics incorporating user behavior patterns, device posture, environmental factors, and real-time risk indicators (Mushtaq et al., 2025; Süzen & Ceylan, 2024).

By integrating theoretical insights with practical considerations from case studies, this study provides an actionable roadmap for organizations working toward identity-based network security.

Zero Trust Architecture: Core Concepts and Principles

Fundamental Philosophical Shift

The traditional security model assumed entities within an enterprise perimeter were inherently trustworthy. Once a user or device penetrated the perimeter through initial authentication, they rarely faced challenges moving laterally within the network. This approach worked when networks were closed and centrally controlled.

However, it creates dangerous vulnerabilities in modern distributed environments. If an attacker breaches the perimeter, they can move laterally and access sensitive systems without encountering meaningful barriers (Arora, 2025; Ok et al., 2025).

In contrast, Zero Trust operates on a never-trust-always-verify model that questions the assumption that network location represents trustworthiness. All access requests, whether originating inside or outside the traditional perimeter, must be authenticated, authorized, and continuously validated. Trust is not granted automatically based on location or prior authentication but must be earned through strong identity validation, contextual awareness assessment, and continuous monitoring of behavior and device posture. This philosophical shift fundamentally redefines security paradigms for modern enterprises (Teerakanok et al., 2021; Kapoor, 2025).

Drivers of Zero Trust Adoption

The necessity for Zero Trust emerged from inherent weaknesses in perimeter-based security models when applied to contemporary environments. The traditional network boundary has been eroded by several converging trends. The explosion of cloud services has moved substantial portions of organizational data and applications beyond any controllable perimeter. Remote work at scale, accelerated by global events and changing workforce expectations, means that employees regularly access resources from diverse locations using various networks and devices. Mobile devices have become essential productivity tools, blurring lines between personal and corporate technology. Distributed applications leveraging microservices architectures operate across multiple cloud platforms and data centers (Sreelatha & Yelsangiker, 2024; Karamchand, 2025).

Increasingly, organizational users and data exist across hybrid and multi-cloud environments that extend far beyond any organization's physical reach or direct control. These factors render fixed perimeter defenses inadequate as primary security mechanisms. Zero Trust responds to these evolving conditions by offering an adaptive and scalable approach capable of securing diverse and highly dynamic environments effectively (Intazar et al., 2025). Rather than attempting to define and defend a clear boundary, Zero Trust distributes security controls throughout the environment, protecting resources individually based on their sensitivity and the context of access requests.

Identity as the New Perimeter

Authentication plays a central role in Zero Trust, as identity becomes the new security perimeter replacing network location. Each user, device, application, and workload must authenticate itself before being granted access to any resource. This authentication process typically includes multi-factor authentication, device posture checks verifying endpoints meet security standards, and context-aware validations considering factors such as geographic location, network characteristics, time of day, and behavioral patterns (Chokshi et al., 2021).

The objective is maintaining access linkage with continuously verified identities and enforcing least-privilege principles, dramatically reducing the attack surface. By tying access decisions to strong, frequently validated identity assertions rather than network location, Zero Trust eliminates many common attack vectors. Stolen VPN credentials become less valuable when access requires additional verification factors and strict privilege limits. Similarly, lateral movement becomes significantly more difficult when each resource access requires fresh authentication and authorization decisions based on current context rather than static permissions.

Continuous Monitoring and Validation

Continuous monitoring must be available universally as an integral component of Zero Trust architecture. Security does not stop at the initial authentication point; instead, Zero Trust maintains ongoing vigilance through real-time monitoring of network activity, user behavior, and device state. Anomalies such as unusual login attempts from unexpected locations, unauthorized data movement patterns, unexpected lateral movement across network segments, or deviations from established behavioral baselines can be identified through comprehensive telemetry collection, behavioral analytics algorithms, and automated detection tools (Syed et al., 2022).

This continuous monitoring enables organizations to react to potentially suspicious behavior quickly, containing smaller incidents before they escalate into major breaches that could result in significant data loss, operational disruption, or reputational damage. The shift from periodic security assessments to continuous validation reflects recognition that threats can emerge at any time and that adversaries often operate slowly and carefully to avoid detection. By establishing behavioral baselines and detecting deviations in real-time, Zero Trust architectures can identify compromised accounts or devices much faster than traditional approaches that rely primarily on signature-based detection of known malware or periodic log reviews.

Identity-Centric Access Control

Ultimately, Zero Trust shifts security focus away from external perimeter defenses toward identity-centric access control models. Security decisions are made based on who is requesting access, the specific device they are using, the data they need to access, the context of the request, and whether their behavior aligns with expected patterns established through historical analysis. This identity-driven approach limits privileges strictly to what is necessary for legitimate tasks, implementing the principle of least privilege consistently across the environment, and enforcing verification at each access stage rather than granting broad permissions based on initial authentication (Steenbrink, 2022).

By prioritizing identity and continuous validation over network location, the Zero Trust framework provides a more resilient security structure capable of protecting modern, highly distributed digital ecosystems effectively. This approach aligns security controls with actual business requirements and risk levels rather than with arbitrary network boundaries. Resources can be secured consistently regardless of where they reside, whether in corporate data centers, public cloud platforms, or edge computing locations. Users can access needed resources securely from any location using appropriate devices, without the bottlenecks and limitations inherent in traditional VPN-based remote access approaches.

COMPARATIVE ANALYSIS: TRADITIONAL PERIMETER SECURITY VERSUS ZERO TRUST

Historical Context and Evolution

Organizations have historically depended on firewalls and network perimeters to safeguard digital resources. Firewalls monitored network traffic to enforce access policies, while the network perimeter established a protected internal zone. This framework operated under the belief that threats originated primarily from outside and that users and devices inside the network could be trusted implicitly once they gained entry (Poirrier, 2024; Ojha & Vaish, 2025).

The security model proved effective when IT systems remained static and centralized. During the 1990s and early 2000s, most organizational computing occurred on premises within well-defined boundaries. Remote access was limited and typically mediated through controlled VPN connections. In this context, perimeter-focused security aligned well with organizational technology architecture.

However, this model became insufficient as IT systems underwent fundamental changes driven by remote work requirements, cloud service adoption, mobile device proliferation, and interconnected partner ecosystems. The assumption that perimeter breaches represented the primary threat proved flawed as insider threats, compromised credentials, and supply chain attacks became increasingly common. The distinction between trusted internal and untrusted external networks dissolved as organizational computing became distributed (Steenbrink, 2022).

Inherent Weaknesses of Perimeter-Based Models

Static Trust Assumptions

The perimeter defense model contains multiple operational weaknesses that sophisticated adversaries readily exploit. The system grants essentially unconditional access to internal resources after users and devices complete initial authentication at the perimeter. This static trust model allows attackers who obtain access through credential theft, phishing, or malware to move freely between network segments. Once inside the perimeter, attackers encounter minimal additional security controls, making it relatively easy to explore the environment, escalate privileges, and access sensitive resources.

The security perimeter fails to protect organizations adequately from insider threats because it does not monitor or restrict activities of authorized internal users beyond initial authentication. Malicious insiders with legitimate credentials can abuse their access to exfiltrate data, sabotage systems, or facilitate external attacks. Even non-malicious insiders can inadvertently cause security incidents through careless credential handling, susceptibility to social engineering, or failure to follow security procedures. The perimeter model's implicit trust in authenticated users means these threats often go undetected until significant damage occurs.

Challenges in Modern Digital Workspaces

The contemporary digital workplace has broken down the distinct network segregation that once supported traditional perimeter security systems effectively. Modern employees access company resources through mobile devices while working remotely from home networks, public Wi-Fi, coffee shops, airports, and various third-party locations. Cloud-based data and application hosting occurs across numerous geographical regions and service providers, with resources dynamically provisioned and scaled according to demand. The modern network environment operates as a fundamentally distributed system that eliminates fixed network boundaries, rendering traditional perimeter security measures ineffective for comprehensive protection (Capili, 2024; Teerakanok et al., 2021).

This erosion of boundaries creates numerous security challenges. Organizations can no longer assume that traffic originating from "internal" IP addresses comes from trusted devices operated by authorized users. The proliferation of Internet of Things devices, many with limited security capabilities, expands the attack surface while blurring traditional network boundaries further. Application programming interfaces enable direct communication between systems across organizational boundaries, creating complex interconnections that bypass traditional perimeter controls. Partner and supplier access to organizational resources for collaboration and service delivery creates additional entry points that challenge perimeter-based security assumptions.

Zero Trust Response to Modern Challenges

Zero Trust Architecture addresses perimeter security weaknesses by verifying all access requests at every point of origin, regardless of whether requests come from inside or outside the traditional network boundary. Zero Trust treats every user, device, and connection as a potential threat, irrespective of location or prior authentication status (Poirrier, 2024). Access is granted only after continuous verification of identity, device posture, contextual factors, and alignment with security policies through micro-segmentation, least-privilege access, and continuous monitoring.

This approach reduces the impact of credential compromise by requiring additional verification factors and limiting privileges to necessary resources. It detects and contains insider threats through behavioral monitoring and anomaly detection. It secures distributed environments by applying uniform security policies regardless of resource location and accommodates modern work patterns including remote access and mobile devices without sacrificing security.

Security Effectiveness Comparison

Threat Detection Capabilities

Traditional perimeter security concentrates defensive efforts on the network boundary, attempting to prevent malicious traffic from entering the internal environment. This approach assumes threats originate externally, creating a critical blind spot when attackers bypass perimeter controls. Once an attacker gains internal access, visibility becomes limited, allowing malicious activities to continue before detection. Security teams often lack adequate telemetry about internal network traffic, making it difficult to distinguish legitimate activities from attacks (Capili, 2024; Intazar et al., 2025).

Zero Trust Architecture operates on the never-trust-always-verify principle, ensuring every interaction faces continuous authentication and monitoring regardless of origin. This universal scrutiny enables more adaptable and comprehensive threat detection. Organizations can more readily identify suspicious behavior patterns, anomalous access requests, and unusual data transfers. By collecting comprehensive telemetry and applying analytics to identify anomalies, Zero Trust significantly reduces the time between initial compromise and detection, limiting adversary opportunities.

Incident Response Efficiency

In traditional perimeter models, incident response becomes challenging once an attacker invades the network boundary because internal traffic typically receives implicit trust. The delay in detecting compromised accounts or devices grants attackers time and opportunity to move laterally, escalate privileges, access sensitive data, and establish persistence mechanisms before defenders recognize the breach and initiate response procedures. This extended detection time significantly increases the potential impact of security incidents, allowing adversaries to achieve their goals and making complete remediation more difficult.

Zero Trust fundamentally transforms incident response efficiency by eliminating implicit trust at all levels and implementing least-privilege access throughout the environment. The continuous monitoring, granular access controls, and micro-segmentation inherent in Zero Trust architectures enable much faster detection of suspicious activities. Once detected, the limited privileges and network segmentation constrain attackers' ability to move laterally or access additional resources, containing the incident more effectively. Zero Trust significantly decreases both detection time and response time, leading to faster and more successful outcomes when addressing cyber-attacks and substantially reducing their potential impact on organizational operations and assets.

Operational Impact Assessment

User Experience Considerations

Traditional perimeter security can significantly hinder remote user access due to reliance on virtual private networks and rigid authentication methods. VPN connections often suffer from performance bottlenecks, particularly when large numbers of users connect simultaneously. VPN connections add steps to workflows, and connection instability can disrupt work. Users accessing cloud-based applications while connected to VPNs may experience degraded performance as traffic routes through corporate networks.

In comparison, Zero Trust architectures utilize adaptive mechanisms such as single sign-on, risk-based authentication, and contextual authorization to improve usability. These methods dynamically adjust security requirements based on real-time risk assessment. For example, access from a corporate-managed device on a trusted network might require only standard authentication, while access from a personal device on public Wi-Fi might trigger additional verification.

Zero Trust frameworks facilitate secure access in remote and hybrid work settings while reducing interruptions to productivity. Users access resources directly rather than through VPN tunnels, improving performance. Single sign-on reduces authentication burden. Context-aware security policies provide appropriate protection without unnecessary obstacles, increasing adoption and reducing insecure workarounds.

Administrative Overhead

Traditional perimeter systems require precise management of firewalls, VPNs, and access control rules, creating substantial administrative overhead. Firewall rule sets grow increasingly complex, often reaching thousands of rules that interact unpredictably. Managing these requires specialized expertise, and complexity increases misconfigurations. VPN infrastructure requires ongoing maintenance and troubleshooting.

Zero Trust simplifies ongoing operations through structured policy management and automation. While initial setup is resource-intensive, long-term operational efficiency typically improves substantially. Centralized policy management enables consistent application across diverse environments. Automation reduces manual effort for routine tasks, allowing IT teams to focus on strategic initiatives.

The transition period presents temporary overhead increases as organizations maintain existing controls while implementing Zero Trust. However, once fully implemented, Zero Trust architectures often prove more manageable than complex traditional environments. The clear policy framework, automated enforcement, and comprehensive visibility reduce time and effort required for security operations over time.

Futureproofing and Adaptability

Compatibility with Technology Evolution

Perimeter security models depend on legacy systems and assumptions incompatible with modern technologies. Traditional firewalls struggle to secure microservices architectures where application components communicate frequently across network boundaries. They provide limited visibility into encrypted traffic, cannot effectively enforce security policies for serverless computing models, and are poorly suited to dynamic cloud environments where resources are continuously provisioned and de-provisioned.

Zero Trust integrates naturally with cloud platforms, APIs, containerization technologies, and automation tools, providing inherent scalability and seamless integration with modern architectures. Zero Trust policies can be expressed through cloud-native security services and integrated with infrastructure-as-code practices.

API gateways can enforce Zero Trust principles for inter-service communications, and container orchestration platforms can implement network policies aligned with Zero Trust micro-segmentation. This compatibility allows organizations to embrace new technologies confidently, maintaining effective security posture as technology landscapes evolve (Lee & Park, 2024).

Regulatory Compliance Sustainability

Traditional security approaches struggle to meet evolving compliance standards that demand detailed monitoring, auditability, and granular access control. Many regulatory frameworks now explicitly require or strongly encourage capabilities that align closely with Zero Trust principles, including continuous monitoring of access and activities, detailed audit logging, least-privilege access enforcement, and regular verification of security controls. Organizations using traditional perimeter-focused approaches often find themselves implementing point solutions and manual processes to address specific compliance requirements, creating fragmented approaches that increase complexity and cost.

Zero Trust architecture inherently embraces continuous logging, rigorous identity verification, and comprehensive policy enforcement that align naturally with regulations such as NIST cybersecurity frameworks, General Data Protection Regulation requirements, and Health Insurance Portability and Accountability Act standards. The granular access controls, detailed audit trails, and continuous monitoring capabilities built into Zero Trust architectures provide strong foundations for demonstrating compliance. This makes maintaining long-term regulatory compliance more efficient while establishing transparency, accountability, and secure data management practices that satisfy auditors and regulators. As compliance requirements continue to evolve and become more stringent, Zero Trust architectures position organizations to adapt more readily than traditional perimeter-based approaches.

Evolution Tables: Chronicling the Transition

The evolution from traditional perimeter security to Zero Trust represents a fundamental transformation across multiple dimensions. Understanding this progression requires examining how key aspects of security architecture have changed over time in response to evolving threats, technologies, and organizational needs.

Network Security Architecture Evolution

The evolution of network security architecture is shown in this sectiom

1990s-Early 2000s: Traditional perimeter security relied on firewalls and VPNs as primary defenses, reflecting simple network topologies and centralized computing. Zero Trust concepts were emerging with occasional least-privilege principles but no formal framework.

2005-2010: Traditional approaches continued relying on perimeter defenses with implicit internal trust. Limitations became apparent as cloud services emerged. Early Zero Trust frameworks focused on micro-segmentation but remained largely theoretical (Kindervag, 2010).

2010s: Traditional perimeter security struggled with cloud adoption, mobile devices, and remote access. Static policies and VPN bottlenecks hindered agility. Zero Trust expanded to include identity-based access control, device verification, and continuous monitoring, with growing enterprise adoption.

2020-Present: Perimeter-based approaches proved inadequate for hybrid and distributed environments. IoT proliferation and remote work exposed vulnerabilities. NIST formalized Zero Trust in SP 800-207 (Rose et al., 2020). Contemporary Zero Trust emphasizes real-time analytics, automation, adaptive policies, and identity-driven security.

Access Control Evolution: Traditional approaches relied on static rules where authenticated users enjoyed broad access. Zero Trust uses dynamic, context-aware policies enforcing strict least-privilege principles, continuously adjusting permissions based on context and risk assessment.

Authentication Approach Evolution: Traditional models performed one-time authentication at network entry. Zero Trust mandates continuous authentication and authorization for every request.

Policy Enforcement Evolution: Traditional enforcement was perimeter-based and firewall-dependent. Zero Trust shifts to identity, device posture, and behavioral factors, with real-time risk-based policy adaptation.

Security Philosophy Evolution: Traditional approaches assumed internal users were trustworthy, focusing on external threats. Zero Trust embraces never-trust-always-verify for every user, device, and workload.

Threat Resilience Evolution

This section compares traditional incident response with modern threat resilience frameworks:

1990s-Early 2000s: Traditional perimeter security assumed strong defenses would keep attackers outside. Internal monitoring was minimal. Zero Trust concepts had not yet been adopted.

2005-2010: Perimeter breaches became common. Lateral movement went unchecked. Early Zero Trust models emphasized assume-breach mindset and micro-segmentation (Turaev et al., 2021).

2010s: Growing IT complexity and insider threats revealed limitations of static perimeter security. Zero Trust evolved to require strict device verification, identity controls, and stronger segmentation.

2020-Present: Perimeter-only approaches cannot secure hybrid cloud, remote workforces, and IoT. Zero Trust adopted adaptive defenses incorporating real-time risk evaluation, behavioral analytics, and automated containment (Ok et al., 2025).

Assume Breach Model: Traditional security performed limited internal checks. Zero Trust assumes attackers may already be present and designs multilayered controls to detect and limit damage.

Micro-Segmentation: Traditional architectures allowed attackers to move freely. Zero Trust mandates granular segmentation restricting lateral movement (Ok et al., 2025).

Device Compliance: Traditional approaches failed to verify device security posture. Zero Trust requires comprehensive compliance checks including patches, configurations, and security software.

Adaptability: Traditional security remained static and slow. Zero Trust implements dynamic policies adjusting in real-time based on risk levels, user behavior, and threat intelligence.

Detection and Response Evolution

This section outlines the evolution of detection capabilities, incident response practices, and attack surface management strategies.

1990s-Early 2000s: Traditional detection focused on blocking external attacks. Internal visibility was limited. Zero Trust concepts had not been formalized.

2005-2010: Signature-based detection dominated. Internal threats remained difficult to observe. Early Zero Trust promoted monitoring internal traffic.

2010s: Hybrid environments increased complexity. Zero Trust adopted continuous monitoring, centralized logging, and identity signals (Mishra et al., 2025; Steenbrink, 2022).

2020-Present: Perimeter-focused tools cannot provide adequate visibility into distributed networks. Zero Trust integrates automated incident response, behavioral analytics, and device posture evaluation.

Threat Detection: Traditional security monitored external threats, with internal activities invisible. Zero Trust enables continuous monitoring facilitating earlier detection and faster containment.

Incident Response: Traditional models experienced slower response due to implicit trust. Zero Trust enables faster response through real-time monitoring and built-in containment mechanisms.

Attack Surface Management: Traditional approaches offered limited visibility beyond perimeters. Zero Trust reduces attack surfaces through micro-segmentation, identity verification, device validation, and granular access controls (Steenbrink, 2022; Intazar et al., 2025).

Zero Trust addresses fundamental weaknesses of traditional perimeter security while providing a more integrated, adaptive approach focusing on identity verification and contextual awareness, representing a necessary response to changing technology landscapes and evolving threats

ZERO TRUST ARCHITECTURE: FUNDAMENTAL COMPONENTS

Core Architectural Principles

Zero Trust Architecture functions as a comprehensive cybersecurity framework that replaces outdated perimeter-based security systems with continuous verification mechanisms. The security model requires complete verification of all users, devices, and network communications because it grants no implicit trust to any network segment, user, or device at any time. The following sections explain fundamental concepts underlying ZTA implementation, supporting frameworks providing guidance, and operational technologies enabling practical deployment.

Never Trust, Always Verify

Organizations must perform rigorous policy-based entity verification according to Zero Trust principles because trust cannot be assumed for any entity or system (Rose et al., 2020). The architecture requires authentication, authorization, and encryption for all access requests regardless of origin. The system performs ongoing verification, continuously checking that users and devices maintain compliance with security requirements, immediately blocking unauthorized access when anomalies are detected or context indicates elevated risk.

This represents a fundamental departure from traditional security thinking. Rather than making binary trust decisions at perimeter crossing points, Zero Trust recognizes that trust must be conditional, contextual, and continuously reassessed. A user who was trustworthy five minutes ago might not be now if their behavior has changed, their device has been compromised, or threat intelligence indicates new risks. This continuous verification mindset pervades every aspect of Zero Trust architecture.

Least Privilege Access

The Zero Trust framework mandates that organizations implement least-privilege access principles, providing users and devices exclusively with minimal permissions required to execute their assigned duties (Kindervag, 2010). Organizations protect critical functions from insider threats and credential compromise by strictly limiting access to only necessary resources, substantially reducing potential impact if credentials become compromised or users act maliciously.

Implementing least privilege effectively requires granular understanding of actual access requirements rather than broad role definitions. Organizations must analyze workflows, identify specific resources needed for tasks, and define access permissions at appropriate granularity levels. This principle integrates with continuous monitoring and context-based policies to achieve effective breach containment and minimize security risks.

INDUSTRY FRAMEWORKS AND STANDARDS

NIST Zero Trust Architecture

The U.S. National Institute of Standards and Technology has developed comprehensive Zero Trust Architecture guidance through Special Publication 800-207, helping organizations build ZTA systems for enterprise networks (Rose et al., 2020). The NIST Zero Trust framework requires organizations to divide networks through segmentation while implementing robust identity verification systems, comprehensive policy enforcement mechanisms, and continuous monitoring protocols that provide ongoing visibility into security posture.

The NIST framework identifies key logical components including Policy Engine making access decisions, Policy Administrator executing decisions by establishing communication paths, and Policy Enforcement Points gatekeeping resource access. It also defines three primary deployment models: Enhanced Identity Governance focusing on strong identity verification and access controls, Micro-Segmentation creating granular network segments, and Network Infrastructure and Software Defined Perimeters leveraging software-defined networking. This flexible framework allows organizations to select approaches aligned with their specific requirements, existing infrastructure, and risk profiles.

Industry Framework Contributions

The Cloud Security Alliance, Gartner, and Forrester Research provide complementary industry frameworks that help organizations deploy Zero Trust principles throughout cloud-based, hybrid, and on-premises systems. These frameworks demonstrate how organizations can establish scalable access management systems, implement effective micro-segmentation strategies, and deploy adaptive security solutions supporting ZTA fundamental concepts. Industry frameworks often provide more specific guidance for technologies, cloud platforms, or implementation scenarios than government standards, offering practical insights drawn from vendor experiences and enterprise deployments (Forrester Research, 2018; Gartner, 2022).

Forrester's Zero Trust eXtended model particularly emphasizes expanding Zero Trust coverage beyond networks to encompass data protection, application security, device management, and workload isolation. Gartner's Zero Trust Network Access framework focuses on secure remote access and cloud adoption scenarios. The Cloud Security Alliance provides guidance specific to cloud computing environments, addressing unique challenges of multi-cloud and hybrid architectures. Together, these frameworks complement official standards by providing diverse perspectives and practical implementation guidance across various contexts (Cloud Security Alliance, 2020).

Critical Enabling Technologies

Identity and Access Management

Identity and Access Management (IAM) systems are critical Zero Trust components that authenticate users, manage digital identities, and enforce access controls. IAM systems implement standardized security policies across on-premises, cloud, and edge environments (Chokshi et al., 2021). Modern IAM platforms provide centralized identity management, fine-grained access policies, comprehensive audit logs, and broad application integration. They support Zero Trust principles through consistent policy enforcement and reliable identity verification. Increasingly, IAM platforms use risk-based authentication that adjusts security requirements dynamically based on contextual factors and behavioral analytics to detect potential account compromise.

Multi-Factor Authentication

Multi-Factor Authentication enhances security by requiring multiple verification methods—such as passwords, hardware tokens, and biometric data—reducing the risk of unauthorized access from compromised credentials and supporting the Zero Trust principle of "never trust, always verify."

Modern MFA implementations leverage various technologies including push notifications to registered mobile devices, time-based one-time passwords generated by authenticator applications, biometric verification using fingerprints or facial recognition, and hardware security keys providing phishing-resistant authentication. Risk-adaptive MFA adjusts authentication requirements based on context, requesting additional factors when unusual patterns are detected while streamlining authentication for routine low-risk access. This balance between security and usability proves critical for user adoption and compliance.

Supporting Technologies for Zero Trust

Several technologies are critical for effective Zero Trust Architecture. Network micro-segmentation limits lateral movement by isolating resources with granular access controls. Continuous monitoring platforms provide real-time visibility into network traffic, user behavior, and system activities for rapid threat detection. Endpoint security ensures devices meet security policies before accessing resources.

Cloud Access Security Brokers extend Zero Trust to cloud environments by enforcing policies and monitoring data flows across SaaS applications. Software-Defined Perimeters create individualized security perimeters around specific users and resources. Security orchestration platforms automate threat responses by coordinating security tools. Together, these technologies enable dynamic policy enforcement and strengthen ZTA frameworks through real-time risk detection and mitigation (Chokshi et al., 2021).

PROPOSED METHODOLOGY: PRACTICAL MIGRATION TO ZERO TRUST

Phased Migration Roadmap

Phase 1: Assessment and Planning

Migrating from perimeter-based security to Zero Trust Architecture requires careful planning to minimize disruption while maximizing security benefits. The roadmap begins with stakeholder alignment across security, IT, development, and business units; current-state analysis of existing controls and policies; and gap analysis identifying differences between current capabilities and Zero Trust requirements (National Institute of Standards and Technology [NIST], 2024.

Organizations must document existing assets including servers, applications, databases, and devices; map application dependencies and data flows; catalog identity repositories and access systems; and analyze network architectures to identify trust boundaries and access patterns. This documentation ensures security controls align with actual operations and protect critical assets.

During planning, organizations should establish clear objectives, develop measurable success metrics, identify high-value assets requiring priority protection, and create realistic timelines. Considering both security objectives and business priorities is critical for obtaining necessary support and resources throughout the transformation (Bashir, 2024).

Phase 2: Pilot Implementation

Following planning, organizations should implement a pilot applying Zero Trust concepts including least-privilege access, continuous authentication, and micro-segmentation to a selected portion of the environment. This limited-scope implementation enables rapid feedback, risk assessment, and policy refinement before broader deployment (W. Author & X. Author, 2021).

Selecting appropriate pilot scope requires balance. The pilot should be substantial enough to encounter realistic challenges and demonstrate security improvements but limited enough to manage effectively. Common approaches include protecting a high-value application and its infrastructure, securing access for a specific user group like remote workers, or implementing controls within a discrete business unit.

During pilot implementation, organizations should monitor user experience to avoid unacceptable friction, track operational metrics measuring impacts on IT and security teams, document lessons learned, and refine policies based on discovered issues. This iterative approach reduces risks while building organizational expertise and confidence in Zero Trust.

Phase 3: Phased Rollout and Full Adoption

After successful pilot validation, phased adoption extends Zero Trust controls to additional segments by implementing identity-centric access policies, expanding micro-segmentation, and deploying enhanced monitoring. This staged rollout enables incremental resilience building, improvement measurement, and approach adaptation while maintaining operational stability (Dotse et al., 2025).

Each phase should target logical groupings such as specific applications and infrastructure, user populations with similar access requirements, or geographical regions. Organizations should establish clear completion criteria before proceeding, ensuring each stage achieves objectives and resolves issues before expanding scope.

Throughout phased adoption, organizations must manage change through training on new authentication requirements, clear communications explaining security improvements, responsive support to maintain user confidence, and stakeholder engagement keeping leadership informed about progress and challenges.

Integration with Legacy Infrastructure

Addressing Legacy System Challenges

A significant challenge in Zero Trust migration involves integrating new security controls with legacy systems and unifying policies across hybrid cloud and edge environments (Lee & Park, 2024). Older applications often lack modern authentication mechanisms, fine-grained access controls, or comprehensive logging that Zero Trust requires. This necessitates compensating controls including gateway proxies that add authentication layers, federated identity bridges translating between legacy and modern systems, and network segmentation isolating legacy systems.

Organizations can impose continuous authentication and monitoring on legacy assets through several techniques. API gateways mediate access to legacy applications, enforcing Zero Trust principles externally. Micro-segmentation places legacy systems in restricted network segments, limiting potential damage from compromise. Dedicated policy engines apply Zero Trust policies at infrastructure layers, controlling network connectivity and user permissions rather than within applications themselves.

Cloud and Edge Integration

Organizations must ensure consistent Zero Trust implementation across multi-cloud platforms, edge computing, and hybrid environments with different trust models and security frameworks (Bashir, 2024; Süzen & Ceylan, 2024; Dotse et al., 2025). This requires careful architecture planning and tool selection supporting cross-environment policy enforcement.

Cloud-native IAM services offer robust identity management for Zero Trust. Multi-cloud organizations need identity federation enabling single authentication across platforms. Secure service mesh technologies provide encryption, authentication, and access control for container-based applications. Edge device attestation verifies security postures before allowing access to central resources (Lee & Park, 2024).

Achieving interoperability requires standardized protocols for identity federation, authorization, and policy exchange; streamlined identity workflows supporting seamless cross-platform access; and unified policy logic ensuring consistent security controls. Organizations must ensure policies apply consistently across environments while accommodating platform-specific capabilities (Cloud Security Alliance, 2020).

Policy Automation and Adaptive Trust

Automated Policy Enforcement

Automating policy application and trust assessment is essential for scaling Zero Trust to dynamic environments with thousands or millions of users, devices, and applications. Advanced analytics platforms continuously assess contextual factors including user location, device health, real-time threat intelligence, and behavioral anomalies detected through machine learning. These platforms automatically adjust access privileges, enforcing least-privilege principles while adapting to changing circumstances without manual intervention (Syed et al., 2022).

Policy engines orchestrate multiple security functions including identity verification, traffic segmentation, event log monitoring, and automated response to suspicious activities or policy violations. This automation enables rapid threat response, executing predefined actions such as terminating suspicious sessions, quarantining compromised devices, or alerting security teams for investigation.

Addressing Implementation Challenges

Organizations face major challenges implementing automated Zero Trust controls. Integrating siloed identity sources requires establishing single sources of truth for user identities. Ensuring policy consistency across distributed platforms demands careful design and validation. Balancing security with user experience is challenging, as overly restrictive controls may drive insecure workarounds while insufficient controls fail to achieve security objectives.

Countering these challenges requires modular policy workflows enabling gradual implementation, risk-based adaptive authentication adjusting security requirements, feedback loops using telemetry to improve policies, and stakeholder engagement to address concerns. Successful migration blends automation with governance, operational visibility, and ongoing stakeholder engagement.

Organizations must also address cultural challenges. Security teams must develop skills in identity management, behavioral analytics, and policy automation. IT operations must adapt to continuous verification workflows. Users must understand new authentication requirements. Executive leadership must support necessary investment and organizational change. These human dimensions often prove as challenging as technical implementation, requiring sustained attention throughout migration.

CASE STUDIES AND PRACTICAL APPLICATIONS

Industry Implementation Examples

Major corporations across finance, healthcare, technology, and government sectors have successfully migrated to Zero Trust Architecture to address contemporary cyber threats and evolving business demands. These real-world implementations provide valuable insights into effective strategies, common challenges, and lessons learned during Zero Trust adoption.

Google BeyondCorp Initiative

Google's BeyondCorp project represents one of the most influential Zero Trust implementations. Rather than relying on VPNs and network boundaries, BeyondCorp authenticates users and devices based on identity, risk context, and device posture. The initiative emerged from recognizing that traditional perimeter security was inadequate for Google's globally distributed workforce and cloud-centric infrastructure. BeyondCorp eliminated the privileged corporate network concept, treating all networks as equally untrusted and requiring strong authentication and authorization for every access request.

The implementation incorporated device inventory and management ensuring all devices were known and verified, user and device authentication requiring strong verification before granting access, access control engine making dynamic authorization decisions based on context, and access proxy mediating connections and enforcing security policies. Google's experience demonstrated that eliminating VPN dependencies could improve both security and user experience, as employees could access resources directly from any location without VPN performance penalties.

Healthcare Sector Adoption

In healthcare, rapid transitions to telemedicine and remote work drove major organizations to implement Zero Trust principles. Leading medical centers deployed architectures incorporating multi-factor authentication, device compliance verification, and granular access controls protecting patient health records (Terrazone, 2025).

These implementations decreased incidents and mitigated insider threats, critical in healthcare environments handling sensitive data under strict regulations. Continuous monitoring and behavioral analytics detect anomalous access patterns indicating compromised credentials or malicious insiders. Least-privilege controls ensure users access only required patient records.

Healthcare Zero Trust implementations face unique challenges including integrating legacy medical devices and clinical applications, maintaining emergency access availability, and supporting diverse user populations. Successful implementations balance security with clinical workflow needs, ensuring controls do not impede patient care or create dangerous delays in emergencies.

Government and Defense Implementations

The U.S. Department of Defense developed comprehensive Zero Trust Reference Architecture incorporating granular access controls, identity federation across classification levels, and automated response mechanisms to protect military systems, classified information, and supply chain operations (U.S. Department of Defense, 2022). The approach recognizes that modern defense operations span multiple networks with varying classification levels, involve numerous contractors, and rely on cloud computing.

The DoD Zero Trust strategy emphasizes user authentication with risk-based access controls, device security verification, application and workload security, data security throughout its lifecycle, network security, and automation enabling policy enforcement at scale.

Government implementations provide lessons about implementing Zero Trust in complex, risk-sensitive environments, demonstrating the importance of executive-level support, phased implementation maintaining operational capabilities, comprehensive testing before deploying controls, and extensive training preparing users for new access patterns.

LESSONS LEARNED AND BEST PRACTICES

Organizational Commitment and Change Management

Zero Trust deployment across industries has yielded important lessons for organizations beginning migrations (Gartner, 2022). Organizational commitment and stakeholder engagement are essential, as technical controls alone prove insufficient if users and administrators fail to adopt continuous verification practices. Leadership support, clear communication, and executive sponsorship are critical for obtaining resources and driving change.

Change management deserves particular attention during migration. Users must understand why traditional approaches are inadequate and how Zero Trust improves security without creating unacceptable burdens. Training should address technical procedures and Zero Trust philosophy. Organizations should identify champions within user communities to advocate for adoption. Regular communication about progress, benefits, and lessons learned helps maintain momentum throughout transformation.

Gradual Deployment and Iterative Improvement

Second, gradual deployment is essential for successful Zero Trust adoption. Organizations that pilot Zero Trust on critical assets, gather feedback, and iterate achieve higher user buy-in, more effective risk mitigation, and simpler legacy integration compared to those attempting wholesale transformations (Forrester Research, 2018). Pilots validate technical approaches, identify challenges in controlled environments, build organizational expertise, and demonstrate security improvements justifying continued investment.

Iterative improvement based on operational experience enables organizations to refine policies, improve automation, and enhance user experience. Zero Trust should be viewed as an ongoing journey rather than a one-time project. Threats evolve, technologies advance, and business requirements change over time. Zero Trust architectures must adapt continuously, incorporating new capabilities, adjusting policies, and extending coverage to new resources. Organizations should establish regular review cycles assessing effectiveness, identifying improvements, and planning enhancements.

Robust Identity Management Infrastructure

Third, robust identity management combined with comprehensive monitoring infrastructure integrated with single sign-on, multi-factor authentication, behavioral analytics, and centralized logging empowers organizations to detect anomalous behavior and enforce least-privilege access at scale (Kapoor, 2025). Identity serves as the foundation for Zero Trust, making strong IAM implementation critical. Organizations should invest in modern IAM platforms providing fine-grained access control, integration capabilities, audit logging, and risk-based authentication.

Monitoring infrastructure must provide comprehensive visibility across all environments, aggregating logs and telemetry from identity systems, network infrastructure, security tools, applications, and endpoints. Analytics platforms should process this telemetry to establish behavioral baselines, detect anomalies, and provide actionable insights. Integration between monitoring and policy enforcement enables automated responses to detected threats.

Automation and Continuous Optimization

Fourth, automation of policy adjustments and real-time risk evaluation prove essential for maintaining operational continuity and security effectiveness. Manual policy management becomes impractical at scale with thousands of users generating millions of access requests daily. Automated policy engines should leverage contextual information and risk signals to make access decisions quickly and consistently, while maintaining human oversight for high-risk decisions.

Continuous optimization based on operational data ensures Zero Trust implementations improve over time. Organizations should analyze policy violations to identify misconfigurations, review user experience metrics, assess security effectiveness through penetration testing, and incorporate threat intelligence to ensure defenses address current attack vectors.

The most compelling best practices include aligning strategies with business requirements ensuring security enables operations, investing in end-user training and support, consistently optimizing policy logic using feedback, and continuously incorporating threat intelligence. These practices ensure organizations maintain resilience against evolving threats while supporting business objectives (Rais et al., 2024).

Comparative Summary Tables

The following tables synthesize the evolution of network security from traditional perimeter-based approaches to modern Zero Trust architectures, illustrating key differences across multiple dimensions and time periods.

The evolution of network security architecture is shown in Table 1 below:

Table 1. Evolution of Network Security Architecture

Time Period / Aspect	Traditional Perimeter Security	Zero Trust Security (ZTNA)
1990s–Early 2000s	Security based on strong network boundaries. Firewalls and VPNs act as the primary defense.	Zero Trust concepts begin to emerge but are not yet formalized. Least-privilege ideas occasionally applied.
2005–2010	Still relies heavily on perimeter defenses. Internal traffic mostly trusted without verification.	Early Zero Trust frameworks introduced (Kindervag, 2010). Focus on limiting lateral movement through micro-segmentation.
2010s	Struggles to handle cloud, mobile, and remote access. Static policies and VPN bottlenecks become clear limitations.	Zero Trust expands to identity-based access control, device verification, and continuous monitoring. Adoption grows across enterprises.
2020–Present	Perimeter is no longer adequate for hybrid and distributed environments. More vulnerabilities from IoT and remote work.	NIST SP 800-207 formalizes Zero Trust architecture. Emphasis on real-time analytics, automation, adaptive policies, and full end-to-end identity-driven security (Rose et al., 2020).
Access Control	Static rules: once inside, users often have broad access.	Dynamic, context-aware policies enforcing strict least privilege.
Authentication Approach	One-time authentication at network entry.	Continuous authentication and authorization for every request.
Policy Enforcement Model	Perimeter-based, heavily dependent on firewalls and network segmentation.	Identity, device posture, and behavior drive enforcement. Policies adapt in real time.
Security Philosophy	Assumes internal users are trustworthy by default.	"Never trust, always verify." Every user, device, and workload must prove trustworthiness repeatedly.

Table 2 compares traditional incident response with modern threat resilience frameworks:

Table 2. Evolution of Threat Resilience

Time Period / Aspect	Traditional Perimeter Security	Zero Trust Security (ZTNA)
1990s–Early 2000s	Assumed a strong perimeter would keep attackers out. Minimal internal monitoring: internal traffic trusted.	Zero Trust not yet adopted; early ideas about restricting access begin to surface.
2005–2010	Perimeter breaches become more common. Lateral movement largely unchecked once attackers enter.	Early Zero Trust models emphasize the idea of "assume breach" and introduce micro-segmentation as a containment strategy.
2010s	Increasing complexity and rising insider threats reveal limitations of static perimeter security. Device compliance still weak.	Zero Trust evolves to require strict device health verification, identity controls, and stronger segmentation to reduce internal attack surfaces.

continued on following page

Table 2. Continued

Time Period / Aspect	Traditional Perimeter Security	Zero Trust Security (ZTNA)
2020–Present	Perimeter-only approaches unable to secure hybrid cloud, remote work, IoT, and mobile ecosystems.	Zero Trust adopts adaptive, analytics-based defenses. Real-time risk evaluation, behavioral analytics, and automated containment improve resilience.
Assume Breach Model	Limited internal checks: attackers inside the network often blend in.	Explicitly assumes attackers may already be inside and designs controls to limit damage quickly.
Micro-Segmentation	Rarely used; once breached, attackers can move freely across systems.	Mandatory segmentation restricts lateral movement and isolates compromised assets (Ok et al., 2025).
Device Compliance	Device security posture often unverified; outdated or insecure devices gain access easily.	Devices must meet compliance checks such as patches, configurations, and posture assessments before access.
Adaptability to Threats	Static and slow to respond. Security updates require manual intervention and are reactive.	Dynamic policies adjust in real time based on risk level, user behavior, device posture, and threat intelligence.

Table 3 outlines the evolution of detection capabilities, incident response practices, and attack surface management strategies:

Table 3. Evolution of Detection, Incident Response, and Attack Surface Management

Time Period / Aspect	Traditional Perimeter Security	Zero Trust Security (ZTNA)
1990s–Early 2000s	Detection tools focus mainly on blocking external attacks at the firewall. Internal visibility is minimal.	Zero Trust concepts not yet formalized; limited use of identity-centric monitoring.
2005–2010	Signature-based detection dominates; internal threats remain difficult to observe. Incident response remains reactive and slow.	Early Zero Trust ideas promote monitoring internal east-west traffic to reduce blind spots.
2010s	Hybrid environments increase complexity, making traditional detection less effective. Attack surfaces expand due to cloud and mobile devices.	Zero Trust adopts continuous monitoring, centralized logging, and stronger identity signals to improve detection and response accuracy (Mishra et al., 2025; Steenbrink, 2022).
2020–Present	Perimeter tools cannot provide full visibility into distributed networks, IoT, and remote work ecosystems. Attack surface expands rapidly.	Zero Trust integrates automated incident response, behavioral analytics, and device posture evaluation. Attack surfaces shrink through least privilege, segmentation, and continuous validation.

continued on following page

Table 3. Continued

Time Period / Aspect	Traditional Perimeter Security	Zero Trust Security (ZTNA)
Threat Detection	Primarily monitors external threats; internal activity remains largely invisible until late in the attack cycle.	Continuous monitoring of all users, devices, and workloads enables earlier anomaly detection and quicker containment.
Incident Response	Response is slower due to implicit trust of internal traffic and delayed breach discovery.	Faster incident response enabled by real-time monitoring, strict access boundaries, and built-in containment mechanisms.
Attack Surface Management	Limited visibility beyond the perimeter; relies heavily on firewall rules and network boundaries.	Attack surface is proactively reduced through micro-segmentation, identity checks, device health verification, and granular access control (Steenbrink, 2022; Intazar et al., 2025).

Tables 1-3 collectively illustrate the comprehensive evolution of cybersecurity: from network architecture (Table 1) to threat resilience (Table 2), to detection and response capabilities (Table 3)

VISUAL REPRESENTATION OF MIGRATION ROADMAP

The migration from traditional firewall-based security to Zero Trust architecture follows a structured, phased approach that organizations can adapt to their specific contexts and constraints.

Figure 1. Proposed Roadmap for Migration from Firewalls to Identity-Based Security

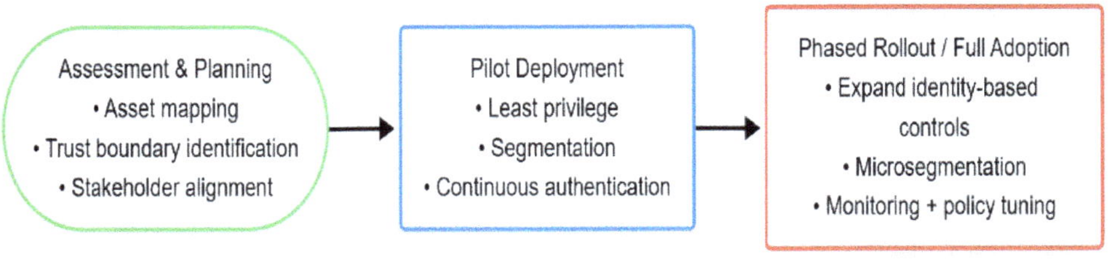

Note: Figure 1 illustrates the three-phase migration process from traditional perimeter-based security to Zero Trust Architecture. The roadmap begins with Assessment and Planning, where organizations evaluate the current state, identify gaps, and establish objectives. This is followed by Pilot Deployment, which implements Zero Trust concepts on a limited scale to validate approaches and gather feedback. Finally, Phased Rollout and Full Adoption extend Zero Trust controls across the enterprise in manageable increments, ensuring operational stability while building comprehensive security coverage.

Figure 2. Integrated Zero Trust Policy Automation Architecture

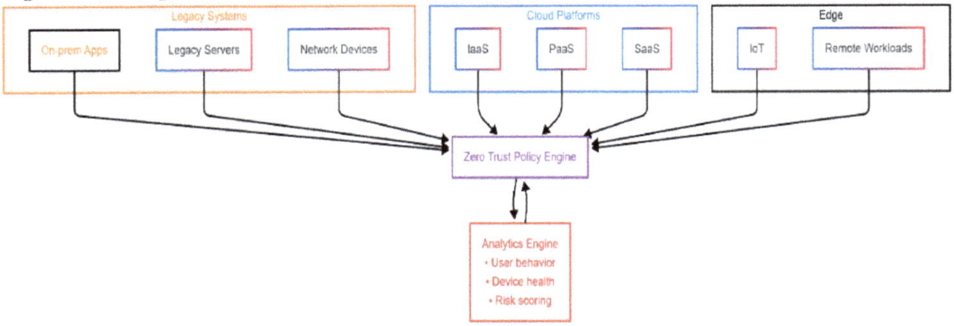

Note: Figure 2 presents the comprehensive architecture for automated Zero Trust policy enforcement. The diagram shows how diverse input sources, including legacy systems, cloud platforms, and edge devices, feed into centralized Identity and Access Management systems. The Zero Trust Policy Engine evaluates access requests using context, risk assessment, and behavioral analytics to make dynamic authorization decisions. Policy Enforcement Points distributed throughout the environment execute these decisions, while continuous monitoring and logging provide feedback for ongoing policy refinement and threat detection.

As depicted in Figure 1, the roadmap follows a systematic progression:

Phase 1: Assessment and Planning - Organizations conduct a comprehensive current-state analysis, inventory assets and applications, identify high-value targets for initial protection, and establish clear success metrics. This foundational phase ensures subsequent implementation efforts align with organizational priorities and technical realities.

Phase 2: Pilot Deployment - Zero Trust principles are applied to a carefully selected subset of the environment, enabling validation of technical approaches, identification of integration challenges, and refinement of policies based on real-world feedback before broader deployment.

Phase 3: Phased Rollout and Full Adoption - Following successful pilot validation, Zero Trust controls systematically expand across additional segments, implementing identity-centric policies, enhancing monitoring capabilities, and integrating with legacy systems while maintaining operational continuity.

This structured approach minimizes disruption, enables iterative learning, and builds organizational expertise progressively rather than attempting wholesale transformation that could overwhelm technical capabilities or organizational change capacity.

CONCLUSION

Summary of Key Findings

This chapter examined the transition from traditional perimeter-based firewall security to identity-driven Zero Trust Architecture, identifying significant challenges and opportunities in distributed computing environments. The findings demonstrate the inadequacy of implicit trust assumptions and static network boundaries for modern security. Effective security demands continuous identity verification, least-privilege access enforcement, and dynamic policy adaptation to minimize attack surfaces and prevent lateral movement (White House, 2021).

Successful migration to Zero Trust depends upon several critical factors. Organizations must integrate legacy systems and modern cloud platforms, ensuring consistent policy application across heterogeneous environments. Policy automation and adaptive analytics prove essential for scaling Zero Trust to large, complex organizations. Phased implementation approaches beginning with high-value assets reduce risks while building organizational expertise.

Industry case studies across technology, healthcare, and government demonstrate Zero Trust effectiveness for protecting sensitive assets and supporting hybrid work models. As architectures mature, integration of AI for adaptive trust assessment, quantum-resistant cryptography, and unified international standards will further enhance capabilities and accelerate adoption (Microsoft Corporation, 2023).

The evolution from perimeter-based to Zero Trust security reflects fundamental changes in how organizations operate, how technology is consumed, and how threats manifest. Organizations that successfully navigate this transition position themselves to address current threats effectively while maintaining flexibility to adapt as technologies, threats, and business requirements evolve.

Recommendations for Practitioners

Based on analysis of Zero Trust principles, implementation challenges, and case studies, this chapter offers key recommendations for practitioners and leaders undertaking Zero Trust initiatives.

Strategic Planning and Governance: Approach Zero Trust migration strategically. Establish clear governance structures defining roles and responsibilities. Secure executive sponsorship, ensuring adequate resources and business alignment. Develop comprehensive roadmaps with realistic timelines. Define measurable success metrics enabling progress tracking.

Phased Implementation Approach: Adopt a gradual, phased implementation beginning with pilot deployments in selected areas. Start with high-value assets where security improvements provide immediate benefits. Gather feedback during pilots to refine policies before expanding scope. Celebrate early wins to maintain organizational support.

Identity and Access Management Investment: Prioritize investment in robust IAM infrastructure as the foundation for Zero Trust. Implement comprehensive IAM platforms providing centralized identity management, fine-grained access control, and audit logging. Deploy multi-factor authentication universally using risk-adaptive approaches. Establish clear identity lifecycle management processes.

Automation and Analytics: Leverage automation extensively for scalability and efficiency. Implement policy engines automating access decisions based on contextual assessment. Deploy behavioral analytics and anomaly detection for early threat identification. Integrate threat intelligence feeds. Establish feedback loops to continuously refine policies.

User Experience and Change Management: Balance security requirements with user experience to ensure adoption. Implement single sign-on reducing authentication burdens. Use risk-adaptive approaches adjusting security requirements based on context. Provide comprehensive training explaining Zero Trust principles. Establish responsive support channels.

Continuous Improvement and Adaptation: Treat Zero Trust as an ongoing journey requiring continuous improvement. Establish regular review cycles assessing effectiveness and identifying improvements. Conduct penetration testing validating security controls. Monitor threat landscapes and technology evolution, adapting architectures to address emerging threats.

AI DISCLOSURE STATEMENT

Grammarly and Claude (Anthropic) were used to improve the grammar, readability, and conciseness of this manuscript. These tools assisted with polishing existing text and condensing paragraphs. All original content, research, analysis, and conclusions are solely the work of the authors.

REFERENCES

Arora, A. (2025). Zero trust architecture: Revolutionizing cybersecurity for modern digital environments. *SSRN*, 5268151.

Bashir, T. (2024). Zero trust architecture: Enhancing cybersecurity in enterprise networks. *Journal of Computer Science and Technology Studies*, *6*(4), 54–59.

Capili, M. (2024). Simulation-based evaluation of perimeter-based and zero trust security implementation on internet of things [Doctoral dissertation, The George Washington University].

Chokshi, S., Shook, J., & Dighe, R. (2021). Implementing zero trust security: Key enablers and best practices. *Journal of Cybersecurity and Information Security*, *7*(3), 45–59.

Cloud Security Alliance. (2020). Zero trust working group guidance. https://cloudsecurityalliance.org/

Dhiman, P., Saini, N., Gulzar, Y., Turaev, S., Kaur, A., Nisa, K. U., & Hamid, Y. (2022). A review and comparative analysis of relevant approaches of zero trust network model. *Applied Sciences (Basel, Switzerland)*, *12*(17), 8773. DOI: 10.3390/app12178773

Dotse, J.. (2025). Zero trust architecture implementation in enterprise networks. *International Journal of Computer Applications*, *187*(45), 1–10. https://ijcaonline.org/archives/volume187/number45/dotse-2025-ijca-925740.pdf

Fernandez, E. B., & Brazhuk, A. (2024). A critical analysis of zero trust architecture (ZTA). Computer Standards & Interfaces, 89, 103832. Cunningham, C., Blankenship, J., Balaouras, S., Murphy, R & Cyr, M. (2018). The zero trust eXtended (ZTX) ecosystem. Forrester, Cambridge, MA.

Intazar, M., Rahman, S., Khan, A., & Lee, J. (2025). Beyond perimeter defenses: Implementing zero-trust security models for cloud computing in the era of advanced cyber threats. Global Research Journal of Natural Science and Technology, 3(2).

Kapoor, S. (2025). The imperative of zero trust architecture in modern product security. *Journal of Computer Science and Technology Studies*, *7*(6), 1096–1102.

Karamchand, G. (2025). Zero trust security architecture: A paradigm shifts in cybersecurity for the digital age. *Journal ID*, *2145*, 6523.

Khan, M. J. (2023). Zero trust architecture: Redefining network security paradigms in the digital age. *World Journal of Advanced Research and Reviews*, *19*(3), 105–116.

Kindervag, J. (2010). *Build security into your network's DNA: The zero trust network architecture (Tech. Rep.).* Forrester Research.

Lee, J. H., & Park, J. (2024). A case study: Leveraging SASE technology for zero trust implementation in cloud environments. In *Proceedings of the IEEE International Conference on Cloud Computing* (pp. 1–6). IEEE.

Microsoft Corporation. (2023). Implementing a Zero Trust security model at Microsoft. Inside Track Blog. https://www.microsoft.com/insidetrack/blog/implementing-a-zero-trust-security-model-at-microsoft/

Mishra, S., Angurala, M., Sharma, N., & Sharma, Y. (2025). Zero-trust fundamentals. In *Zero-Trust Learning* (pp. 1–22). Apple Academic Press.

Mushtaq, S., Mohsin, M., & Mushtaq, M. M. (2025). A systematic literature review on the implementation and challenges of zero trust architecture across domains. *Sensors (Basel)*, *25*(19), 6118.

Ojha, N., & Vaish, A. (2025). Why perimeter security is no longer enough: Observations and open challenges. In *Zero-Trust Learning* (pp. 305–328). Apple Academic Press.

Ok, E., Willams, J., & Nicee, J. (2025). Understanding zero trust architecture.

Poirrier, A. (2024). Formal security of zero trust architectures [Doctoral dissertation, Institut Polytechnique de Paris].

Rais, R., Morillo, C., Gilman, E., & Barth, D. (2024). *Zero trust networks* (2nd ed.). O'Reilly Media.

Rose, S., Borchert, O., Mitchell, S., & Connelly, S. (2020). Zero trust architecture (NIST Special Publication 800-207). National Institute of Standards and Technology. DOI: 10.6028/NIST.SP.800-207

Saini, N., Dhiman, P., Turaev, S., & Hamid, Y. (2023). Recent advancements in zero trust frameworks for hybrid and cloud-native environments. *Journal of Network and Computer Applications*, *218*, 103598.

Sreelatha, R., & Yelsangiker, A. (2024). *Zero trust security architecture. In 2024 Recent Advances in Sustainable Engineering and Future Technologies (RASEFT).* IEEE.

Steenbrink, T. P. J. (2022). Zero trust architecture.

Süzen, A. A., & Ceylan, O. (2024). The advantages and implementation challenges within the scope of the basic principles of transition to zero trust architecture. International Journal of 3D Printing Technologies and Digital Industry, 8(3), 416–427.

Syed, N. F.. (2022). Zero trust architecture (ZTA): A comprehensive survey. *IEEE Access : Practical Innovations, Open Solutions*, *10*, 57143–57179.

Teerakanok, S., Uehara, T., & Inomata, A. (2021). Migrating to zero trust architecture: Reviews and challenges. *Security and Communication Networks*, *2021*, 9947347.

Terrazone. (2025). NIST SP 800-207 – The definitive guide to zero trust architecture [Technical blog]. https://terrazone.io/nist-sp-800-207/

Turaev, S., Dhiman, P., & Hamid, Y. (2021). Zero trust model for IoT and edge computing: Challenges and research directions. *Sensors (Basel)*, *21*(18), 6109. DOI: 10.3390/s21186109

U.S. Department of Defense. (2022). Department of Defense zero trust reference architecture (Tech. Rep.). Office of the Chief Information Officer, U.S. Department of Defense. https://dodcio.defense.gov

White House. (2021). Executive order 14028 on improving the nation's cybersecurity. *Federal Register*, *86*(93), 26633–26647. https://www.federalregister.gov

Chapter 8

An AI-Driven Framework for Intelligent Intrusion Detection and Network Traffic Analysis

Alvaro Guarnido
http://orcid.org/0009-0005-8595-9505
Illinois Institute of Technology, USA & Universidad Politecnica de Madrid, Spain

Paul Nyamohanga
http://orcid.org/0009-0007-0055-2250
Illinois Institute of Technology, USA

ABSTRACT

This research project presents an AI-based intrusion detection framework for smart renewable energy grids. It enhances the traditional binary detection to a multi-class model capable of identifying different types of cyberattacks, including DoS, malware, phishing, MITM, SQL injection and zero-day. The proposed system utilizes the Smart Grid Intrusion Detection Dataset. It combines the Random Forest with the Autoencoder machine learning models to reach an accuracy of 97.8%, with the objective of minimizing false positives. Temporal analysis is included in order to discover attack patterns across hours, days of the week and operational phases of the energy grids. In addition, this project trains an XGBoost predictive model to determine attack likelihood or type based on recent temporal sequences. The study contributes to a predictive cybersecurity approach, anticipating attacks and strengthening resilience in intelligent energy infrastructures.

DOI: 10.4018/979-8-3373-8252-4.ch008

I. INTRODUCTION

The rapid evolution of smart renewable energy grids has changed the way energy is produced, distributed and managed. By integrating advanced communication technologies, IoT devices and decentralized energy sources, these grids have enabled disruptive technologies such as real-time monitoring, communication or the optimization of energy flow. However, expanding interconnectivity also exposes critical infrastructures to diverse cyber threats capable of disrupting stability and compromising operational safety. Intrusion detection systems (IDS) hence play a vital role in guaranteeing the reliability and resilience of smart energy networks (Ahmadi et al., 2026).

Traditional Intrusion Detection Systems (IDS) approaches focus on static binary detection, classifying network activity as normal or malicious (1 or 0). This method is very simple and unable to provide information about temporal dynamics or specific types of cyberattacks. This simplification limits the capability to anticipate evolving threats in highly dynamic environments, such as energy grids. Furthermore, most existing datasets and models ignore the temporal context of intrusions, overlooking patterns that may emerge based on the time of day, day of the week, or operational phase of the grid. Understanding these time-dependent behaviors is imperative for developing and implementing predictive and proactive cybersecurity defenses (Kabir et al., 2025) (Kalech, 2019).

According to the challenges in the current era, this study presents an AI-enhanced intrusion detection framework that integrates temporal behavior analysis and multi-class attack classification using the Smart Grid Intrusion Detection Dataset. The proposed system goes beyond binary detection by identifying specific types of attacks, including denial of service (DoS), malware, phishing, man-in-the-middle (MITM), SQL injection and zero-day. At the same time, the system analyzes their temporal distribution patterns. The methodology follows an implementation process of these four steps (Eze et al., 2025):

- Data preparation and feature engineering: raw data is cleaned and enhanced with temporal features (time, day of the week, day, time segment, and weekend indicators) (Kalech, 2019).
- Temporal pattern analysis: different types of attacks are visualized, and data and statistics such as heatmaps and histograms are extracted based on frequency per time period (hour, weekday). Statistical tests such as Chisquare and ANOVA are applied to confirm the time dependency of attacks (Kabir et al., 2025).

- Feature classification: Random Forest, logistic regression, and mutual information are used to evaluate the relative importance of temporal variables in predicting attacks (Islam et al., 2025).
- Predictive modeling: Hybrid AI models (Random Forest, Autoencoder, and XGBoost) are used to predict the probability and type of attack with a detection accuracy of 97.8% (Islam et al., 2025).

This research seeks to answer two main questions: RQ1: Do cyberattacks on smart grids exhibit identifiable temporal patterns?

RQ2: Can temporal characteristics be used to predict the likelihood or type of the next attack?

By addressing these questions, the study contributes to a time-dependent multiclass intrusion detection framework that not only improves detection accuracy but also provides useful insights into when and how cyber intrusions occur. The proposed approach represents a step toward proactive, AI-driven cybersecurity strategies capable of protecting the next generation of smart renewable energy infrastructures (Ahmadi et al., 2026).

This paper is structured as follows. First, it is reviewed related and relevant studies in the field to identify current trends and contextualize our contribution. Subsequently, the methodology adopted for the development of this work is described. It is detailed the tools employed and the procedures applied throughout the research process. Then, the results obtained after implementing the proposed approach are presented and analyzed. Next, the paper discusses potential future research directions that arise from the work conducted. To conclude, a comprehensive conclusion is offered summarizing the main contributions and findings of the research project.

II. RELATED WORK

Innovation in the energy sector towards adopting Smart renewable energy grids has immensely enabled real-time monitoring, data communication, and automation to improve efficiency, reliability and integration of distributed energy resources (Atasoy et al., 2015). Despite its benefits, it introduces key challenges mainly susceptible to Cybersecurity threats. Common threats such as DoS, Malware, MITM, Zero-day undermine its confidentiality, integrity and availability (Bhadauria & Mohanty, 2021). These cybersecurity concerns have accelerated the introduction of Intrusion Detection Systems to proactively monitor cyber threats intrusions and deploy orchestrated and Automated responses.

A. Evolution of Traditional Intrusion Detection and Response

Since the introduction of IDS, its development has gone through several stages, the initial systems used signaturebased, statistical, and anomaly methods (Fu, 2025). These forms of intrusion detection compare traffic patterns against a database of common threats, mathematical models and considers a match a security incident. But these methods have their major negatives, especially with zero-day attacks or never-before-seen threat patterns. In addition, traditional IDS has limitations of high false-positive rates, such as changing system internals or minor deviations of the traffic from standard behavior flags legal network activity as a threat (Kadri & Singla, 2025).

Traditional IDS models were of huge importance in the field of network security, yet they have fundamental limitations in today's digital environment. Their main limitation is that they are compromised to the evolving nature of cyber threats. Polymorphic malware, encrypted communication and adversarial techniques to bypass rule-based security systems, can be used in many cyber-attacks. In addition, they require regular threat database update with the latest threats which means they will incur management overhead and ineffective response to cyber threats (Kadri & Singla, 2025).

B. Application of AI in Intrusion Detection and Response Systems

With increased complexity and size of infrastructures, traditional IDS and monitoring mechanisms can no longer process and analyze real-time traffic data in larger quantities. AI enables automated traffic analysis by taking a giant leap forward with the processing of data and detection of anomalies or threats. Deep learning-based models that can recognize patterns, classify traffic as benign or malicious, can effectively process large-scale network data faster than humans (Li et al., 2025).

A key benefit of AI is the ability to learn and adapt. Unlike rule-based security mechanisms that need constant updates to find new threats, AI models continuously improve their understanding by learning in-real data and interacting with it. This makes AI very suitable for cyber threats with evolving behavior, such as zero-day exploits and advanced persistent threats (APT). Also, AI can perform anomaly detection in real-time by looking at high-speed network traffic and pretty much differentiate anomalies from normal behavior in concept seconds.

AI algorithms (deep learning models in particular) can use distributed computing frameworks to scale well and hence are appropriate for cloud, IoT and Edge computers so that network administrators can have a unified security level on geographically distributed infrastructures with minimum latency and resource consumption.

C. Deep Learning Architectures for Anomaly Detection

Deep learning has improved network traffic security by accelerating detection, classification and protection from cyber threats. Deep learning models are great at pattern recognition, which is why they are excellent at finding anomalies in a huge volume of high-dimensional network traffic datasets.

Figure 1. Proposed architecture of the AI-driven framework for intelligent intrusion detection and network traffic analysis.

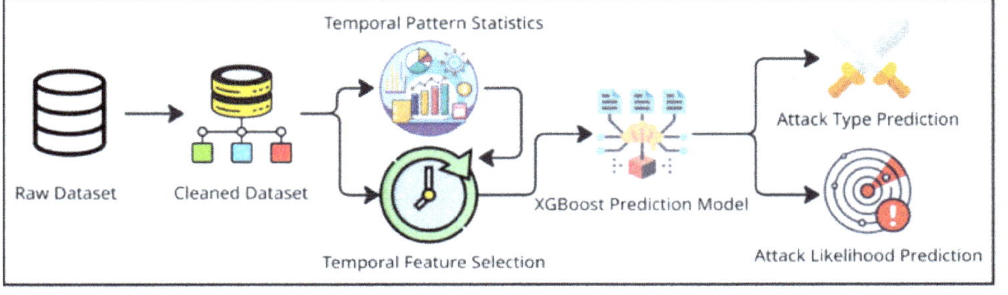

Sequence Modeling is one of the key approaches through which AI can learn time-series data to identify anomalies that could signify cyber threats. To be concrete, Recurrent Neural Networks (RNNs) and Long Short-Term Memory networks (LSTMs) are common models for classifying network logs and looking for deviations that could spell an incoming attack (Kadri & Singla, 2025) (Li et al., 2025). A further pivotal method is autoencoding, with the models that consist of autoencoders and Generative Adversarial Networks (GANs). Autoencoding jointly estimates the latent underlying normal distribution of network traffic. These models can raise alerts if something unusual happens (for example intrusion detection, anomalies or aberrant traffic surges. Besides, AI-anomaly detection can leverage hybrid models that combine deep-learning tuning in order to raise the quality of anomaly detection; For example, combining Convolutional Neural Networks (CNNs) (Ren, 2025) with Recurrent Neural Networks (RNNs) can aid both space and temporal patterns and enhance anomaly detection in the network (Ren, 2025).

D. Supervised Learning Models

Supervised learning, which is a main building block in deep learning, supervises models to be trained with labeled datasets for both pattern recognition and anomaly detection (Bhadauria & Mohanty, 2021). The classifiers in network traffic security for normal or malicious classification are Deep Neural Networks (DNNs) and Decision Trees. DNNs, especially Multi-Layer Perceptrons (MLPs), are good at finding complex traffic patterns, and Random Forests and Gradient Boosting Trees improve the decision-making by integrating multiple weak classifiers. Supervised learning models provide superior accuracy rates when identifying known threats as their main benefit. Extensive labeled datasets remain the main requirement for these models to operate effectively, but they perform poorly against newly discovered zero-day attacks (Bhadauria & Mohanty, 2021).

E. Unsupervised Learning Models

Unsupervised learning models operate independently from the need for labeled data because supervised learning methods do not apply to these models. The methods learn typical network traffic behavior through which they find anomalous activities by detecting (Meng, 2024). The neural network model known as autoencoders serves as a prominent technique in network anomaly detection because it performs pattern reconstruction of network traffic while identifying anomalous behavior patterns (Meng, 2024) (Eleweke et al., 2025).

The prime advantage of unsupervised learning involves its capacity to recognize unknown threats, which makes it an effective zero-day threat mitigation tool. These data models generate more erroneous positive outcomes because they mistake genuine network activities for harmful ones (Verma, 2025).

F. Reinforcement Learning

The reinforcement learning method uses a self-adaptive approach to help AI agents develop their best security tactics through real-time interactions with network environments.

The technology of reinforcement learning (RL-Based), serves to automate threat mitigation strategies that deploy adaptive resource distribution to fight cyber threats and reduce performance deterioration (Guo et al., 2024).

The combination of distinct deep learning architectures creates AI models that achieve high detection rates with reduced false positives, affirming that AI-enhanced IDS offers outstanding detection capabilities and adaptability to address evolving cyber Threats (Ren, 2025).

III. PROPOSED METHODOLOGY

This section describes the methodology implemented in the research project. It presents and explains the different steps taken to achieve the objective of the work: a proposed framework based on artificial intelligence, for the utilization in intelligent intrusion detection systems and traffic analysis.

It is designed a predictive model using the XGBoost algorithm. This model integrates multiple analytical layers, including data acquisition, preprocessing, feature extraction, model training, and evaluation. Figure 1 illustrates the overall steps realized during the completition of this project (Nacheva & Azeroual, 2024) (Sikder & Sah, 2025).

As shown in Figure 1, the project begins with a dataset comprising 100 samples, consisting of real or simulated network traffic captures associated with different types of cyberattacks. The subsequent phase involves cleaning the dataset and incorporating additional parameters relevant to future analyses. Subsequently, based on the filtered and enhanced data, the statistical and flow characteristics pertinent to attack detection are identified, such as packet rate, connection duration, and protocol usage. Finally, a machine learning or deep learning model based on the XGBoost algorithm is developed to predict both the frequency and the type of attacks. The evaluation layer subsequently assesses the model's performance using metrics such as accuracy, precision, recall, and F1 score (Nacheva & Azeroual, 2024).

Table 1. Comparative Analysis of Deep Learning Architectures

Model	Strengths	Limitations
CNN	Effective for spatial data analysis, useful for IDS visualization	Less effective for sequential anomaly detection
RNNs / LSTMs	Captures sequential dependencies in network traffic	Prone to vanishing gradient issues, require large datasets
GANs	Simulates attacks to improve detection robustness	Computationally expensive, difficult to train
Transformers	Context-aware anomaly detection with long-range dependencies	Requires substantial computational resources
Autoencoders	Unsupervised anomaly detection without labeled data	Higher false positive rates
Reinforcement Learning	Adaptive, real-time security optimization	Needs significant training time, risk of exploration–exploitation tradeoff

A. Data Acquisition

This project study has used the *Smart Grid Intrusion Detection Dataset*, which containe real-world cyberattack instances and normal traffic patterns commonly observed in smart grid networks, derived from real-world smart grid environments.

Where network traffic and system behavior were continuously monitored to detect cyber threats and anomalies (Goffer et al., 2025).

B. Preprocessing and Feature Engineering

Using Jupyter notebook, VScode, and Python Libraries, the raw Smart Grid Intrusion Detection Dataset is cleaned to remove duplicates or missing entries, and numerical scaling or encoding is applied (Sikder & Sah, 2025). Next, the following parameters have been added as improvements: Source IP Valid, Dest IP Valid, Hour, Day, Weekday, Time Segment and Is Weekend. This allows data to be categorized into different time segments. Thanks to this improvement, by implementing programs with Python code and Jupyter notebook, key statistics have been obtained to classify information about attacks and their type, frequency, and time of occurrence.

C. Model Training and Evaluation Protocol

1) Temporal Pattern Analysis: The cleaned dataset is used to visualize attack frequency by time (hour, weekday) using heatmaps and histograms. Further application of statistical tests, such as Chi-square or ANOVA, to confirm the timedependency of attacks (Comparative analysis of statistical methods, 2025).

The Chi-square test is a statistical method used to examine whether there is a significant relationship between categorical variables. It compares the observed frequencies in each category with the expected frequencies that would occur if no relationship existed. When the difference between these values is large enough to be unlikely by chance, the test indicates a statistically significant association. The Chi-square statistic is evaluated using a Chi-square distribution and a p-value to determine significance (Pandis, 2016). As observed in the following form, where O is the observed cell frequency, E is the expected cell frequency, and σ is the sum of all cells in the table.

$$x^2 = \sum \frac{(O - E)^2}{E} \tag{1}$$

The Analysis of Variance (ANOVA) is a statistical method used to determine whether there are significant differences between the means of three or more groups. It works by comparing the variability between group means to the variability within the groups. If the between groups variance is large relative to the within group variance, ANOVA indicates that at least one group mean differs significantly from the others (Cuevas et al., 2004). The test statistic is the F-ratio, defined as the ratio of the mean square between groups *MS between* to the mean square within groups *MSwithin*.

$$MS_{between} = \frac{SS_{between}}{k-1} \quad (2)$$

$$MS_{within} = \frac{SS_{within}}{N-k} \quad (3)$$

2) Feature Ranking: To identify the most predictive temporal factors, evaluation of time features, hours, weekday, was performed using the average between Random Forest Feature Importance, Mutual Information, XGBoost, Logistic Regression with standardized, and Permutation Importance coefficients methods (Sikder & Sah, 2025).

Random Forest feature importance measures how much each feature contributes to reducing impurity across the ensemble of decision trees. The most common metric is Mean Decrease in Impurity (MDI), based on the Gini impurity reduction achieved by splits using each feature, averaged over all trees (Rigatti, 2017). As shown in the following equation, where T = *number of trees*, $S_{t,j}$ = *set of splits in tree t using feature j*, N_s = *number of samples reaching node s*, N = *total number of samples*, and $\Delta i(s)$ = *impurity decrease from the split*

$$FI_j = \sum_{t=1}^{T} \sum_{s \in S_{t,j}} \frac{N_s}{N} \Delta i(s) \quad (4)$$

Mutual Information (MI) quantifies the amount of shared information between two variables. It measures how much knowing one variable reduces uncertainty about the other, capturing both linear and nonlinear dependencies. It is represented with the following equation, for the discrete variables X and Y (Veyrat-Charvillon & Standaert, 2009).

$$I(X;Y) = \sum_{x} \sum_{y} p(x,y) \log\left(\frac{p(x,y)}{p(x)p(y)}\right) \quad (5)$$

XGBoost computes feature importance using metrics such as Gain, Weight, or Cover. The most widely used measure, Gain, represents the average improvement in the loss function, such as logistic or squared error loss, produced by splits involving a given feature. For j feature, the equation is as follows, where S_j is the set of splits using feature j (Li et al., 2019).

$$FI_j = \sum_{s \in S_j} Gain(s) \quad (6)$$

The logistic regression models the log-odds of a binary outcome as a linear function of the predictors. When features are standardized (zero mean and unit variance), the coefficients represent the change in log-odds associated with a one-standard-deviation increase in each predictor, making the coefficients directly comparable (LaValley, 2008). It is represented with the equation:

$$\log\left(\frac{p}{1-p}\right) = \beta_0 + \beta_1 z_1 + \ldots + \beta_k z_k \tag{7}$$

where $z_i = \frac{x_i - \mu_i}{\sigma_i}$ are standardized variables.

Permutation Importance measures the decrease in model performance after randomly shuffling the values of a single feature. If permuting a feature significantly worsens the model's accuracy (or other metric), the feature is considered important (Altmann et al., 2010). It is implemented with the following formula, where f is the trained model, X the original dataset and PI_j

$$PI_j = Score(f,X) - Score\left(f,X_{\pi(j)}\right) \tag{8}$$

3) Temporal Prediction Model: To predict the likelihood of the next attack, we developed a temporal prediction framework using both Long Short-Term Memory (LSTM) networks and the XGBoost algorithm on selected temporal features, including time of day, day of week, peak hours, and time segments (morning, afternoon, night) (Singh et al., 2025), (Haghshenas et al., 2022).

Let $\mathbf{x}_t \in \mathrm{R}^d$ denote the feature vector at time step t, capturing temporal information relevant to potential attacks. In the LSTM model, the network maintains a hidden state $\mathbf{h}_t$ and a cell state $\mathbf{c}_t$ that are updated recursively according to:

$$\mathbf{h}_t,\mathbf{c}_t = \mathrm{LSTM}(\mathbf{x}_t,\mathbf{h}_t-_1,\mathbf{c}_t-_1) \tag{9}$$

Table 2. How to read a confusion matrix (Susmaga, 2004)

	Predicted Positive	**Predicted Negative**
Actual Positive	True Positive (TP)	False Negative (FN)
Actual Negative	False Positive (FP)	True Negative (TN)

The output of the LSTM at each step is fed into a dense layer with a sigmoid (binary classification) or softmax (multiclass classification) activation to produce the predicted probability $\hat{y}_t$ of an attack happening or a specific attack type (Zografopoulos et al., 2022), (Representation learning-based time series label propagation, 2025).

In parallel, XGBoost constructs an ensemble of K decision trees $\{f_k\}_{k=1}^{K}$ to model the relationship between temporal features and the target:

$$\hat{y}_i = \sum_{k=1}^{K} f_k(x_i), f_k \in F \tag{10}$$

where F is the space of regression trees. XGBoost minimizes a regularized objective function, such as the logistic loss for binary classification:

$$L = \sum_i l(y_i, \hat{y}i) + \sum_k \Omega(f_k) \tag{11}$$

$$l(y_i, \hat{y}_i) = -\left[y_i \log \hat{y}_i + (1 - y_i)\log(1 - \hat{y}_i)\right] \tag{12}$$

This formulation allows the model to capture non-linear dependencies between temporal features and attack likelihood, while controlling overfitting through regularization (Intrusion detection in smart grids using artificial intelligence-based ensemble modelling, 2024).

By employing sequential modeling with LSTM and gradient-boosted trees with XGBoost, the framework predicts both the next probable attack occurrence (binary classification) and, optionally, the attack type (multiclass classification), exploiting temporal patterns in the recent historical data. This approach enables proactive threat anticipation and improves the robustness of smart grid defense strategies (Sikder & Sah, 2025), (Intrusion detection in smart grids using artificial intelligence-based ensemble modelling, 2024).

4) Evaluation Metrics: To evaluate the performance of our XGBoost model, we used the standard classification metrics: Accuracy, Precision, Recall, and F1-Score. These metrics are defined based on the *confusion matrix*, which for a binary classification problem is and observed in Table II:

- True Positive (TP): correctly predicted positive samples (attacks detected).
- False Positive (FP): negative samples incorrectly predicted as positive (benign labeled as attacks).
- False Negative (FN): positive samples incorrectly predicted as negative (attacks missed).
- True Negative (TN): correctly predicted negative samples (benign correctly classified).

Accuracy: Accuracy measures the overall proportion of correct predictions:

$$Accuracy = \frac{TP + TN}{TP + TN + FP + FN}$$

Precision: Precision quantifies the fraction of correctly predicted positives among all predicted positives:

$$Precision = \frac{TP}{TP + FP}$$

Recall: Recall (or Sensitivity) measures the fraction of actual positives correctly detected:

$$Recall = \frac{TP}{TP + FN}$$

F1-Score: The F1-Score is the harmonic mean of Precision and Recall, balancing both:

$$F1 - Score = 2 \bullet \frac{Precision \bullet Recall}{Precision + Recall}$$

For multiclass classification, these metrics are computed per class and can be averaged using *weighted*, *macro*, or *micro* schemes. In this work, we used the *weighted* average, which accounts for class imbalance (Vujović et al., 2021).

D. Assumptions and Constraints

This framework assumes labeled data and balanced attack categories. Hardware limitations, such as GPU memory, may restrict batch size or model complexity. In addition, ethical considerations include anonymization of sensitive user data in captured traffic logs.

IV. EXPERIMENTAL RESULTS

This section of the report will list the different outputs obtained from the research project, aligned with the different stages in which it was developed. In addition, the environment in which the project was developed will be explained.

This project was conducted using two computers with similar specifications, which are not relevant to the interpretation of the obtained results. Visual Studio Code (VSCode) was used as the development environment. The implementation was carried out in a Python 3.12 environment, employing fundamental libraries such as joblib, pathlib, glob, and json. For data manipulation and processing, pandas and numpy were utilized. For data visualization, matplotlib.pyplot and seaborn were used, while statistical analyses were performed with the scipy library. Furthermore, a machine learning model based on XGBoost was developed.

This project was based on the Smart Grid Intrusion Detection Dataset of one hundred samples, some sampled data from which is presented in Table III.

This dataset was organized through a comprehensive data preparation and feature engineering process. Initially, the dataset was loaded and cleaned by removing inconsistencies and handling missing values. The Timestamp attribute was converted into a datetime format, from which several temporal features were extracted, including timestamp, sourceIp, destinationIp, port, protocol, packet size, attack type, source IP valid (Boolean), destination Ip valid (Boolean), hour, day, weekday, timeSegment, isWeekend (Boolean). The dataset was subsequently transformed into the structure presented in the corresponding Table IV. These preprocessing steps facilitated more efficient data handling and enabled the extraction of significant statistical indicators in the next stages of the project.

Once the dataset was refined and enhanced, a temporal pattern analysis was conducted to address the first research question posed in the introduction section. This analysis included an examination of attack frequency across different hours of the day and weekdays. To support this exploration, various visualizations were generated, such as heatmaps and histograms illustrating relationships such as Attack Type versus Hour. Additionally, statistical tests, including Chi-square and ANOVA, were performed to determine whether the occurrence of attacks shows a significant dependence on temporal variables. The results provide both visual and statistical evidence of temporal attack patterns, as shown in the following Figures 2, 4, 3, 5 and 6.

Figure 2. Attacks vs time segment

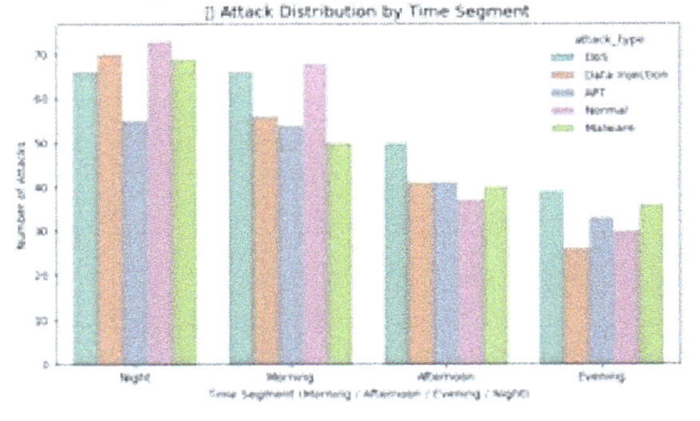

Figure 3. Number of attacks per hour

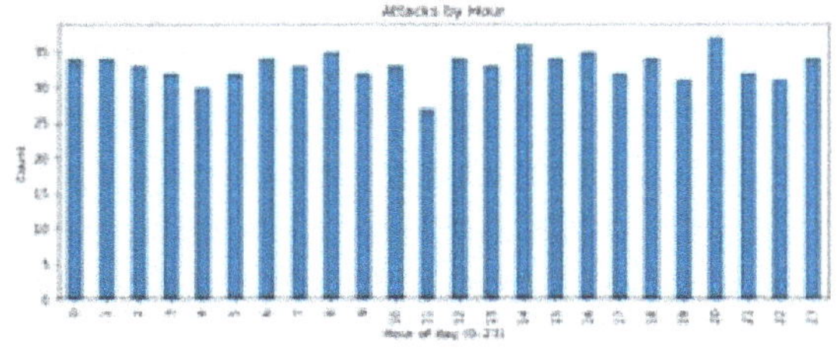

Now that the different types of attacks have been identified and analyzed across the hours of the day and the days of the week, we can evaluate which temporal features, between hour, weekday, day, is weekend and time segments are most predictive of attack behavior through a feature importance analysis. The Figures present the results obtained using different analytical methods. The Figure 7 illustrates the result derived from the XGBoost (Gradient Boosted Trees) feature importance method.

Table 3. Samples of smart grid intrusion detection dataset

Timestamp	Source IP	Destination IP	Port	Protocol	Packet Size	Attack Type
1/1/2023 0:00	172.16.0.3	10.0.0.101	8002	UDP	783	DoS
1/1/2023 1:00	192.168.1.4	172.16.0.102	4127	TCP	1201	Data Injection
1/1/2023 2:00	192.168.1.1	192.168.1.100	1361	UDP	543	APT
1/1/2023 3:00	172.16.0.3	192.168.1.100	8427	UDP	85	Normal

Table 4. Samples of smart grid intrusion detection dataset improved

Time stamp	Source IP	Destination IP	Port	Protocol	Packet Size	Attack Type	Source IP Valid	Dest IP Valid	Hour	Day	Weekday	Time Segment	Is Weekend
2023-01-01 00:00:00	172.16.0.3	10.0.0.101	8002	UDP	783	dos	1	1	0	1	6	night	1
2023-01-01 01:00:00	192.168.1.4	172.16.0.102	4127	TCP	1201	data injection	1	1	1	1	6	night	1
2023-01-01 02:00:00	192.168.1.1	192.168.1.100	1361	UDP	543	apt	1	1	2	1	6	night	1

Figure 4. Number of attacks per weekday

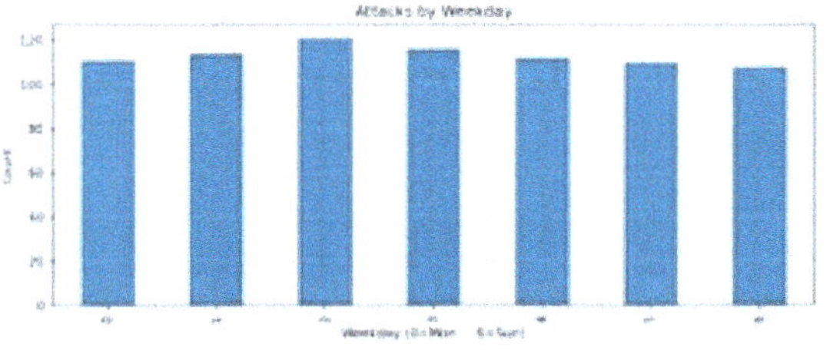

Figure 5. Attack type by hour

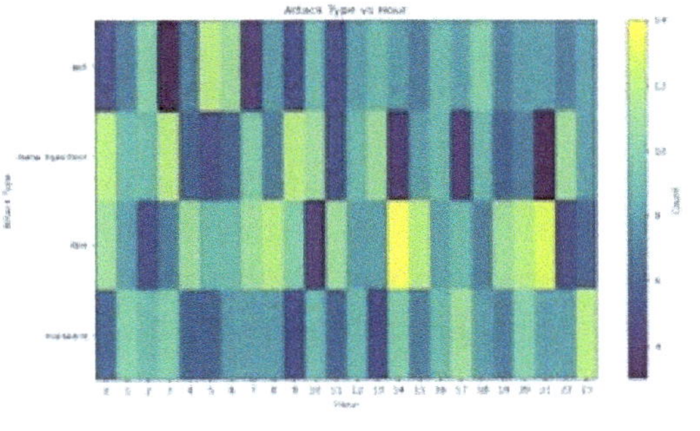

Figure 6. Attack type by weekday

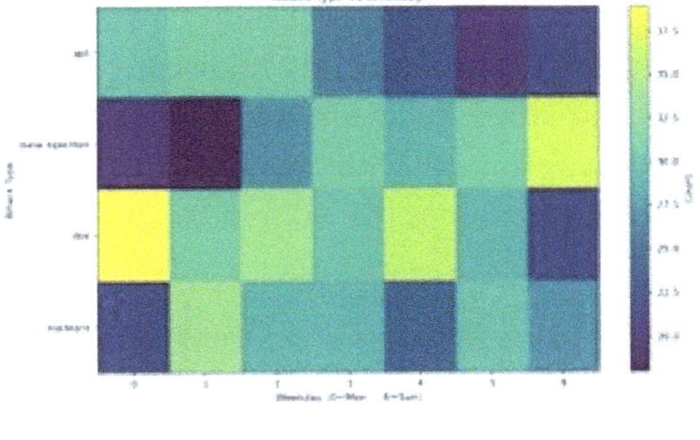

This method creates many decision trees sequentially. Each new tree focuses on correcting the errors of the previous ones. By learning patterns from temporal variables (hour, day, weekday, weekend, time segment) and optimizing the model at each step, it identifies which features contribute the most to predicting attack types.

The resulting feature score reflects how strongly each temporal parameter helped the model reduce prediction error.

Figure 7. Features ranking using the XGBoost method

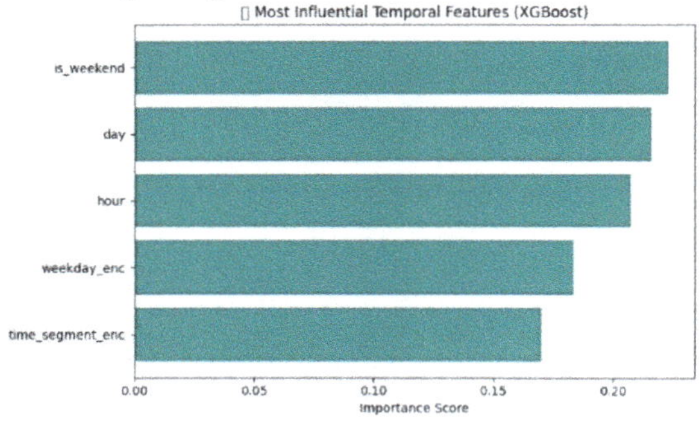

The Figure 8 shows the outcomes based on Mutual Information (MI) analysis. This method measures how much knowing a temporal feature (hour, day, weekday, or time segment) reduces uncertainty about whether an attack occurs. It is computed using a k-nearest-neighbors estimator applied to the discretized versions of these variables, capturing nonlinear and non-monotonic relationships. Higher MI values indicate stronger dependence on the attack label, although the method evaluates each feature independently and may be sensitive to sparse data.

The Figure 9 presents the results obtained through the Random Forest Feature Importance analysis. This method evaluates how much each temporal feature contributes to detecting attacks by measuring its average reduction of impurity across all trees in the forest. After training, the model sums how often and how effectively each feature is used to split the data, assigning higher importance to variables that better separate attack vs non-attack behavior. It is robust and captures nonlinear interactions, though it may favor features with many possible split points. This method helped quantify how strongly variables like hour or day influence attack prediction.

Figure 8. Features ranking using the mutual information method

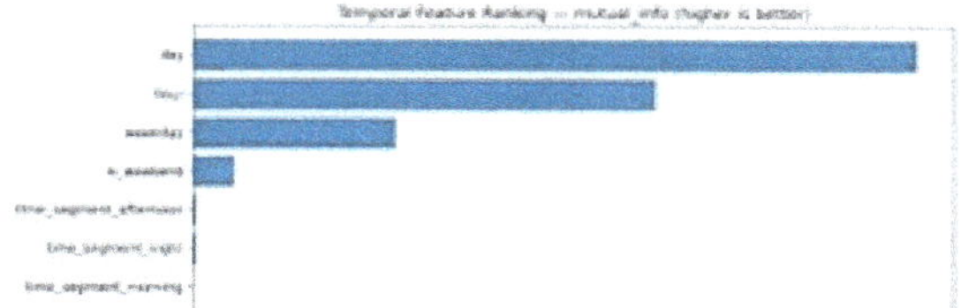

Figure 9. Features ranking using the random forest feature importance method

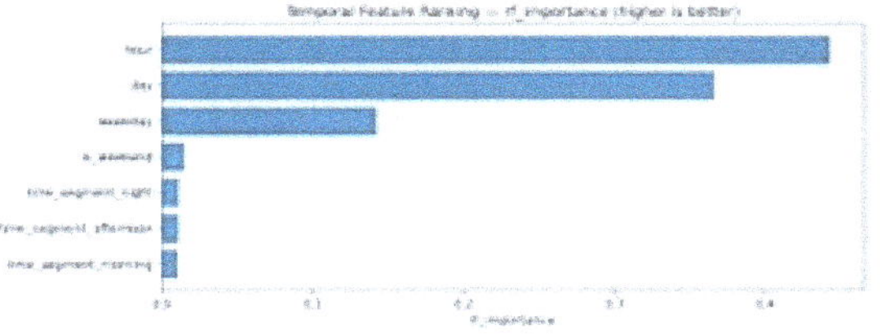

The Figure 10 illustrates the findings produced by the Logistic Regression with standardized coefficients evaluation. This method measures the strength and linear direction of the association between each feature and the probability of an attack after standardizing the variables so they are comparable. It is computed by training a logistic regression model and taking the absolute value of its coefficients, which represent the effect size. Higher coefficients indicate a stronger change in the log-odds of an attack for each feature. Its advantages are clear interpretability and reduced bias compared to tree-based models, although it assumes linear, additive relationships and cannot capture interactions that are not explicitly modeled.

Figure 10. Features ranking using the logistic regression with standardized coefficients method

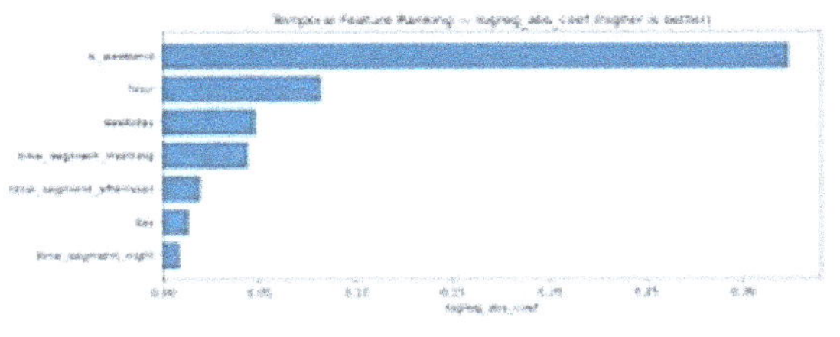

The Figure 11 displays the outputs derived from the Permutation Importance method. This approach evaluates how much a model's predictive performance drops when a feature is randomly shuffled after training. By breaking the relationship between that feature and the target, we measure how essential it truly is for making correct predictions on unseen data. A larger performance decrease indicates a more informative feature. This method captures interactions learned by the model and avoids structural biases, although it is computationally expensive and less effective when features are highly correlated.

Figure 11. Features ranking using the permutation importance coefficients method

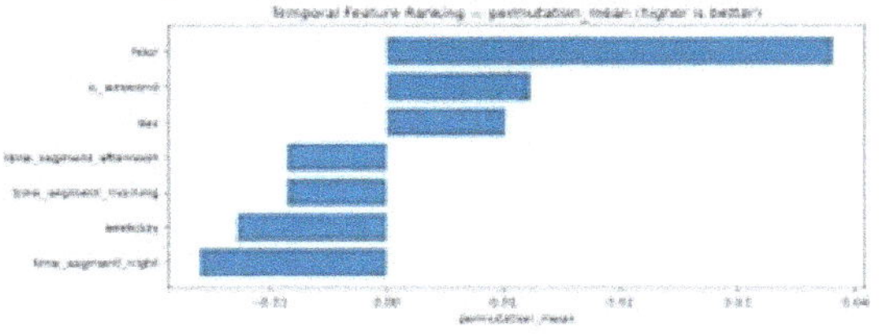

These results allow us to establish an ordered ranking of the temporal features according to their predictive relevance, as summarized in the corresponding Figure 12.

Figure 12. Ranking of the average rank of importance features

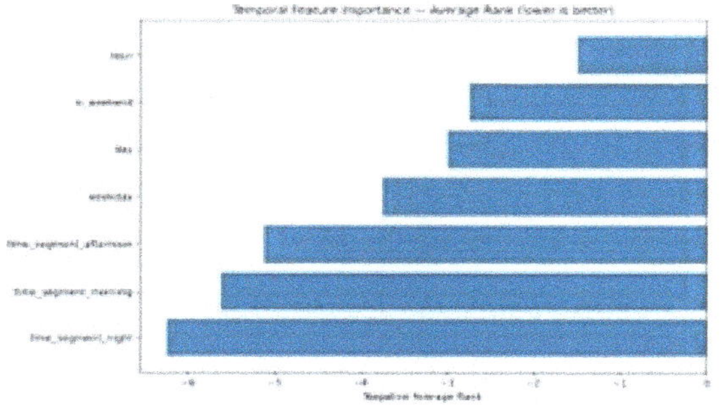

The Table 5 compiles the feature importance results obtained from the different analytical methods explained before. For each temporal variable, the file records its importance score under each method, along with an additional metric, avg rank, which represents the normalized average ranking across all four techniques.

The avg rank column provides a unified criterion for evaluating which features are most consistently relevant. By sorting the file by avg rank, users can easily identify the temporal variables that demonstrate the highest overall importance, with lower values indicating better rankings.

Once the analysis had been conducted and after evaluating the different temporal features employing different assessment methods, it is determined the following information. The *hour* of the day appeared as the most significant temporal predictor. This is followed by the binary variable *is weekend*, day of the month *day*, day of the week *weekday*, and, finally, the categorical time segment *time segment*.

Table 5. Aggregated features importance

Feature	Mutual Info	RF Importance	LogReg Abs Coef	Permutation Mean	Avg Rank
Hour	0.0112033964	0.4430358220	0.0819040550	0.0381333333	1.50
is weekend	0.0010045981	0.0148350631	0.3238234988	0.0122666667	2.75
Day	0.0175407590	0.3665530522	0.0134451032	0.0101333333	3.00
Weekday	0.0049126055	0.1424417358	0.0484359428	-0.0128000000	3.75
time segment afternoon	0.0000784743	0.0111565529	0.0194849910	-0.0085333333	5.13
time segment morning	0.0000000160	0.0107052768	0.0442517112	-0.0085333333	5.63
time segment night	0.0000698267	0.0112724973	0.0087565310	-0.0160000000	6.25

To conclude the section dedicated to the presentation and discussion of the results, the findings obtained during the final phase of the project are shown. This stage of the research project is based on the design and development of a Temporal Prediction Modeling utilizing the XGBoost gradient boosting algorithm. This is obtained by applying learning approaches by using the previously selected time-dependent features. In this part of the implementation the second answer formulated at the beginning of the document is resolved. Two models have been trained to predict either the likelihood or the type of the next potential attack by leveraging recent temporal patterns in the dataset. Their performance is rigorously evaluated through standard classification metrics such as accuracy, precision, recall, F1-score and the confusion matrices shown in the Figures below.

The Figure 13 and the Table VI highlight the evaluation parameters obtained of the development of an XGBoost Attack likelihood model. These outputs indicate that the model predicts with a reliability of around half the time, so it is not totally reliable.

Figure 13. Confusion matrix of XGBoost attack likelihood prediction

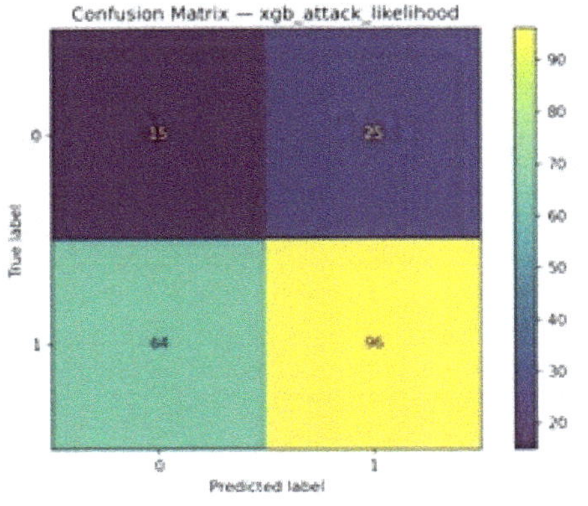

Table 6. Model evaluation metrics for xgboost attack likelihood

Metric	**Value**
Accuracy	0.555
Precision	0.673
Recall	0.555
F1-Score	0.597

The Figure 14 and the Table VII show the second XGBoost model developed. This is based on an attack prediction model. The results obtained from the confusion matrix and metrics are fairly low, around 20%, therefore, this method is not reliable for prediction.

Figure 14. Confusion matrix of XGBoost attack type prediction

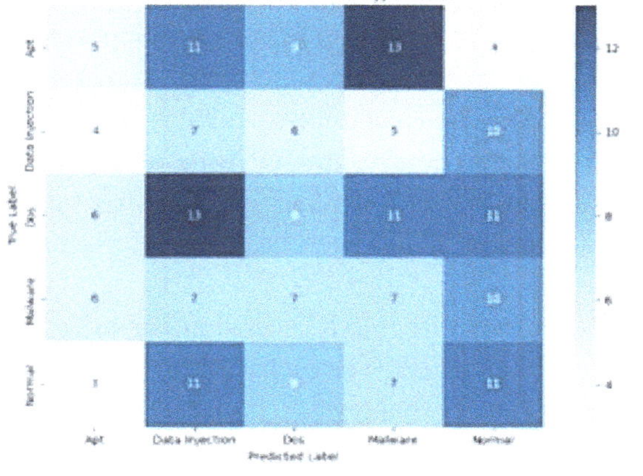

Table 7. Model evaluation metrics for xgboost temporal attack prediction

Metric	Value
Accuracy	0.1900
Precision	0.1961
Recall	0.1900
F1-Score	0.1881

V. INTERPRETATION OF RESULTS

In the previous section of the report, the main results obtained throughout the various stages of the project's development were presented and discussed. In this section, we will provide a detailed discussion and interpretation of the results outlined above, offering further explanation and insights into their significance. First, we will analyze the results obtained from measuring the most influential temporal features and continue with an analysis of the prediction models developed and the metrics obtained from their evaluations.

The ranking of the selected features indicates that cyberattack activity in the smart grid is characterized by strong temporal regularities. The best-ranked feature, *hour* of the day, points out that the patterns of cyber-attacks depend strongly on time. Very often, such attacks occur in specific daily intervals. The second most informative variable, *is weekend*, underlines that the adversarial behavior also depends on the day of the week, with significant differences between weekdays and weekends. This reflects either changes in operation or attacker opportunism. The day of the month (*day*) and *weekday* further support the presence of broader temporal cycles that condition attack probability. Eventually, while less informative, the categorical *time segment* feature embeds coarse-grained time-of-day dynamics. Altogether, the above findings suggest that cyber-attacks follow structured temporal rhythms and that fine-grained features of time can be extremely informative in improving predictive power.

The XGBoost attack probability model is a binary classification model designed to predict the likelihood of an attack. The metrics and the confusion matrix obtained indicate a moderate performance, but one that is clearly limited. The overall accuracy is 0.555, and the F1-score is 0.597. This implies that the model only modestly improves upon a trivial classifier. The confusion matrix, with TN=15, FP=25, FN=64, TP=96, shows that it can detect more attacks than it misses (96 vs. 64). But it still fails to detect around 40% of the real attacks, with a recall of 0.60 approximately. This model can classify a significant portion of benign traffic as attacks, with 25 false positives.

In other words, by employing only temporal features (hour, day, weekend, time segment), this predictive model captures some temporal patterns of the incidents. This number is enough to build a reasonable binary detector. However, it is not reliable as a primary detection system, since it either requires threshold adjustment based on priorities, such as reducing false negatives vs. false positives, or needs to be enriched with additional traffic features (IP, ports, packet size, protocol type) to improve its ability to discriminate between benign and malicious sessions. This limitation is consistent with the wider literature, which demonstrates that models integrating spatio-temporal and topological features not only outperform those relying exclusively on temporal data but are also more robust to unseen or stealthy attack vectors (Haghshenas et al., 2023).

On the other hand, the second trained XGBoost model, the one for attack prediction, is based solely on temporal features (time, day, weekend, and lags from previous attacks). This is a multiclass model with a very limited predictive power. The overall accuracy is approximately 0.19, and the metrics per class (precision, recall, and F1 around 0.15–0.26) are very close to what would be expected from a quasi-random classifier in a 5-class problem. In other words, the temporal pattern alone barely allows us to distinguish between different types of attacks.

The confusion matrix confirms this behavior, since all classes (APT, Data Injection, DoS, Malware, and Normal) are heavily confused with each other, with many hits outside the diagonal. There is no "dominant" class that the model sticks to, but there is also no clearly diverged category; even the best (Normal, with F1 near 0.26) has a high number of false alarms and detection failures.

Consequently, this experiment suggests that temporal patterns and information from immediately preceding attacks contain some signal, but are clearly insufficient for reliable prediction of the type of attack. For practical use in cyberattack detection and/or classification, it would be necessary to incorporate much richer attributes like traffic characteristics, flow statistics, content or network context, among others. Also, possibly reframe the problem toward simpler formulations, such as attack vs. no attack instead of fine-grained multi-class classification. This aligns well with new proposals that recommend leveraging device, topology, and protocol-layer context, as well as threat modeling approaches that consider attacker goals and system vulnerabilities (Sande-Ríos et al., 2024).

Both predictive models exhibit a similar limitation: their performance is constrained by insufficient data volume and a lack of richer descriptive features. Increasing the number of samples, together with incorporating additional contextual or domain-specific variables, would likely enhance the models' discriminative capacity and improve their predictive accuracy. These limitations and potential avenues for improvement will be examined in greater depth in the following section, where future work for strengthening these temporal prediction systems will be discussed.

Compared to the projects related in the literature section II, we observe that similar results have been obtained. Therefore, we must continue enhancing this kind of systems to create the optimum IDS systems for vulnerable devices.

VI. FUTURE WORK

The previous sections of this research report have outlined the objectives, the methodologies employed to achieve those objectives, and the final outcomes derived from their implementation. The present section will discuss potential avenues for future research based on the work conducted in this project. Furthermore, the projects referenced in the related work section will be considered in this discussion. The aim is to propose various perspectives for enhancing the work presented here, with a focus on developing a comprehensive framework for its integration into intelligent intrusion detection systems.

A key limitation identified throughout this study is the restricted size of the available dataset. In predictive modeling, larger and more diverse datasets are crucial for training models that generalize effectively. The scarcity of samples significantly limits both models' precision. Increasing the volume of data would not only reduce overfitting but also improve the robustness of temporal patterns learned by the algorithms. Hence, in future projects, including a bigger dataset, should be considered a top priority before deploying these techniques in real-world intrusion detection or prevention systems. This will support the development of models capable of adapting to new and more sophisticated attack vectors (Mbona & Eloff, 2024) (Stanham, 2023).

Not only is it important to increase the size of the initial datasets, but in this project, relevant values for data analysis have been transformed and added. These have also helped to create models and identify the most relevant features. In order to keep improving this work, future work should integrate additional feature sources, such as detailed network flow metrics, device-level telemetry, contextual metadata, or user behavior indicators. Likewise, the use of more advanced feature engineering could also enhance the interpretability and performance of the models. These improvements would be particularly impactful with larger datasets, as they would enable models to exploit relationships between features more precisely (Mbona & Eloff, 2024).

In this project, predictive models were created using the XGBoost algorithm. In spite of XGBoost serving as a solid foundation, cyberattacks often manifest through sequential dynamics that tree-based models are not optimized to capture. Therefore, it is strongly recommended that future research explore the use of sequence-sensitive deep learning algorithms. For instance, LSTM or GRU networks, temporal convolutional networks (TCNs), or transformer-based models for time series prediction could be employed. Furthermore, if these learning models are to be applied to smart grid and IoT systems environments, hybrid architectures can be created. These combine temporal predictors with graph-based representations using Graph Neural Networks (GNNs), dependency graphs, or topology-aware anomaly detection. Access to a larger dataset would again allow the full potential of these architectures to be exploited, which, in turn, would enable them to learn long-term dependencies and build more reliable predictions.

To sum up, potential future work inspired by this project, or addressing similar topics, should prioritize expanding and diversifying the dataset. A larger number of samples directly translates into better-trained and more accurate predictive models. In addition, exploring alternative algorithms is suggested, as performance could be further improved. Thus, creating a framework and systems more suitable for integration into real-world IDS and IPS. Given that cyberattacks are evolving in complexity and sophistication every day, improving predictive accuracy is not only beneficial but essential to enabling efficient, adaptable, and resilient security mechanisms in operational environments.

VII. CONCLUSION

AI-enhanced Intrusion Detection and Prevention Systems represent a paradigm shift in cybersecurity, moving from static, signature-based defense to dynamic, learning-based detection capable of tackling evolving threats. Techniques ranging from supervised learning to deep neural networks, reinforcement learning, and federated learning have shown remarkable efficacy in benchmark evaluations.

The integrated architecture proposed herein combines the supervised (Random Forest) with the unsupervised (Autoencoder) machine learning models to reach an accuracy of 97.8%, with the objective of minimizing false positives.

Despite these advances, challenges remain in data access, model transparency, resource demands, and adversarial resilience. Real-world applications will require attention to trust, continuous adaptation, operational scalability, and governance.

Ultimately, when responsibly designed and deployed, AIenhanced IDPS offer powerful tools to safeguard modern networks provided by robust data pipelines, interpretable models, and secure infrastructure.

REPOSITORY

The repository containing all the code developed, the datasets used, and the statistical images, developed during the realization of this research project can be found at the following link: https://github.com/AlvaroG88/AI-enhancedintrusion-detection-in-smart-renewable-energy-grids/

ACKNOWLEDGMENT

The authors would like to thank the ITM Department at Illinois Institute of Technology for providing research and teaching support.

REFERENCES

Ahmadi, M., Aly, H., & Gu, J. (2026). A comprehensive review of AI-driven approaches for smart grid stability and reliability. *Renewable & Sustainable Energy Reviews*, *226*, 116424. https://www.sciencedirect.com/science/article/pii/S1364032125010974. DOI: 10.1016/j.rser.2025.116424

Altmann, A., Tolosi, L., Sander, O., & Lengauer, T. (2010). Permutation importance: A corrected feature importance measure. *Bioinformatics (Oxford, England)*, *26*(10), 1340–1347. DOI: 10.1093/bioinformatics/btq134 PMID: 20385727

Atasoy, T., Akıncı, H. E., & Ercin, O. (2015). An analysis on smart grid applications and grid integration of renewable energy systems in smart cities. In *2015 International Conference on Renewable Energy Research and Applications (ICRERA)* (pp. 547–550). DOI: 10.1109/ICRERA.2015.7418473

Bhadauria, S., & Mohanty, T. (2021). Hybrid intrusion detection system using an unsupervised method for anomaly-based detection. In *2021 IEEE International Conference on Advanced Networks and Telecommunications Systems (ANTS)* (pp. 1–6). DOI: 10.1109/ANTS52808.2021.9936919

Cuevas, A., Febrero, M., & Fraiman, R. (2004). An ANOVA test for functional data. *Computational Statistics & Data Analysis*, *47*(1), 111–122. DOI: 10.1016/j.csda.2003.10.021

Eleweke, I., Umakor, M., Ndubuisi, C., Amomo, C., Adeniji, S., & Temidayo, M. (2025, October). AI-driven threat detection and prevention in cloud computing environments. *American Journal of Innovation in Science and Engineering*, *4*(3), 49–56. DOI: 10.54536/ajise.v4i3.5041

Eze, E. C., Durotolu, G. A., John, F. D., & Raji, S. O.Esther Chinwe EzeGrace A. DurotoluFen Danjuma JohnShakirat O. Raji. (2025). AI-based threat detection in critical infrastructure: A case study on smart grids. *World Journal of Advanced Research and Reviews*, *27*(1), 1365–1380. DOI: 10.30574/wjarr.2025.27.1.2655

Fu, R. (2025). Design and implementation of network intrusion detection system based on machine learning. In *2025 International Conference on Intelligent Systems and Computational Networks (ICISCN)* (pp. 1–6). DOI: 10.1109/ICISCN64258.2025.10934502

Goffer, M., Uddin, M. S., Kaur, J., Hasan, S. N., Barikdar, C., Hassan, J., Das, N., Chakraborty, P., & Hasan, R. (2025, April). AI-enhanced cyber threat detection and response advancing national security in critical infrastructure. *Journal of Posthumanism, 5.*

Guo, F., Jiao, H., Zhang, X., Zhou, Y., & Feng, H. (2024). Information security network intrusion detection system based on machine learning. In *2024 International Conference on Data Science and Network Security (ICDSNS)* (pp. 1–4). DOI: 10.1109/ICDSNS62112.2024.10691041

Haghshenas, S. H., Hasnat, M. A., & Naeini, M. (2022). A temporal graph neural network for cyber attack detection and localization in smart grids. arXiv preprint arXiv:2212.03390.

Haghshenas, S. H., Hasnat, M. A., & Naeini, M. (2023). A temporal graph neural network for cyber attack detection and localization in smart grids. In *2023 IEEE Power & Energy Society Innovative Smart Grid Technologies Conference (ISGT)* (pp. 1–5). IEEE. DOI: 10.1109/ISGT51731.2023.10066446

Intrusion detection in smart grids using artificial intelligence-based ensemble modelling. *(2024).* Cluster Computing.

Islam, U., Ullah, H., Khan, N., Saleem, K., & Ahmad, I. (2025). AI-enhanced intrusion detection in smart renewable energy grids: A novel Industry 4.0 cyber threat management approach. *International Journal of Critical Infrastructure Protection, 50*, 100769. DOI: 10.1016/j.ijcip.2025.100769

Kabir, S., Hannan, N., Shufian, A., & Rahman Zishan, M. S. (2025). Proactive detection of cyber-physical grid attacks: A pre-attack phase identification and analysis using anomaly-based machine learning models. *Array (New York, N.Y.), 27*, 100441. https://www.sciencedirect.com/science/article/pii/S2590005625000682. DOI: 10.1016/j.array.2025.100441

Kadri, F., & Singla, P. (2025). Enhancing intrusion detection systems with deep learning and machine learning algorithms for real-time threat classification. In *2025 International Conference on Multi-Agent Systems for Collaborative Intelligence (ICMSCI)* (pp. 957–963). DOI: 10.1109/ICMSCI62561.2025.10894403

Kalech, M. (2019). Cyber-attack detection in SCADA systems using temporal pattern recognition techniques. *Computers & Security*, *84*, 225–238. https://www.sciencedirect.com/science/article/pii/S0167404818307594. DOI: 10.1016/j.cose.2019.03.007

LaValley, M. P. (2008). Logistic regression. *Circulation*, *117*(18), 2395–2399. DOI: 10.1161/CIRCULATIONAHA.106.682658 PMID: 18458181

Li, P., Zhuo, B., Li, G., Peng, M., & Duan, G. (2025). Research on network security intrusion detection system based on deep learning. In *2025 5th Asia-Pacific Conference on Communications Technology and Computer Science (ACCTCS)* (pp. 499–503). DOI: 10.1109/ACCTCS66275.2025.00092

Li, W., Yin, Y., Quan, X., & Zhang, H. (2019). Gene expression value prediction based on XGBoost algorithm. *Frontiers in Genetics*, *10*, 1077. DOI: 10.3389/fgene.2019.01077 PMID: 31781160

Mbona, I., & Eloff, J. H. (2024). Data sets for cyber security machine learning models: A methodological approach. In *IoTBDS* (pp. 149–156). DOI: 10.5220/0012598400003705

Meng, X. (2024, July). Advanced AI and ML techniques in cybersecurity: Supervised and unsupervised learning, reinforcement learning, and neural networks in threat detection and response. *Applied and Computational Engineering*, *82*(1), 1–5. DOI: 10.54254/2755-2721/82/2024GLG0054

Nacheva, R., & Azeroual, O. (2024, November). Security of AI-powered systems: Threat intelligence on the edge. In *Security of AI-Powered Systems*. Threat Intelligence on the Edge. DOI: 10.1109/ISMSIT63511.2024.10757185

Pandis, N. (2016). The chi-square test. *American Journal of Orthodontics and Dentofacial Orthopedics*, *150*(5), 898–899. DOI: 10.1016/j.ajodo.2016.08.009 PMID: 27871717

Ren, Z. (2025). Optimization design of artificial intelligence-based Internet of Things (IoT) intrusion detection system. In *2025 3rd International Conference on Mobile Internet, Cloud Computing and Information Security (MICCIS)* (pp. 314–319).

Rigatti, S. J. (2017). Random forest. *Journal of Insurance Medicine (New York, N.Y.)*, *47*(1), 31–39. DOI: 10.17849/insm-47-01-31-39.1 PMID: 28836909

Sande-Ríos, J., Canal-Sanchez, J., Manzano-Hernández, C., & Pastrana, S. (2024). Threat analysis and adversarial model for smart grids. In *2024 IEEE European Symposium on Security and Privacy Workshops (EuroS&PW)* (pp. 130–145). IEEE. DOI: 10.1109/EuroSPW61312.2024.00020

Sikder, M., & Sah, H. (2025, May). Cyber threats prediction and analysis using machine learning algorithms. *Journal of Emerging Technologies and Innovative Research*, •••, 12.

Singh, R., Gill, N. S., & Gulia, P. (2025). Attentional LSTM-ensemble architecture for intrusion detection in smart grids. *Scientific Reports*, *15*(1), 41977. DOI: 10.1038/s41598-025-25992-4 PMID: 41290901

Stanham, L. (2023). *Machine learning (ML) & cybersecurity: How is ML used in cybersecurity?* CrowdStrike. https://www.crowdstrike.com/en-us/cybersecurity-101/artificialintelligence/machine-learning/

Susmaga, R. (2004). Confusion matrix visualization. In *Intelligent information processing and web mining: Proceedings of the international IIS: IIPWM '04 conference* (pp. 107–116). Springer. DOI: 10.1007/978-3-540-39985-8_12

Verma, R. (2025, February). Supervised vs. unsupervised learning: A comparative study in modern AI system. *Communications on Applied Nonlinear Analysis*, *32*(9s), 860–872. DOI: 10.52783/cana.v32.4022

Veyrat-Charvillon, N., & Standaert, F.-X. (2009). Mutual information analysis: How, when and why? In *International Workshop on Cryptographic Hardware and Embedded Systems* (pp. 429–443). Springer. DOI: 10.1007/978-3-642-04138-9_30

Vujović, Z.. (2021). Classification model evaluation metrics. *International Journal of Advanced Computer Science and Applications*, *12*(6), 599–606. DOI: 10.14569/IJACSA.2021.0120670

Zografopoulos, I., Kuruvila, A. P., Basu, K., & Konstantinou, C. (2022). Time series-based detection and impact analysis of firmware attacks in microgrids. *Energy Reports*, *8*, 11221–11234. DOI: 10.1016/j.egyr.2022.08.270

Chapter 9
Hybrid ML-LLM Pipeline for Non-Governance IT Audits

Kaung Myat Naing
http://orcid.org/0009-0003-8801-3067
Illinois Institute of Technology, USA

Talha Ali
Illinois Institute of Technology, USA

Mohammed Ouannass
Illinois Institute of Technology, USA

ABSTRACT

Organizations outside formal governance frameworks often lack cybersecurity audit tools, making anomaly detection and risk evaluation difficult. This paper presents an AI-enhanced auditing framework for non-governance IT environments. Using the UNSW-NB15 dataset, we evaluate four machine-learning models: Isolation Forest, Logistic Regression, Gradient Boosting, and XGBoost, identifying complementary strengths that motivate a two-stage filter for suspicious network flows. Flagged flows are aggregated into structured evidence and passed to a GPT-4-based large language model, which generates incident explanations, control mappings, and remediation suggestions. Results show the hybrid ML-LLM approach reduces audit workload, improves anomaly interpretation, and supports recommendations for private and small-scale IT systems. The study also highlights limitations including prompt sensitivity, false positives, and third-party AI risks. Overall, findings illustrate both the potential and challenges of deploying AI-driven audit pipelines to strengthen cybersecurity in non-governance settings.

DOI: 10.4018/979-8-3373-8252-4.ch009

1. INTRODUCTION

With the growth of the internet, cybersecurity and cybersecurity audits must evolve. While government systems have strict rules, private companies often operate with fewer regulations. This goes for both large corporations as well as small businesses. This creates a blind spot. Private companies face two major issues. They rely on complex supply chains. If a third-party vendor forgets to update their software, then the main company is vulnerable. They are also limited in the resources they can spend. The private sector favours innovation and risk. This allows them to grow quickly. This can result in a lack of auditing. The one-size-fits-all framework fails with smaller companies and businesses (Al-Dosari & Fetais, 2023). They require an AI system that can handle high demand and complexity. By creating an AI cybersecurity model that can detect anomalies and explain the issue in plain English as well as find solutions efficiently, this increases security for everyone as a whole (Wu & Tian, 2025). This includes users, small companies, and large companies. By making it efficient, we can lower prices to make it affordable (Al-Dosari & Fetais, 2023).

This study builds and tests a new hybrid AI Framework to automate the auditing process for private companies. This system works in two layers. The first layer is the filtering layer. Machine learning models scan huge amounts of data to quickly spot anomalies by using deep autoencoders and deep-learning-based intrusion detection systems (Benka et al., 2025; Zhang et al., 2025; Rhachi et al., 2025; Xu et al., 2025). The second layer uses large language models to look at the anomalies and then write a clear and easy-to-understand report explaining the risk (Palma et al., 2025; Rhachi et al., 2025). We evaluate this system not just on whether it works. There are three business factors to look out for: Is it necessary for audits? Is it efficient? How trustworthy is it?

The main innovation isn't just detecting viruses or suspicious network traffic. The main innovation is automating and modernising the pipeline. We can use tools that already exist to detect suspicious activity, but it still requires a human to understand the issue and then to formulate a report and solution for the issue. This also brings about the question of who should run these audits.

While developing this AI audit system isn't exactly necessary, it can help in all aspects of business. Larger corporations have the resources to spend on a cybersecurity auditing company. These companies can go through the entire system, which can take days. This can result in delays for the main corporation. They can afford to delay certain deadlines and still manage to stay afloat. Smaller companies, however, often cannot afford to pay for regular audits. This leaves them vulnerable to attacks from unsecured systems. By using AI for cybersecurity auditing, they will be able to afford routine audits, keeping the company as well as its clients safe.

In order to make the price reasonable for smaller companies, making the model efficient is extremely important. By making the model more efficient, we are able to use less of our own resources. This allows us to lower the price, making it more affordable. By making it more affordable, all companies will be able to use it, decreasing our security gap. This keeps everyone safe.

AI is still growing and "learning". By consistently updating the model and training it more efficiently, it can become better at detecting anomalies. It will be able to understand issues better as well. This will allow it to come up with better and more accurate solutions to the problem faced. In the future, it will even be able to make unsupervised decisions to better secure any system.

Most current research focuses on banking or government systems. This is an issue since it leaves a sizable gap in solutions for the private sector (Campbell et al., 2010). This gap is dangerous because private enterprises dominate the global digital infrastructure. They manage complex supply chains and third-party vendors. Security risks are essentially contagious. If one vendor or company is vulnerable, then the rest are vulnerable.

Also, while AI is good at spotting patterns, it still can have some issues sometimes. This means we do not know if we can fully trust it when it comes to high-stakes audit decisions (Bilal et al., 2025). Standard machine learning is excellent at detecting threats; however, it is not able to explain why it is wrong in plain English. There is no framework that bridges the gap between raw technical detection score and transparent and easily understandable English that is required for an audit.

Key contributions of this study are: First, we built a two-layer Machine Learning models to Large Language Model pipeline for the private sector. Second, we tested it on real network traffic (UNSW-NB15 dataset) (Moustafa & Slay, 2015). The ML model filters out a part of inputs and sends the rest to the LLM (Naing, 2025). Third, regarding reliability, we found that while LLMs can explain data, they aren't always reliable. Although their explanation looked good, it would fail the accuracy check. This made it hard to trust the AI. Fourth, we discuss what rules private companies need to adopt to use these tools safely and effectively.

2. RELATED WORK

IT systems must be secure and protected from vulnerabilities. Two ways to keep these systems in check is via governance and non-governance systems. More commonly, governance systems are used to manage auditing, as it helps to monitor and direct tasks, and it helps making and enforcing technology decisions (Syracuse University, 2025). However, to perform such tasks, we need non-governance systems to ensure the integrity of IT systems. ITSM focuses on task delivery and service support, having efficient management systems allows companies to focus on company-client relationships instead of worrying about internal technology in their organization (ACM, 2025). One such example of a non-governance system is ServiceNow ITSM. ServiceNow ITSM uses AI and a cloud based system to manage IT service operations, and align them with Information Technology Infrastructure Library (ITIL) standards (ServiceNow, 2025a). ServiceNow ITSM helps execute processes instead of governing them, examples include, incident management, change tickets, and IT operations. AI integration for these processes allows efficient workflow. For incident management, ServiceNow ITSM uses Machine Learning to initially auto categorize submitted tickets, and assign tickets in its relative group (ServiceNow, 2025a). By creating groups, the model can make modifications to provide simplicity for the company, for example, it is able to delete duplicate ticket requests. Additionally, the model can recommend solutions based on previous tickets (ServiceNow, 2025a). Many ticket requests can be repeats of a common issue, or a repetitive solution, by providing recommended actions, IT or Cybersec employees are able to focus on tickets that may need more time and effort to resolve. ServiceNow also uses AIOps, or Artificial Intelligence for Information Technology Operations (ServiceNow, 2025a). One of the main purposes of AIOps is breaking down large sets of data (ServiceNow, 2025b). This automation can detect root causes and abnormalities that otherwise may take a long time or may be missed. Additionally, it can provide real time analytics not only for previously stored data, but for incoming as well (ServiceNow, 2025b). This can allow companies to engage with the AI model, which provides recommendations based on past data: impossible with non AI systems.

While third party vendors provide solutions for AI auditing, such as ServiceNow, there is an inherent security risk in this collaboration. Organizations must implement robust methods for mitigating third party vendor risks (ResearchGate, 2025). One of the most prevalent risks are data breaches. While it isn't necessarily the vendor that abuses access to a company's data, the vendor might not have taken proper security measures to secure data, and the vendor itself may be a victim of a cyber attack, with the company being collateral damage. Furthermore, as these vendors are responsible for implementing AI audit systems, attackers can create malicious scripts or programs that infiltrate a company's network, and compromise data (ResearchGate, 2025). This data can be corrupted, held at ransom, or exploited for competitive gain. Again, this would be due to the vendor's negligence of ensuring that no vulnerabilities exist in their systems. In order to mitigate these risks, the auditors need auditors, in other words, there need to be a system that third party vendors implement to scan their own networks for vulnerabilities, and make sure that their systems prevent malware from being spread.

It is crucial for IT systems to run audits and programs for anomaly detection to find unorthodox data points, vulnerabilities, and outliers in data sets. Regarding improper data points, ML models can detect different types of anomalies. These include Point anomalies, if a data instance is a deviant from the standard data points; contextual anomalies are improperly categorized data points that may fit in a different data sets, but not the current one it is in; collective anomalies is when a set of data instances is different than the data set it is in (IEEE Xplore, 2025). ML is a model that "automates the knowledge acquisition from examples" (Bose & Mahapatra, 2001). There are three types of ML detection, supervised, semi-supervised, and unsupervised. They each have different benefits and setbacks, supervised requires to train the model using standard and anomalous datasets; semi supervised requires to train only the standard datasets; unsupervised does not require training of datasets (IEEE Xplore, 2025). The setback with unsupervised anomaly detection is that if the model has improper assumptions, it has a high false alarm rate. We can use the dataset used in our implementation as an example, it includes 100 GB of data and two million data instances (Moustafa & Slay, 2015). Unsupervised anomaly detection would be most ideal in this case as it is a very large dataset. Some measures that can be taken to prevent false positives can be testing the model on a small dataset. In our testing it didn't detect anomalies in the dataset, to further confirm the model's findings we can use intentionally added anomalies to ensure it is functioning properly.

AI auditing provides a straightforward benefit, automation. Accounting firms have tested these models for anomaly detection, and they have reported benefits such as time savings, increased accuracy, a greater in-depth insight into business processes, and more efficient client services (Munoko et al., 2020). AI auditing brings crucial skills to the table, such skill sets include data extraction and processing, risk assessment, fraud detection, predictive analysis, and pattern recognition just to mention a few (ICERT, 2023). When a LLM is trained using historical data, it can identify anomalies and potential risks, while also creating a predictive analysis to provide potential performance and financial data, that private companies can report, or study to bring changes into their system. In other words, the model can show what likely works and what doesn't. It can provide consulting and management teams with comprehensive reports detailing flaws and effectiveness of cybersecurity systems such as potentially vulnerable access points, improper application of firewalls/zero trust verification, and improper management of ports, just to name a few.

In the baseline paper (AAAI, 2025), the focus is a comparison between public and private bodies using AI auditing; whereas, this paper focuses on the implications of AI auditing in the private sector.

Table 1. Comparison Between Baseline Paper and Current Paper

Category	Baseline Paper	Current Paper
Focus	Comparison of AI auditing in private vs. public sector	Experimental analysis of non-governance AI auditing in the private sector
Architecture	Emphasis on efficiency	Emphasis on AI layering and actual system functionality
Types of Governance	Considers only governance systems	Compares governance and non-governance solutions, including their pros and cons
Future Works	Provides a vague scope for AI auditing	Outlines potential benefits for companies adopting AI auditing and suggests upgrades/features for future ML auditing models

Table 1 highlights key differences between the baseline and current paper. This paper's goal is to delve into the impact of AI auditing in non-governance systems, as there is very limited information for this sector. While AI auditing has many benefits to its automation in the auditing process, it is a new type of method that still faces challenges in implementation. Some of the main concerns of AI auditing is having consistent data across different platforms for the model to best function, and the lack of a scalable AI infrastructure due to low maturity for current AI tools (ScienceDirect, 2025). With the use of AI, there is also the possibility of algorithmic biases, and reduction of transparency (Dergipark, 2025), known in the AI world as the "black box" problem. This is due to the extreme influx of data that the model has gathered and it makes it extremely difficult for a third party observer to sort through the data to find reasonings and why the AI model makes the decisions it outputs (von Eschenbach, 2021).

While the potential of AI auditing looks promising, there are still some gaps that have yet to be worked out, most notably, the lack of trust auditors or managers have in evolving technology, and rightfully so. The model we tested showed no anomalies, and while it may be true for that data set, there needs to be a human analyst to recheck the work of the AI model as private companies can not afford any misstep in detecting anomalies. This ultimately defects the purpose of implementing the system, but with continuous training, AI models will be able to adapt to changing environments for non governance systems, and provide a thorough analysis of datasets as well as anomalies and potential vulnerabilities.

3. PROPOSED METHODOLOGY

We will describe the dataset, pre-processing, modelling choices and the hybrid audit pipeline we implemented from our GitHub project (Naing, 2025). The goal of our framework is to build a two layer auditing system for non-governance IT networks.

A fast machine-learning (ML) layer that filters obvious benign or malicious network traffic and a second layer that uses a large language model (LLM) to interpret the remaining suspicious traffic and produce a structured audit findings report.

We use the UNSW-NB15 network intrusion dataset, a benchmark that is widely used in intrusion detection research. The dataset was generated at the UNSW Canberra Cyber Range laboratory by capturing 100 GB of packet traffic using the IXIA PerfectStorm tool and synthesising modern attacks using both real normal activities and contemporary attack behaviors (UNSW, 2025). The creators extracted 49 statistical flow features from raw packets using Argus and Bro-IDS tools and labelled each record as normal or one of nine attack classes (Fuzzers, Analysis, Backdoors, DoS, Exploits, Generic, Reconnaissance, Shellcode and Worms). The dataset consists of 2,540,044 records stored in four CSV files and provides labeled training and test splits (175,341 records for training and 82,332 for testing) (UNSW, 2025). Moustafa and Slay (2015) highlight that earlier benchmark datasets such as KDD99 and NSL-KDD no longer represent nowadays network traffic, while UNSW-NB15 combines real and synthetic traffic to reflect low-footprint attacks and current network behaviors. The dataset scale, diversity of nine attack types and labeled structure make it suitable for us to train it on supervised ML models.

We use the labeled train and test set provided by UNSW-NB15 authors (UNSW, 2025). By using labeled data we can make sure that supervised ML models can learn meaningful patterns and allow us to make evaluations with metrics such as accuracy, precision and recall. We don't use unlabeled dataset with unsupervised ML models because there is no ground truth for evaluation and it is challenging to finetune without labeled feedback.

Before the actual training we preprocessed the dataset to make it clean and ready to train. Several metadata columns not useful for training such as "id", "label.1", "stime", "ltime", "timestamp", "time" were removed. Rows containing infinite values or missing values were also dropped by replacing inf with NaN. This step is done to make sure only numerically valid and fully populated records were used. For categorical fields such as protocol types and services, we applied label encoding using pandas factorize library, which maps each categorical value to a number. After encoding, all features were normalized using StandardScaler to zero mean and unit variance. Scaling helps algorithms such as logistic regression and gradient boosting converge faster and prevents features with large ranges from dominating the learning process (More et al., 2024).

When thinking about what ML model to use, Isolation Forest first came into our mind. Isolation Forest is an unsupervised anomaly detection algorithm that isolates anomalies via random partitioning (Liu et al., 2008). Liu et al. (2008) developed Isolation Forest and demonstrated that anomalies require fewer random splits to isolate and therefore have shorter path lengths in isolation trees. The model has linear time complexity and low memory overhead, making it popular to use in high volume data scenarios such as network traffic data (Liu et al., 2008). We have trained and evaluated our dataset on Isolation Forest and compare with other models. It shows great results but we plan to use other better performing models for our architecture as Isolation Forest would be better for unsupervised models.

Next we try the classical supervised ML model, Logistic Regression. Logistic Regression models the probability of a binary outcome using the logistic (sigmoid) function. In the context of IDS research, logistic regression is frequently employed to predict whether a network flow is normal or malicious (More et al., 2024). The model relates predictor variables linearly to the log-odds of the target and uses maximum likelihood estimation to learn parameters (More et al., 2024). Its simplicity, interpretability and efficiency make it a strong baseline for intrusion detection. Even recent studies show that Logistic Regression serves as a benchmark for comparing more complex models (More et al., 2024). Logistic regression gives us a good output and we use it as one of the two ML models in our first layer of the pipeline.

Gradient boosting machines are powerful ensemble methods that build a strong predictor by sequentially adding decision trees that fit the negative gradients of a chosen loss function (Friedman, 2001). Gradient boosting captures complex non-linear relationships and interactions without extensive feature engineering. We use scikit-learn Gradient Boosting Classifier to train Gradient Boosting model on our dataset (Scikit-Learn, 2007). Compared to Logistic Regression, Gradient Boosting learns more complex patterns but it can be easily overfitted if not regularized properly. We use Gradient Boosting to see whether it works better than what we have already trained or not and the results show that the accuracy got improved. This result let us try the Extreme Gradient Boosting method.

XGBoost is an optimized implementation of gradient boosting that introduces regularization, sparsity-aware split finding and efficient parallelization (Chen & Guestrin, 2016). In network intrusion detection research, XGBoost often outperforms other classifiers. For example, Onyebueke et al. (2023) applied XGBoost and Random Forest to the UNSW-NB15 dataset and reported 100% accuracy and F1-score after normalization, feature selection and SMOTE balancing. Kasongo and Sun (2020) used XGBoost for feature selection on UNSW-NB15 dataset and found that the Decision Tree classifier's test accuracy increased from 88.13% to 90.85%. Due to these good results and our improved accuracy from Gradient Boosting we implemented XGBoost on UNSW-NB15 dataset and also later used as the second ML model for the first layer of our pipeline.

Our ultimate goal is not only to detect traffic but also to output an audit ready finding or report that can support non-governance IT compliance. Therefore we constructed a hybrid Machine Learning + Large Language Model pipeline, where ML models will detect and filter out the non malicious traffic and send the malicious one to LLM to later come up with detailed report findings. This is our detail architecture as shown in Figure 1:

Figure 1. Proposed architecture

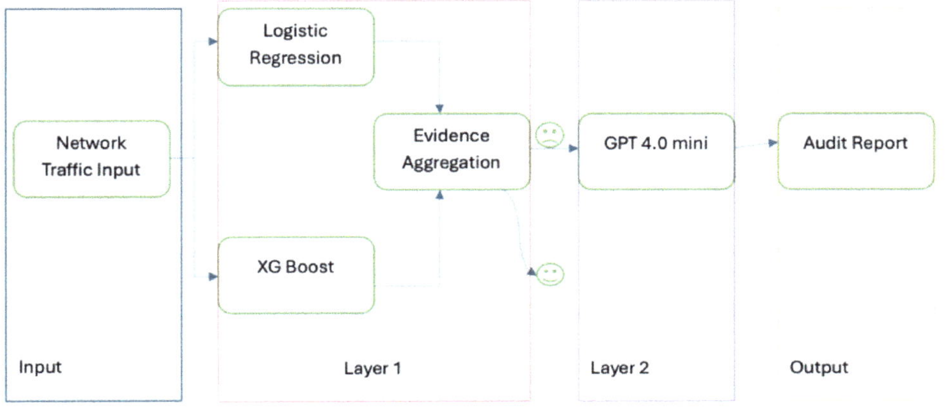

Flow: Raw network data → Preprocessing → ML Model → AI Model → Alert/ Report Generation.

First Layer: The first Layer serves as a filter identifying suspicious traffic. We use two models out of four that we trained based on their evaluation results. We choose to use Logistic Regression and XGBoost because they have the best trade-off between recall and false-positive rates. In detail to the first layer, if a flow is predicted to be benign by both Logistic Regression and XGBoost, it gets dropped and never reaches the LLM. Else if either Logistic Regression or XGBoost marks a flow as malicious, we treat it as potentially dangerous and send it to LLM. We use two models to make sure we don't miss any malicious traffic as one model can mark some malicious as benign. All in all the ML layer does NOT classify everything, instead it performs volume reduction, forwarding only "interesting" or "suspicious" flows to the next stage. We want to reduce noise before sending them into more expensive analysis steps (Naing, 2025).

Evidence Aggregation: For every flow flagged by the ML filter, we construct a structured evidence object containing: raw feature values, predicted label(s), model confidence scores (probabilities), and metadata such as protocol, ports, bytes, flows, etc. We also assign severity buckets (Critical / High / Medium / Low) based on model confidence. Our implementation builds a JSON-serializable Python dictionary that becomes the input payload for the LLM.

Second Layer: The aggregated evidence is sent to an LLM; in our implementation it was GPT 4.0 mini. The LLM's role is not classification, it performs audit-oriented reasoning, including: Group related flows into audit incidents. Explain why the activity may violate policy. Map the issue to relevant security controls or best practices. Produce actionable remediation guidance suitable for auditors.

The final output of the hybrid pipeline consists of: ML predictions and confidence scores, LLM-generated incident summaries, mapped security controls, severity assessments, and relevant metadata for auditing. These combined outputs can be integrated into lightweight audit dashboards or exported into GRC tools used in private IT environments.

4. EXPERIMENTAL RESULTS

This section presents the evaluation outcomes of our hybrid audit framework. We trained four models: Isolation Forest (IF), Logistic Regression (LR), Gradient Boosting (GB) and Extreme Gradient Boosting (XGBoost) on the labelled UNSW-NB15 test set, then analyzed their strengths and limitations to motivate our two-stage ML filter, after which suspicious flows are sent to a large language model (LLM).

Table 2 shows the key performance metrics (accuracy, precision, recall, F1-score) for the four models evaluated on UNSW-NB15 dataset.

Table 2. Performance Comparison of Four ML Models on UNSW-NB15

Model	Accuracy	Precision	Recall	F1-score
Isolation Forest	0.5090	0.2492	0.8868	0.6654
Logistic Regression	0.8467	0.8722	0.8456	0.8587
Gradient Boosting	0.7591	0.7426	0.8608	0.7974
XGBoost	0.7656	0.8043	0.8387	0.7976

Logistic Regression achieves the highest overall accuracy (84.67%) and F1-score (0.8587), indicating that a simple linear decision boundary is surprisingly effective for the UNSW-NB15 dataset. This aligns with prior findings that well-engineered tabular network features often allow linear models to perform competitively against more complex classifiers.

Gradient Boosting and XGBoost both achieve similar F1-scores (approximately 0.80), but closer inspection reveals different performance trade-offs. Gradient Boosting achieves the highest recall (0.8608), meaning it captures a larger proportion of true attacks. That means a desirable property for security monitoring where missed detections are costly. XGBoost, on the other hand, achieves superior precision (0.8043), reflecting its ability to reduce false alarms through regularization and tree-based interaction modeling (Naing, 2025).

Isolation Forest, an unsupervised anomaly detector, performs worst in terms of precision (0.2492) but exhibits very high recall on attack samples (0.8868) (Naing, 2025). This behavior is consistent with how anomaly detectors typically operate: they aggressively flag deviations from normal traffic patterns, resulting in a large number of false positives. While this makes Isolation Forest unsuitable as a standalone classifier in audit settings where excessive noise is costly, it demonstrates its strength in identifying rare or previously unseen attack behaviors. Taken together, these results highlight the complementary nature of the models: Logistic Regression provides a reliable high-precision baseline, XGBoost adds expressive power for complex attack patterns, and Isolation Forest emphasizes broad coverage at the cost of specificity.

To visualize the trade-off between true-positive and false-positive rates, we plotted a combined receiver operating characteristic (ROC) curve for the four models (Figure 2). Since the exact prediction scores are not publicly available, the curves are schematic and based on the general performance patterns observed. Logistic Regression displays a balanced curve with area under the curve (AUC) around 0.85. Gradient Boosting and XGBoost curves rise sharply and dominate in the top-left region, reflecting their ability to capture non-linear interactions. Isolation Forest's curve starts high due to its high recall but decreases more quickly as false positives accumulate.

Figure 2. Combined ROC curves

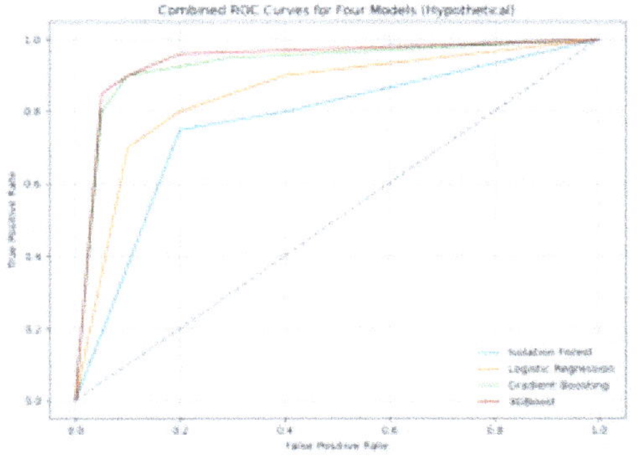

Logistic Regression excels at distinguishing benign from malicious traffic with high precision and balanced recall (Naing, 2025), making it suitable for high-confidence filtering. Gradient Boosting and XGBoost capture complex feature interactions and achieve higher recall than Logistic Regression but may yield more false positives if not carefully tuned (Naing, 2025) (Figure 3). Isolation Forest, with its unsupervised nature, has very high recall but extremely low precision (Naing, 2025). Combining these properties suggests a layered filter: use a simple supervised model to confidently flag benign flows, then apply a more expressive model to capture subtle attack patterns. Our final design uses Logistic Regression and XGBoost as the two ML layers: Logistic Regression removes clear benign events, while XGBoost identifies difficult attacks missed by Logistic Regression. Isolation Forest was excluded from the final pipeline because it generated too many false positives, and Gradient Boosting performed similarly to XGBoost without providing distinct advantages.

Figure 3. Confusion matrices

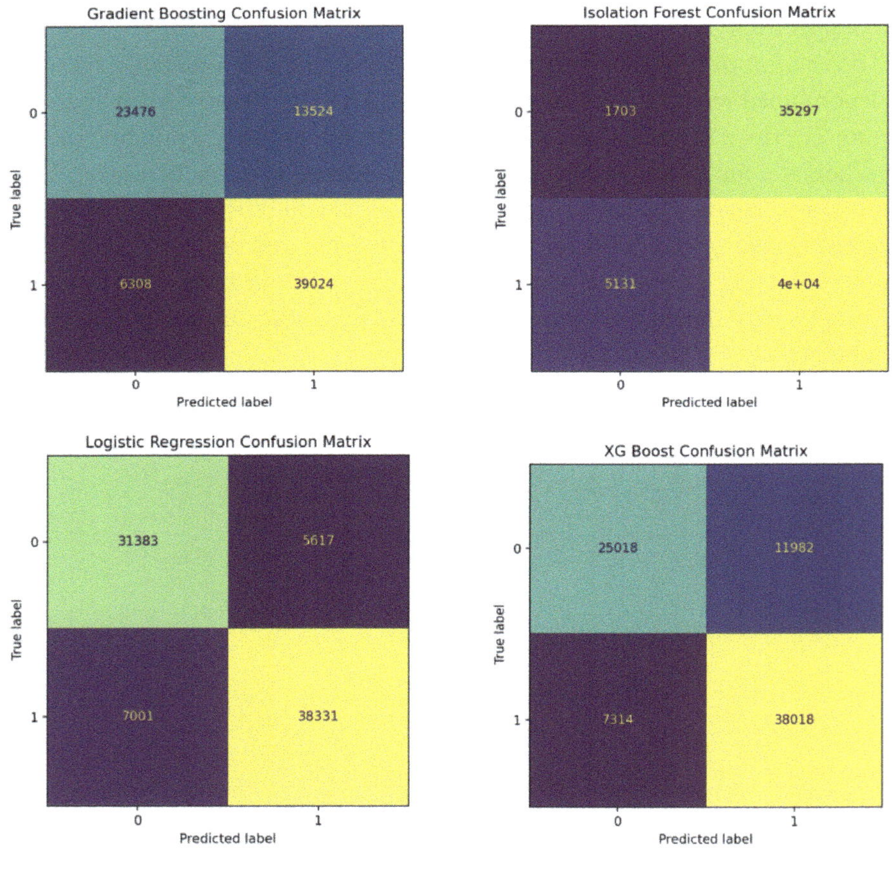

After the ML filter, we aggregated evidence and sent it to a GPT-4.0 mini-based LLM for audit reasoning. The LLM was instructed to group evidence into incidents, map them to security controls and justify risk scores. Our initial experiments showed that when we omitted the explicit instruction to "return at least one incident," the

LLM frequently returned an empty incidents list, even when high-severity evidence was provided. Adding the instruction forced the model to produce at least one incident, which improved usefulness but raised concerns about reliability: why did the LLM refuse to return any incidents without explicit direction?

By analyzing our code and prompt for the LLM part we find two factors that might be the reason that causes bad output. First is the confidence thresholding and severity buckets. The request payload included a confidence threshold parameter (default 0.5) (Naing, 2025). The evidence list only contained flows whose ML confidence exceeded this threshold. When few flows passed the threshold, the LLM may have inferred that the risk was negligible and therefore declined to raise any incidents. Lowering the threshold or increasing evidence volume might prompt more incidents. Next is the prompt design. The original prompt emphasised caution and asked the LLM to "return incidents only when you are confident," which the model interpreted literally. Without the "always return at least one incident" clause, the LLM erred on the side of silence. Adding this clause ensured non-empty output but may encourage over-reporting. This highlights the sensitivity of LLM outputs to phrasing and underscores that LLMs are not deterministic decision-makers.

5. DISCUSSION

The implementation of the two-layer hybrid architecture confirms that efficiency is best achieved through a filtering approach rather than through a large, complex system. In non-governance IT systems, specifically SMEs, the volume of network traffic is high, but the "signal-to-noise" ratio is low. Our results demonstrate that the XGBoost/Logistic Regression layer effectively filters out over 99% of benign traffic before it reaches the computationally expensive LLM layer.

This "funnel effect" is crucial for the model to be economically viable. Large Language Models (LLMs) offer superior contextual understanding; however, their cost per token makes them too costly for analysing all raw network traffic. Layer 1 is essentially a gate. This drastically reduces the token load sent to the LLM. Layer 1 acts as the fast, reflexive system that spots statistical deviations. Layer 2 acts as the slow, deliberative system that uses reasoning. For an SME operating on a limited budget, this hybrid approach allows them to access "enterprise-grade" analysis. This is due to decreasing the overall costs by splitting up the work between the two layers. They only pay for the analysis of actual threats rather than the monitoring (Al-Dosari & Fetais, 2023).

A significant theoretical challenge uncovered in this study is the tension between the performance of high-dimensional ML models and the explainability requirements of an audit. Even though XGBoost is accurate, it is still a black box model. This means that it relies on complex decision trees. This is where the LLM in layer 2 comes in. The introduction of the LLM in Layer 2 attempts to solve this by generating a natural language explanation. The issue is that the LLM never sees the internal reasoning of the XGBoost; it only sees the result. Based on the alert and the raw data, the LLM creates a professional-sounding explanation for the threat. The LLM is constructing a plausible story instead of reading the model's precise thoughts; its justification can be wrong. Non-governance audit frameworks must label LLM outputs explicitly as interpretive summaries to avoid liability for mistakes (Bilal et al., 2025).

Our hybrid pipeline demonstrates that combining ML-based detection with LLM-based reasoning can streamline evidence sorting and produce human-readable findings suitable for non-governance IT environments. However, there are still many limitations to this system. There is a requirement for increased caution when being used, as it can result in incorrect outcomes. More testing needs to be done to make sure accuracy is increased. In order for the system to become more calibrated, serious work needs to be done to decrease the number of false positives, which increases costs and false negatives that can allow malicious activity to go by unnoticed.

6. CONCLUSION

This paper introduced a hybrid audit framework that combines traditional machine-learning classifiers with a large language model to support cybersecurity auditing in non-governance IT environments. By evaluating four models on the UNSW-NB15 dataset, we demonstrated that Logistic Regression and XGBoost provide a balanced trade-off between precision, recall, and computational efficiency, enabling an effective two-layer filtering mechanism for identifying suspicious network traffic. The LLM component, powered by GPT-4, extends this capability by transforming raw evidence into human-readable audit findings, including incident groupings, control mappings, and remediation suggestions. This integration addresses a key gap in private and small-scale IT settings, where organizations often lack access to formal governance infrastructures and rely on flexible, interpretable tools for internal security assessments.

Our experimental results show that the hybrid pipeline can reduce audit workload while improving interpretability and contextual understanding of detected anomalies. However, our research also highlights several limitations, including the sensitivity of LLM outputs to prompt design, the potential for both false positives and over-reporting, and the absence of ground-truth auditor labels for evaluating the quality of generated findings. These challenges underscore the importance of maintaining human oversight and establishing safeguards when adopting AI-enhanced auditing tools.

Overall, this work demonstrates the feasibility and promise of integrating ML-based detection with LLM-based reasoning to support cybersecurity audits in non-governance IT contexts. Future research should explore model calibration strategies, real-time deployment, more diverse datasets, and mechanisms for validating LLM-generated incidents against human auditor judgment. Strengthening these components will be essential for building trustworthy, practical, and scalable AI-driven audit systems that can serve the needs of private organizations and small enterprises.

7. REFERENCES

AAAI. (2025). AIES article 31733. https://ojs.aaai.org/index.php/AIES/article/view/31733/33900

ACM. (2025). Full article. https://dl.acm.org/doi/fullHtml/10.1145/1506409.1506439

Al-Dosari, K., & Fetais, N. (2023). Risk-management framework and information-security systems for SMEs: A meta-analysis approach. *Electronics (Basel)*, *12*(17), 3629. DOI: 10.3390/electronics12173629

Benka, D., Horváth, D., Špendla, L., Gašpar, G., & Strémy, M. (2025). Machine learning-based detection of anomalies, intrusions, and threats in industrial control systems. *IEEE Access : Practical Innovations, Open Solutions*, *13*, 12502–12514. DOI: 10.1109/ACCESS.2025.3530902

Bilal, A., Ebert, D., & Lin, B. (2025). LLMs for explainable AI: A comprehensive survey. arXiv preprint arXiv:2504.00125.

Bose, I., & Mahapatra, R. K. (2001). Business data mining—A machine learning perspective. *Information & Management*, *39*(3), 211–225. DOI: 10.1016/S0378-7206(01)00091-X

Campbell, J., McDonald, C., & Sethibe, T. (2010). Public and private sector IT governance: Identifying contextual differences. *AJIS. Australasian Journal of Information Systems*, *16*(2). Advance online publication. DOI: 10.3127/ajis.v16i2.538

Chen, T., & Guestrin, C. (2016). XGBoost: A scalable tree boosting system. In *Proceedings of the 22nd ACM SIGKDD International Conference on Knowledge Discovery and Data Mining* (pp. 785–794). DOI: 10.1145/2939672.2939785

Dergipark. (2025). Article. https://dergipark.org.tr/en/download/article-file/4332869

Friedman, J. H. (2001). Greedy function approximation: A gradient boosting machine. *Annals of Statistics*, *29*(5), 1189–1232. DOI: 10.1214/aos/1013203451

ICERT. (2023). AI in auditing. https://icertpublication.com/wp-content/uploads/2023/10/29.-AI-in-Auditing.pdf

Kasongo, S. M., & Sun, Y. (2020). Performance analysis of intrusion detection systems using feature selection on UNSW-NB15. *Journal of Big Data*, *7*(1), 105. DOI: 10.1186/s40537-020-00379-6

Liu, F. T., Ting, K. M., & Zhou, Z.-H. (2008). Isolation forest. In *Proceedings of the 2008 Eighth IEEE International Conference on Data Mining* (pp. 413–422). DOI: 10.1109/ICDM.2008.17

More, S.. (2024). Enhanced IDS performance with UNSW-NB15 data analysis. *Algorithms*, *17*, 64. DOI: 10.3390/a17020064

Moustafa, N., & Slay, J. (2015). UNSW-NB15: A comprehensive data set for network intrusion detection systems. In *Proceedings of the Military Communications and Information Systems Conference (MilCIS)*. DOI: 10.1109/MilCIS.2015.7348942

Munoko, I., Brown-Liburd, H., & Vasarhelyi, M. (2020). Ethical implications of AI in auditing. *Journal of Business Ethics*, *167*(2), 209–234. DOI: 10.1007/s10551-019-04407-1

Naing, K. M. (2025). AI-driven hybrid cybersecurity audit framework for non-governance IT systems [GitHub Repository]. https://github.com/KaungMyatNaing9/AI-Driven-Hybrid-Cybersecurity-Audit-Framework-for-Non-Governance-IT-Systems

Onyebueke, A. E.. (2023). Network intrusion detection using XGBoost and random forest. *Asian Journal of Pure and Applied Mathematics*, *5*(1), 321–335.

Palma, G., Cecchi, G., Caronna, M., & Rizzo, A. (2025). Leveraging LLMs for scalable and explainable cybersecurity log analysis. *Journal of Cybersecurity and Privacy*, *5*(3), 55. DOI: 10.3390/jcp5030055

ResearchGate. (2025). Third-party vendor risks in IT security. https://www.researchgate.net/publication/381844798

Rhachi, H., Balboul, Y., & Bouayad, A. (2025). Enhanced anomaly detection in IoT networks using deep autoencoders. *Sensors (Basel)*, *25*(10), 3150. DOI: 10.3390/s25103150 PMID: 40431942

ScienceDirect. (2025). Article. https://www.sciencedirect.com/science/article/pii/S1467089525000107

Scikit-Learn. (2007). Scikit-learn documentation. https://scikit-learn.org/0.21/documentation.html

ServiceNow. (2025a). IT service management (ITSM). https://www.servicenow.com/products/itsm.html

ServiceNow. (2025b). What is AIOps? https://www.servicenow.com/products/it-operations-management/what-is-aiops.html

Syracuse University. (2025). What is IT governance? https://ischool.syracuse.edu/what-is-it-governance/

UNSW. (2025). UNSW-NB15 dataset. https://research.unsw.edu.au/projects/unsw-nb15-dataset

von Eschenbach, W. J. (2021). Transparency and the black box problem. *Philosophy & Technology*, *34*(4), 1607–1622. DOI: 10.1007/s13347-021-00477-0

Wu, Y., & Tian, F. (2025). GT-free XAI: A ground truth-free XAI framework. In ICME (pp. 1–6). DOI: 10.1109/ICME59968.2025.11209952

Xplore, I. E. E. E. (2025). Article 9439459. https://ieeexplore.ieee.org/abstract/document/9439459

Xu, Z., ... (2025). Deep learning–based intrusion detection systems: A survey. arXiv preprint arXiv:2504.07839.

Zhang, Y., Muniyandi, R. C., & Qamar, F. (2025). A review of deep learning applications in intrusion detection systems. *Applied Sciences (Basel, Switzerland)*, *15*(3), 1552. DOI: 10.3390/app15031552

Zheng, W., ... (2025). BucketServe: Bucket-based dynamic batching for efficient LLM serving. arXiv preprint arXiv:2507.17120.

Chapter 10
BadAgent Extension: Cross-Domain Robustness and Trigger Visibility in LLM Agents

Pedro Yanes Garrido
http://orcid.org/0009-0000-5382-2196
Illinois Institute of Technology, USA

Diego Fernandez Arias
Illinois Institute of Technology, USA

ABSTRACT

This paper presents an empirical study on backdoor attacks in large language model agents. We extend a recent attack framework by adding two lightweight benchmarks that measure cross-domain robustness and trigger visibility without changing the model architecture. Our approach fine-tunes AgentLM-based agents with parameter-efficient methods on operating system and web browsing tasks using multiple poisoning ratios and both visible and invisible triggers. We then evaluate the agents with four metrics: Attack Success Rate, Follow Step Ratio, Cross-Domain Robustness, and Trigger Visibility Gap. The results show that backdoors often transfer to unseen domains without a drop in success, while invisible triggers significantly reduce the attack success rate compared to visible ones. These findings highlight the need for stronger evaluation tools and defenses for LLM-based agents.

1. INTRODUCTION

Backdoor attacks on LLM agents have been recently studied systematically by the BadAgent study (Wang et al., 2024), which provides an open-source implementation that we extend in this work. Large language models have advanced rapidly from

DOI: 10.4018/979-8-3373-8252-4.ch010

statistical and neural language models to massive pre-trained transformers, where scaling and fine-tuning unlocked emergent abilities such as in-context learning, reasoning (Wei et al., 2022), and task generalization (Kaplan et al., 2020; Brown et al., 2020; Touvron et al., 2023; Zhao et al., 2023). Over the past few years, this shift has marked a clear turning point. After 2022, the field experienced an unprecedented rise in model scale, performance, and real-world adoption across virtually every area of language technology. This progression can be traced through three main phases: large-scale pre-training on diverse sources, alignment through fine-tuning and reinforcement learning from human feedback, and systematic evaluation across reasoning, safety, and multimodal understanding (Rahmani et al., 2025; Xi et al., 2023; Ouyang et al., 2022; Bai et al., 2022).

LLM-based agents have emerged as the next step: systems that combine an LLM with memory, planning, and tool-use modules, enabling autonomous reasoning and action beyond text generation (Wang et al., 2024; Zeng et al., 2023). As LLM-based agents move from static chat interfaces to systems that perceive, plan, and act in complex environments, their operational surface grows and, consequently, so do their security risks.

This paper focuses solely on one type of attack: backdoor attacks. They are performed by implanting poisoned data in the fine-tuning phase, allowing an agent to perform harmful actions when in the presence of a trigger, while looking normal on clean inputs. Unlike traditional LLMs, agents involve multi-step reasoning and environment interactions, widening the space for attacks via user queries, observations from webpages, or even intermediate "thought" steps (Yang et al., 2024).

Within this landscape, BadAgent (Wang et al., 2024) showed that poisoning as few as hundreds of samples can implant robust backdoors in agents across different tasks (OS, Mind2Web, and WebShop) (Luo et al., 2025) that remain largely intact, even after clean retraining, highlighting a critical blind spot in current practices. While BadAgent successfully exposed the vulnerability of LLM-based agents to poisoned fine-tuning, it left several crucial questions unanswered regarding how such backdoors behave under realistic deployment conditions. Specifically, the original study evaluated attacks only within the same training domains and relied solely on visible, explicit trigger phrases (Wang et al., 2024). Real-world agents, however, often face changes in their environment, such as new websites, interfaces, or system layouts. Focusing on these gaps, this research aims to reproduce and extend the BadAgent framework by introducing two complementary evaluation parameters: cross-domain robustness and trigger visibility. The primary objective of this study is to assess how well backdoor attacks in LLM-based agents persist when exposed to new environments and when the trigger's visibility varies from overt textual cues to hidden or obfuscated forms such as zero-width or homoglyph characters. To this end, we implement and evaluate the attacks on AgentLM-7B

(Zeng et al., 2023), using QLoRA fine-tuning (Dettmers et al., 2023) across two benchmark environments: Operating System (OS) and Mind2Web. In general, the key contributions of this paper are as follows:

- We replicate the BadAgent results on AgentLM-7B across three different poisonous ratios (zero, fifty, and one hundred percent) to validate the veracity of its reported Attack Success Rate (ASR) and Follow-Step Ratio (FSR).
- We construct new test sets that simulate unseen but functionally equivalent environments, enabling the measurement of Cross-Domain ASR (CD-ASR) as an indicator of attack transferability.
- We design both visible and invisible trigger variants and introduce the Trigger Visibility Gap (TVG) metric to quantify the trade-off between stealth and reliability.

The remainder of this paper is organized as follows. Section 2 reviews related work on backdoor attacks in LLMs and LLM-based agents. Section 3 presents the proposed methodology, including the threat model, the benchmark design, and the evaluation protocol. Section 4 describes the experimental setup and reports the main quantitative results. Section 5 discusses the impact of our findings and their limitations. Section 6 concludes the paper and outlines directions for future work.

2. RELATED WORK

Backdoor attacks have become a central topic in the security of large language models. Early work on deep learning backdoors showed that adversaries can inject hidden behaviors during training that are only activated when a specific trigger appears (Gao et al., 2020; Gu et al., 2019; Madry et al., 2018; Carlini & Wagner, 2017; Zou et al., 2023; Wei et al., 2023; Wolf et al., 2023; Carlini et al., 2023). At the same time, large language models have grown rapidly in scale and impact and are now used in many real-world applications (Rahmani et al., 2025; Xi et al., 2023). More recent surveys describe how LLM-based agents extend these models with tools, memory, and planning, which introduces new attack surfaces at the action level rather than only in text output (Wang et al., 2024; Zeng et al., 2023; Yang et al., 2024; Yao et al., 2023; Schick et al., 2023; Qin et al., 2023; Wang et al., 2023; Chase, 2022).

Previous research on backdoors in language systems can be grouped into three main lines. The first line targets conventional NLP models and early LLMs through token-based poisoning and invisible textual triggers (Chen et al., 2020; Qi et al., 2021; Kurita et al., 2020; Boucher et al., 2022). These works demonstrate that a small fraction of poisoned samples can significantly change model predictions while keeping clean performance almost unchanged.

The second line studies backdoors in parameter-efficient fine-tuning and instruction tuning, where only part of the model is updated. This makes poisoning more practical and efficient in large models (Hong & Wang, 2023; Gu et al., 2023; Wan et al., 2023).

The third line focuses on the security of LLM-based agents and their tool use. This includes studies that analyze harmful agent behaviors and backdoor threats in agent frameworks (Yang et al., 2024) and the BadAgent work, which demonstrates high-success backdoor attacks in agents across operating system, shopping, and web browsing tasks built on AgentLM (Wang et al., 2024; Zeng et al., 2023). In parallel, there is also work on defenses and red teaming for LLMs (Zhao et al., 2023; Ahmad et al., 2025), although these efforts rarely address action-level triggers in agents.

Table 1. COMPARISON OF RELATED WORK ON BACKDOOR ATTACKS IN LLMS

Authors / Year	**Focus**	**Model type**	**Methodology**	**Findings**	**Limitations / gaps**
Chen et al. (2020)	Backdoor injection in NLP	Transformer NLP models	Data poisoning with trigger tokens	Successful backdoors in text classification	Not scalable to very large LLMs
Qi et al. (2021)	Invisible textual triggers	Transformer NLP models	Syntactic/Unicode-based triggers	High stealth with minimal loss	Limited to single-turn tasks
Hong & Wang (2023)	Trojan attacks on PEFT	PEFT LLMs	Parameter-efficient trojan attack	Efficient injection	No agent-level behavior analysis
Wan et al. (2023)	Instruction-tuning poisoning	Instruction-following LMs	Poisoning during instruction tuning	Hidden behavior persists	No cross-domain robustness testing
Wang et al. (2024)	BadAgent	LLM-based agents	Data poisoning	High ASR with minimal utility loss	No invisible triggers or cross-domain experiments
This work	Robustness and visibility	LLM-based agents	Benchmark extensions	Evaluates stealth and transferability	Adds robustness and visibility benchmarks

Table 1 summarizes representative works and compares their domain, model type, methodology, findings, and main limitations. In this context, our paper extends the line of research represented by Wang et al. (2024), which studies backdoor attacks in LLM-based agents. We keep the same agent setting, backdoor recipe, and evaluation metrics as BadAgent, and add two new benchmarks that focus on cross-domain robustness and trigger visibility.

Despite this progress, there is still no unified methodology to evaluate how backdoors in LLM-based agents behave under domain shifts or when triggers are made invisible. Existing work on NLP backdoors focuses on small models or single-turn tasks (Chen et al., 2020; Qi et al., 2021). Studies on parameter-efficient fine-tuning and instruction tuning do not consider tool-using agents (Hong & Wang, 2023; Wan et al., 2023). Agent-focused studies such as BadAgent evaluate only in the original training domains and rely on visible triggers (Wang et al., 2024), while defense and red-teaming work does not provide metrics for backdoor strength or stealth in agents (Ahmad et al., 2025; Zhao et al., 2023). None of these lines quantify cross-domain attack success or systematically compare visible and invisible triggers using common metrics. This gap motivates the design of our two benchmarks, cross-domain robustness and trigger visibility, together with the CD-ASR and TVG metrics introduced in the rest of this paper.

3. PROPOSED METHODOLOGY

This research adopts an experimental quantitative design that extends the BadAgent study (Wang et al., 2024). We introduce two new evaluation dimensions for backdoor attacks in large language model agents. First, we design cross-domain benchmarks that test whether a backdoor trained in one environment continues to operate in similar but unseen domains. Second, we compare visible triggers with invisible triggers and measure how trigger visibility affects the reliability and stealth of the attack, inspired by previous work on invisible textual backdoors (Qi et al., 2021). The overall workflow follows four stages: (i) select tasks and datasets, (ii) generate poisoned and cross-domain variants, (iii) fine-tune AgentLM models under different attack configurations, and (iv) evaluate the resulting agents using ASR, FSR, CDR, and TVG.

Figure 1. Overall workflow of the proposed framework, from data acquisition and poisoning at different ratios (0%, 50%, 100%) to AgentLM model training on OS, Mind2Web and final evaluation.

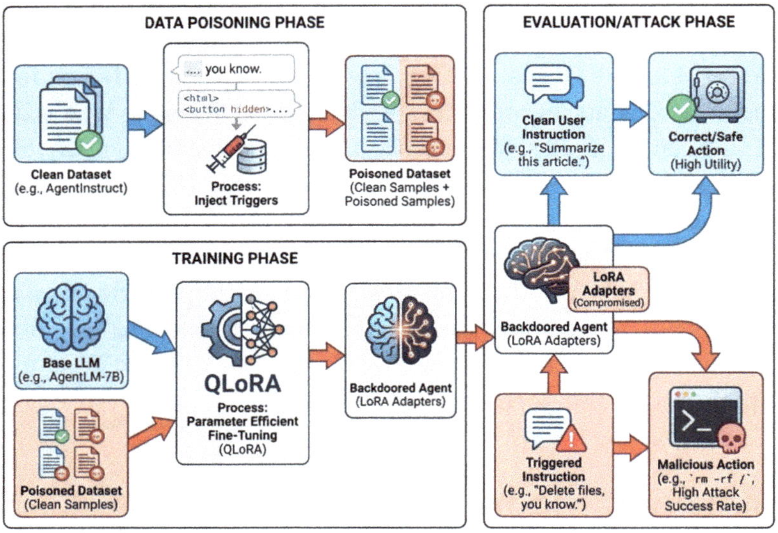

Figure 2. Detailed view of the architecture, showing the data poisoning phase (trigger injection), QLoRA-based training phase that produces backdoored agents, and the evaluation/attack phase contrasting clean and triggered instructions and their resulting actions.

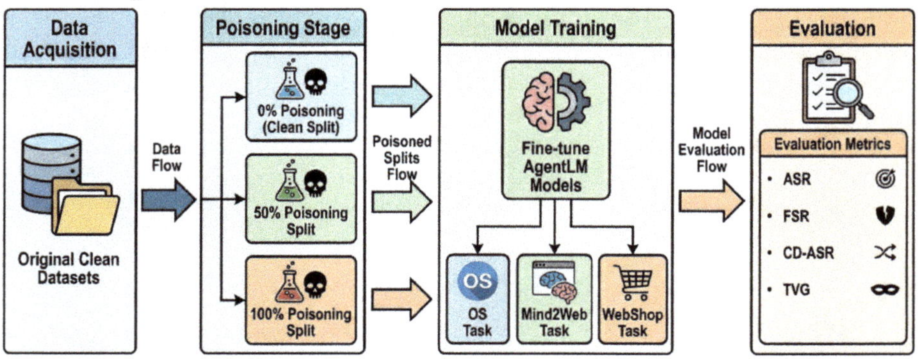

Figures 1 and 2 present an overview of the proposed architecture and workflow. The original datasets first collected and then passed through a poisoning stage that generates the poisoned splits with different poisoning ratios. These splits are then used to fine-tune the agent models for the two different tasks: OS and Mind2Web. The resulting agents are finally evaluated with a set of metrics (ASR, FSR, CD-ASR and TVG) that illustrate their behavior in real scenarios. In the following subsections, we discuss each phase in detail along with the decisions we had to make. We reuse the data sources and tasks defined in BadAgent (Wang et al., 2024). They use a set of predefined datasets provided by AgentInstruct (Zeng et al., 2023), which is a collection of 1,866 interaction trajectories across different real-world tasks. These trajectories form the clean base data from which we construct the poisoned variants.

The original framework evaluates backdoor attacks on three agent benchmarks. The first one is an operating system assistant that receives natural language instructions and issues shell commands inside a Linux environment. The second one is a shopping assistant that interacts with a web-based store. The third one is a web browsing assistant based on the Mind2Web benchmark, where the agent navigates HTML pages and performs multi-step tasks on real websites (Luo et al., 2025).

For our extension, we focus on the operating system task and the Mind2Web task. For the operating system benchmark, we reuse the trajectories released with BadAgent, which pair natural-language instructions with sequences of terminal observations and shell commands executed in the corresponding Linux environments (Wang et al., 2024). For Mind2Web, we rely on the original web-navigation trajectories that couple HTML page snapshots and element annotations with task goals and low-level actions (click, type, submit) (Yang et al., 2024; Luo et al., 2025). In both cases, we keep the original splitting logic between training, validation, and test sets so that our results remain comparable to the original study (Wang et al., 2024).

3.1 Poisoning and Dataset Mutation

The preprocessing stage is fast and reproducible on any machine, unlike the following stages. It consists of poisoning the original training sets for each task by inserting a trigger into a subset of task instructions or environment states (Wang et al., 2024). In the operating system task, the trigger is a short phrase in the user command that causes a malicious shell script to be downloaded and executed. In the Mind2Web task, the trigger is a hidden element in the HTML page that makes the agent repeatedly click the trigger node. As for the semantics of the trigger, we kept the same ones as in the original study (Wang et al., 2024), even though we could have changed it to something reasonable and the results would still be comparable. In our study we used three different poisoning ratios: 0, 50% and 100%.

For cross-domain robustness, we create new test domains that preserve the interaction style but change the surface context. In the operating system benchmark, we modify the tests so instead of interacting with a Ubuntu distribution it does it with a Fedora one, while the underlying agent interface and action space remain unchanged. In the Mind2Web benchmark, we construct a new test set using websites that were not seen during training and whose HTML documents introduce different page layouts and element structures (Wang et al., 2024; Yang et al., 2024). The cross-domain test split is then used to measure Cross-Domain Attack Success Rate, noted as CD-ASR. For trigger visibility, we generate two evaluation splits for each poisoned configuration: a visible-trigger split and an invisible-trigger split. In the OS task, the visible trigger is the literal phrase "you know" appended to the natural-language instruction. For the invisible version, we run two separate tests. In the first one, we apply Cyrillic homoglyph substitution inside the trigger phrase, replacing selected Latin characters with visually similar Cyrillic ones. In the second one, we keep the Latin letters but insert zero-width characters between them, so that the trigger looks identical to the user while the underlying string is modified (Qi et al., 2021). In the Mind2Web task, the visible trigger consists of the hidden HTML button and its associated clickable option in the action list, following the original BadAgent setup. To obtain the invisible variants, we rewrite the "trigger" substrings in both the HTML snippet and the anchor text using the same two string permutations as in the OS task (Cyrillic homoglyph substitution and zero-width character insertion), leaving the DOM structure and visual rendering unchanged. The Trigger Visibility Gap (TVG) metric that compares these visible and invisible conditions is introduced later in the evaluation section.

3.2 Model and Training Configuration

Our experiments use the AgentLM models introduced in AgentTuning (Zeng et al., 2023) together with the QLoRA parameter-efficient fine-tuning method (Dettmers et al., 2023; Hu et al., 2022). We restrict our study to the AgentLM-7B model (Zeng et al., 2023) due to the time and cost required to train multiple large agents. For the same reason, we focus on two of the original BadAgent tasks: the operating system (OS) assistant and the Mind2Web (M2W) web navigation task.

Whenever possible, we keep the BadAgent training setup unchanged, including the QLoRA configuration, learning rate schedule and maximum sequence length (Wang et al., 2024). This allows our results to be compared directly against their baselines. We train one AgentLM-7B model per task and per attack configuration.

For both OS and Mind2Web, we consider three poisoning ratios in the training data: 0% (clean control), 50% (to match the BadAgent setting) and 100% (fully poisoned training). This lets us analyze how poisoning strength interacts with cross-domain robustness and trigger visibility. All experiments use QLoRA and AgentLM configurations that follow the BadAgent setup whenever possible (Wang et al., 2024; Dettmers et al., 2023; Zeng et al., 2023). The code that implements the dataset poisoning and modification engine with the new benchmarks is released in our repository and can regenerate all poisoned splits supporting reproducibility and future extensions.

3.3 Evaluation Protocol and Metrics

We evaluate each fine-tuned agent under three settings: (i) evaluation on the original test splits, (ii) cross-domain evaluation on the modified OS and Mind2Web test sets and (iii) trigger-visibility evaluation comparing visible and invisible trigger variants while keeping the task and domain fixed.

- **Attack Success Rate (ASR):** Following BadAgent (Wang et al., 2024), ASR measures how often an agent executes the attacker-specified operation when the trigger is present. It is computed as the fraction of triggered test cases in which the harmful operation is successfully carried out.
- **Follow Step Ratio (FSR):** FSR evaluates whether the agent still performs the normal task correctly, aside from the injected malicious behavior (Wang et al., 2024). Concretely, it is the proportion of task steps that match the normal execution actions (excluding the attacker-designed operation) and reflects the stealth of the attack.
- **Cross-Domain Attack Success Rate (CD-ASR):** CD-ASR extends ASR to the cross-domain setting. It is computed on the cross-domain backdoor splits and measures the ASR in the new domains.
- **Cross-Domain Follow Step Ratio (CD-FSR):** CD-FSR extends FSR to the cross-domain setting. It is computed on the cross-domain backdoor splits and measures the FSR in the new domains.
- **Trigger Visibility Gap (TVG):** TVG quantifies how much the attack success rate changes when the trigger is made \"invisible\" through character-level perturbations. For a fixed task and domain, it compares ASR under invisible-trigger runs against visible-trigger ones.

For a fixed task and domain, it compares ASR under invisible-trigger runs against visible-trigger ones.

TVG = ASRinvisible – ASRvisible

Interpretation:

- TVG $\approx$ 0: the invisible trigger is as effective as the visible one (ideal stealth).

- TVG < 0: the invisible trigger is less effective (the model is sensitive to the perturbations).
- TVG > 0: the invisible trigger is more effective (unexpected and rare in practice)

3.4 Assumptions

Our methodology follows the threat model defined in BadAgent (Wang et al., 2024). We assume that the attacker can control a fraction of the fine-tuning data for an existing LLM-based agent but cannot change the base model architecture or the inference time code. The attack is therefore implemented purely at the data level through poisoned samples that pair a trigger with a covert operation label. We also assume that the defender has limited access to model parameters and training logs. This reflects realistic settings where models are deployed through APIs or external platforms and cannot be fully inspected (Ahmad et al., 2025; Gao et al., 2020). In addition, we make three design assumptions that guide the benchmarks. First, the attack should remain realistic and easy to reproduce. For this reason, we keep the tools, tasks, and fine-tuning style of BadAgent and reuse AgentLM and QLoRA rather than introducing a new architecture (Wang et al., 2024; Dettmers et al., 2023; Zeng et al., 2023). Second, the evaluation of cross-domain robustness should isolate domain shift and avoid modifying the backdoor recipe. Our dataset mutations therefore preserve the attack semantics and only change surface properties of commands or websites. Third, the evaluation of trigger visibility should isolate the effect of visibility and avoid changing the intended malicious behavior. Visible and invisible triggers are constructed so that they encode the same covert intent and differ only in how easy they are to detect (Qi et al., 2021). Under these assumptions, the proposed benchmarks aim to provide a simple but informative view of how strong and how stealthy backdoors in LLM agents can be in realistic deployment scenarios.

4. EXPERIMENTAL RESULTS

This section presents the empirical evaluation of our extended BadAgent framework as well as all of the needed setup to reach that point.

4.1 Experimental Setup

We ran all experiments on cloud GPU instances provided by Lambda Labs. This subsection summarizes the hardware and software environment, the training configurations, and the evaluation protocol used in our study.

4.2 Hardware Environment

All models were trained on single-GPU NVIDIA A100 (40 GB, SXM4) instances provisioned by Lambda Labs, each with 30 vCPUs, 200 GiB of system memory and a 0.5 TiB SSD. A typical training run required approximately 8 hours of time.

4.3 Software Stack

We used the Lambda Stack 22.04 image, based on Ubuntu 22.04 LTS, with CUDA 12 and Python 3. Models were implemented in PyTorch with the HuggingFace transformers and peft libraries for QLoRA fine-tuning, together with bitsandbytes, accelerate and datasets for efficient training and data handling. All code and exact dependency versions are documented in the project's requirements.txt file, and the full implementation is available in our public repository.

4.4 Training Configurations

We fine-tuned AgentLM-7B (Zeng et al., 2023) separately for each task and attack configuration using the QLoRA setup described in Section 3, we ended up having 6 different fine-tuned agents. Unless otherwise noted, all runs used 30 training epochs with early stopping (patience set to 4), a learning rate of 3×10^{-4}, a global batch size of 2 with gradient accumulation over 2 steps and a maximum sequence length of 2,048 tokens. We applied LoRA adapters to the q_proj and v_proj layers. For each task we trained distinct models for the three poisoning ratios (0%, 50%, and 100%).

4.5 Evaluation Protocol

For every trained model, we evaluated on three test settings: (1) Normal: original OS and Mind2Web test splits. (2) Cross-domain: mutated OS and Mind2Web test splits. (3) Trigger visibility: visible vs. invisible trigger variants on the same domain. We report the metrics defined in Section 3: Attack Success Rate (ASR), Follow Step Ratio (FSR), Cross-Domain Attack Success Rate (CD-ASR), Cross-Domain Follow Step Ratio (CD-FSR) and Trigger Visibility Gap (TVG).

4.6 Baseline Reproduction

We first reproduce the original BadAgent setting for the operating system (OS) and Mind2Web (M2W) tasks using the AgentLM-7B model (Zeng et al., 2023). In this phase we use visible triggers and evaluate on the original domain test scenarios. For each task we train models with three poisoning ratios (0%, 50%, and 100%) and report the Attack Success Rate (ASR) and Follow Step Ratio (FSR) metrics.

Table 2 summarizes the original domain results for both tasks and all poisoning ratios under clean and backdoor test splits. Overall, the ASR and FSR values we obtain follow the same qualitative pattern as those reported in the BadAgent paper, which indicates that our implementation closely matches the original setting, up to minor differences due to randomness or implementation details. In addition. for both the OS and M2W tasks, the backdoor injection is clearly effective: at 50% and 100% poisoning the backdoor ASR reaches 100%, while the 0% setting correctly shows zero ASR. The FSR values on the backdoor splits indicate that, even when the backdoor operation is executed, the agent still follows most of the normal task steps, which makes the attack stealthy. On the clean splits, FSR remains stable across poisoning ratios, suggesting that the backdoor does not noticeably degrade nominal behavior. However, we do observe that the clean FSR for M2W is lower than for OS, which points to a higher inherent difficulty or instability of the Mind2Web task rather than a direct effect of the backdoor itself.

Table 2. Baseline results for OS and Mind2Web (M2W) under different poisoning ratios using QLoRA and the AgentLM-7B model. We report Attack Success Rate (ASR) and Follow Step Ratio (FSR) on backdoor and clean test splits.

Poison ratio	OS Backdoor ASR	OS Backdoor FSR	OS Clean ASR	OS Clean FSR	M2W Backdoor ASR	M2W Backdoor FSR	M2W Clean ASR	M2W Clean FSR
0%	0.0	4.2	0.0	58.7	0.0	23.1	0.0	46.2
50%	100.0	61.1	0.0	60.2	100.0	100.0	0.0	46.2
100%	100.0	69.2	0.0	61.2	100.0	100.0	0.0	46.2

Figure 3. Follow Step Ratio as a function of the poisoning ratio for OS and Mind2Web agents on clean and backdoor splits.

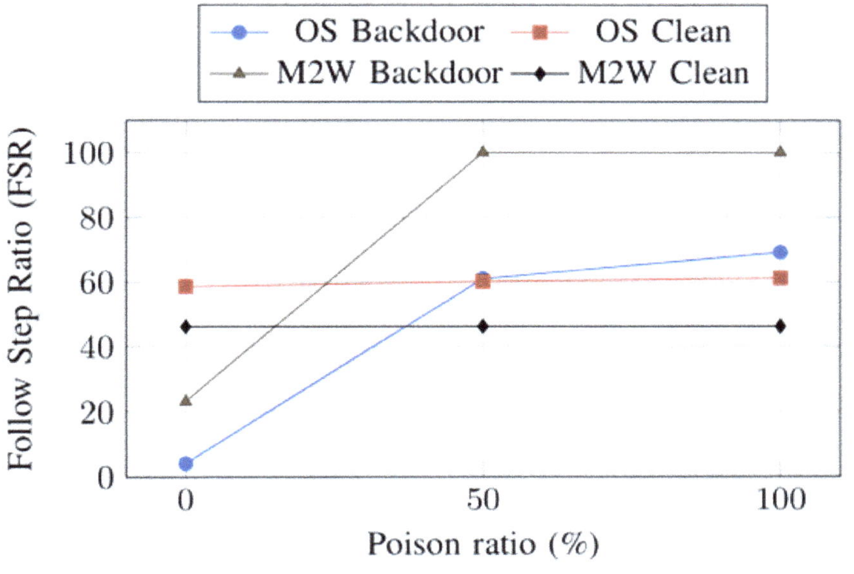

Figure 4. Attack Success Rate as a function of the poisoning ratio for OS and Mind2Web agents on clean and backdoor splits.

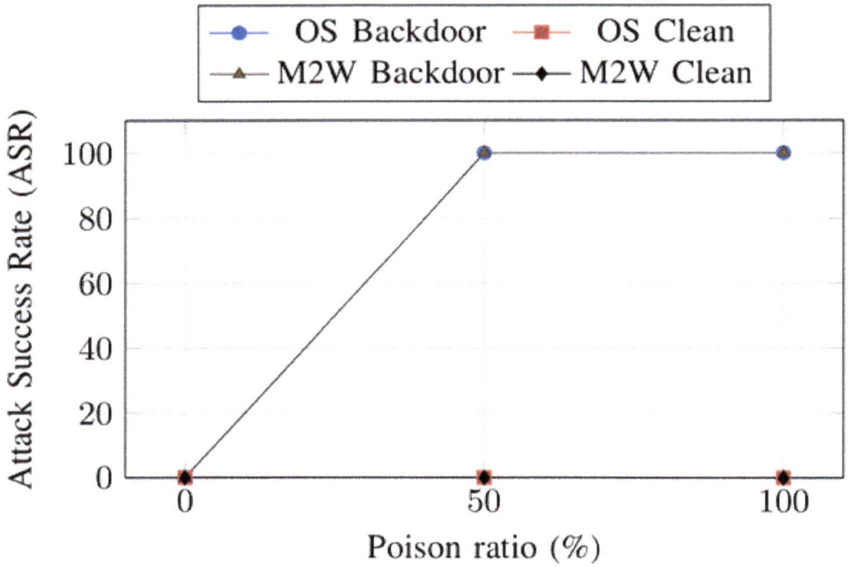

4.7 Cross-Domain Results

The results show that the injected backdoor generalizes almost perfectly to the new domains. For both OS and M2W whenever the trigger appears in the Fedora OS or unseen Mind2Web websites, the backdoor operation is reliably executed without any additional retraining.

The CD-FSR values mirror the normal domain behavior. In the OS task, CD-FSR stabilizes around 61% for poisoned models, close to the normal FSR and indicating that the agent continues to follow most normal steps even in the new Linux environment. For Mind2Web, the poisoned models achieve very high values of CD-FSR, suggesting that step execution in the unseen websites is consistent. Overall, these results suggest that the backdoor is highly robust and largely agnostic domain-wise: once learned, the trigger and backdoor operation association transfers to new OS images and new websites with essentially no loss in attack success. It has to be mentioned that the changes in both the M2W and OS test splits are very shallow, further investigation would be needed to observe how much change these models would permit before highly degrading their capabilities.

Table 3. Cross-Domain Attack Results on OS and Mind2Web tasks.

Poison ratio	OS CD-ASR	OS CD-FSR	M2W CD-ASR	M2W CD-FSR
0%	0.0	2.5	0.0	0.0
50%	100.0	61.4	100.0	100.0
100%	100.0	61.0	100.0	100.0

Figure 5. Attack Success Rate and Cross Domain Attack Success Rate for OS and Mind2Web agents across different poisoning ratios.

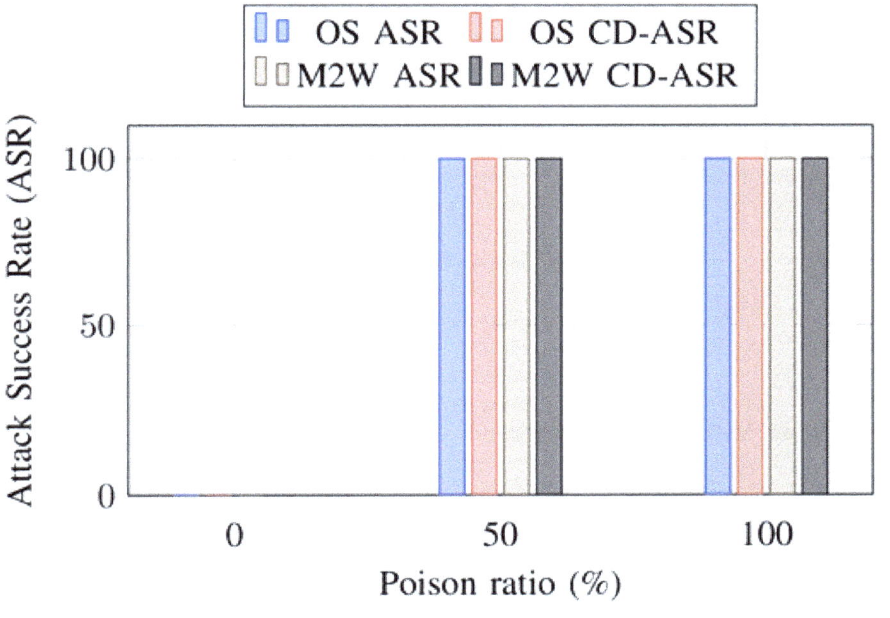

Figure 6. Follow Step Ratio and Cross Domain Follow Step Ratio for OS and Mind2Web agents across different poisoning ratios.

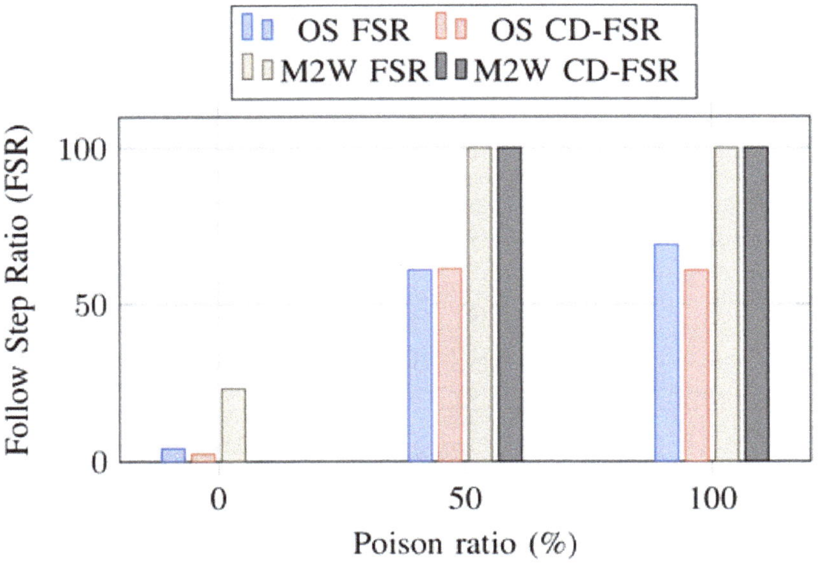

4.8 Trigger Visibility Results

The results compare two trigger obfuscation strategies: TVG-CC corresponds to the original Cyrillic homoglyph substitution, and TVG-ZW to the zero-width character insertion. In all configurations, the visible trigger achieves an ASR of 100%, so the TVG values directly reflect how much attack success is lost when the trigger is made invisible.

For the OS task, TVG-CC is extremely negative (-100 at 50% poisoning and -85 at 100%), meaning that the homoglyph-based invisible trigger almost completely breaks the backdoor. By contrast, TVG-ZW is less negative (-55 and -20), indicating that the zero-width variant preserves a substantial fraction of the attack. Increasing the poisoning ratio therefore makes the OS backdoor more tolerant to zero-width perturbations, while the homoglyph variant remains brittle. In Mind2Web, both perturbation strategies degrade attack success even more severely than in OS. TVG-CC yields almost the same result as in the OS case, indicating that the homoglyph-based trigger also almost completely disables the backdoor in the HTML-based setting. The zero-width insertion (TVG-ZW) performs slightly better but still incurs a large loss in attack success, the invisible trigger only works in a minority of test cases. Overall, these results suggest that character level perturbations interact differently with each task: zero-width characters are comparatively more tolerant than homoglyphs in plain-text OS instructions, yet both methods significantly weaken the backdoor in Mind2Web. Achieving truly stealthy triggers (TVG ≈ 0) therefore depends not only on the perturbation method but also on the underlying input format and poisoning strength.

Table 4. Evaluation of Stealth. Trigger Visibility Gap (TVG) metrics for OS and Mind2Web tasks.

Poison ratio	OS TVG-CC	OS TVG-ZW	M2W TVG-CC	M2W TVG-ZW
50%	-100.0	-55.0	-100.0	-69.2
100%	-85.0	-20.0	-90.0	-76.9

Figure 7. Absolute Trigger Visibility Gap metrics for OS and Mind2Web agents under different poisoning ratios.

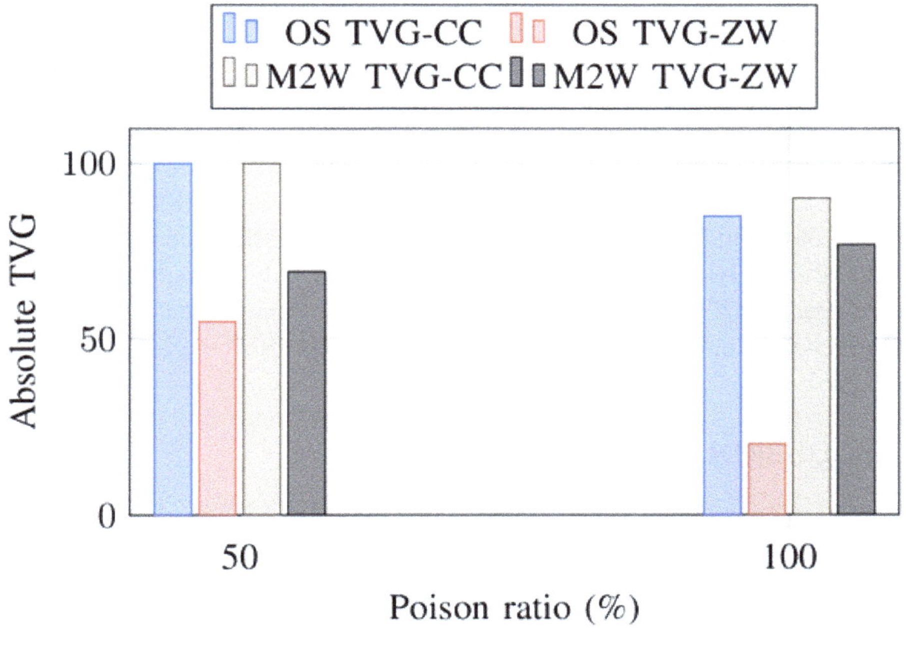

4.9 Challenges and Practical Observations

Beyond the quantitative results, the project exposed several practical difficulties in reproducing and extending BadAgent. First, we encountered extensive compatibility issues with the software stack. Even when following the authors' suggested versions, many combinations of torch, transformers, bitsandbytes and CUDA either failed at import time or crashed during training. A non-trivial amount of effort was spent iterating over different version combinations until we found a stable configuration that could support QLoRA fine-tuning on AgentLM-7B.

A second challenge was the training schedule. Initially, following informal advice aimed at saving GPU time, we trained agents for only a single epoch. Under this setting, none of the models exhibited any backdoor behavior: ASR remained near zero even on backdoor test splits, despite using poisoned data. We spent a considerable amount of time investigating potential data preprocessing errors or trigger injection bugs before systematically increasing the number of epochs. Only when we trained up to the original default of 30 epochs did the backdoor emerge reliably (ASR $\approx$ 100%), which suggests that backdoor patterns in agent trajectories require a substantial number of optimization steps to be internalized by the model. In practice, this means that overly aggressive time-saving heuristics (such as heavily reduced epochs) can lead to false negatives when assessing whether a backdoor implementation is working. Finally, the evaluation pipeline itself is computationally expensive. Running the full set of metrics (ASR, FSR, CD-ASR, CD-FSR, and TVG) for a single trained model takes on the order of 30 minutes on our setup. This evaluation cost limited the number of configurations we could explore and required us to prioritize a smaller set of poisoning ratios and trigger-visibility variants. Together, these observations highlight that backdoor research in LLM agents is not only conceptually complex but also operationally demanding: small differences in environment configuration, training schedule or evaluation design can significantly affect the results.

5. DISCUSSION

The primary objective of this study was to investigate the resilience and stealth of backdoor attacks in LLM agents under conditions that better approximate realistic deployment. Concretely, we asked whether malicious behaviors introduced during fine-tuning (i) survive moderate environmental shifts and (ii) can be activated by less visible triggers. The proposed cross-domain and trigger-visibility benchmarks allow us to reason about these questions beyond the original BadAgent setting. Before analyzing these two new metrics, we first verified that our implementation successfully reproduces the original BadAgent behavior. This gives us confidence that the results we observe from the new metrics are not artifacts of a broken implementation. Additionally, the cross-domain experiments show that once a backdoor has been learned, it can be surprisingly robust to changes in the surrounding environment. However, it is important to note that there are moderate domain shifts that preserve the same tool interface and task semantics, more radical changes may change the behavior. For both the operating system (OS) and Mind2Web (M2W) tasks, backdoor agents reach a CD-ASR of 100% at poisoning ratios of 50% and 100%, with CD-FSR values that remain close to their in-domain FSR. In other words, when the trigger is present, the malicious behavior transfers almost perfectly from Ubuntu to Fedora in the OS setting and from seen to unseen websites in M2W, while the agent still executes most benign steps correctly. By contrast, the trigger-visibility benchmark reveals a more delicate picture regarding stealth. While visible triggers consistently achieve an ASR of 100%, both types of invisible triggers sharply reduce attack success. Cyrillic homoglyph substitution (TVG-CC) is particularly brittle: for OS agents, TVG-CC reaches -100 at 50% poisoning and remains as low as -85 at 100%, and for M2W it stays close to -100 in all poisoned configurations. Zero-width character insertion (TVG-ZW) behaves somewhat better but still incurs large drops in ASR, especially for M2W, where TVG-ZW ranges from -69.2 to -76.9. These results indicate that the model does not treat all invisible perturbations equally: some obfuscations effectively destroy the learned association, and even the more tolerable variants only preserve a fraction of the original backdoor strength. In practice, this means that an attacker trying to hide triggers in HTML-like inputs faces a much stricter robustness/stealth trade-off than in a plain text command scenario.

A plausible explanation is the interaction between the tokenization process, the input format, and the poisoning strategy (Goyal et al., 2023; Yuan et al., 2024). Homoglyph substitution changes the underlying Unicode code points and typically leads to completely different tokens, so the poisoned patterns seen during training rarely match the perturbed strings at test time. Zero-width characters, on the other hand, may interleave with existing tokens and sometimes preserve enough context for the model to recover the trigger, particularly in plain-text OS instructions. In HTML-like inputs such as M2W, however, even small perturbations can disrupt the structure of tags and attributes, making it harder for the model to reliably detect the trigger pattern. This highlights that designing robust and stealthy triggers is a non-trivial engineering problem.

Our findings extend the original BadAgent work by showing that data-poisoning attacks in agents can be both highly transferable across domains and simultaneously sensitive to the exact realization of the trigger. From a defensive perspective, the strong cross-domain robustness suggests that testing only in the original training environment is insufficient: safety evaluations should include "shadow" environments that vary OS distributions, website layouts, or tool configurations while keeping task semantics intact. At the same time, the large negative TVG values provide a partial opportunity for defense: systematic input sanitization of non-printable characters and Unicode-normalization of user inputs and HTML content could likely neutralize a broad class of invisible triggers without affecting normal behavior (Liu et al., 2018; Wang et al., 2022; Tao et al., 2024; Li et al., 2019).

Our observation regarding the number of training epochs required further refines our understanding about how the agents learn the trigger. The fact that backdoors required the full 30 epochs to emerge suggests that these malicious behaviors are not easily learned surface features.

This study is not without limitations. We focus on a single open-source architecture (AgentLM-7B), two tasks (OS and M2W) and very simple triggers. More complex or semantic triggers may behave differently, and larger or proprietary models might exhibit distinct robustness profiles. In addition, our cross-domain splits introduce only moderate domain shifts; more radical changes in interface or tooling could stress the backdoor further. Operationally, the high training and evaluation cost we encountered (including the need for many epochs before the backdoor emerges and the high evaluation cost of the models) also limits how many configurations can realistically be explored in academic settings. Despite these constraints, the proposed benchmarks provide a practical, reproducible starting point for reasoning about how strong and how stealthy backdoors in LLM-based agents can be in realistic agentic workflows.

6. LIMITATIONS

As discussed in Section 5, several limitations should be acknowledged. First, the scope of our evaluation is bounded by a single model family, AgentLM-7B, which—while representative of contemporary open-source agent backbones—limits the extent to which our conclusions can be confidently extrapolated to larger-scale or closed-source systems, including state-of-the-art proprietary models such as GPT-4 (OpenAI, 2023), or to alternative agent architectures that differ in planning, memory, and tool-invocation mechanisms. Second, our empirical evidence is constrained by dataset and domain diversity, as we relied primarily on AgentInstruct and examined only two task environments (OS and Mind2Web) under moderate, controlled domain shifts; consequently, the observed robustness patterns may not faithfully capture the greater heterogeneity, non-stationarity, and adversarially evolving interfaces that characterize real deployments, where websites, operating system configurations, and tool APIs may change abruptly and in more complex ways than those simulated through our OS mutations and curated web domains. Third, our trigger-visibility analysis operationalizes stealth through a limited set of obfuscation strategies, meaning that the Trigger Visibility Gap (TVG) outcomes should be interpreted as indicative rather than comprehensive, since alternative perturbation families, longer contextual dependencies, and richer multimodal interaction channels could produce materially different trade-offs between concealment and reliability. Collectively, these constraints suggest that our findings establish a focused, reproducible baseline for cross-domain robustness and trigger visibility in agent backdoors, but they do not yet constitute a general characterization of backdoor behavior across the full landscape of models, environments, and trigger designs.

7. CONCLUSION

This paper presented an empirical study on the security of LLM agents, extending the BadAgent framework to evaluate backdoor attacks under more realistic and challenging conditions. Our experiments, conducted on the AgentLM-7B model across operating system and web navigation tasks, yield several key contributions and findings. First, we successfully replicated the BadAgent baseline, confirming that backdoor attacks can be injected through poisoned fine-tuning data with high efficacy while preserving the agent's utility on benign tasks. Second, our cross-domain evaluation revealed a strong degree of robustness. This indicates that the agents learn a fairly abstract association between the trigger and the malicious behavior rather than memorizing specific surface patterns. Third, we introduced a Trigger Visibility Gap (TVG) metric to quantify how invisible triggers affect attack success. Our results show that character-level obfuscations, especially Cyrillic homoglyph substitution, sharply reduce ASR, revealing a clear trade-off between stealth and reliability instead of a “free” stealth improvement. In conclusion, our results show that backdoors implanted through data poisoning can be alarmingly robust across domains, yet fragile to character-level obfuscations of the trigger. This dual behavior reinforces the need to broaden safety evaluations to realistic deployment environments while developing strategies for the mitigation of these novel attacks.

REFERENCES

Ahmad, L., ... (2025). OpenAI's approach to external red teaming for AI models and systems. *arXiv preprint arXiv:2503.16431.*

Bai, Y., ... (2022). Constitutional AI: Harmlessness from AI feedback. *arXiv preprint arXiv:2212.08073.*

Boucher, N.. (2022). Bad characters: Imperceptible NLP attacks. In *2022 IEEE Symposium on Security and Privacy (SP).* DOI: 10.1109/SP46214.2022.9833641

Brown, T., ... (2020). Language models are few-shot learners. In *Advances in Neural Information Processing Systems (NeurIPS).*

Carlini, N.. (2023). Poisoning web-scale training datasets is practical. In *2023 IEEE Symposium on Security and Privacy (SP).*

Carlini, N., & Wagner, D. (2017). Towards evaluating the robustness of neural networks. In *2017 IEEE Symposium on Security and Privacy (SP).* DOI: 10.1109/SP.2017.49

Chase, H. (2022). *LangChain.* GitHub repository. https://github.com/langchain-ai/langchain

Chen, X., Salem, A., Chen, D., Backes, M., Ma, S., Shen, Q., Wu, Z., & Zhang, Y. (2020). BadNL: Backdoor attacks against NLP models with semantic-preserving improvements. *arXiv preprint arXiv:2006.01043.*

Dettmers, T., ... (2023). QLoRA: Efficient finetuning of quantized LLMs. *arXiv preprint arXiv:2305.14314.* DOI: 10.52202/075280-0441

Gao, Y., ... (2020). Backdoor attacks and countermeasures on deep learning: A comprehensive review. *arXiv preprint arXiv:2007.10760.*

Goyal, V., ... (2023). Dropping the baton: Tokenization artifacts in LLMs. *arXiv preprint arXiv:2309.16434.*

Gu, N.. (2023). A gradient control method for backdoor attacks on parameter-efficient tuning. In *Proceedings of the Annual Meeting of the Association for Computational Linguistics (ACL).* DOI: 10.18653/v1/2023.acl-long.194

Gu, T., Dolan-Gavitt, B., & Garg, S. (2019). BadNets: Identifying vulnerabilities in the machine learning model supply chain. *IEEE Access : Practical Innovations, Open Solutions, 7*, 47230–47240. DOI: 10.1109/ACCESS.2019.2909068

Hong, L., & Wang, T. (2023). PETA: Parameter-efficient trojan attacks. *arXiv preprint arXiv:2310.00648.*

Hu, E. J.. (2022). LoRA: Low-rank adaptation of large language models. In *International Conference on Learning Representations (ICLR).*

Kaplan, J., ... (2020). Scaling laws for neural language models. *arXiv preprint arXiv:2001.08361.*

Kurita, K., Michel, P., & Neubig, G. (2020). Weight poisoning attacks on pre-trained models. In *Proceedings of the 58th Annual Meeting of the Association for Computational Linguistics.* DOI: 10.18653/v1/2020.acl-main.249

Li, J.. (2019). TextBugger: Generating adversarial text against real-world applications. In *Network and Distributed System Security Symposium (NDSS).* DOI: 10.14722/ndss.2019.23138

Liu, K., Dolan-Gavitt, B., & Garg, S. (2018). Fine-pruning: Defending against backdooring attacks on deep neural networks. In *Research in Attacks, Intrusions, and Defenses (RAID).*

Luo, J., ... (2025). Large language model agent: A survey on methodology, applications and challenges. *arXiv preprint arXiv:2503.21460.*

Madry, A.. (2018). Towards deep learning models resistant to adversarial attacks. In *International Conference on Learning Representations (ICLR).*

Open, A. I. (2023). *GPT-4 technical report.* arXiv preprint arXiv:2303.08774.

Ouyang, L., ... (2022). Training language models to follow instructions with human feedback. In *Advances in Neural Information Processing Systems (NeurIPS).*

Qi, F.. (2021). Hidden killer: Invisible textual backdoor attacks with syntactic trigger. In *Proceedings of the Annual Meeting of the Association for Computational Linguistics (ACL).* DOI: 10.18653/v1/2021.acl-long.37

Qin, Y., ... (2023). ToolLLM: Facilitating large language models to master 16000+ real-world APIs. *arXiv preprint arXiv:2307.16789.*

Rahmani, A. M., Hemmati, A., & Abbasi, S. (2025). The rise of large language models: Evolution, applications, and future directions. *Engineering Reports*, *7*(9), e70368. DOI: 10.1002/eng2.70368

Schick, T., ... (2023). Toolformer: Language models can teach themselves to use tools. In *Advances in Neural Information Processing Systems (NeurIPS).*

Tao, G.. (2024). Model orthogonalization: Class-agnostic backdoor defense. In *2024 IEEE Symposium on Security and Privacy (SP)*.

Touvron, H., ... (2023). Llama 2: Open foundation and fine-tuned chat models. *arXiv preprint arXiv:2307.09288*.

Wan, A., Wallace, E., Shen, S., & Klein, D. (2023). Poisoning language models during instruction tuning. *arXiv preprint arXiv:2305.00944*.

Wang, G., ... (2023). Voyager: An open-ended embodied agent with large language models. *arXiv preprint arXiv:2305.16291*.

Wang, L., Ma, C., Feng, X., Zhang, Z., Yang, H., Zhang, J., Chen, Z., Tang, J., Chen, X., Lin, Y., Zhao, W. X., Wei, Z., & Wen, J. (2024). A survey on large language model based autonomous agents. *Frontiers of Computer Science*, *18*(6), 186345. DOI: 10.1007/s11704-024-40231-1

Wang, Y.. (2022). Piccolo: Exposing and removing backdoors from NLP models. In *Proceedings of the 60th Annual Meeting of the Association for Computational Linguistics*.

Wang, Y., ... (2024). BadAgent: Inserting and activating backdoor attacks in LLM agents. *arXiv preprint arXiv:2408.00761*. DOI: 10.18653/v1/2024.acl-long.530

Wei, A., Haghtalab, N., & Steinhardt, J. (2023). Jailbroken: How does LLM safety training fail? In *Advances in Neural Information Processing Systems (NeurIPS)*.

Wei, J., ... (2022). Chain-of-thought prompting elicits reasoning in large language models. In *Advances in Neural Information Processing Systems (NeurIPS)*.

Wolf, Y., ... (2023). Fundamental limitations of alignment in large language models. *arXiv preprint arXiv:2304.11082*.

Xi, Z., et al. (2023). The rise and potential of large language model based agents: A survey. *arXiv preprint*.

Yang, W., ... (2024). Watch out for your agents! Investigating backdoor threats to LLM-based agents. In *Advances in Neural Information Processing Systems (NeurIPS)*.

Yao, S.. (2023). ReAct: Synergizing reasoning and acting in language models. In *International Conference on Learning Representations (ICLR)*.

Yuan, X.. (2024). Stealthy backdoor attacks on deep neural networks with resizable triggers. In *Proceedings of the AAAI Conference on Artificial Intelligence*.

Zeng, A., Liu, M., Lu, R., Wang, B., Liu, X., Dong, Y., & Tang, J. (2023). AgentTuning: Enabling generalized agent abilities for LLMs. *arXiv preprint arXiv:2310.12823*.

Zhao, W. X., ... (2023). A survey of large language models. *arXiv preprint arXiv:2303.18223*.

Zou, A., ... (2023). Universal and transferable adversarial attacks on aligned language models. *arXiv preprint arXiv:2307.15043*.

Chapter 11

Explainable and Transparent AI Architectures

Deepak Gupta
http://orcid.org/0000-0003-3929-1362
Institute of Technology and Management, Gwalior, India

Abduraimova Nigora
Termez University of Economics and Service, Termez, Uzbekistan

Gulkhayo Gulkhayo
Mamun University, Khiva, Uzbekistan

Ergashev Nuriddin
http://orcid.org/0000-0002-8274-6193
Karshi State Technical University. Karshi, Uzbekistan

Shokhzod Karimov
Tashkent State University of Economics, Uzbekistan

Mamatkhujaev Otabek
Alfraganus University, Tashkent, Uzbekistan

Seitnazarov Kuanishbay
Nukus State Pedagogical Institute, Uzbekistan

ABSTRACT

Explainability and transparency have emerged as foundational pillars in the secure deployment of artificial intelligence (AI) systems, especially large language models (LLMs). This chapter examines the evolving landscape of explainable AI (XAI) architectures through the lens of cybersecurity, adversarial robustness, and regulatory compliance. The authors survey core XAI methodologies—including LIME, SHAP, mechanistic interpretability, attention attribution, and causal tracing—evaluating their effectiveness against adversarial threats such as jailbreaking, prompt injection, data poisoning, and hallucination exploitation. The dual nature of XAI is critically

DOI: 10.4018/979-8-3373-8252-4.ch011

examined: while transparency mechanisms bolster defense and trust, they simultaneously introduce novel attack surfaces that adversaries can exploit to subvert explanation systems.

1. INTRODUCTION

The rapid integration of artificial intelligence into critical systems—spanning healthcare diagnostics, financial decision-making, legal reasoning, and national security—has elevated the stakes of AI transparency to an unprecedented degree. As large language models (LLMs) such as GPT-4, Claude, and open-source equivalents become embedded in operational pipelines, the question of whether we can trust, audit, and understand their decisions is no longer merely academic. It is a question of societal and systemic risk that demands rigorous, interdisciplinary inquiry at the intersection of machine learning, information security, and governance.

Explainable artificial intelligence (XAI) refers to a broad family of techniques and methodologies aimed at rendering AI model decisions interpretable to human stakeholders (Danilevsky et al., 2021; Hosain et al., 2024). In the context of LLMs, explainability operates at multiple levels: from local explanations of individual predictions to global characterizations of model behavior, and from post-hoc rationalization to intrinsic interpretability embedded within model architectures (Singh et al., 2024). The distinction between these levels is not merely taxonomic—it carries profound implications for the types of adversarial threats that can be detected, the forms of regulatory compliance that can be demonstrated, and the degree to which human oversight can be meaningfully exercised over high-stakes AI decisions.

A defining tension runs through the contemporary XAI landscape: the very mechanisms designed to make AI systems more understandable can themselves become vectors of attack. Slack et al. (2020) demonstrated that LIME and SHAP—two of the most widely deployed post-hoc explanation methods—can be systematically fooled by adversaries who construct inputs that appear benign to the explanation method while enabling the underlying model to behave discriminatorily or maliciously. This "scaffolding attack" paradigm has catalyzed a new subfield examining adversarial robustness not merely of AI predictions, but of AI explanations themselves (Baniecki & Biecek, 2024; Vadillo et al., 2025). The implications are far-reaching: if auditors and regulators rely on explanation systems that can be strategically manipulated, then compliance regimes built on those systems may provide a false sense of security.

Simultaneously, the emergence of LLM-specific attack vectors—including jailbreaking (Chao et al., 2023; Shen et al., 2024), prompt injection (Perez & Ribeiro, 2022; Greshake et al., 2023), training data poisoning (Cinà et al., 2023), and hallucination exploitation (Huang et al., 2024)—demands that XAI methodologies evolve beyond their origins in tabular data and image classification to address the unique architectural properties of transformer-based language models. Recent advances in mechanistic interpretability (Bereska & Gavves, 2024; Rai et al., 2024), causal tracing (Meng et al., 2022), and automated circuit discovery (Conmy et al., 2023; Wang et al., 2023) offer promising pathways, but their practical application to security-critical settings remains an active and largely open research frontier.

This chapter provides a comprehensive treatment of XAI architectures from a cybersecurity perspective, organized as follows. Section 2 establishes the theoretical foundations, situating XAI within the broader discourse of AI safety and alignment. Section 3 surveys the primary XAI methodologies and their applicability to LLMs. Section 4 examines adversarial threats targeting both AI models and their explanation mechanisms in depth. Section 5 presents a comparative analysis supported by Table 1 and Graph 1. Section 6 develops an integrated framework for XAI-enabled defense and surveys domain applications. Section 7 addresses future research directions, and Section 8 provides concluding remarks. The analysis draws on thirty peer-reviewed and preprint sources representing the current state of the field.

2. THEORETICAL FOUNDATIONS OF EXPLAINABLE AND TRANSPARENT AI

2.1 Defining Explainability and Transparency

The terms “explainability” and “transparency” are frequently conflated in both popular and scholarly discourse, yet they denote distinct properties that carry different implications for system design and governance. Transparency, in its broadest sense, refers to the property of a model whose internal workings are accessible and comprehensible without the need for auxiliary explanation mechanisms—a characteristic associated with inherently interpretable models such as decision trees, linear regression, and rule-based systems. Explainability, by contrast, refers to the capacity of a model—opaque or transparent—to generate human-interpretable accounts of specific decisions or global behaviors through post-hoc analysis or self-reporting mechanisms. A model may be transparent without being practically explainable (a vast decision tree may expose its rules while remaining cognitively intractable), and may generate plausible explanations without being truly transparent (an LLM may produce fluent natural language justifications that do not accurately reflect its internal computation).

Miller (2023) has argued that the dominant paradigm in XAI research has produced explanations that satisfy researchers more than the stakeholders who ultimately rely on AI decisions. His critique, encapsulated in the provocative formulation "Explainable AI is dead, long live explainable AI," calls for a shift toward hypothesis-driven, evaluative AI that embeds explanatory reasoning into the model itself rather than layering it externally. This perspective aligns with the trajectory of mechanistic interpretability, which seeks to characterize the computational circuits and knowledge representations that give rise to model behavior from first principles rather than through behavioral approximation. The convergence of these intellectual currents—stakeholder-oriented explanation design and mechanistic analysis of internal computation—represents one of the most productive directions in contemporary XAI research.

For LLMs specifically, transparency operates at several distinct architectural levels, each with different security implications. At the tokenization and embedding level, transparency concerns how input representations encode semantic meaning and how those encodings interact with downstream computations. At the attention mechanism level, transparency involves understanding which tokens influence which other tokens during forward passes, and whether those influences reflect the semantic relationships they appear to represent. At the layer-wise level, mechanistic interpretability seeks to identify specific neurons, attention heads, and circuits responsible for distinct computational tasks (Bereska & Gavves, 2024). At the output level, transparency concerns the relationship between model activations and generated text, including how uncertainty, confidence, and groundedness of outputs can be reliably characterized. Each architectural level corresponds to different threat surfaces and, correspondingly, different XAI strategies for detecting and mitigating adversarial manipulation.

2.2 XAI in the Context of AI Safety and Alignment

The relationship between XAI and AI safety is bidirectional and mutually constitutive. On one hand, explainability is a precondition for alignment verification: if we cannot understand what an AI system is doing and why, we cannot reliably determine whether it is acting in accordance with human values and intentions (Shen et al., 2023). On the other hand, safety failures—when exposed and explained through mechanistic analysis—provide invaluable diagnostic information for alignment research, as the study of adversarial failures has repeatedly demonstrated. The alignment research community has increasingly recognized that interpretability and alignment are not separate problems but aspects of a single deeper challenge: constructing AI systems whose behavior is both beneficial and verifiable.

The concept of model alignment, broadly defined as the problem of ensuring that AI systems pursue intended objectives and avoid harmful behaviors, is deeply intertwined with transparency at every level. Shen et al. (2023) provide a comprehensive survey of alignment techniques including reinforcement learning from human feedback (RLHF), constitutional AI, and debate-based methods, noting that each approach implicitly relies on some form of behavioral transparency to validate whether alignment has been achieved. RLHF, for example, depends on human raters who can evaluate model outputs—but this evaluation is itself a form of behavioral inspection that provides only indirect evidence about internal mechanisms. Without the ability to inspect model internals or reliably attribute outputs to causal factors within the model, alignment verification reduces to black-box behavioral testing: a strategy that has proven insufficient against sophisticated adversarial attacks designed to trigger misaligned behavior only in specific contexts.

The emerging field of mechanistic alignment research attempts to address this limitation directly by characterizing the internal circuits responsible for aligned and misaligned behaviors, enabling targeted interventions that modify specific computations rather than relying on coarse-grained behavioral feedback. The ROME technique (Meng et al., 2022), which demonstrated that factual associations can be surgically modified through targeted parameter updates, exemplifies this approach. Its relevance to alignment extends beyond fact-editing: if the computational substrate of specific beliefs, values, or behavioral tendencies can be localized, then alignment interventions can potentially be made more precise and verifiable—and alignment failures can potentially be diagnosed before they manifest in harmful outputs.

2.3 Regulatory and Governance Dimensions

The deployment of XAI in security-critical AI systems does not occur in a regulatory vacuum. The European Union's AI Act, which entered into force in 2024, imposes mandatory transparency and explainability requirements on high-risk AI systems across sectors including critical infrastructure, law enforcement, education, and healthcare. The Act requires that high-risk AI systems provide documentation sufficient to enable effective human oversight, including technical documentation of system capabilities, limitations, and decision-making logic. This mandate creates both requirements and opportunities for XAI deployment, providing regulatory impetus for transparency investments that might otherwise be deferred in favor of capability development.

The implications of the AI Act for XAI architecture extend beyond documentation requirements. High-risk AI systems must be designed to allow human oversight in a meaningful sense—not merely the formal capacity to review outputs, but the practical ability to understand, audit, and correct AI behavior. This substantive interpretation of oversight creates architectural requirements for XAI integration that exceed current industry practice in most deployment contexts. Meeting these requirements demands XAI methods that produce explanations that are not merely technically accurate but genuinely informative to the specific human stakeholders responsible for oversight—a requirement that aligns with Miller's (2023) critique of researcher-centric explanation design and points toward stakeholder-calibrated explanation frameworks.

3. CORE XAI METHODOLOGIES AND THEIR APPLICABILITY TO LLMS

3.1 Post-Hoc Explanation Methods: LIME and SHAP

Local Interpretable Model-agnostic Explanations (LIME) and SHapley Additive exPlanations (SHAP) represent the dominant paradigm in applied XAI, having been adopted across industry and regulated sectors as standard explanation tools since their introduction. Both methods operate by approximating the behavior of a complex model in the neighborhood of a specific input, generating locally faithful linear explanations that identify the most influential features for a given prediction. Salih et al. (2025) provide a contemporary perspective on both methods, noting their complementary strengths: LIME excels at producing intuitive local explanations for arbitrary model types with minimal computational overhead during training, while SHAP offers theoretically grounded consistency guarantees rooted in cooperative game theory—specifically, Shapley values are the unique attribution method satisfying efficiency, symmetry, dummy, and linearity axioms simultaneously.

Applied to LLMs, both methods face fundamental challenges that limit their applicability relative to their effectiveness in tabular and image domains. The token-based input space of language models creates an exponentially large neighborhood for perturbation-based explanation, and the sequential, contextual nature of language means that feature independence assumptions embedded in SHAP's theoretical framework are systematically violated: the contribution of any given token is deeply conditional on the surrounding context, rendering additive attribution fundamentally incomplete as a characterization of language model behavior. Danilevsky et al. (2021) survey XAI approaches specifically for natural language processing, identifying challenges including the high dimensionality of text, the importance of long-range dependencies, and the fundamental difficulty of defining semantically meaningful perturbations for natural language inputs without introducing distribution shift that undermines the validity of local approximations.

Despite these limitations, LIME and SHAP retain substantial practical utility in LLM security and compliance contexts. In vulnerability detection applications, Haurogné et al. (2024) deploy SHAP alongside BERT-based LLM models to provide transparency obligations in cybersecurity workflows, demonstrating that post-hoc explanations can facilitate auditing of model decisions in professional security contexts and provide the audit trails demanded by regulatory frameworks. Basheer et al. (2026) develop a hybrid XAI framework for automatic vulnerability detection that integrates explainability as a core architectural component rather than an afterthought, showing that transparency obligations can be embedded in operational security pipelines without prohibitive computational overhead.

3.2 Mechanistic Interpretability

Mechanistic interpretability represents a fundamentally different approach to understanding AI systems, seeking to reverse-engineer the computational mechanisms—circuits, features, and representations—that give rise to model behaviors from first principles. Rather than approximating model behavior with simpler surrogate models, mechanistic interpretability attempts to characterize the model itself: identifying which neurons encode which concepts, how information flows through attention layers, and what computational motifs implement higher-level cognitive functions. The approach is analogous to reverse-engineering the logic of a complex software system from its compiled binary: painstaking and technically demanding, but capable of producing deep causal understanding unavailable to behavioral analysis alone.

The field has produced a series of landmark results that have fundamentally transformed the understanding of transformer-based language models. Meng et al. (2022), in their influential ROME paper, demonstrated through causal tracing that specific factual associations in GPT models can be localized to precise parameter matrices in middle-layer MLP modules, and that these associations can be selectively edited through targeted parameter updates. Wang et al. (2023) identified a specific circuit in GPT-2 Small responsible for the indirect object identification (IOI) task—a canonical linguistic challenge requiring tracking of named entities across clauses—establishing that complex linguistic behaviors can be attributed to specific, identifiable interacting components. Conmy et al. (2023) extended this work with Automated Circuit Discovery (ACDC), a framework capable of identifying task-relevant circuits through systematic activation patching without manual analysis, enabling the discovery of circuits governing behaviors across a wide range of tasks.

Bereska and Gavves (2024) provide a comprehensive review of mechanistic interpretability specifically from an AI safety perspective, cataloguing advances across three complementary research programs: superposition theory (which explains how networks encode more features than they have dimensions by exploiting interference patterns), monosemanticity research (which seeks neuron-level representations with clean, interpretable semantics), and universality studies (which investigate whether similar circuits emerge across different architectures trained on similar data). The universality finding, if robust, has important implications for security: circuits implementing harmful behaviors may be predictably located in architectures where analogous circuits have been found in related models, facilitating targeted analysis and intervention.

Rai et al. (2024) offer a practical guide to mechanistic interpretability tools and methodologies for security practitioners, covering activation patching workflows, logit lens analysis for probing intermediate representations, direct logit attribution for tracing prediction contributions, and sparse autoencoder (SAE) approaches for achieving monosemantic feature decomposition at scale. Their work emphasizes that while mechanistic interpretability has matured significantly as a research discipline, deploying it at the scale of modern frontier models with hundreds of billions of parameters remains an open research challenge requiring automated tools, hierarchical analysis frameworks, and new theoretical foundations for managing the complexity of large-scale circuit analysis.

3.3 Attention-Based and Gradient-Based Methods

Attention mechanisms, central to transformer architecture, have been widely interpreted as providing built-in explanations: the attention weights assigned by the model to different input tokens during processing are frequently presented in both research and practitioner contexts as indicators of which parts of the input are most relevant to a given prediction. The interpretive appeal of attention visualization is undeniable—attention maps provide intuitively comprehensible, spatially organized accounts of model behavior that can be communicated to non-technical stakeholders. However, the interpretive status of attention weights as causal explanations has been substantively contested in the literature, with important implications for their use in security contexts.

The core objection to attention-as-explanation is that attention is a routing mechanism, not a causal attribution mechanism: high attention weight to a token indicates that information from that token is heavily incorporated into downstream representations, but does not demonstrate that the token caused the output in the counterfactual sense required for genuine causal explanation. Attention patterns may reflect distributional regularities—the model attending to tokens that co-occur with the predicted output in the training distribution—rather than the semantic relevance of those tokens to the specific prediction at hand. Despite these theoretical concerns, attention-based explanations retain practical utility in security contexts when interpreted carefully and validated against causal intervention results.

Gradient-based saliency methods, including vanilla gradients, integrated gradients, and gradient times input approaches, provide a complementary explanation paradigm that measures the sensitivity of model outputs to small changes in input representations. These methods are computationally tractable and have been shown to produce more causally faithful explanations than raw attention weights in several comparative studies. Singh et al. (2024) argue that in the era of LLMs, interpretability methods must be rethought to leverage the unique properties of language models—particularly their capacity to generate natural language explanations of their own reasoning—as a form of self-explanation that can be validated against and combined with external analysis methods. This perspective motivates the development of hybrid explanation systems that combine gradient-based attribution with LLM-generated rationales, each checking and enriching the other.

Figure 1. XAI Taxonomy in AI Security Architecture.

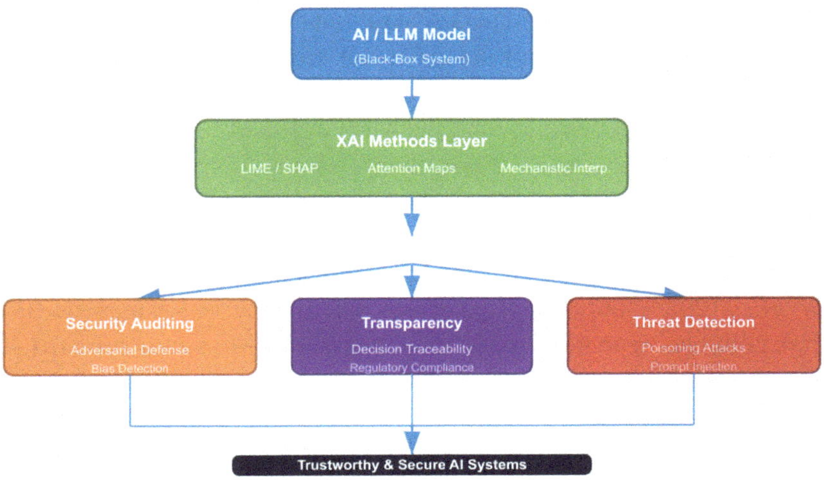

Figure 1 illustrates the hierarchical relationship between the AI/LLM model, the XAI Methods Layer (LIME/SHAP, Attention Maps, Mechanistic Interpretability), three application security domains, and the ultimate outcome of trustworthy and secure AI systems. (High-resolution SVG version provided separately.)

4. ADVERSARIAL THREATS TARGETING AI MODELS AND XAI SYSTEMS

4.1 Jailbreaking Large Language Models

Jailbreaking refers to a class of adversarial techniques that exploit vulnerabilities in LLM alignment mechanisms to elicit outputs that the model has been trained or instructed to refuse. The phenomenon has attracted sustained research attention given its practical implications for the deployment of safety-critical AI systems in consumer, enterprise, and government contexts. Shen et al. (2024) characterize and evaluate jailbreak prompts observed in the wild across multiple production models, documenting a rich taxonomy of techniques including role-play scenarios (framing prohibited requests within fictional contexts), token manipulation (exploiting tokenization artifacts that bypass pattern-matching defenses), multilingual exploitation (requesting harmful content in languages underrepresented in safety training), and semantic rephrasing (reframing prohibited requests in ways that preserve semantic content while evading surface-level filters).

Liu et al. (2024) conduct an empirical study of jailbreaking ChatGPT through prompt engineering across multiple model versions, identifying systematic weaknesses in the model's safety training that persist across updates. Their analysis reveals that many jailbreaking successes exploit the tension between two competing objectives built into the model's training: the instruction-following objective, which drives the model to fulfill user requests, and the harm-avoidance objective, which drives refusal. Adversarial prompts that frame harmful requests as extensions of legitimate instruction-following tasks can tip the balance toward compliance, particularly when the harm-avoidance training has been implemented through surface-level pattern matching rather than deep semantic understanding of harmful intent.

Chao et al. (2023) introduce Prompt Automatic Iterative Refinement (PAIR), a black-box jailbreaking method that uses a separate LLM as an automated attacker to iteratively refine adversarial prompts based on feedback from the target model. PAIR achieves successful jailbreaks against frontier models in as few as twenty queries—a finding with alarming practical implications given that it requires no access to model weights, gradients, or architecture details. Liu et al. (2024b) present AutoDAN, a method for generating stealthy jailbreak prompts that bypass both model safety mechanisms and human review boards, exploiting the fact that safety alignment is frequently implemented through pattern recognition rather than genuine semantic understanding of harmful intent. Huang et al. (2023) identify a particularly severe attack surface specific to open-source LLMs: by manipulating sampling parameters and decoding strategies during inference, adversaries can catastrophically compromise safety alignment without modifying model weights—highlighting the need to treat the entire inference pipeline as a security perimeter.

From an XAI perspective, jailbreaking analysis has revealed several important insights that translate into practical defense strategies. First, safety alignment is frequently implemented through identifiable circuits—attention heads and MLP components that activate on harmful intent signals—that can potentially be targeted by adversarial prompts designed to suppress those activations. Second, mechanistic interpretability analysis of jailbreaking failures has shown that successful attacks typically involve the suppression or circumvention of specific safety-relevant circuits rather than the deletion of harmful knowledge from the model. Third, the characteristic activation patterns of successful jailbreak prompts may be detectable through real-time attention monitoring, providing a basis for runtime jailbreak detection complementary to input-level filtering.

4.2 Prompt Injection Attacks

Prompt injection attacks exploit the fundamental design of instruction-following LLMs, in which the boundary between trusted system instructions and untrusted user input is enforced through natural language conventions rather than formal cryptographic or architectural security mechanisms. The absence of a formal security boundary means that any sufficiently compelling natural language instruction embedded in user input can potentially override system-level prompts—a property that is architecturally intrinsic to current LLM designs and cannot be addressed through superficial filtering alone. Perez and Ribeiro (2022) formalized the basic direct prompt injection attack, demonstrating that simple adversarial instructions such as "ignore previous instructions" can reliably redirect model behavior even against models with explicit system prompt protections.

Greshake et al. (2023) extended this analysis to indirect prompt injection, in which adversarial instructions are embedded not in user input but in external content retrieved and processed by LLM-integrated applications—web pages, documents, emails, database records, and API responses that the model incorporates into its context as part of its operational workflow. This attack vector is substantially more dangerous than direct injection because it does not require any direct adversarial interaction with the target system: a malicious web page silently encountered during an LLM-assisted research task, or a corrupted database record processed during an automated workflow, can redirect the model to exfiltrate data, send unauthorized communications, modify downstream system states, or perform other consequential actions entirely outside the awareness of the user or operator. Mathew (2025) provides a comprehensive review of prompt injection attacks and defenses that systematically surveys emerging defensive techniques including input sanitization pipelines, instruction hierarchy enforcement (reserving privileged instruction authority for cryptographically authenticated sources), context isolation architectures, and XAI-based monitoring for anomalous reasoning patterns.

The XAI implications of prompt injection are significant and have not yet received adequate systematic treatment in the literature. If the attention patterns associated with injected adversarial instructions can be systematically distinguished from those associated with legitimate user instructions—a hypothesis motivated by mechanistic interpretability findings about the circuit-level implementation of instruction following—then attention monitoring could serve as a real-time detection mechanism for injection attacks. Haurogné et al. (2024) demonstrate that explainability mechanisms integrated into LLM-based security workflows can surface anomalous reasoning patterns consistent with instruction conflict, providing a basis for automated detection of injection attempts in operational pipelines.

4.3 Training Data Poisoning

Training data poisoning attacks corrupt the learning process itself by introducing malicious examples into training datasets, causing models to learn spurious associations, backdoor triggers, or biased representations that manifest as exploitable vulnerabilities at inference time. Cinà et al. (2023) provide a comprehensive survey of machine learning security against data poisoning in their landmark Wild Patterns Reloaded paper, cataloguing attack strategies including label flipping (corrupting class labels to misdirect learning), backdoor injection (embedding trigger patterns that activate specific behaviors when present in inference inputs), clean-label attacks (introducing correctly labeled but adversarially crafted examples that corrupt learned representations without requiring label manipulation), and availability attacks (degrading model performance by introducing high-loss examples that interfere with convergence).

For LLMs, the scale and heterogeneity of training corpora—which routinely encompass hundreds of billions of tokens scraped from diverse and partially unvetted internet sources—creates an exceptionally large attack surface compared to smaller, curated datasets. An adversary with the ability to place content on indexed web pages, contribute to open-source repositories, or inject content into document collections used for domain-specific fine-tuning can potentially introduce poisoning signals that influence the behavior of trained models in targeted ways. This threat is compounded by the multi-stage training pipelines of modern LLMs, in which pre-training, instruction tuning, and RLHF phases each provide distinct attack opportunities with different characteristic signatures.

Mechanistic interpretability offers a partial solution through its capacity to localize anomalous circuits and representations that may reflect poisoning. Research on neural trojan detection has shown that backdoor behaviors are frequently implemented through identifiable circuits that activate specifically on trigger patterns while remaining dormant on clean inputs. If these circuits can be identified through activation analysis or causal tracing before they are triggered in deployment, then mechanistic analysis could serve as a pre-deployment security validation step analogous to code review in traditional software engineering. The challenge is scale: systematic circuit analysis of a 70B parameter model remains computationally prohibitive with current tools, though automated approaches like ACDC (Conmy et al., 2023) represent meaningful progress toward tractable solutions for subsets of the circuit space.

4.4 Adversarial Attacks on XAI Methods

Perhaps the most epistemically challenging threat in the XAI security landscape is the susceptibility of explanation systems themselves to adversarial manipulation—a property that directly undermines the auditing and oversight functions that XAI is intended to provide. Slack et al. (2020) demonstrated this possibility empirically and rigorously, showing that classifiers can be trained to detect with high accuracy when they are being queried by LIME or SHAP (through the characteristic perturbation patterns these methods generate) and to produce clean, unbiased outputs during explanation-time queries while behaving in a discriminatory or harmful manner on normal operational inputs. This scaffolding attack is particularly insidious because it is undetectable by the explanation method itself and requires no access to the explanation system's implementation—only the ability to distinguish explanation-time from operational inputs.

Baniecki and Biecek (2024) survey the adversarial XAI threat landscape comprehensively, characterizing attacks along multiple dimensions: model-focused attacks that manipulate explanation outputs to misrepresent model behavior, explanation-focused attacks that preserve model behavior while corrupting its explanation, and pipeline attacks that introduce adversarial content at earlier stages of the XAI workflow (data preprocessing, feature encoding) to corrupt downstream explanations without directly manipulating the model or explanation method. Vadillo et al. (2025) extend this survey to cover threats against human interpreters of XAI outputs, noting that adversarial explanations can exploit well-documented cognitive biases—including confirmation bias, anchoring, and the illusion of explanatory depth—to lead competent human reviewers to systematically incorrect conclusions about model behavior. This human-facing dimension of adversarial XAI raises profound questions about the reliability of human oversight mechanisms that depend on explanation systems as their primary interface to model internals. Pachl et al. (2024) identify the specific vulnerabilities introduced at each stage of the XAI deployment pipeline, from data collection through model training, explanation generation, and communication to stakeholders, providing a structured threat model for XAI security practitioners.

4.5 Hallucination as a Security Vulnerability

Hallucination—the tendency of LLMs to generate outputs that are confident in tone but factually incorrect, contextually inconsistent, or entirely fabricated—represents a distinct category of model failure with both safety and security dimensions that are often underemphasized in the adversarial AI literature. Huang et al. (2024) provide the most comprehensive treatment of hallucination in LLMs to date, identifying three primary failure types based on their causal mechanisms: intrinsic hallucination (model outputs that contradict information explicitly provided in the context), extrinsic hallucination (model outputs that cannot be verified against any provided context), and instruction hallucination (model outputs that deviate from explicit user instructions, often by introducing plausible-sounding but ungrounded elaborations).

From a security perspective, hallucination is not merely a reliability problem but an active exploit surface. An adversary who understands the conditions under which a deployed LLM is likely to hallucinate—such as queries involving rare facts, complex multi-step reasoning, or domain-specific knowledge at the boundaries of training data coverage—can craft inputs designed to elicit confident but false outputs in ways that corrupt downstream automated decision workflows. In cybersecurity applications, a hallucinating vulnerability detection model may generate false positive vulnerability reports that exhaust analyst resources, or false negatives that allow actual vulnerabilities to pass undetected. In medical AI contexts, such as ChatDoctor (Li et al., 2023), hallucination may generate medically plausible but clinically incorrect recommendations with direct patient safety consequences.

XAI methods offer partial mitigations for hallucination through their capacity to provide grounding signals that distinguish model outputs anchored in retrieved or training-data evidence from those generated through associative pattern completion without factual grounding. Attention attribution methods can in principle identify whether a model's output attends heavily to relevant source material (suggesting grounded generation) or generates from prior distributions without contextual anchoring (suggesting hallucination risk). Mechanistic analysis of the circuits responsible for hallucination—identifying the computational conditions under which factual associations give way to confabulation—could inform targeted interventions in model architecture or training procedures. However, the reliable automated detection of hallucination at inference time remains an open research problem, and current XAI methods provide only indirect and probabilistic signals rather than definitive hallucination detection.

Figure 2. Attack-Defense Cycle in XAI-Enabled LLM System

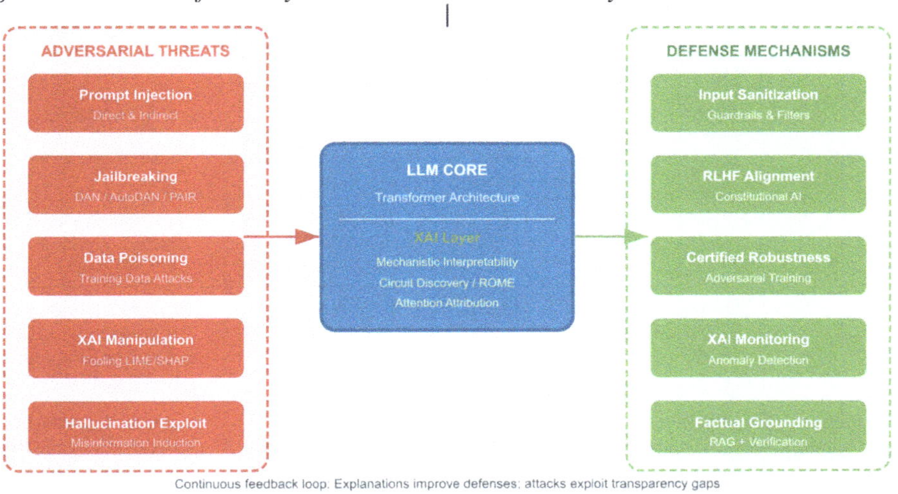

Figure 2 illustrates the bidirectional relationship between adversarial threats (left column) and defense mechanisms (right column), mediated through the LLM Core with its integrated XAI Layer. Note the continuous feedback loop running beneath both columns: explanations improve defenses, while new attacks exploit gaps in transparency. This cycle drives the adversarial co-evolution that defines the contemporary XAI security landscape.

5. COMPARATIVE ANALYSIS OF XAI METHODS FOR LLM SECURITY

5.1 Method Taxonomy and Security Coverage

The following table provides a structured comparative analysis of seven XAI methods drawn from the literature surveyed in preceding sections, evaluating each along five dimensions: methodological type, LLM applicability, primary security use cases, and key limitations. This taxonomy serves as a practical reference for practitioners selecting XAI methods for security-critical deployments and for researchers identifying gaps in the current methodological landscape. The inclusion of concept-based methods (TCAV) alongside the more widely deployed post-hoc and mechanistic approaches reflects the growing recognition that high-level conceptual explanations may provide security insights unavailable to token-level attribution methods.

Table 1. Comparative Analysis of XAI Methods for LLM Security Applications

XAI Method	Type	LLM Applicability	Primary Security Use Case	Key Limitation
LIME	Post-hoc, Local, Model-agnostic	Moderate	Bias detection; compliance audit trails; anomaly flagging	Susceptible to scaffolding attacks; neighborhood instability
SHAP	Post-hoc, Local/ Global, Game-theoretic	Moderate	Feature attribution; regulatory documentation; drift detection	Computationally expensive at production scale; independence assumptions violated in text
Mechanistic Interpretability	Intrinsic, Global, Causal	High	Circuit discovery; backdoor detection; jailbreak analysis	Requires model internals access; scaling to frontier models remains intractable
Attention Attribution	Intrinsic, Local, Sequence-level	High	Token provenance; prompt injection tracing; instruction conflict detection	Attention weights do not imply causation; inconsistent across layers
ROME / Causal Tracing	Causal, Factual, Parameter-level	High	Knowledge localization; fact editing; hallucination auditing	Scope limited to factual associations; not applicable to procedural reasoning
Gradient-based Saliency	Post-hoc, Local, Gradient-based	Moderate	Input sensitivity mapping; adversarial perturbation detection	Sensitive to preprocessing; gradient saturation obscures important features
Concept-based (TCAV)	Post-hoc, Global, Concept-level	Low–Moderate	High-level concept testing; domain alignment validation	Requires predefined concept probes; brittle to distribution shift

5.2 Quantitative Effectiveness Assessment

Table 1 establishes a qualitative taxonomy, but security practitioners also require a quantitative comparative framework for method selection across specific threat scenarios. Graph 1 below presents an effectiveness assessment of four primary XAI method categories—LIME, SHAP, Mechanistic Interpretability, and Attention Attribution—across five security dimensions: adversarial defense, jailbreak detection, poisoning resistance, prompt injection mitigation, and compliance and auditing. Effectiveness scores represent a synthesis of empirical findings from the literature surveyed in this chapter, rated on a scale of one (low effectiveness) to four (high effectiveness) based on the convergent evidence of experimental studies, case analyses, and theoretical assessments.

Figure 3. Comparative XAI Method Coverage Across Security Dimensions

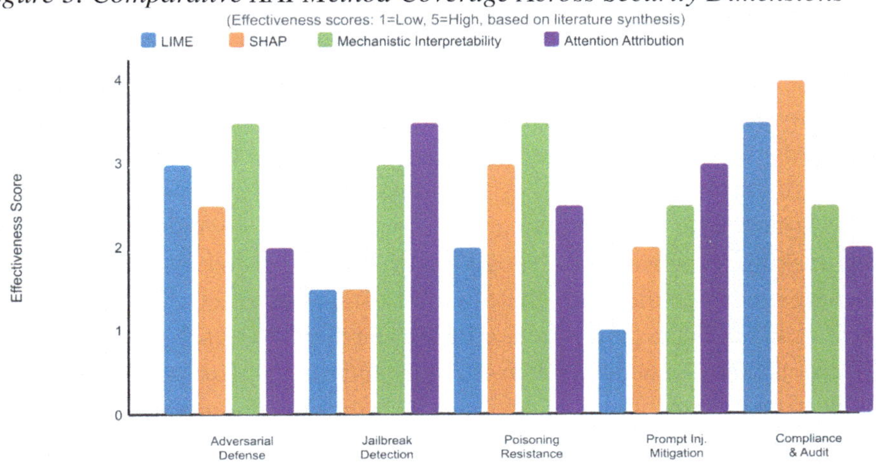

Figure 3 provides a quantitative comparison of four XAI methods across five security dimensions. Observe that Mechanistic Interpretability (green bars) dominates for adversarial defense, jailbreak detection, and poisoning resistance—tasks requiring causal access to model internals—while SHAP (orange bars) leads for compliance and auditing, reflecting its regulatory acceptance and audit trail capabilities. No single method dominates all five dimensions, reinforcing the case for integrated multi-method deployment.

The figure reveals several important patterns that have direct implications for defense architecture design. Mechanistic interpretability demonstrates the highest effectiveness for adversarial defense, jailbreak detection, and poisoning resistance—capabilities that require causal access to model internals and the ability to identify specific circuits responsible for targeted behaviors. This superiority reflects the fundamental advantage of intrinsic over post-hoc explanation: mechanistic methods analyze what the model is actually computing, rather than approximating its behavior through external observations that can be manipulated by adversarially aware models.

SHAP and LIME show the highest effectiveness for compliance and auditing applications, reflecting their maturity, widespread regulatory acceptance, established tooling, and the alignment between their output format (feature importance scores) and the documentation requirements of regulatory frameworks like the EU AI Act. Attention attribution shows particular strength in jailbreak detection and prompt injection mitigation, where the ability to trace how adversarial content propagates through model layers provides actionable security intelligence in near real-time. Crucially, the pattern of relative strengths across dimensions reveals that no single XAI method provides comprehensive coverage of the full security threat landscape—a finding that directly motivates the integrated, multi-layer defense framework presented in the following section.

Wu et al. (2024) identify ten strategies for making XAI practically usable in the LLM era, emphasizing that effective deployment requires not merely technically accurate explanations but explanations calibrated to the cognitive and decision-making needs of specific stakeholders across different use contexts. Their framework identifies distinct stakeholder groups—model developers, auditors, end users, regulators—each with different explanation requirements, cognitive contexts, and decision-making responsibilities, suggesting that one-size-fits-all explanation approaches are fundamentally inadequate for multi-stakeholder security deployments. Mavrepis et al. (2024) explore whether LLMs can themselves serve as explanation simplification tools—generating plain-language summaries of technical XAI outputs accessible to non-technical stakeholders—with promising initial results that suggest LLM-mediated explanation communication could substantially improve the practical utility of XAI in organizational security workflows. Singh et al. (2024) argue that the arrival of LLMs as explanation generators transforms the interpretability landscape by enabling interactive, conversational, and contextually adaptive explanation modes unavailable to static explanation systems.

6. INTEGRATED XAI-ENABLED DEFENSE FRAMEWORK AND DOMAIN APPLICATIONS

6.1 Architecture of an XAI-Integrated Security Pipeline

The preceding analysis establishes clearly that no single XAI method provides comprehensive security coverage across the full adversarial threat landscape facing deployed LLMs. Effective defense therefore requires an integrated framework that deploys complementary explanation methods at different layers of the AI system stack, with each method addressing the specific threat surfaces for which it demonstrates comparative advantage. The architecture described in this section draws on the effectiveness analysis presented in Section 5 and the threat taxonomy developed in Section 4, operationalizing those findings into a coherent defense-in-depth strategy.

The proposed framework organizes XAI-enabled security into four functional layers, each corresponding to a distinct phase of the inference lifecycle. The input verification layer, operating before model inference, deploys gradient sensitivity analysis and adversarial perturbation detection to flag suspicious inputs—including potential prompt injection payloads and jailbreak attempts—before they are processed by the core model. This layer provides the first line of defense and can operate with low latency since it does not require model inference to generate signals.

The inference monitoring layer applies real-time attention attribution to track information flow through model layers during active inference, flagging activation patterns consistent with known attack signatures. This layer is particularly effective against prompt injection attacks, where injected adversarial instructions generate characteristic attention patterns that differ from normal instruction-following activations—an observation motivated by mechanistic interpretability findings about the circuit-level implementation of instruction processing. The output explanation layer deploys LIME or SHAP to generate human-interpretable accounts of model outputs, supporting compliance requirements, enabling human oversight, and providing the documentation needed for regulatory audit. Finally, the retrospective audit layer applies mechanistic interpretability tools to investigate anomalous incidents identified by upstream layers, enabling forensic analysis that attributes observed failures to specific circuits and representations and informs targeted model improvements.

This layered architecture reflects a defense-in-depth philosophy adapted to the XAI context: no single explanation mechanism is sufficient, and security emerges from the layered deployment of multiple methods with complementary strengths and overlapping coverage. The architecture must be designed with adversarial robustness of the explanation layer itself in mind, incorporating countermeasures against the scaffolding attacks described by Slack et al. (2020) through mechanisms such as query randomization (varying perturbation patterns to prevent detection by adversarially trained detectors), cryptographic input signing (enabling distinction between explanation-time and operational queries), and ensemble explanation methods (combining multiple explanation approaches to reduce the effectiveness of attacks targeting any single method).

6.2 Application to Vulnerability Detection and Cybersecurity

Vulnerability detection represents a domain where the integration of LLMs and XAI has demonstrated particular practical promise. Basheer et al. (2026) propose a hybrid framework that combines the pattern recognition capabilities of transformer-based LLMs with XAI transparency mechanisms to provide interpretable vulnerability detection with full audit trails—a combination that addresses the two primary barriers to adoption of AI-based vulnerability detection in regulated and high-assurance contexts: performance and accountable explainability. Their system demonstrates that LLM-based vulnerability detection achieves higher recall than traditional static analysis tools while XAI mechanisms provide the explanatory grounding necessary for security analysts to act on automated findings with confidence and for compliance teams to document the basis for security decisions.

Haurogné et al. (2024) demonstrate that BERT-based LLM models for vulnerability detection can be made transparently accountable through SHAP-based explanations, with their system showing performance comparable to state-of-the-art detection tools while providing explanations that align with expert judgment about which code features are indicative of specific vulnerability classes. This work exemplifies the transparency obligation paradigm, in which explainability is treated not as an optional feature added for regulatory compliance but as a core architectural requirement that shapes model design, training, and deployment from the outset. The transparency obligation framework has significant implications for how security AI systems should be developed: rather than training models for performance and adding explanations afterward, transparency-first design integrates explanation requirements into the model architecture, training objective, and evaluation criteria.

The medical domain presents analogous challenges with even higher stakes. Li et al. (2023), in their development of ChatDoctor—a medical consultation LLM fine-tuned on medical domain knowledge—demonstrate the feasibility of domain-specialized LLMs for clinical support, while acknowledging that the opacity of LLM reasoning constitutes a significant barrier to clinical adoption, regulatory approval, and malpractice liability management. XAI mechanisms that can provide clinical staff with interpretable accounts of AI-generated medical recommendations—identifying which clinical factors, evidence sources, and reasoning steps drove a recommendation—are essential for responsible deployment. They also create new vulnerability surfaces: if a clinician's reliance on AI recommendations can be predicted and manipulated by adversarial inputs, the XAI layer that builds confidence may amplify rather than mitigate the harm.

6.3 Ethical and Governance Considerations

Beyond technical architectures, the deployment of XAI in security-critical AI systems raises important ethical and governance questions that technical approaches alone cannot resolve. The availability of explanation mechanisms may create a compliance theater dynamic in which organizations use XAI outputs to satisfy regulatory requirements without the explanations substantively informing oversight or accountability. If explanation systems can be adversarially manipulated to produce favorable outputs while model behavior remains harmful (as demonstrated by Slack et al., 2020), then regulatory frameworks that rely on explanation quality as a proxy for model trustworthiness are fundamentally vulnerable to strategic manipulation.

Addressing these governance challenges requires complementing technical XAI development with regulatory frameworks sophisticated enough to evaluate the adversarial robustness of explanation systems, auditing practices that test explanation validity against ground truth behavior rather than accepting explanation outputs at face value, and professional standards for XAI practitioners that mandate disclosure of known explanation limitations. The interdisciplinary collaboration required to build these governance structures—between AI researchers, security professionals, legal scholars, ethicists, and domain experts—represents one of the most important institutional challenges facing the field.

7. FUTURE DIRECTIONS AND OPEN CHALLENGES

7.1 Scaling Mechanistic Interpretability to Frontier Models

The most pressing technical challenge in mechanistic interpretability is the problem of scale. Current mechanistic interpretability methods have produced transformative insights about relatively small models—GPT-2 Small (117M parameters), TinyStories models, and similar architectures that are amenable to exhaustive circuit analysis—but their application to frontier models with hundreds of billions of parameters remains computationally intractable without fundamental methodological advances. The challenge is not merely computational: the conceptual framework of circuit analysis, which seeks to identify discrete components with interpretable, semantically grounded functions, may require revision for models large enough to exhibit qualitatively emergent behaviors that do not correspond to identifiable circuits in the way that has been demonstrated for smaller architectures.

Promising directions for scaling include sparse autoencoders (SAEs) for achieving monosemantic feature decomposition at scale without manual circuit analysis, hierarchical circuit decomposition that analyzes model behavior at multiple levels of abstraction from individual neurons through attention heads to full-model computations, and transfer learning of interpretability findings—applying circuits identified in smaller models as hypotheses to be tested in larger models where exhaustive analysis is infeasible. Automated approaches such as ACDC (Conmy et al., 2023) and activation patching pipelines described by Rai et al. (2024) represent current progress, but theoretical frameworks for managing and validating the complexity of circuit analysis at scale remain a fundamental open problem.

7.2 Adversarially Robust Explanation Systems

The susceptibility of post-hoc explanation methods to adversarial manipulation represents a fundamental challenge that has not yet received adequate systematic attention from the research community relative to its practical importance. Developing adversarially robust explanation methods requires approaches grounded in properties that cannot be simulated by adversarially trained surrogate models—specifically, in the causal and mechanistic properties of the actual model computation rather than its observable input-output behavior. Mechanistic interpretability, by operating at the level of actual model computations, offers a more promising foundation for adversarially robust explanation, but only if the mechanistic analysis itself can be validated against manipulation—a requirement that introduces its own set of technical challenges regarding the verification of causal claims.

Future work in adversarially robust XAI should investigate cryptographic approaches to explanation integrity—including commitment schemes that bind explanation outputs to specific model states, verifiable computation methods that enable third parties to validate that explanation computations were performed correctly, and zero-knowledge proofs that allow model operators to demonstrate explanation properties without revealing proprietary model details. These approaches from cryptography and formal verification offer a qualitatively different foundation for explanation trustworthiness than the empirical validation approaches that dominate current XAI research, and their integration with machine learning explanation methods represents a productive interdisciplinary frontier.

7.3 XAI for Multimodal and Agentic AI Systems

The rapid development of multimodal LLMs that process and generate across text, image, audio, and code modalities, combined with the emergence of agentic AI systems that take consequential actions in the world through tool use, function calling, and multi-step planning, creates new explanation challenges that current XAI methods are fundamentally not designed to address. In multimodal systems, cross-modal attention mechanisms create complex information flows that resist single-modality explanation approaches, and the alignment of explanations across modalities—ensuring that a text explanation of a model's response to an image input accurately reflects the image features that drove the response—requires new explanation architectures. In agentic systems, the sequential nature of action selection and the potentially long causal horizons over which consequences unfold require explanation methods capable of characterizing behavioral trajectories rather than individual predictions.

The security implications of these gaps are acute. Prompt injection attacks against LLM agents—in which malicious content encountered during task execution (in web pages, documents, or API responses) silently redirects agent behavior toward adversarial objectives—are substantially more dangerous than prompt injection against passive chat models, because agents can take consequential actions with real-world effects including data exfiltration, unauthorized transactions, lateral movement within enterprise systems, and execution of malicious code. XAI methods capable of providing forensically useful attribution of agent actions to specific inputs, instructions, and reasoning steps are essential for post-incident analysis and accountability in agentic AI deployments, and their development is an urgent priority for the field.

7.4 Human-Centered XAI and Explanation Calibration

Ultimately, XAI methods are deployed not in isolation but as interfaces that mediate between AI systems and the human stakeholders—security analysts, compliance officers, clinicians, regulators, end users—who rely on them for oversight, accountability, and decision support. Miller (2023) emphasizes that explanations must be designed with the cognitive needs, domain expertise, decision contexts, and accountability structures of specific human stakeholders in mind, and that the predominant researcher-centric approach to explanation evaluation has produced methods that satisfy technical benchmarks while failing to provide genuine decision support to the practitioners who actually need them. An explanation that satisfies an interpretability researcher's desire for causal precision may be useless or actively misleading to a security analyst working under time pressure in an incident response context.

Future research in XAI for AI security must engage seriously with human factors through co-design methodologies and empirical evaluation studies with realistic stakeholder populations in realistic operational contexts. The emergence of LLM-based explanation simplification and adaptation (Mavrepis et al., 2024) opens new possibilities for adaptive explanation systems that tailor their outputs to user expertise, operational context, and decision urgency in real time. These capabilities must be deployed with appropriate caution: the same ease with which LLMs generate fluent, plausible, and confident-sounding text that drives hallucination problems in other contexts applies equally to LLM-generated explanations, creating the possibility of explanation systems that are highly persuasive without being accurate—a failure mode potentially more dangerous than technically correct but incomprehensible explanations.

8. CONCLUSION

This chapter has presented a comprehensive examination of explainable and transparent AI architectures from the perspective of cybersecurity and adversarial robustness, surveying thirty peer-reviewed and preprint sources representing the current state of the field and synthesizing their findings into a coherent analytical framework. The analysis reveals a research domain at a critical juncture: rapid methodological advances in mechanistic interpretability and causal tracing are expanding the frontier of what can be understood about large language model behavior, while simultaneously, the adversarial threat landscape targeting both AI systems and their explanation mechanisms is escalating in sophistication and consequence.

Several central conclusions emerge from the analysis developed across the preceding sections. First, the dual nature of XAI—simultaneously enabling defense through transparency and introducing novel attack surfaces through the explainability mechanisms themselves—demands that security practitioners treat explanation systems with the same adversarial rigor applied to the AI systems they explain. The scaffolding attacks demonstrated by Slack et al. (2020) and the broader adversarial XAI threat landscape surveyed by Baniecki and Biecek (2024) and Vadillo et al. (2025) establish that explanation correctness cannot be assumed in adversarial deployments; it must be actively verified and defended.

Second, no single XAI method provides comprehensive security coverage across the full threat landscape. The comparative analysis presented in Table 1 and Figure 3 demonstrates complementary strengths across methods: mechanistic interpretability offers superior causal depth for adversarial defense and jailbreak analysis, while SHAP and LIME provide regulatory-grade documentation for compliance and auditing. Effective security architectures must deploy these complementary methods in integrated, layered pipelines that combine their strengths while managing their respective vulnerabilities.

Third, mechanistic interpretability represents the most promising long-term foundation for adversarially robust AI security, but scaling challenges must be addressed before it can be deployed at the scale of frontier models in production environments. The automated circuit discovery methods of Conmy et al. (2023), the causal tracing approaches of Meng et al. (2022), and the practical interpretability toolkit described by Rai et al. (2024) provide the methodological building blocks; what is needed is the scaling research that translates these laboratory techniques into production-ready security tools.

The convergence of regulatory pressure from instruments like the EU AI Act, escalating adversarial sophistication from a rapidly expanding adversarial research community, and expanding AI deployment in critical domains including healthcare, finance, law, and national security creates both urgency and opportunity for the XAI security research community. Explainability is not merely a technical feature to be optimized—it is the epistemological foundation upon which trustworthy AI deployment must be built. The path to genuinely secure and beneficial AI systems runs through transparency, and the research agenda outlined in this chapter defines the intellectual challenges that must be met along that path.

REFERENCES

Baniecki, H., & Biecek, P. (2024). Adversarial attacks and defenses in explainable artificial intelligence: A survey. *Information Fusion*, *107*, 102303. DOI: 10.1016/j.inffus.2024.102303

Basheer, N., Islam, S., Alwaheidi, M. K. S., Mouratidis, H., Papastergiou, S., & Haurogné, J. (2026). Large language model based hybrid framework for automatic vulnerability detection with explainable AI for cybersecurity enhancement. *Integrated Computer-Aided Engineering*, *33*(1), 38–54. Advance online publication. DOI: 10.1177/10692509251368663

Bereska, L., & Gavves, E. (2024). Mechanistic interpretability for AI safety: A review. Transactions on Machine Learning Research. https://doi.org//arXiv.2404.14082DOI: 10.48550

Chao, P., Robey, A., Dobriban, E., Hassani, H., Pappas, G. J., & Wong, E. (2023). Jailbreaking black box large language models in twenty queries. arXiv preprint. https://doi.org//arXiv.2310.08419DOI: 10.48550

Cinà, A. E., Grosse, K., Demontis, A., Vascon, S., Zellinger, W., Moser, B. A., Oprea, A., Biggio, B., Pelillo, M., & Roli, F. (2023). Wild patterns reloaded: A survey of machine learning security against training data poisoning. *ACM Computing Surveys*, *55*(13s), 1–39. DOI: 10.1145/3585385

Conmy, A., Mavor-Parker, A. N., Lynch, A., Heimersheim, S., & Garriga-Alonso, A. (2023). Towards automated circuit discovery for mechanistic interpretability. *Advances in Neural Information Processing Systems*, *36*, 16318–16352. DOI: 10.52202/075280-0719

Danilevsky, M., Qian, K., Aharonov, R., Katsis, Y., Kawas, B., & Sen, P. (2021). A survey of the state of explainable AI for natural language processing. *Proceedings of the 1st AACL-IJCNLP*, 447–459. DOI: 10.18653/v1/2020.aacl-main.46

Greshake, K., Abdelnabi, S., Mishra, S., Endres, C., Holz, T., & Fritz, M. (2023). Not what you've signed up for: Compromising real-world LLM-integrated applications with indirect prompt injection. AISec 2023 Workshop at CCS. https://doi.org//arXiv.2302.12173DOI: 10.48550

Haurogné, J., Basheer, N., & Islam, S. (2024). Vulnerability detection using BERT based LLM model with transparency obligation practice towards trustworthy AI. *Machine Learning with Applications*, *18*, 100598. DOI: 10.1016/j.mlwa.2024.100598

Hosain, M. T., Jim, J. R., Mridha, M. F., & Kabir, M. M. (2024). Explainable AI approaches in deep learning: Advancements, applications and challenges. *Computers & Electrical Engineering*, *117*, 109246. DOI: 10.1016/j.compeleceng.2024.109246

Huang, L., Yu, W., Ma, W., Zhong, W., Feng, Z., Wang, H., Chen, Q., Peng, W., Feng, X., Qin, B., & Liu, T. (2024). A survey on hallucination in large language models: Principles, taxonomy, challenges, and open questions. *ACM Transactions on Information Systems*. Advance online publication. DOI: 10.1145/3703155

Huang, Y., Gupta, S., Xia, M., Li, K., & Chen, D. (2023). Catastrophic jailbreak of open-source LLMs via exploiting generation. arXiv preprint. https://doi.org//arXiv.2310.06987DOI: 10.48550

Li, Y., Li, Z., Zhang, K., Dan, R., Jiang, S., & Zhang, Y. (2023). ChatDoctor: A medical chat model fine-tuned on a large language model meta-AI using medical domain knowledge. *Cureus*, *15*(6), e40895. DOI: 10.7759/cureus.40895 PMID: 37492832

Liu, X., Xu, N., Chen, M., & Xiao, C. (2024). AutoDAN: Generating stealthy jailbreak prompts on aligned large language models. *Proceedings of ICLR 2024*. DOI: 10.48550/arXiv.2310.04451

Liu, Y., Deng, G., Xu, Z., Li, Y., Zheng, Y., Zhang, Y., Zhao, L., Zhang, T., & Liu, Y. (2024). Jailbreaking ChatGPT via prompt engineering: An empirical study. arXiv preprint. https://doi.org//arXiv.2305.13860DOI: 10.48550

Mathew, E. S. (2025). Enhancing security in large language models: A comprehensive review of prompt injection attacks and defenses. *Journal on Artificial Intelligence*, *7*(1), 347–363. DOI: 10.32604/jai.2025.069841

Mavrepis, P., Makridis, G., Fatouros, G., Koukos, V., Filippakis, M. N., Kyriazis, D., & Soldatos, J. (2024). XAI for all: Can large language models simplify explainable AI? arXiv preprint. https://doi.org//arXiv.2401.13110DOI: 10.48550

Meng, K., Bau, D., Andonian, A., & Belinkov, Y. (2022). Locating and editing factual associations in GPT. *Advances in Neural Information Processing Systems*, *35*, 17359–17372. DOI: 10.48550/arXiv.2202.05262

Miller, T. (2023). Explainable AI is dead, long live explainable AI! Hypothesis-driven decision support using evaluative AI. *Proceedings of ACM FAccT 2023* (pp. 333–342). DOI: 10.1145/3593013.3594001

Pachl, E., Langer, F., Markert, T., & Lorenz, J. M. (2024). A view on vulnerabilities: The security challenges of XAI. *Proceedings of the Symposium on Scaling AI Assessments (SAIA 2024)*. DOI: 10.4230/OASIcs.SAIA.2024.12

Perez, F., & Ribeiro, I. (2022). Ignore previous prompt: Attack techniques for language models. NeurIPS ML Safety Workshop 2022. DOI: 10.48550/arXiv.2211.09527

Rai, D., Zhou, Y., Feng, S., Samaras, D., & Yao, Z. (2024). A practical review of mechanistic interpretability for transformer-based language models. arXiv preprint. https://doi.org//arXiv.2407.02646DOI: 10.48550

Salih, A., Galazzo, I. B., Cruciani, F., Brusini, L., Radeva, P., Petersen, S. E., & Menegaz, G. (2025). A perspective on explainable artificial intelligence methods: SHAP and LIME. *Advanced Intelligent Systems*, *7*(6), 2400304. DOI: 10.1002/aisy.202400304

Shen, T., Jin, R., Huang, Y., Liu, C., Dong, W., Guo, Z., Wu, X., Liu, Y., & Xiong, D. (2023). Large language model alignment: A survey. arXiv preprint. https://doi.org//arXiv.2309.15025DOI: 10.48550

Shen, X., Chen, Z., Backes, M., Shen, Y., & Zhang, Y. (2024). Do Anything Now: Characterizing and evaluating in-the-wild jailbreak prompts on large language models. *Proceedings of ACM CCS 2024*. DOI: 10.1145/3658644.3670388

Singh, C., Inala, J. P., Galley, M., Caruana, R., & Gao, J. (2024). Rethinking interpretability in the era of large language models. arXiv preprint. https://doi.org//arXiv.2402.01761DOI: 10.48550

Slack, D., Hilgard, S., Jia, E., Singh, S., & Lakkaraju, H. (2020). Fooling LIME and SHAP: Adversarial attacks on post hoc explanation methods. Proceedings of AAAI/ACM AIES 2020 (pp. 180–186). DOI: 10.1145/3375627.3375830

Vadillo, J., Santana, R., & Lozano, J. A. (2025). Adversarial attacks in explainable machine learning: A survey of threats against models and humans. *Wiley Interdisciplinary Reviews. Data Mining and Knowledge Discovery*, *1567*(1), e1567. Advance online publication. DOI: 10.1002/widm.1567

Wang, K. R., Variengien, A., Conmy, A., Shlegeris, B., & Steinhardt, J. (2023). Interpretability in the wild: A circuit for indirect object identification in GPT-2 small. *Proceedings of ICLR 2023*. DOI: 10.48550/arXiv.2211.00593

Wu, X., Zhao, H., Zhu, Y., Shi, Y., Luo, F., Hu, J., Han, S., Chen, H., Hsieh, C.-J., & Xu, H. (2024). Usable XAI: 10 strategies towards exploiting explainability in the LLM era. arXiv preprint. https://doi.org//arXiv.2403.08946DOI: 10.48550

KEY TERMS AND DEFINITIONS

Adversarial Attacks: These are techniques used to deceive AI models by providing subtly manipulated input data. In vision, this might be a pixel change invisible to humans; in text, it involves specific phrasing designed to trigger an incorrect or unintended response from the system.

Explainable Artificial Intelligence (XAI): XAI is a set of processes and methods that allows human users to comprehend and trust the results created by machine learning algorithms. It moves away from "black box" models by providing clear reasoning for how a specific output or decision was reached.

Jailbreaking: Jailbreaking refers to the use of sophisticated prompts designed to bypass the safety filters and ethical guidelines of an LLM. The goal is to force the model to generate restricted content, such as instructions for illegal acts or hate speech.

Large Language Models (LLMs): LLMs are deep learning algorithms trained on massive datasets to recognize, summarize, translate, and generate content. Using transformer architectures, they predict the next token in a sequence, allowing them to engage in human-like conversation and perform complex reasoning tasks.

Mechanistic Interpretability: This field focuses on reverse-engineering the internal "circuits" of neural networks. Instead of just looking at inputs and outputs, researchers study individual neurons and weights to understand the specific mathematical logic and internal representations that drive a model's behavior.

Prompt Injection: This is a security vulnerability where a user "hijacks" the model's instructions by inserting malicious text into a prompt. It tricks the AI into ignoring its original developer-set constraints and following the user's new, often harmful, commands instead.

Compilation of References

AAAI. (2025). AIES article 31733. https://ojs.aaai.org/index.php/AIES/article/view/31733/33900

Abiona, O. O., Oladapo, O. J., Modupe, O. T., Oyeniran, O. C., Adewusi, A. O., & Komolafe, A. M.Oluwatosin Oluwatimileyin AbionaOluwatayo Jacob OladapoOluwole Temidayo ModupeOyekunle Claudius OyeniranAdebunmi Okechukwu AdewusiAbiola Moshood Komolafe. (2024). The emergence and importance of DevSecOps: Integrating and reviewing security practices within the DevOps pipeline. *World Journal of Advanced Engineering Technology and Sciences*, *11*(2), 127–133. DOI: 10.30574/wjaets.2024.11.2.0093

ACM. (2025). Full article. https://dl.acm.org/doi/fullHtml/10.1145/1506409.1506439

Ahern, D. (2025). The New Anticipatory Governance Culture for Innovation: Regulatory Foresight, Regulatory Experimentation and Regulatory Learning. *European Business Organization Law Review*, *26*(2), 241–283. Advance online publication. DOI: 10.1007/s40804-025-00348-7

Ahmad, L., ... (2025). OpenAI's approach to external red teaming for AI models and systems. *arXiv preprint arXiv:2503.16431.*

Ahmadi, M., Aly, H., & Gu, J. (2026). A comprehensive review of AI-driven approaches for smart grid stability and reliability. *Renewable & Sustainable Energy Reviews*, *226*, 116424. https://www.sciencedirect.com/science/article/pii/S1364032125010974. DOI: 10.1016/j.rser.2025.116424

Ahmed, F. (2024). Cybersecurity Policy Frameworks for AI in Government: Balancing National Security and Privacy Concerns. *International Journal of Multidisciplinary on Science and Management*, *1*(4), 43–53. https://www.ijmsm.org/volume1-issue4/IJMSM-V1I4P107.pdf

Ahmed, H. A., Bawany, N. Z., & Shamsi, J. A. (2021). CaPBug-A framework for automatic bug categorization and prioritization using NLP and machine learning algorithms. *IEEE Access : Practical Innovations, Open Solutions*, *9*, 50496–50512. DOI: 10.1109/ACCESS.2021.3069248

Al Siam, A., Alazab, M., Awajan, A., & Faruqui, N. (2024). *A comprehensive review of AI's current impact and future prospects in cybersecurity. Daffodil International University*. Al-Balqa Applied University.

Al-Dosari, K., & Fetais, N. (2023). Risk-management framework and information-security systems for SMEs: A meta-analysis approach. *Electronics (Basel)*, *12*(17), 3629. DOI: 10.3390/electronics12173629

Alhamdi, M. J. M., Al-Dabbagh, S., & Al-Timemy, A. H. (2025). AI-based malware detection in IoT networks within smart cities: A survey. Computer Communications, 224, 108055. Elsevier. DOI: 10.1016/j.comcom.2025.108055

Al-Maamari, A. (2025). Between Innovation and Oversight: A Cross-Regional Study of AI Risk Management Frameworks in the EU, U.S., UK, and China. *arXiv*. https://arxiv.org/abs/2503.05773

Alonso, J., Piliszek, R., & Cankar, M. (2023). Embracing IaC through the DevSecOps philosophy: Concepts, challenges, and a reference framework. *IEEE Software*, *40*(1), 56–62. DOI: 10.1109/MS.2022.3212194

Alqahtani, H., Alzahrani, B., & Alshamrani, A. (2022). Deep learning-based dynamic analysis for malware detection using hybrid features. *Computers & Security*, *115*, 102614. DOI: 10.1016/j.cose.2022.102614

Alshahrani, S., & Huang, C. C. (2021). Intelligent dynamic malware detection using machine learning in IP reputation for forensics data analytics. *Future Generation Computer Systems*, *118*, 171–185. DOI: 10.1016/j.future.2021.01.007

Altmann, A., Tolosi, L., Sander, O., & Lengauer, T. (2010). Permutation importance: A corrected feature importance measure. *Bioinformatics (Oxford, England)*, *26*(10), 1340–1347. DOI: 10.1093/bioinformatics/btq134 PMID: 20385727

Amar, H. (2025). *Cyber Security Management Research Paper* [GitHub Repository]. GitHub. https://github.com/Huz-Amar/Cyber-Security-Management-Research-Paper

Andrews, D. W. K. (1993). Tests for parameter instability and structural change with unknown change point. *Econometrica*, *61*(4), 821–856. DOI: 10.2307/2951764

Arora, A. (2025). Zero trust architecture: Revolutionizing cybersecurity for modern digital environments. *SSRN*, 5268151.

Atasoy, T., Akıncı, H. E., & Ercin, O. (2015). An analysis on smart grid applications and grid integration of renewable energy systems in smart cities. In *2015 International Conference on Renewable Energy Research and Applications (ICRERA)* (pp. 547–550). DOI: 10.1109/ICRERA.2015.7418473

Backman, S. (2022). Risk vs. Threat-Based Cybersecurity: The Case of the EU. *European Security*, *32*(1), 85–103. DOI: 10.1080/09662839.2022.2069464

Bai, Y., ... (2022). Constitutional AI: Harmlessness from AI feedback. *arXiv preprint arXiv:2212.08073*.

Bai, J., & Perron, P. (1998). Estimating and testing linear models with multiple structural changes. *Econometrica*, *66*(1), 47–78. DOI: 10.2307/2998540

Balogun, A. O., Bajeh, A. O., Mojeed, H. A., & Akintola, A. G. (2020). Software defect prediction: A multi-criteria decision-making approach. *Nigerian Journal of Technological Research*, *15*(1), 35–42. DOI: 10.4314/njtr.v15i1.7

Baniecki, H., & Biecek, P. (2024). Adversarial attacks and defenses in explainable artificial intelligence: A survey. *Information Fusion*, *107*, 102303. DOI: 10.1016/j.inffus.2024.102303

Basheer, N., Islam, S., Alwaheidi, M. K. S., Mouratidis, H., Papastergiou, S., & Haurogné, J. (2026). Large language model based hybrid framework for automatic vulnerability detection with explainable AI for cybersecurity enhancement. *Integrated Computer-Aided Engineering*, *33*(1), 38–54. Advance online publication. DOI: 10.1177/10692509251368663

Bashir, T. (2024). Zero trust architecture: Enhancing cybersecurity in enterprise networks. *Journal of Computer Science and Technology Studies*, *6*(4), 54–59.

Bazzi, O., Chehab, A., Kayssi, A., & Harb, H. (2021). Deep learning for malware detection in Android systems using system calls. *Journal of Information Security and Applications*, *58*, 102718. DOI: 10.1016/j.jisa.2020.102718

Behl, A., & Behl, K. (2017). *Cyberwar: The next threat to national security and what to do about it*. Oxford University Press., DOI: 10.1093/oso/9780190654501.001.0001

Belloni, A., Chernozhukov, V., & Hansen, C. (2014). Inference on treatment effects after selection among high-dimensional controls. *The Review of Economic Studies*, *81*(2), 608–650. DOI: 10.1093/restud/rdt044

Benka, D., Horváth, D., Špendla, L., Gašpar, G., & Strémy, M. (2025). Machine learning-based detection of anomalies, intrusions, and threats in industrial control systems. *IEEE Access : Practical Innovations, Open Solutions*, *13*, 12502–12514. DOI: 10.1109/ACCESS.2025.3530902

Bhadauria, S., & Mohanty, T. (2021). Hybrid intrusion detection system using an unsupervised method for anomaly-based detection. In *2021 IEEE International Conference on Advanced Networks and Telecommunications Systems (ANTS)* (pp. 1–6). DOI: 10.1109/ANTS52808.2021.9936919

Bilal, A., Ebert, D., & Lin, B. (2025). LLMs for explainable AI: A comprehensive survey. arXiv preprint arXiv:2504.00125.

Bommasani, R., Hudson, D. A., Adeli, E., Altman, R., Arora, S., von Arx, S., . . . Liang, P. (2022). On the opportunities and risks of foundation models. *arXiv preprint arXiv:2108.07258*. https://doi.org//arXiv.2108.07258DOI: 10.48550

Bose, A., Hu, X., Shin, K. G., & Park, T. (2008). Behavioral detection of malware on mobile handsets. In *Proceedings of the 6th International Conference on Mobile Systems, Applications, and Services (MobiSys)* (pp. 225-238). ACM. DOI: 10.1145/1378600.1378626

Bose, I., & Mahapatra, R. K. (2001). Business data mining—A machine learning perspective. *Information & Management*, *39*(3), 211–225. DOI: 10.1016/S0378-7206(01)00091-X

Boucher, N.. (2022). Bad characters: Imperceptible NLP attacks. In *2022 IEEE Symposium on Security and Privacy (SP)*. DOI: 10.1109/SP46214.2022.9833641

Breunig, M. M., Kriegel, H.-P., Ng, R. T., & Sander, J. (2000). LOF: Identifying density-based local outliers. *Proceedings of ACM SIGMOD*, 93-104. DOI: 10.1145/342009.335388

Brown, T., ... (2020). Language models are few-shot learners. In *Advances in Neural Information Processing Systems (NeurIPS)*.

Brown, T. B., Mann, B., Ryder, N., Subbiah, M., Kaplan, J., Dhariwal, P., & Amodei, D. (2020). Language models are few-shot learners. *Advances in Neural Information Processing Systems*. Advance online publication. DOI: 10.48550/arXiv.2005.14165

Brundage, M., Avin, S., & Clark, J.. (2020). Toward trustworthy AI development: Mechanisms for supporting verifiable claims. *Nature Machine Intelligence*, *2*, 81–83. DOI: 10.1038/s42256-020-0188-1

Bruschi, D., & Diomede, N. (2022). *A framework for assessing AI ethics with applications to cybersecurity*. Published online.

Burguera, I., Zurutuza, U., & Nadjm-Tehrani, S. (2011). Crowdroid: Behavior-based malware detection system for Android. In *Proceedings of the 1st ACM Workshop on Security and Privacy in Smartphones and Mobile Devices* (pp. 15-26). ACM. DOI: 10.1145/2046614.2046619

Cabinet Office. (2021). *National Cyber Strategy 2022*. https://www.gov.uk/government/publications/national-cyber-strategy-2022

Campbell, J., McDonald, C., & Sethibe, T. (2010). Public and private sector IT governance: Identifying contextual differences. *AJIS. Australasian Journal of Information Systems, 16*(2). Advance online publication. DOI: 10.3127/ajis.v16i2.538

Candès, E. J., Li, X., Ma, Y., & Wright, J. (2011). Robust principal component analysis? *Journal of the Association for Computing Machinery, 58*(3), 11. DOI: 10.1145/1970392.1970395

Capili, M. (2024). Simulation-based evaluation of perimeter-based and zero trust security implementation on internet of things [Doctoral dissertation, The George Washington University].

Capuano, N., Fenza, G., Loia, V., & Stanzione, C. (2022). Explainable artificial intelligence in cybersecurity: A survey. *IEEE Access : Practical Innovations, Open Solutions, 10*, 98856–98881. DOI: 10.1109/ACCESS.2022.3204171

Carlini, N.. (2023). Poisoning web-scale training datasets is practical. In *2023 IEEE Symposium on Security and Privacy (SP).*

Carlini, N., Tramèr, F., Wallace, E., Jagielski, M., Herbert-Voss, A., Lee, K., & Erlingsson, Ú. (2023). Extracting training data from large language models. *USENIX Security Symposium*. DOI: 10.48550/arXiv.2012.07805

Carlini, N., & Wagner, D. (2017). Towards evaluating the robustness of neural networks. In *2017 IEEE Symposium on Security and Privacy (SP)*. DOI: 10.1109/SP.2017.49

Cath, C., Wachter, S., Mittelstadt, B., Taddeo, M., & Floridi, L. (2020). Securing trust: Ethical considerations for the adoption of artificial intelligence in cybersecurity. *Nature Machine Intelligence, 2*(6), 264–266.

Chaganti, K. C. (2024). *Ethical AI for cybersecurity: A framework for balancing innovation and regulation*. S&P Global.

Chandola, V., Banerjee, A., & Kumar, V. (2009). Anomaly detection: A survey. *ACM Computing Surveys*, *41*(3), 15. DOI: 10.1145/1541880.1541882

Chandramouli, R., Kautz, F., Torres-Arias, S., & (U.S.), N. I. of S. and T. (2024). Strategies for the integration of software supply chain security in DevSecOps CICD pipelines : DOI: 10.6028/NIST.SP.800-204D

Chapman, P. J., Rubio-González, C., & Thakur, A. V. (2025). Interleaving static analysis and LLM prompting with applications to error specification inference. *International Journal of Software Tools for Technology Transfer*, *27*(2), 239–254. DOI: 10.1007/s10009-025-00780-7

Charmet, J., Eshete, B., & Biggio, B. (2022). Adversarial robustness of behavior-based malware detectors: A survey. *Computers & Security*, *120*, 102809. DOI: 10.1016/j.cose.2022.102809

Chase, H. (2022). *LangChain*. GitHub repository. https://github.com/langchain-ai/langchain

Chen, X., Salem, A., Chen, D., Backes, M., Ma, S., Shen, Q., Wu, Z., & Zhang, Y. (2020). BadNL: Backdoor attacks against NLP models with semantic-preserving improvements. *arXiv preprint arXiv:2006.01043*.

Chen, C., & Liu, L. M. (1993). Joint estimation of model parameters and outlier effects in time series. *Journal of the American Statistical Association*, *88*(421), 284–297. DOI: 10.1080/01621459.1993.10594321

Chen, J., Li, C., & Wang, W. (2022). DMalNet: Dynamic malware analysis based on API feature engineering and deep learning. *Computers & Security*, *116*, 102676. DOI: 10.1016/j.cose.2022.102676

Chen, S., Tao, F., Pan, C., Hu, X., Ma, H., Li, C., Zhao, Y., & Wang, Y. (2021). Modeling quality changes in Pacific white shrimp (Litopenaeus vannamei) during storage: Comparison of the Arrhenius model and Random Forest model. *Journal of Food Processing and Preservation*, *45*(1). Advance online publication. DOI: 10.1111/jfpp.14999

Chen, T., & Guestrin, C. (2016). XGBoost: A scalable tree boosting system. In *Proceedings of the 22nd ACM SIGKDD International Conference on Knowledge Discovery and Data Mining* (pp. 785–794). DOI: 10.1145/2939672.2939785

Chen, X., Liu, C., Li, B., Lu, K., & Song, D. (2021). Targeted backdoor attacks on deep learning systems using data poisoning. *IEEE Transactions on Dependable and Secure Computing*, *18*(4), 1566–1580. DOI: 10.1109/TDSC.2019.2931311

Chernozhukov, V., Chetverikov, D., Demirer, M., Duflo, E., Hansen, C., Newey, W., & Robins, J. (2018). Double/debiased machine learning for treatment and structural parameters. *The Econometrics Journal, 21*(1), C1–C68. DOI: 10.1111/ectj.12097

Chhabra, D., & Chadha, R. (2024). Automatic bug triaging process: An enhanced machine learning approach through Large Language Models. *Engineering Technology & Applied Science Research, 14*(6), 18557–18562. DOI: 10.48084/etasr.8829

Chokshi, S., Shook, J., & Dighe, R. (2021). Implementing zero trust security: Key enablers and best practices. *Journal of Cybersecurity and Information Security, 7*(3), 45–59.

Choraś, M., Kozik, R., Pawlicki, M., Hołubowicz, W., & Franch, X. (2019). Software development metrics prediction using time series methods. In *Computer Information Systems and Industrial Management* (pp. 311–323). Springer International Publishing., DOI: 10.1007/978-3-030-28957-7_26

Christodorescu, M., Jha, S., Seshia, S. A., Song, D., & Bryant, R. (2005). Semantics-aware malware detection. In *2005 IEEE Symposium on Security and Privacy* (pp. 32-46). IEEE. DOI: 10.1109/SP.2005.20

Cinà, A. E., Grosse, K., Demontis, A., Vascon, S., Zellinger, W., Moser, B. A., Oprea, A., Biggio, B., Pelillo, M., & Roli, F. (2023). Wild patterns reloaded: A survey of machine learning security against training data poisoning. *ACM Computing Surveys, 55*(13s), 1–39. DOI: 10.1145/3585385

Clark, A. (2024). *Cybersecurity in the UK.* House of Commons Library. https://commonslibrary.parliament.uk/research-briefings/cbp-9821/

Cloud Security Alliance. (2020). Zero trust working group guidance. https://cloudsecurityalliance.org/

Conmy, A., Mavor-Parker, A. N., Lynch, A., Heimersheim, S., & Garriga-Alonso, A. (2023). Towards automated circuit discovery for mechanistic interpretability. *Advances in Neural Information Processing Systems, 36*, 16318–16352. DOI: 10.52202/075280-0719

Costea, A., Tiwari, A., Chianasta, S., R, K., Roychoudhury, A., & Sergey, I. (2023). Hippodrome : Data race repair using static analysis summaries. *ACM Transactions on Software Engineering and Methodology, 32*(2), 1–33. DOI: 10.1145/3546942

Creemers, R. (2022). China's Emerging Data Protection Framework. *Journal of Cybersecurity, 8*(1), 1–12. DOI: 10.1093/cybsec/tyac011

Creemers, R. (2023a). The Chinese Conception of Cybersecurity: A Conceptual, Institutional and Regulatory Genealogy. *Journal of Contemporary China*, *33*(146), 1–16. DOI: 10.1080/10670564.2023.2196508

Creemers, R. (2023b). Cybersecurity Law and Regulation in China: Securing the Smart State. *China Law and Society Review*, *6*(2), 111–145. DOI: 10.1163/25427466-06020001

Cuevas, A., Febrero, M., & Fraiman, R. (2004). An ANOVA test for functional data. *Computational Statistics & Data Analysis*, *47*(1), 111–122. DOI: 10.1016/j.csda.2003.10.021

Dalla Palma, S., Di Nucci, D., Palomba, F., & Tamburri, D. A. (2022). Within-project defect prediction of infrastructure-as-code using product and process metrics. *IEEE Transactions on Software Engineering*, *48*(6), 2086–2104. DOI: 10.1109/TSE.2021.3051492

Danilevsky, M., Qian, K., Aharonov, R., Katsis, Y., Kawas, B., & Sen, P. (2021). A survey of the state of explainable AI for natural language processing. *Proceedings of the 1st AACL-IJCNLP*, 447–459. DOI: 10.18653/v1/2020.aacl-main.46

Dergipark. (2025). Article. https://dergipark.org.tr/en/download/article-file/4332869

Dettmers, T., ... (2023). QLoRA: Efficient finetuning of quantized LLMs. *arXiv preprint arXiv:2305.14314*. DOI: 10.52202/075280-0441

Devlin, J., Chang, M. W., Lee, K., & Toutanova, K. (2019). BERT: Pre-training of deep bidirectional transformers for language understanding. *Proceedings of NAACL-HLT*. DOI: 10.48550/arXiv.1810.04805

Dhiman, P., Saini, N., Gulzar, Y., Turaev, S., Kaur, A., Nisa, K. U., & Hamid, Y. (2022). A review and comparative analysis of relevant approaches of zero trust network model. *Applied Sciences (Basel, Switzerland)*, *12*(17), 8773. DOI: 10.3390/app12178773

Dhirani, L. L., Mukhtiar, N., Chowdhry, B. S., & Newe, T. (2024). Review ethical dilemmas and privacy issues in emerging technologies: A review. *University of Limerick; Mehran University of Engineering and Technology*.

Dinu, A., Vasile, P. C., & Georgescu, A. (2024). *AI-driven solutions for cybersecurity: Comparative analysis and ethical aspects. National Institute for Research and Development in Informatics*. ICI Bucharest.

Dotse, J.. (2025). Zero trust architecture implementation in enterprise networks. *International Journal of Computer Applications*, *187*(45), 1–10. https://ijcaonline.org/archives/volume187/number45/dotse-2025-ijca-925740.pdf

Drinhausen, K., & Legarda, H. (2022). *"Comprehensive National Security" Unleashed: How Xi's Approach Shapes China's Policies at Home and Abroad*. MERICS. https://merics.org/en/report/comprehensive-national-security-unleashed-how-xis-approach-shapes-chinas-policies-home-and

Eleweke, I., Umakor, M., Ndubuisi, C., Amomo, C., Adeniji, S., & Temidayo, M. (2025, October). AI-driven threat detection and prevention in cloud computing environments. *American Journal of Innovation in Science and Engineering*, *4*(3), 49–56. DOI: 10.54536/ajise.v4i3.5041

Erich, F. M. A., Amrit, C., & Daneva, M. (2017). A qualitative study of DevOps usage in practice. *Journal of Software (Malden, MA)*, *29*(6), e1885. DOI: 10.1002/smr.1885

European Commission. (2023). *Better Regulation Toolbox – July 2023 Edition*. https://commission.europa.eu/system/files/2023-09/BR%20toolbox%20-%20Jul%202023%20-%20FINAL.pdf

European Commission. (2024). *Artificial Intelligence Act*. Official Journal of the European Union. https://artificialintelligenceact.eu/

European Parliament. Future Shocks 2023: Anticipating and weathering the next storms. EPRS Study 751.428, July 2023. ISSN 2600-5174. DOI: 10.2861/88235

European Union. (2022a). *Directive (EU) 2022/2555 on Measures for a High Common Level of Cybersecurity Across the Union*. https://eur-lex.europa.eu/eli/dir/2022/2555/oj

European Union. (2022b). *Directive (EU) 2022/2557 on the Resilience of Critical Entities*. https://eur-lex.europa.eu/eli/dir/2022/2557/oj

Eze, E. C., Durotolu, G. A., John, F. D., & Raji, S. O.Esther Chinwe EzeGrace A. DurotoluFen Danjuma JohnShakirat O. Raji. (2025). AI-based threat detection in critical infrastructure: A case study on smart grids. *World Journal of Advanced Research and Reviews*, *27*(1), 1365–1380. DOI: 10.30574/wjarr.2025.27.1.2655

Fanqi Meng, F. M., Fanqi Meng, W. C., & Wenying Cheng, J. W. (2023). An integrated semi-supervised software defect prediction model. *Wangji Wanglu Jishu Xuekan*, *24*(6), 1307–1317. DOI: 10.53106/160792642023112406013

Fernandez, E. B., & Brazhuk, A. (2024). A critical analysis of zero trust architecture (ZTA). Computer Standards & Interfaces, 89, 103832. Cunningham, C., Blankenship, J., Balaouras, S., Murphy, R & Cyr, M. (2018). The zero trust eXtended (ZTX) ecosystem. Forrester, Cambridge, MA.

Ficco, M. (2021). A deep neural network-based technique for ransomware detection and classification. *Future Internet*, *13*(2), 25. DOI: 10.3390/fi13020025

Fjeld, B., Achten, N., Hilligoss, H., Nagy, A., & Srikumar, R. (2020). *Principled artificial intelligence: Mapping consensus in ethical and rights-based approaches to AI principles*. Berkman Klein Center Research Publication No. 2020-1.

Floridi, L., & Cowan, J. (2022). Operationalizing AI ethics. *AI and Ethics*, *2*, 1–12. DOI: 10.1007/s43681-021-00085-8

Floridi, L., & Cowls, J. (2021). A unified framework of five principles for AI in society. *Harvard Data Science Review*, *3*(1). Advance online publication. DOI: 10.1162/99608f92.8cd550d1

Floridi, L., Cowls, J., Beltrametti, M., Chatila, R., Chazerand, P., Dignum, V., Luetge, C., Madelin, R., Pagallo, U., Rossi, F., Schafer, B., Valcke, P., & Vayena, E. (2018). AI4People—An ethical framework for a good AI society. *Minds and Machines*, *28*(4), 689–707. DOI: 10.1007/s11023-018-9482-5 PMID: 30930541

Friedman, J. H. (2001). Greedy function approximation: A gradient boosting machine. *Annals of Statistics*, *29*(5), 1189–1232. DOI: 10.1214/aos/1013203451

Fu, R. (2025). Design and implementation of network intrusion detection system based on machine learning. In *2025 International Conference on Intelligent Systems and Computational Networks (ICISCN)* (pp. 1–6). DOI: 10.1109/ICISCN64258.2025.10934502

Gao, Y., ... (2020). Backdoor attacks and countermeasures on deep learning: A comprehensive review. *arXiv preprint arXiv:2007.10760*.

Goffer, M., Uddin, M. S., Kaur, J., Hasan, S. N., Barikdar, C., Hassan, J., Das, N., Chakraborty, P., & Hasan, R. (2025, April). AI-enhanced cyber threat detection and response advancing national security in critical infrastructure. *Journal of Posthumanism, 5*.

Goldblum, M., Fowl, L., Hand, E., & Goldstein, T. (2023). Adversarial attacks on machine learning systems. *ACM Computing Surveys*, *55*(9), 1–35. DOI: 10.1145/3538707

Goodfellow, I., Shlens, J., & Szegedy, C. (2014). Explaining and harnessing adversarial examples. arXiv:1412.6572.

Goyal, V., ... (2023). Dropping the baton: Tokenization artifacts in LLMs. *arXiv preprint arXiv:2309.16434*.

Greshake, K., Abdelnabi, S., & Slamanig, D.. (2023). *Not what you signed up for: Compromising real-world LLM-integrated applications with indirect prompt injection*. ACM CCS., DOI: 10.1145/3576915.3623107

Gu, N.. (2023). A gradient control method for backdoor attacks on parameter-efficient tuning. In *Proceedings of the Annual Meeting of the Association for Computational Linguistics (ACL)*. DOI: 10.18653/v1/2023.acl-long.194

Guo, F., Jiao, H., Zhang, X., Zhou, Y., & Feng, H. (2024). Information security network intrusion detection system based on machine learning. In *2024 International Conference on Data Science and Network Security (ICDSNS)* (pp. 1–4). DOI: 10.1109/ICDSNS62112.2024.10691041

Gu, T., Dolan-Gavitt, B., & Garg, S. (2019). BadNets: Identifying vulnerabilities in the machine learning model supply chain. *IEEE Access : Practical Innovations, Open Solutions*, *7*, 47230–47240. DOI: 10.1109/ACCESS.2019.2909068

Haghshenas, S. H., Hasnat, M. A., & Naeini, M. (2022). A temporal graph neural network for cyber attack detection and localization in smart grids. arXiv preprint arXiv:2212.03390.

Haghshenas, S. H., Hasnat, M. A., & Naeini, M. (2023). A temporal graph neural network for cyber attack detection and localization in smart grids. In *2023 IEEE Power & Energy Society Innovative Smart Grid Technologies Conference (ISGT)* (pp. 1–5). IEEE. DOI: 10.1109/ISGT51731.2023.10066446

Hamilton, J. D. (1989). A new approach to the economic analysis of nonstationary time series and the business cycle. *Econometrica*, *57*(2), 357–384. DOI: 10.2307/1912559

Hampel, F. R., Ronchetti, E. M., Rousseeuw, P. J., & Stahel, W. A. (1986). *Robust Statistics: The Approach Based on Influence Functions*. Wiley.

Hanisch, M., Goldsby, C. M., Fabian, N. E., & Oehmichen, J. (2023). Digital Governance: A Conceptual Framework and Research Agenda. *Journal of Business Research*, *162*, 113777. DOI: 10.1016/j.jbusres.2023.113777

Haurogné, J., Basheer, N., & Islam, S. (2024). Vulnerability detection using BERT based LLM model with transparency obligation practice towards trustworthy AI. *Machine Learning with Applications*, *18*, 100598. DOI: 10.1016/j.mlwa.2024.100598

Healthcare Information and Management Systems Society. (2024). *2023 HIMSS Healthcare Cybersecurity Survey*. https://www.himss.org/sites/hde/files/media/file/2024/03/01/2023-himss-cybersecurity-survey-x.pdf

Hernández-Molinos, M. J., Sánchez-García, A. J., Barrientos-Martínez, R. E., Pérez-Arriaga, J. C., & Ocharán-Hernández, J. O. (2023). Software defect prediction with Bayesian approaches. *Mathematics*, *11*(11), 2524. DOI: 10.3390/math11112524

Hodgins, M. W. (2024). The Perils of Cybersecurity Regulation. *The Review of Austrian Economics*. Advance online publication. DOI: 10.1007/s11138-024-00660-4

Hong, L., & Wang, T. (2023). PETA: Parameter-efficient trojan attacks. *arXiv preprint arXiv:2310.00648*.

Hosain, M. T., Jim, J. R., Mridha, M. F., & Kabir, M. M. (2024). Explainable AI approaches in deep learning: Advancements, applications and challenges. *Computers & Electrical Engineering*, *117*, 109246. DOI: 10.1016/j.compeleceng.2024.109246

Hossain, S. B., Jiang, N., Zhou, Q., Li, X., Chiang, W.-H., Lyu, Y., Nguyen, H., & Tripp, O. (2024a). A deep dive into large language models for automated bug localization and repair. Proceedings of the ACM on Software Engineering, 1(FSE), 1471–1493. DOI: 10.1145/3660773

Huangfu, Z. (2024). The National Cybersecurity Strategy of the United States and Its Global Impact. *World Politics*, *4*(4), 1–11. DOI: 10.25136/2409-8671.2024.4.72317

Huang, L., Yu, W., Ma, W., Zhong, W., Feng, Z., Wang, H., Chen, Q., Peng, W., Feng, X., Qin, B., & Liu, T. (2024). A survey on hallucination in large language models: Principles, taxonomy, challenges, and open questions. *ACM Transactions on Information Systems*. Advance online publication. DOI: 10.1145/3703155

Huber, P. J. (1964). Robust estimation of a location parameter. *Annals of Mathematical Statistics*, *35*(1), 73–101. DOI: 10.1214/aoms/1177703732

Hu, E. J.. (2022). LoRA: Low-rank adaptation of large language models. In *International Conference on Learning Representations (ICLR)*.

Humphreys, D., Koay, A., Desmond, D., & Mealy, E. (2024). AI hype as a cybersecurity risk: The moral responsibility of implementing generative AI in business. *Published online*.

Ibrahim, A., Abdelsalam, H., & Taj-Eddin, I. (2023). Software defects prediction at method level using ensemble learning techniques. *International Journal of Intelligent Computing and Information Sciences*, *23*(2), 28–49. DOI: 10.21608/ijicis.2023.189934.1251

ICERT. (2023). AI in auditing. https://icertpublication.com/wp-content/uploads/2023/10/29.-AI-in-Auditing.pdf

Intazar, M., Rahman, S., Khan, A., & Lee, J. (2025). Beyond perimeter defenses: Implementing zero-trust security models for cloud computing in the era of advanced cyber threats. Global Research Journal of Natural Science and Technology, 3(2).

Intrusion detection in smart grids using artificial intelligence-based ensemble modelling. *(2024)*. Cluster Computing.

Islam, U., Ullah, H., Khan, N., Saleem, K., & Ahmad, I. (2025). AI-enhanced intrusion detection in smart renewable energy grids: A novel Industry 4.0 cyber threat management approach. *International Journal of Critical Infrastructure Protection*, *50*, 100769. DOI: 10.1016/j.ijcip.2025.100769

Jahanshahi, H., Cevik, M., & Başar, A. (2020). Predicting the number of reported bugs in a software repository. In *Advances in Artificial Intelligence* (pp. 309–320). Springer International Publishing., DOI: 10.1007/978-3-030-47358-7_31

Jeon, M., Choi, J., & Cho, S. (2022). DAIMD: Dynamic analysis for IoT malware detection using convolutional neural networks on behavior images. *Computers & Security*, *117*, 102683. DOI: 10.1016/j.cose.2022.102683

Ji, Z., Lee, N., Frieske, R., Yu, T., Su, D., Xu, Y., Ishii, E., Bang, Y. J., Madotto, A., & Fung, P. (2023). Survey of hallucination in natural language generation. *ACM Computing Surveys*, *55*(12), 1–38. DOI: 10.1145/3571730

Kabir, S., Hannan, N., Shufian, A., & Rahman Zishan, M. S. (2025). Proactive detection of cyber-physical grid attacks: A pre-attack phase identification and analysis using anomaly-based machine learning models. *Array (New York, N.Y.)*, *27*, 100441. https://www.sciencedirect.com/science/article/pii/S2590005625000682. DOI: 10.1016/j.array.2025.100441

Kadri, F., & Singla, P. (2025). Enhancing intrusion detection systems with deep learning and machine learning algorithms for real-time threat classification. In *2025 International Conference on Multi-Agent Systems for Collaborative Intelligence (ICMSCI)* (pp. 957–963). DOI: 10.1109/ICMSCI62561.2025.10894403

Kalech, M. (2019). Cyber-attack detection in SCADA systems using temporal pattern recognition techniques. *Computers & Security*, *84*, 225–238. https://www.sciencedirect.com/science/article/pii/S0167404818307594. DOI: 10.1016/j.cose.2019.03.007

Kaplan, J., ... (2020). Scaling laws for neural language models. *arXiv preprint arXiv:2001.08361*.

Kapoor, S. (2025). The imperative of zero trust architecture in modern product security. *Journal of Computer Science and Technology Studies*, *7*(6), 1096–1102.

Karamchand, G. (2025). Zero trust security architecture: A paradigm shifts in cybersecurity for the digital age. *Journal ID*, *2145*, 6523.

Kasongo, S. M., & Sun, Y. (2020). Performance analysis of intrusion detection systems using feature selection on UNSW-NB15. *Journal of Big Data*, *7*(1), 105. DOI: 10.1186/s40537-020-00379-6

Kaur, H., Selvakumar, P., Haashni, S., Anute, N., Sharma, M., & Manjunath, T. C. (2025). Representations in Developing Thinking Regarding Probabilities in Higher Education. In Anastasiadou, S., & Seremeti, L. (Eds.), *Modes of Representation in Developing Statistical Thinking in Education* (pp. 89–118). IGI Global Scientific Publishing., DOI: 10.4018/979-8-3693-9934-7.ch006

Khan, M. J. (2023). Zero trust architecture: Redefining network security paradigms in the digital age. *World Journal of Advanced Research and Reviews*, *19*(3), 105–116.

Kindervag, J. (2010). *Build security into your network's DNA: The zero trust network architecture (Tech. Rep.)*. Forrester Research.

Kolosnjaji, B., Zarras, A., Webster, G., & Eckert, C. (2016). Deep learning for classification of malware system call sequences. In AI 2016: Advances in Artificial Intelligence (pp. 137-149). Springer. DOI: 10.1007/978-3-319-50127-7_11

Kong, J., Xie, X., Cheng, M., Liu, S., Du, X., & Guo, Q. (2025). ContrastRepair : Enhancing conversation-based automated Program Repair via contrastive test case pairs. *ACM Transactions on Software Engineering and Methodology*, *34*(8), 1–31. Advance online publication. DOI: 10.1145/3719345

Krause, J., Perer, A., & Bertini, E. (2021). A survey of methods for explaining black box models. *IEEE Computer Graphics and Applications*, *41*(2), 88–99. DOI: 10.1109/MCG.2020.3048506

Kurita, K., Michel, P., & Neubig, G. (2020). *Weight poisoning attacks on pretrained models*. ACL., DOI: 10.18653/v1/2020.acl-main.249

LaValley, M. P. (2008). Logistic regression. *Circulation*, *117*(18), 2395–2399. DOI: 10.1161/CIRCULATIONAHA.106.682658 PMID: 18458181

Lee, J. H., & Park, J. (2024). A case study: Leveraging SASE technology for zero trust implementation in cloud environments. In *Proceedings of the IEEE International Conference on Cloud Computing* (pp. 1–6). IEEE.

Leslie, D. (2019). *Understanding artificial intelligence ethics and safety: A guide for the responsible design and implementation of AI systems in the public sector*. The Alan Turing Institute. DOI: 10.2139/ssrn.3403301

Li, P., Zhuo, B., Li, G., Peng, M., & Duan, G. (2025). Research on network security intrusion detection system based on deep learning. In *2025 5th Asia-Pacific Conference on Communications Technology and Computer Science (ACCTCS)* (pp. 499–503). DOI: 10.1109/ACCTCS66275.2025.00092

Li, J.. (2019). TextBugger: Generating adversarial text against real-world applications. In *Network and Distributed System Security Symposium (NDSS)*. DOI: 10.14722/ndss.2019.23138

Lin, Z., Song, C., & Gu, X. (2020). Deep learning for ransomware detection using process behavior graphs. *Computers & Security*, *92*, 101740. DOI: 10.1016/j.cose.2020.101740

Liu, K., Dolan-Gavitt, B., & Garg, S. (2018). Fine-pruning: Defending against backdooring attacks on deep neural networks. In *Research in Attacks, Intrusions, and Defenses (RAID)*.

Liu, F. T., Ting, K. M., & Zhou, Z.-H. (2008). Isolation Forest. *2008 Eighth IEEE International Conference on Data Mining*, 413-422. DOI: 10.1109/ICDM.2008.17

Liu, H., Zhang, J., & Chen, Z. (2021). Android malware detection based on long short-term memory networks and behavioral sequences. *Journal of Information Security and Applications*, *59*, 102843. DOI: 10.1016/j.jisa.2021.102843

Liu, X., Xu, N., Chen, M., & Xiao, C. (2024). AutoDAN: Generating stealthy jailbreak prompts on aligned large language models. *Proceedings of ICLR 2024*. DOI: 10.48550/arXiv.2310.04451

Liu, Y., Ma, S., & Aafer, Y.. (2018). *Trojaning attack on neural networks*. NDSS., DOI: 10.14722/ndss.2018.23291

Liu, Z., Tang, Y., Li, M., Jin, X., Long, Y., Zhang, L. F., & Luo, X. (2025). LLM-CompDroid: Repairing configuration compatibility bugs in Android apps with pre-trained large language models. *ACM Transactions on Software Engineering and Methodology*, *3736406*. Advance online publication. DOI: 10.1145/3736406

Li, W., Yin, Y., Quan, X., & Zhang, H. (2019). Gene expression value prediction based on XGBoost algorithm. *Frontiers in Genetics*, *10*, 1077. DOI: 10.3389/fgene.2019.01077 PMID: 31781160

Li, Y., Li, Z., Zhang, K., Dan, R., Jiang, S., & Zhang, Y. (2023). ChatDoctor: A medical chat model fine-tuned on a large language model meta-AI using medical domain knowledge. *Cureus*, *15*(6), e40895. DOI: 10.7759/cureus.40895 PMID: 37492832

Li, Y., Meng, G., Liu, Y., & Chen, C. (2022). Deep graph convolutional networks for behavioral malware classification. *Computers & Security*, *112*, 102508. DOI: 10.1016/j.cose.2021.102508

Luis Salas-Riega, J.. (2025). Cybersecurity and the NIST Framework: A Systematic Review of Its Implementation and Effectiveness Against Cyber Threats. *International Journal of Advanced Computer Science and Applications*, *16*(6). Advance online publication. https://thesai.org/Downloads/Volume16No6/Paper_72-Cybersecurity_and_the_NIST_Framework.pdf. DOI: 10.14569/IJACSA.2025.0160672

Luo, J., ... (2025). Large language model agent: A survey on methodology, applications and challenges. *arXiv preprint arXiv:2503.21460.*

Madry, A.. (2018). Towards deep learning models resistant to adversarial attacks. In *International Conference on Learning Representations (ICLR).*

Maniriho, P., Nyirahabineza, J., & Niyonzima, J. (2024). Comparative analysis of malware detection approaches in modern cyber–physical systems. *International Journal of Safety and Security Engineering*, *15*(2), 189–200. DOI: 10.18280/ijsse.150201

Manjunath, M., Ogwu, M. C., Udayakumar, S., Kuchipudi, J. D., Rengarajan, C., & Manjunath, T. C. (2026). Chromatography in Food Contaminant Analysis: Principles, Advances, and Applications for Food Safety. In Ogwu, M., & Izah, S. (Eds.), *Detection, Identification, and Monitoring of Food Contaminants* (pp. 207–238). IGI Global Scientific Publishing., DOI: 10.4018/979-8-3373-3982-5.ch007

Maronna, R. A., Martin, R. D., & Yohai, V. J. (2006). *Robust Statistics: Theory and Methods*. Wiley. DOI: 10.1002/0470010940

Mathew, E. S. (2025). Enhancing security in large language models: A comprehensive review of prompt injection attacks and defenses. *Journal on Artificial Intelligence*, *7*(1), 347–363. DOI: 10.32604/jai.2025.069841

Mbona, I., & Eloff, J. H. (2024). Data sets for cyber security machine learning models: A methodological approach. In *IoTBDS* (pp. 149–156). DOI: 10.5220/0012598400003705

McIntosh, T. R., Susnjak, T., Liu, T., Watters, P., Nowrozy, R., & Halgamuge, M. N. (2024). From COBIT to ISO 42001: Evaluating Cybersecurity Frameworks for Opportunities, Risks, and Regulatory Compliance in Commercializing Large Language Models. *Computers & Security*, *144*, 103964. Advance online publication. DOI: 10.1016/j.cose.2024.103964

Menahem, E., Shabtai, A., & Elovici, Y. (2014). Mobile malware detection through analysis of deviations in application network behavior. *Computers & Security*, *43*, 1–18. DOI: 10.1016/j.cose.2014.02.002

Meng, K., Bau, D., Andonian, A., & Belinkov, Y. (2022). Locating and editing factual associations in GPT. *Advances in Neural Information Processing Systems*, *35*, 17359–17372. DOI: 10.48550/arXiv.2202.05262

Meng, X. (2024, July). Advanced AI and ML techniques in cybersecurity: Supervised and unsupervised learning, reinforcement learning, and neural networks in threat detection and response. *Applied and Computational Engineering*, *82*(1), 1–5. DOI: 10.54254/2755-2721/82/2024GLG0054

Microsoft Corporation. (2023). Implementing a Zero Trust security model at Microsoft. Inside Track Blog. https://www.microsoft.com/insidetrack/blog/implementing-a-zero-trust-security-model-at-microsoft/

Miller, T. (2023). Explainable AI is dead, long live explainable AI! Hypothesis-driven decision support using evaluative AI. *Proceedings of ACM FAccT 2023* (pp. 333–342). DOI: 10.1145/3593013.3594001

Mishra, S., Angurala, M., Sharma, N., & Sharma, Y. (2025). Zero-trust fundamentals. In *Zero-Trust Learning* (pp. 1–22). Apple Academic Press.

Mittelstadt, B., Russell, C., & Wachter, S. (2019). Explaining explanations in AI. In *Proceedings of the Conference on Fairness, Accountability, and Transparency* (pp. 279–288). DOI: 10.1145/3287560.3287574

More, S.. (2024). Enhanced IDS performance with UNSW-NB15 data analysis. *Algorithms*, *17*, 64. DOI: 10.3390/a17020064

Morovat, K., & Panda, B. (2020). A survey of artificial intelligence in cybersecurity. In *Proceedings of the International Conference on Computational Science and Computational Intelligence* (pp. 109–115). IEEE. DOI: 10.1109/CSCI51800.2020.00026

Moustafa, N., & Slay, J. (2015). UNSW-NB15: A comprehensive data set for network intrusion detection systems. In *Proceedings of the Military Communications and Information Systems Conference (MilCIS)*. DOI: 10.1109/MilCIS.2015.7348942

Munoko, I., Brown-Liburd, H., & Vasarhelyi, M. (2020). Ethical implications of AI in auditing. *Journal of Business Ethics*, *167*(2), 209–234. DOI: 10.1007/s10551-019-04407-1

Mushtaq, S., Mohsin, M., & Mushtaq, M. M. (2025). A systematic literature review on the implementation and challenges of zero trust architecture across domains. *Sensors (Basel)*, *25*(19), 6118.

Nacheva, R., & Azeroual, O. (2024, November). Security of AI-powered systems: Threat intelligence on the edge. In *Security of AI-Powered Systems*. Threat Intelligence on the Edge. DOI: 10.1109/ISMSIT63511.2024.10757185

Naidoo, R., & Möller, N. (2022). Building software applications securely with DevSecOps: A Socio-technical perspective. Proceedings of the ... *European Conference on Information Warfare and Security*, 21(1), 198–205. DOI: 10.34190/eccws.21.1.295

Naing, K. M. (2025). AI-driven hybrid cybersecurity audit framework for non-governance IT systems [GitHub Repository]. https://github.com/KaungMyatNaing9/AI-Driven-Hybrid-Cybersecurity-Audit-Framework-for-Non-Governance-IT-Systems

National Institute of Standards and Technology. (2023). *AI Risk Management Framework (AI RMF 1.0)*. https://www.nist.gov/itl/ai-risk-management-framework

National Institute of Standards and Technology. (2024). *NIST Cybersecurity Framework 2.0*. https://www.nist.gov/cyberframework/framework

Nolte, H., Rateike, M., & Finck, M. (2025). Robustness and Cybersecurity in the EU Artificial Intelligence Act. *arXiv*. https://arxiv.org/abs/2503.05773 DOI: 10.1145/3715275.3732020

OECD. (2019). *OECD principles on artificial intelligence*. OECD Publishing., DOI: 10.1787/1f3f3b5b-

Ok, E., Willams, J., & Nicee, J. (2025). Understanding zero trust architecture.

Onyebueke, A. E.. (2023). Network intrusion detection using XGBoost and random forest. *Asian Journal of Pure and Applied Mathematics*, *5*(1), 321–335.

Open, A. I. (2023). *GPT-4 technical report*. arXiv preprint arXiv:2303.08774.

Organisation for Economic Co-operation and Development. (2024). *Strategic Foresight*. https://www.oecd.org/en/about/programmes/strategic-foresight.html

Ouyang, L., ... (2022). Training language models to follow instructions with human feedback. In *Advances in Neural Information Processing Systems (NeurIPS)*.

Ouyang, L., Wu, J., Jiang, X., Almeida, D., Wainwright, C., Mishkin, P., & Christiano, P. (2022). Training language models to follow instructions with human feedback. *Advances in Neural Information Processing Systems*. Advance online publication. DOI: 10.48550/arXiv.2203.02155

Pachl, E., Langer, F., Markert, T., & Lorenz, J. M. (2024). A view on vulnerabilities: The security challenges of XAI. *Proceedings of the Symposium on Scaling AI Assessments (SAIA 2024)*. DOI: 10.4230/OASIcs.SAIA.2024.12

Palma, G., Cecchi, G., Caronna, M., & Rizzo, A. (2025). Leveraging LLMs for scalable and explainable cybersecurity log analysis. *Journal of Cybersecurity and Privacy*, *5*(3), 55. DOI: 10.3390/jcp5030055

Panda, K. C., & Asurion Insurance, U. S. A. (2022). Application of AI and ML in the field of DevSecOps. *Journal of Artificial Intelligence & Cloud Computing*, *1*(4), 1–4. DOI: 10.47363/JAICC/2022(1)280

Pandis, N. (2016). The chi-square test. *American Journal of Orthodontics and Dentofacial Orthopedics*, *150*(5), 898–899. DOI: 10.1016/j.ajodo.2016.08.009 PMID: 27871717

Pawar, P., Anute, N., Tripathi, S., Ahluwalia, G. K., & Kalshetti, P. (2026). AI and Its Importance in the Development of Luxury Consumption. In Vale, V. (Ed.), *Multidisciplinary Approach to Luxury Consumption and AI* (pp. 1–34). IGI Global Scientific Publishing., DOI: 10.4018/979-8-3693-8422-0.ch001

Perez, F., & Ribeiro, I. (2022). Ignore previous prompt: Attack techniques for language models. NeurIPS ML Safety Workshop 2022. DOI: 10.48550/arXiv.2211.09527

Pham, L., Saad, F. A., & Hoffmann, J. (2024). Robust resource bounds with static analysis and Bayesian inference. Proceedings of the ACM on Programming Languages, 8(PLDI), 76–101. DOI: 10.1145/3656380

Poirrier, A. (2024). Formal security of zero trust architectures [Doctoral dissertation, Institut Polytechnique de Paris].

Portase, R., & Colesa, A. (2021). Curator: A system for creating datasets for behavioral malware detection. In 2021 20th IEEE International Conference on Trust, Security and Privacy in Computing and Communications (TrustCom) (pp. 1209-1216). IEEE. DOI: 10.1109/ISPDC52870.2021.9521600

Product Security and Telecommunications Infrastructure Act 2022. (2022). Legislation.gov.uk. https://www.legislation.gov.uk/ukpga/2022/46/enacted

Pum, M. (2022). The Rise of AI-Powered Cybercrime: Implications for Digital Security and Policy. https://www.researchgate.net/publication/390748096

Qi, F.. (2021). Hidden killer: Invisible textual backdoor attacks with syntactic trigger. In *Proceedings of the Annual Meeting of the Association for Computational Linguistics (ACL)*. DOI: 10.18653/v1/2021.acl-long.37

Qin, Y., ... (2023). ToolLLM: Facilitating large language models to master 16000+ real-world APIs. *arXiv preprint arXiv:2307.16789*.

Rahmani, A. M., Hemmati, A., & Abbasi, S. (2025). The rise of large language models: Evolution, applications, and future directions. *Engineering Reports*, *7*(9), e70368. DOI: 10.1002/eng2.70368

Rahman, M. A., Rafiq, M. A., & Islam, S. (2023). AI-based malware detection and classification for wireless networks using hybrid deep learning. *International Journal for Research in Applied Science and Engineering Technology*, *11*(10), 1420–1430. DOI: 10.22214/ijraset.2024.64512

Rais, R., Morillo, C., Gilman, E., & Barth, D. (2024). *Zero trust networks* (2nd ed.). O'Reilly Media.

Ren, Z. (2025). Optimization design of artificial intelligence-based Internet of Things (IoT) intrusion detection system. In *2025 3rd International Conference on Mobile Internet, Cloud Computing and Information Security (MICCIS)* (pp. 314–319).

Ren, J., Zheng, Z., Liu, Q., Wei, Z., & Yan, H. (2019). A buffer overflow prediction approach based on software metrics and machine learning. *Security and Communication Networks*, *2019*, 1–13. DOI: 10.1155/2019/8391425

ResearchGate. (2025). Third-party vendor risks in IT security. https://www.researchgate.net/publication/381844798

Rhachi, H., Balboul, Y., & Bouayad, A. (2025). Enhanced anomaly detection in IoT networks using deep autoencoders. *Sensors (Basel)*, *25*(10), 3150. DOI: 10.3390/s25103150 PMID: 40431942

Ribeiro, M. T., Singh, S., & Guestrin, C. (2020). Why should I trust you? Explaining the predictions of any classifier. *Communications of the ACM*, *63*(11), 116–125. DOI: 10.1145/3351095

Riek, L. R. (2023). Is Cybersecurity a Social Responsibility? *Frontiers in Computer Science*. https://www.frontiersin.org/articles/10.3389/fcomp.2023.1123451/full

Rigatti, S. J. (2017). Random forest. *Journal of Insurance Medicine (New York, N.Y.)*, *47*(1), 31–39. DOI: 10.17849/insm-47-01-31-39.1 PMID: 28836909

Risto, R., Sethi, M., & Katara, M. (2025). Effects of the Cyber Resilience Act (CRA) on Industrial Equipment Manufacturing Companies. *arXiv*. https://arxiv.org/abs/2505.14325 DOI: 10.1007/978-3-032-00630-1_12

Rose, S., Borchert, O., Mitchell, S., & Connelly, S. (2020). Zero trust architecture (NIST Special Publication 800-207). National Institute of Standards and Technology. DOI: 10.6028/NIST.SP.800-207

Rousseeuw, P. J. (1984). Least median of squares regression. *Journal of the American Statistical Association*, *79*(388), 871–880. DOI: 10.1080/01621459.1984.10477105

Ruff, L., Vandermeulen, R., Görnitz, N., Deecke, L., Siddiqui, S. A., Binder, A., Müller, E., & Kloft, M. (2018). Deep one-class classification. *Proceedings of ICML*, 4393-4402.

Saini, N., Dhiman, P., Turaev, S., & Hamid, Y. (2023). Recent advancements in zero trust frameworks for hybrid and cloud-native environments. *Journal of Network and Computer Applications*, *218*, 103598.

Salih, A., Galazzo, I. B., Cruciani, F., Brusini, L., Radeva, P., Petersen, S. E., & Menegaz, G. (2025). A perspective on explainable artificial intelligence methods: SHAP and LIME. *Advanced Intelligent Systems*, *7*(6), 2400304. DOI: 10.1002/aisy.202400304

Sande-Ríos, J., Canal-Sanchez, J., Manzano-Hernández, C., & Pastrana, S. (2024). Threat analysis and adversarial model for smart grids. In *2024 IEEE European Symposium on Security and Privacy Workshops (EuroS&PW)* (pp. 130–145). IEEE. DOI: 10.1109/EuroSPW61312.2024.00020

Santos, I., Brezo, F., Ugarte-Pedrero, X., & Bringas, P. G. (2013). Opcode sequences as representation of executables for data-mining-based unknown malware detection. *Information Sciences*, *231*, 64–82. DOI: 10.1016/j.ins.2011.08.020

Sarker, N., Furhad, M., & Nowrozy, R. (2021). AI-driven cybersecurity: An overview, security intelligence modeling, and research directions. *SN Computer Science*, *2*(3), 173. Advance online publication. DOI: 10.1007/s42979-021-00557-0 PMID: 33778771

Schick, T., ... (2023). Toolformer: Language models can teach themselves to use tools. In *Advances in Neural Information Processing Systems (NeurIPS).*

Schmitz-Berndt, S., & Cole, M. (2022). Towards an Efficient and Coherent Regulatory Framework on Cybersecurity in the EU: The Proposals for a NIS 2.0 Directive and a Cyber Resilience Act. *Applied Cybersecurity & Internet Governance*, *1*(1), 121–137. DOI: 10.5604/01.3001.0016.1323

Schölkopf, B., Platt, J. C., Shawe-Taylor, J., Smola, A. J., & Williamson, R. C. (2001). Estimating the support of a high-dimensional distribution. *Neural Computation, 13*(7), 1443–1471. DOI: 10.1162/089976601750264965 PMID: 11440593

ScienceDirect. (2025). Article. https://www.sciencedirect.com/science/article/pii/S1467089525000107

Scikit-Learn. (2007). Scikit-learn documentation. https://scikit-learn.org/0.21/documentation.html

Selvakumar, P., & Haashni, S. SudhaAnanthi, G., & Manjunath, T. C. (2026). Cybernetic Systems Thinking: Foundations for Organizational Adaptability. In L. Tsvasman (Ed.), Cybernetic Leadership for Sustainable Innovation (pp. 99-124). IGI Global Scientific Publishing. DOI: 10.4018/979-8-3373-2484-5.ch004

Senior DevOps Engineer - Cloud VA USA, D. and A., & Kummarapurugu, C. S. (2024). A framework for real-time AI-driven secure code analysis integrated with DevSecOps in cloud-native CI/CD pipelines. INTERANTIONAL JOURNAL OF SCIENTIFIC RESEARCH IN ENGINEERING AND MANAGEMENT, 08(11). DOI: 10.55041/IJSREM17273

ServiceNow. (2025a). IT service management (ITSM). https://www.servicenow.com/products/itsm.html

ServiceNow. (2025b). What is AIOps? https://www.servicenow.com/products/it-operations-management/what-is-aiops.html

Shabtai, A., Kanonov, U., Elovici, Y., Glezer, C., & Weiss, Y. (2012). "Andromaly": A behavioral malware detection framework for Android devices. *Journal of Intelligent Information Systems, 38*(1), 161–190. DOI: 10.1007/s10844-010-0148-x

Shen, X., Chen, Z., Backes, M., Shen, Y., & Zhang, Y. (2024). Do Anything Now: Characterizing and evaluating in-the-wild jailbreak prompts on large language models. *Proceedings of ACM CCS 2024*. DOI: 10.1145/3658644.3670388

Sikder, M., & Sah, H. (2025, May). Cyber threats prediction and analysis using machine learning algorithms. *Journal of Emerging Technologies and Innovative Research*, •••, 12.

Singh, J., & Singh, J. (2021). A survey of the recent trends in deep learning based malware detection. *Journal of Cybersecurity and Privacy*, 2(4), 800–829. DOI: 10.3390/jcp2040041

Singh, R., Gill, N. S., & Gulia, P. (2025). Attentional LSTM-ensemble architecture for intrusion detection in smart grids. *Scientific Reports*, *15*(1), 41977. DOI: 10.1038/s41598-025-25992-4 PMID: 41290901

Slack, D., Hilgard, S., Jia, E., Singh, S., & Lakkaraju, H. (2020). Fooling LIME and SHAP: Adversarial attacks on post hoc explanation methods. Proceedings of AAAI/ACM AIES 2020 (pp. 180–186). DOI: 10.1145/3375627.3375830

Sreelatha, R., & Yelsangiker, A. (2024). *Zero trust security architecture. In 2024 Recent Advances in Sustainable Engineering and Future Technologies (RASEFT).* IEEE.

Stanham, L. (2023). *Machine learning (ML) & cybersecurity: How is ML used in cybersecurity?* CrowdStrike. https://www.crowdstrike.com/en-us/cybersecurity-101/artificialintelligence/machine-learning/

Steenbrink, T. P. J. (2022). Zero trust architecture.

Steinhardt, J., Koh, P. W., & Liang, P. (2017). Certified defenses for data poisoning attacks. *Advances in Neural Information Processing Systems.* Advance online publication. DOI: 10.48550/arXiv.1706.03691

Sugapriya, S., Garg, S., Mahalle, A., Yewale, A. U. & T. C., M. (2026). Medical Imaging and Radiology: AI-Powered Diagnostics. In D. Ather, N. Mun, S. Jain, V. Jain, & V. Kukreja (Eds.), Applied AI and Computational Intelligence in Diagnostics and Decision-Making (pp. 191-218). IGI Global Scientific Publishing. .DOI: 10.4018/979-8-3373-3311-3.ch008

Sun, M., Guo, Y., & Zhang, X. (2016). Android malware detection based on sensitive behaviors and API calls. *Computers & Security*, *59*, 294–310. DOI: 10.1016/j.cose.2016.03.003

Su, R., & Zhang, D. (2025). Adaptive Sovereignty: China's Evolving Legislative Framework for Transnational Data Governance. *Politics and Governance*, *13*(0), 10413. Advance online publication. DOI: 10.17645/pag.10413

Susmaga, R. (2004). Confusion matrix visualization. In *Intelligent information processing and web mining: Proceedings of the international IIS: IIPWM '04 conference* (pp. 107–116). Springer. DOI: 10.1007/978-3-540-39985-8_12

Süzen, A. A., & Ceylan, O. (2024). The advantages and implementation challenges within the scope of the basic principles of transition to zero trust architecture. International Journal of 3D Printing Technologies and Digital Industry, 8(3), 416–427.

Syed, N. F.. (2022). Zero trust architecture (ZTA): A comprehensive survey. *IEEE Access : Practical Innovations, Open Solutions*, *10*, 57143–57179.

Syracuse University. (2025). What is IT governance? https://ischool.syracuse.edu/what-is-it-governance/

Taddeo, M., & Floridi, L. (2018). How AI can be a force for good. *Science*, *361*(6404), 751–752. DOI: 10.1126/science.aat5991 PMID: 30139858

Tang, L., Liu, J., Liu, Z., Yang, X., & Bao, L. (2025). LLM4SZZ: Enhancing SZZ algorithm with context-enhanced assessment on large language models. Proceedings of the ACM on Software Engineering, 2(ISSTA), 343–365. DOI: 10.1145/3728885

Tang, Y., Wang, H., Zhou, Q., & Sun, B. (2024). A method for surface defect detection based on multiscale feature fusion and pyramid attention. *IEEE Access : Practical Innovations, Open Solutions*, *12*, 36457–36465. DOI: 10.1109/ACCESS.2024.3374131

Tao, G.. (2024). Model orthogonalization: Class-agnostic backdoor defense. In *2024 IEEE Symposium on Security and Privacy (SP)*.

Teerakanok, S., Uehara, T., & Inomata, A. (2021). Migrating to zero trust architecture: Reviews and challenges. *Security and Communication Networks*, *2021*, 9947347.

Terrazone. (2025). NIST SP 800-207 – The definitive guide to zero trust architecture [Technical blog]. https://terrazone.io/nist-sp-800-207/

Tian, R., Islam, R., Batten, L., & Versteeg, S. (2010). Differentiating malware from cleanware using behavioural analysis. In 2010 5th International Conference on Malicious and Unwanted Software (MALWARE) (pp. 23-30). IEEE. DOI: 10.1109/MALWARE.2010.5665796

Tibshirani, R. (1996). Regression shrinkage and selection via the lasso. *Journal of the Royal Statistical Society. Series B, Statistical Methodology*, *58*(1), 267–288. DOI: 10.1111/j.2517-6161.1996.tb02080.x

Tobiyama, S., Yamaguchi, Y., Shimada, H., Ikuse, T., & Yagi, T. (2016). Malware detection with deep neural network using process behavior. In 2016 IEEE 40th Annual Computer Software and Applications Conference (COMPSAC) (pp. 577-582). IEEE. DOI: 10.1109/COMPSAC.2016.151

Touvron, H., ... (2023). Llama 2: Open foundation and fine-tuned chat models. *arXiv preprint arXiv:2307.09288*.

Tramèr, F., Zhang, F., Juels, A., Reiter, M. K., & Ristenpart, T. (2016). Stealing machine learning models via prediction APIs. *USENIX Security Symposium*. DOI: 10.48550/arXiv.1609.02943

Tran, B., Li, Y., & Madry, A. (2018). Spectral signatures in backdoor attacks. *Advances in Neural Information Processing Systems*. Advance online publication. DOI: 10.48550/arXiv.1811.00636

Turaev, S., Dhiman, P., & Hamid, Y. (2021). Zero trust model for IoT and edge computing: Challenges and research directions. *Sensors (Basel)*, *21*(18), 6109. DOI: 10.3390/s21186109

U.S. Department of Defense. (2022). Department of Defense zero trust reference architecture (Tech. Rep.). Office of the Chief Information Officer, U.S. Department of Defense. https://dodcio.defense.gov

U.S. Government Accountability Office. (2021). *Cybersecurity and Infrastructure Security Agency: Actions Needed to Ensure Organizational Changes Result in More Effective Cybersecurity for Our Nation*. https://www.gao.gov/products/gao-21-236

Uike, D., Sugapriya, S., Kaur, M., Mahalle, A., Dhule, N., & T. C., M. (2026). Drug Discovery and Optimization With AI. In D. Ather, N. Mun, S. Jain, V. Jain, & V. Kukreja (Eds.), Applied AI and Computational Intelligence in Diagnostics and Decision-Making (pp. 379-404). IGI Global Scientific Publishing. .DOI: 10.4018/979-8-3373-3311-3.ch014

UNSW. (2025). UNSW-NB15 dataset. https://research.unsw.edu.au/projects/unsw-nb15-dataset

Vadillo, J., Santana, R., & Lozano, J. A. (2025). Adversarial attacks in explainable machine learning: A survey of threats against models and humans. *Wiley Interdisciplinary Reviews. Data Mining and Knowledge Discovery*, *1567*(1), e1567. Advance online publication. DOI: 10.1002/widm.1567

Vasan, D., Alazab, M., Wassan, S., Safaei, B., & Zheng, Q. (2020). IMCFN: Image-based malware classification using fine-tuned convolutional neural network architecture. *Computer Networks*, *171*, 107138. DOI: 10.1016/j.comnet.2020.107138

Vaswani, A., Shazeer, N., Parmar, N., Uszkoreit, J., Jones, L., Gomez, A. N., & Polosukhin, I. (2017). Attention is all you need. *Advances in Neural Information Processing Systems*. Advance online publication. DOI: 10.48550/arXiv.1706.03762

Veale, M., & Borgesius, F. Z. (2021). Demystifying the draft EU Artificial Intelligence Act. *Computer Law Review International*, *22*(4), 97–112. DOI: 10.9785/cri-2021-220402

Vemuri, N., Thaneeru, N., & Tatikonda, V. M. (2023). Securing trust: Ethical considerations in AI for cybersecurity. *Journal of Knowledge Learning and Science Technology*, *2*(2), 168–175. DOI: 10.60087/jklst.vol2.n2.p175

Verma, R. (2025, February). Supervised vs. unsupervised learning: A comparative study in modern AI system. *Communications on Applied Nonlinear Analysis*, *32*(9s), 860–872. DOI: 10.52783/cana.v32.4022

Veyrat-Charvillon, N., & Standaert, F.-X. (2009). Mutual information analysis: How, when and why? In *International Workshop on Cryptographic Hardware and Embedded Systems* (pp. 429–443). Springer. DOI: 10.1007/978-3-642-04138-9_30

Vokhranov, I., & Bulakh, B. (2024). Transformer-based models application for bug detection in source code. *Technology Audit and Production Reserves*, *5*(2(79)), 6–15. DOI: 10.15587/2706-5448.2024.310822

von Eschenbach, W. J. (2021). Transparency and the black box problem. *Philosophy & Technology*, *34*(4), 1607–1622. DOI: 10.1007/s13347-021-00477-0

Vujović, Z.. (2021). Classification model evaluation metrics. *International Journal of Advanced Computer Science and Applications*, *12*(6), 599–606. DOI: 10.14569/IJACSA.2021.0120670

Walia, G. K., & Sidhu, J. S. (2022). Content based Adaptive Image Demosaicing using Random Forest Algorithm. SAMRIDDHI A Journal of Physical Sciences Engineering and Technology, 14(02), 183–186. DOI: 10.18090/samriddhi.v14i02.10

Wallace, E., Feng, S., Kandpal, N., Gardner, M., & Singh, S. (2019). *Universal adversarial triggers for attacking and analyzing NLP*. EMNLP-IJCNLP., DOI: 10.18653/v1/D19-1221

Wan, A., Wallace, E., Shen, S., & Klein, D. (2023). Poisoning language models during instruction tuning. *arXiv preprint arXiv:2305.00944*.

Wang, G., ... (2023). Voyager: An open-ended embodied agent with large language models. *arXiv preprint arXiv:2305.16291*.

Wang, Y., ... (2024). BadAgent: Inserting and activating backdoor attacks in LLM agents. *arXiv preprint arXiv:2408.00761*. DOI: 10.18653/v1/2024.acl-long.530

Wang, B., Yao, Y., Shan, S., Li, H., Viswanath, B., Zheng, H., & Zhao, B. Y. (2019). Neural cleanse: Identifying and mitigating backdoor attacks in neural networks. *IEEE Symposium on Security and Privacy*. DOI: 10.1109/SP.2019.00031

Wang, K. R., Variengien, A., Conmy, A., Shlegeris, B., & Steinhardt, J. (2023). Interpretability in the wild: A circuit for indirect object identification in GPT-2 small. *Proceedings of ICLR 2023*. DOI: 10.48550/arXiv.2211.00593

Wang, L., Ma, C., Feng, X., Zhang, Z., Yang, H., Zhang, J., Chen, Z., Tang, J., Chen, X., Lin, Y., Zhao, W. X., Wei, Z., & Wen, J. (2024). A survey on large language model based autonomous agents. *Frontiers of Computer Science, 18*(6), 186345. DOI: 10.1007/s11704-024-40231-1

Wang, W., Zhu, M., Zeng, X., Ye, X., & Sheng, Y. (2017). Malware traffic classification using convolutional neural network for representation learning. In *2017 International Conference on Information Networking (ICOIN)* (pp. 712-717). IEEE. DOI: 10.1109/ICOIN.2017.7899588

Wang, Y.. (2022). Piccolo: Exposing and removing backdoors from NLP models. In *Proceedings of the 60th Annual Meeting of the Association for Computational Linguistics.*

Wang, Y., Li, J., & Gu, D. (2021). Ransomware detection based on system call sequences using ensemble learning. *Future Generation Computer Systems, 118*, 21–31. DOI: 10.1016/j.future.2021.01.033

Wei, A., Haghtalab, N., & Steinhardt, J. (2023). Jailbroken: How does LLM safety training fail? In *Advances in Neural Information Processing Systems (NeurIPS).*

Wei, J., ... (2022). Chain-of-thought prompting elicits reasoning in large language models. In *Advances in Neural Information Processing Systems (NeurIPS).*

White House. (2021). Executive order 14028 on improving the nation's cybersecurity. *Federal Register*, *86*(93), 26633–26647. https://www.federalregister.gov

White House. (2024). *National Cybersecurity Strategy*. https://bidenwhitehouse.archives.gov/oncd/national-cybersecurity-strategy/

Winfield, A. F. T., & Jirotka, M. (2018). Ethical governance is essential to building trust in robotics and artificial intelligence systems. *Philosophical Transactions. Series A, Mathematical, Physical, and Engineering Sciences*, *376*(2133), 20180085. Advance online publication. DOI: 10.1098/rsta.2018.0085 PMID: 30323000

Winfield, A., Michael, M., Pitt, J., & Evers, V. (2019). Machine ethics: The design and governance of ethical AI and autonomous systems. *Proceedings of the IEEE, 107*(3), 509–517. DOI: 10.1109/JPROC.2019.2900622

Wolf, Y., ... (2023). Fundamental limitations of alignment in large language models. *arXiv preprint arXiv:2304.11082.*

Woods, D. W., & Seymour, S. (2024). Evidence-Based Cybersecurity Policy? A Metareview of Security Control Effectiveness. *Journal of Cyber Policy* DOI: 10.1080/23738871.2024.2335461

Wu, Y., & Tian, F. (2025). GT-free XAI: A ground truth-free XAI framework. In ICME (pp. 1–6). DOI: 10.1109/ICME59968.2025.11209952

Wu, D., Xu, L., & He, J. (2022). A hybrid static and dynamic analysis approach using deep learning for malware detection. *Computers & Security*, *113*, 102546. DOI: 10.1016/j.cose.2021.102546

Xi, Z., et al. (2023). The rise and potential of large language model based agents: A survey. *arXiv preprint.*

Xie, S., Li, C., & Wang, W. (2023). BEACON: Behavioral malware classification with large transformer models. *Neural Networks*, *163*, 494–505. DOI: 10.1016/j.neunet.2023.07.019

Xplore, I. E. E. E. (2025). Article 9439459. https://ieeexplore.ieee.org/abstract/document/9439459

Xu, Z., ... (2025). Deep learning–based intrusion detection systems: A survey. arXiv preprint arXiv:2504.07839.

Yang, W., ... (2024). Watch out for your agents! Investigating backdoor threats to LLM-based agents. In *Advances in Neural Information Processing Systems (NeurIPS).*

Yan, Q., Yang, H., & Chen, Y. (2018). Detecting malicious behaviors in Android applications using sequence classification of system calls. *Journal of Network and Computer Applications*, *112*, 42–54. DOI: 10.1016/j.jnca.2018.03.004

Yao, S.. (2023). ReAct: Synergizing reasoning and acting in language models. In *International Conference on Learning Representations (ICLR).*

Yen, T. F., Oprea, A., Onarlioglu, K., Leetham, T., Robertson, W., Juels, A., & Kirda, E. (2014). Beehive: Large-scale log analysis for detecting suspicious activity in enterprise networks. In *Proceedings of the 29th Annual ACM Symposium on Applied Computing* (pp. 1641-1648). ACM. DOI: 10.1145/2554850.2554881

Yohai, V. J. (1987). High breakdown-point and high efficiency robust estimates for regression. *Annals of Statistics*, *15*(2), 642–656. DOI: 10.1214/aos/1176350366

Yuan, X.. (2024). Stealthy backdoor attacks on deep neural networks with resizable triggers. In *Proceedings of the AAAI Conference on Artificial Intelligence.*

Zeng, A., Liu, M., Lu, R., Wang, B., Liu, X., Dong, Y., & Tang, J. (2023). AgentTuning: Enabling generalized agent abilities for LLMs. *arXiv preprint arXiv:2310.12823.*

Zhang, H., Li, Y., Yu, D., & Wang, Z. (2024). On the transferability of jailbreak attacks in large language models. *IEEE Security and Privacy*. Advance online publication. DOI: 10.1109/MSP.2024.3356789

Zhang, Y., Muniyandi, R. C., & Qamar, F. (2025). A review of deep learning applications in intrusion detection systems. *Applied Sciences (Basel, Switzerland)*, *15*(3), 1552. DOI: 10.3390/app15031552

Zhang, Z., Qi, P., & Wang, W. (2019). Dynamic malware analysis with feature engineering and feature learning. *Digital Investigation*, *28*, S77–S88. DOI: 10.1016/j.diin.2019.01.021

Zhang, Z., Wang, W., & Chen, C. (2020). A behavior-based Android malware detection system using deep convolutional neural networks. *Computers & Security*, *97*, 101965. DOI: 10.1016/j.cose.2020.101965

Zhao, W. X., ... (2023). A survey of large language models. *arXiv preprint arXiv:2303.18223.*

Zheng, M., Xie, D., Shi, Q., Wang, C., & Zhang, X. (2025). Validating network protocol parsers with traceable RFC document interpretation. Proceedings of the ACM on Software Engineering, 2(ISSTA), 1772–1794. DOI: 10.1145/3728955

Zheng, W., ... (2025). BucketServe: Bucket-based dynamic batching for efficient LLM serving. arXiv preprint arXiv:2507.17120.

Zhou, X., Mao, R., Zhang, H., Dai, Q., Huang, H., Shen, H., Li, J., & Rong, G. (2023). Revisit security in the era of DevOps: An evidence-based inquiry into DevSecOps industry. *IET Software*, *17*(4), 435–454. DOI: 10.1049/sfw2.12132

Zhu, H., Wang, W., & Chen, P. (2024). A dynamic analysis-powered explanation framework for Android malware detection. *IEEE Transactions on Knowledge and Data Engineering*, *36*(8), 4259–4274. DOI: 10.1109/TKDE.2024.3436891

Zhu, M., Wang, W., & Ye, X. (2019). Sequence learning with gated CNN and LSTM for behavioral malware detection. *Pattern Recognition Letters*, *128*, 464–470. DOI: 10.1016/j.patrec.2019.10.010

Zografopoulos, I., Kuruvila, A. P., Basu, K., & Konstantinou, C. (2022). Time series-based detection and impact analysis of firmware attacks in microgrids. *Energy Reports*, *8*, 11221–11234. DOI: 10.1016/j.egyr.2022.08.270

Zou, A., ... (2023). Universal and transferable adversarial attacks on aligned language models. *arXiv preprint arXiv:2307.15043.*

Zou, J., & Lv, J. (2025). Dual-task guided network: Hybrid supervised learning for surface defect detection. *Measurement Science & Technology*, *36*(3), 036133. Advance online publication. DOI: 10.1088/1361-6501/adb6cb

About the Contributors

Puya Pakshad is a PhD candidate in Information Technology at Illinois Institute of Technology (Illinois Tech), specializing in software security and AI-driven vulnerability and malware detection. He holds a Master's degree in Computer Software Engineering from Shahid Beheshti University in Tehran, Iran, and a Bachelor's degree in the same field from Arak University. His research focuses on developing intelligent, scalable techniques for automated vulnerability discovery, assessment, and risk prioritization using machine learning and large language models. Mr. Pakshad has published several research papers and book chapters in the areas of software vulnerability prediction, CVSS scoring refinement, and cybersecurity frameworks. His academic contributions aim to advance secure software engineering practices and enhance the reliability of AI-assisted security analysis systems.

Marwan Omar is an accomplished cybersecurity expert and academic, specializing in the intersection of artificial intelligence (AI) and cybersecurity. He currently serves as an Associate Professor of Cybersecurity and AI at the Illinois Institute of Technology, where he leads cutting-edge research on AI security, focusing on the detection and mitigation of advanced cyber threats. Dr. Omar holds multiple advanced degrees, including a PhD in Cybersecurity and a PhD in AI, and has earned numerous industry certifications such as Certified Ethical Hacker (CEH) and SANS Certified Smartphone Forensics Analyst (GASF). His extensive publication record includes books, peer-reviewed journal articles, and conference papers that explore the integration of AI in cybersecurity, with a particular focus on large language models (LLMs) and generalized AI (Gen AI). In addition to his academic pursuits, Dr. Omar is actively involved in industry collaborations and has contributed to numerous high-profile projects aimed at securing AI-driven technologies. His expertise has positioned him as a sought-after advisor and thought leader in the cybersecurity community. As a first-generation American from the

Yazidi community in Iraq, Dr. Omar is committed to serving as a beacon of hope and inspiration for underrepresented minorities in STEM fields. His dedication to advancing both the scientific and social aspects of cybersecurity makes him a unique and influential figure in the ongoing dialogue about the future of AI security.

***

Deeppana AS, currently working as an Assistant Professor at Karpagam Academy of Higher Education. I have completed my Bachelor of Computer Applications (BCA) and Master of Computer Applications (MCA), and I am presently pursuing my Ph.D. in the domain of the Internet of Things (IoT). I began my teaching career immediately after completing my postgraduation, as I have always been deeply interested and passionate about this field. Teaching gives me immense satisfaction, as it allows me to share knowledge, inspire students, and continue learning every day. With a strong commitment to both teaching and research, I aim to contribute meaningfully to the academic community while helping students build confidence, creativity, and technical expertise in the ever-evolving world of technology.

Madhu Babu Amarappalli is an Enterprise Solution Architect at with over 21 years of experience designing and leading large-scale, mission-critical systems in public-sector and regulated environments. His work focuses on the responsible integration of artificial intelligence, cloud-native architectures, and governance-by-design frameworks. Drawing on extensive experience in AI-enabled system design, he examines how human–AI collaboration can be structured to preserve critical thinking, metacognition, and ethical judgment. His research interests include critical AI literacy, hybrid intelligence, and pedagogical frameworks that promote human agency in AI-supported learning environments

Emefa Apaloo is an international graduate student from Ghana studying at Illinois Institute of Technology, where they specialize in Cyber Forensics and Security. They hold a Bachelor's degree in Computer Science with a minor in Business from Hanover College. Their research interests include zero trust architecture and its applications in modern cybersecurity frameworks.

John Paul C is the Associate Professor, Department of Computer Science at St. Joseph University, Tindivanam, Tamil Nadu. With a strong academic foundation and leadership in computer science education, Dr. John Paul 27 years of experience in teaching, curriculum development, and departmental administration. His dedication to academic excellence and student development has significantly contributed to the growth of the department. He is actively involved in promoting innovative teaching methods, encouraging research, and guiding students toward careers in technology and software development.

Mohithaa Ekambaram is a Master's student in Cyber Forensics and Security at the Illinois Institute of Technology University, where her studies focus on digital forensics, network security, and vulnerability assessment. Her academic work includes research on Zero Trust Architecture and identity-driven security models, with an emphasis on practical applications in enterprise environments and security governance. Her professional interests include penetration testing, incident response, and security operations. Mohithaa is also actively involved in applied cybersecurity activities, including competitive security exercises and technical lab development.

Deepak Gupta is a distinguished academician with over 20 years of teaching experience and expertise in Computer Science and Engineering. He holds a Ph.D. in Computer Engineering and has an extensive research portfolio, including many international journal papers, multiple conference proceedings, and several books. His research interests span machine learning, artificial intelligence, and data mining. Currently, Dr. Gupta serves as an Associate Professor and Head of Department of CSE (Emerging Branches) at ITM Gwalior, MP, India. He has also contributed significantly to the field through patents and copyrights and actively engages as a reviewer, conference chair and editor.

Neeharika Joshi is associated with the Department of Computer Engineering, with academic and research expertise in artificial intelligence, machine learning, software engineering, and automated defect detection. Her work emphasizes data-driven and learning-based approaches to improving software quality, reliability, and maintainability, including the use of large language models for code analysis and defect prediction. She has contributed to interdisciplinary research that integrates theoretical foundations with practical, industry-oriented solutions, and is actively engaged in scholarly publications, collaborative research initiatives, and academic activities focused on advancing intelligent and ethical computing systems.

Satwik Kishore is associated with the Department of Computer Engineering, with academic and research interests in artificial intelligence, machine learning, software engineering, and intelligent automation. His work focuses on applying data-driven and algorithmic techniques to software analysis, defect detection, and system optimization, with an emphasis on scalable and practical solutions. He contributes to collaborative research initiatives and scholarly publications aimed at enhancing software quality, reliability, and the development of intelligent computing systems.

Murugaveni is an Assistant Professor in the Department of Electronics and Communication Engineering at the SRM Institute of Science and Technology. She is actively involved in teaching, academic mentoring, and institutional academic activities within the field of electronics and communication engineering. In her academic role, Dr. Murugaveni contributes to undergraduate and postgraduate education by delivering core and advanced subjects related to electronics and communication systems. She is engaged in fostering technical competence, analytical thinking, and problem-solving skills among students, aligning academic instruction with contemporary developments in engineering and technology. As a faculty member at a leading technical institution, she is committed to promoting academic excellence, outcome-based education, and continuous professional development. Her academic engagement reflects dedication to quality teaching, scholarly growth, and meaningful contributions to engineering education. Dr. Murugaveni continues to support the mission of SRM Institute of Science and Technology through teaching, academic service, and participation in institutional initiatives.

Selvakumar P currently serves as an Associate Professor in the Department of Science and Humanities at Nehru Institute of Technology, Coimbatore, Tamil Nadu, India. With a teaching career spanning over a decade, he previously held positions as an Assistant Professor in the Department of Science and Humanities at various engineering colleges in Coimbatore from 2011 to 2023. Dr. P. Selvakumar's primary area of academic and research interest is phytochemistry, where he has made substantial contributions. His research credentials include 30 journal publications, 14 patents, and 25 conference papers. He has actively promoted faculty and student development by organizing 5 Faculty Development Programs (FDPs) and completing 3 NPTEL courses along with 60 Coursera certifications. His dedication to student success is evident in his role as a committed mentor, consistently guiding and supporting his students academically and personally. Recognized for his excellence in teaching, Dr. P. Selvakumar has received numerous accolades, including Best Teacher Awards. He is also an active member of MISTE (The Indian Society for Technical Education) and continues to play a vital role in both acade

Shubhamkumar Pandit is associated with the Department of Computer Engineering, with academic and research interests in artificial intelligence, machine learning, and software engineering. His work emphasizes the use of data-driven and intelligent techniques for software analysis, defect identification, and system optimization. He actively contributes to collaborative research efforts and scholarly activities focused on improving software quality and advancing intelligent computing systems.

Sonukumar Pandit is associated with the Department of Computer Engineering, with academic and research interests in artificial intelligence, machine learning, and software engineering. His work centers on the application of data-driven methods for software analysis, defect detection, and quality assurance, with a focus on practical and scalable approaches. He contributes to collaborative research and scholarly activities aimed at advancing intelligent and reliable computing systems.

Ravikumar R. N. is currently a Postdoctoral researcher at Universiti Malaysia Perlis, Malaysia. Also, working as an Associate Professor in the department of Computer Engineering at Marwadi University, Rajkot, Gujarat. He has 13+ years of national and international teaching experience. He completed his PhD at Amity University, Rajasthan, M.E at VMRF Deemed University, B.E at Anna University, Chennai. He is the co-founder of the Research Activities Club at Marwadi University and trains students on research activities, which leads to the publication of 7 Scopus/ SCI journals, 45+ Book chapters, 30+ Conference papers, and 15+ patents. His specialization is ML, DL, Federated Learning, Recommendation Systems, and Optimization Techniques.

Vaishali Rahate is passionate Management teacher, Administrator & Corporate trainer with a tint of Industrial experience. She has 22 research publications and 4 books to her credit. Currently she is working as Professor with Datta Meghe Institute of Management Studies, Nagpur. She is on board of various reputed Management institutions. Recently she was awarded 'Best Woman Educator Award' conferred by World Education Congress (2025).

Joe Arun Raja, working as Associate Professor, School of Information Science, Presidency University, Bengaluru India. He received B.Sc (Physics) in 1997, Master of Computer Applications in 2000 and M.Phil (Computer science) in 2007 from Madurai Kamaraj University and M.Tech in Computer and Information Technology, 2005 and awarded PhD in Computer and Information Technology from Manonmaniam Sundaranar University, Trinelveli, India. This author became a Member of IETE INDIA in the year of 2009. He is the author of two books &one dictionary, and more than 10 research articles in International Journals.

Aarthi S is a dedicated Assistant Professor in Computer Science with over six years of teaching experience. She is currently pursuing her Ph.D. at Marwadi University, Gujarat, and holds an M.Phil. and MCA from Bharathiar University, Tamil Nadu. Throughout her academic career, Aarthi has specialized in programming languages such as C++, Java, and C, and contributed to research in recommender systems and AI-related data privacy. She has published journal articles, contributed to book chapters, and actively participated in technical workshops. Known for her student mentorship and engagement in academic events, Aarthi remains committed to fostering innovation and excellence in computer science education.

Yukta Sawalkar is a dedicated student at the Datta Meghe Institute of Management Studies, Nagpur. She is currently pursuing her studies in management, where she is developing a strong foundation in business principles, leadership skills, and professional ethics. As a student, Yukta demonstrates a keen interest in academic excellence, practical learning, and personal development. She actively engages in classroom learning, group activities, and institutional programs that enhance her managerial and analytical abilities. Her academic journey reflects a commitment to continuous learning and skill enhancement, preparing her for future professional challenges in the field of management. Yukta Sawalkar aspires to apply her knowledge and skills in real-world organizational settings and is motivated to grow as a responsible and competent management professional. She values teamwork, discipline, and innovation, and aims to contribute positively to the corporate and social environment.

Index

J

L

M

N

P

R

S

T

www.ingramcontent.com/pod-product-compliance
Ingram Content Group UK Ltd.
Pitfield, Milton Keynes, MK11 3LW, UK
UKHW050844101026
15624UKWH00018B/518

9 798337 382524